DEAD
PRESIDENTS

AN AMERICAN ADVENTURE

INTO THE STRANGE DEATHS

AND SURPRISING AFTERLIVES

OF OUR NATION'S LEADERS

DEAD PRESIDENTS

BRADY CARLSON

W. W. NORTON & COMPANY
Independent Publishers Since 1923
NEW YORK • LONDON

For information about permission to reproduce selections from this book,
write to Permissions, W. W. Norton & Company, Inc.,
500 Fifth Avenue, New York, NY 10110

For information about special discounts for bulk purchases, please contact W. W.
Norton Special Sales at specialsales@wwnorton.com or 800-233-4830

Manufacturing by Quad Graphics Fairfield
Book design by Brooke Koven
Production manager: Julia Druskin

Library of Congress Cataloging-in-Publication Data

Carlson, Brady, author.
Dead presidents : an American adventure into the strange deaths and surprising
afterlives of our nation's leaders / Brady Carlson. — First edition.
pages cm
Includes bibliographical references and index.
ISBN 978-0-393-24393-2 (hardcover)
1. Presidents—United States—Death. 2. Presidents—United States—Biography. I.
Title.
E176.1.C23 2016
973.09'9—dc23
[B]
2015032329

W. W. Norton & Company, Inc.
500 Fifth Avenue, New York, N.Y. 10110
www.wwnorton.com

W. W. Norton & Company Ltd.
Castle House, 75/76 Wells Street, London W1T 3QT

1 2 3 4 5 6 7 8 9 0

For Owen,
who has malice toward none and charity for all

That's all a man can hope for during his
lifetime—to set an example—and when he is dead,
to be an inspiration for history.

WILLIAM McKINLEY

Being president is like running a cemetery:
you've got a lot of people under you and nobody's
listening.

BILL CLINTON

CONTENTS

PRESIDENTS OF THE UNITED STATES

George Washington (1732–1799)	1789–1797
John Adams (1735–1826)	1797–1801
Thomas Jefferson (1743–1826)	1801–1809
James Madison (1751–1836)	1809–1817
James Monroe (1758–1831)	1817–1825
John Quincy Adams (1767–1848)	1825–1829
Andrew Jackson (1767–1845)	1829–1837
Martin Van Buren (1782–1862)	1837–1841
William Henry Harrison (1773–1841)	1841
John Tyler (1790–1862)	1841–1845
James K. Polk (1795–1849)	1845–1849
Zachary Taylor (1784–1850)	1849–1850
Millard Fillmore (1800–1874)	1850–1853

Franklin Pierce (1804–1869)   1853–1857

James Buchanan (1791–1868)   1857–1861

Abraham Lincoln (1809–1865)   1861–1865

Andrew Johnson (1808–1875)   1865–1869

Ulysses S. Grant (1822–1885)   1869–1877

Rutherford B. Hayes (1822–1893)   1877–1881

James A. Garfield (1831–1881)   1881

Chester Arthur (1829–1886)   1881–1885

Grover Cleveland (1837–1908)   1885–1889, 1893–1897

Benjamin Harrison (1833–1901)   1889–1893

William McKinley (1843–1901)   1897–1901

Theodore Roosevelt (1858–1919)   1901–1909

William Howard Taft (1857–1930)   1909–1913

Woodrow Wilson (1856–1924)   1913–1921

Warren G. Harding (1865–1923)   1921–1923

Calvin Coolidge (1872–1933)   1923–1929

Herbert Hoover (1874–1964)   1929–1933

Franklin D. Roosevelt (1882–1945)   1933–1945

Harry S. Truman (1884–1972)   1945–1953

Dwight D. Eisenhower (1890–1969)   1953–1961

John F. Kennedy (1917–1963)   1961–1963

Lyndon B. Johnson (1908–1973)   1963–1969

Richard Nixon (1913–1994)   1969–1974

Gerald Ford (1913–2006)   1974–1977

Jimmy Carter (1924–)   1977–1981

Ronald Reagan (1911–2004)   1981–1989

George H. W. Bush (1924–)   1989–1993

Bill Clinton (1946–)   1993–2001

George W. Bush (1946–)   2001–2009

Barack H. Obama (1961–)   2009–2017

DEAD
PRESIDENTS

INTRODUCTION

WHAT IS the job of a dead president? Before answering this peculiar question—and there are several ways to answer—I should explain that this is not the question I would have asked when my fascination with presidents began in elementary school. Back then, it was the *lives* of our leaders that interested me, thanks to a little paperback book called *Mr. President* by George Sullivan, which I read over and over. I had a pretty limited understanding of what a president actually did, but whatever it was, I knew these guys *mattered*. They led wars, signed legislation into law, showed up on coins and on television screens. I studied the presidents' portraits and gleaned every detail about their life stories, signature talents, and achievements. Thomas Jefferson could "break a horse, dance a minuet and play the violin"; Teddy Roosevelt charged up San Juan Hill with his Rough Riders; Grover Cleveland's fat-shaming contemporaries nicknamed him "Uncle Jumbo." I once convinced my fifth-grade teacher to turn the class over to me for an afternoon of presidential trivia, and while I was clearly the only one in the room

3

with any enthusiasm for the impromptu lesson, I like to think that, to this day, every one of the kids in Mr. Butsch's class at Lester School in Downers Grove, Illinois, remembers that John Quincy Adams was the first president to have his clothes stolen while swimming naked in the Potomac.

Five years after I first thumbed through my copy of *Mr. President*, my parents drove my sister and me to Springfield to take in the city's Abraham Lincoln history. I was going to *see* my first president. It was thrilling. I drank in scenes from Lincoln's early life at New Salem village, and marveled as I stood in the house where Abraham and Mary Lincoln set down their roots, raised their kids, and set about building a political career that would change the world. And then, Oak Ridge Cemetery, to see the man himself.

The monument at Oak Ridge broke my brain. I grew up in a flat suburban landscape where the tallest building was the three-story Wieboldt's building at the mall, or maybe a water tower, and here was a giant stone obelisk stretching 117 feet into the air, encircled by elaborate terraces and striking bronze figures of Civil War soldiers. I hurried inside and came to a room of marble where I found a massive, flag-flanked red stone sarcophagus. "ABRAHAM LINCOLN," it said, "1809–1865." High on the wall behind it stood the words Secretary of War Edwin Stanton spoke upon Lincoln's death: "Now he belongs to the ages."

Even as a kid I could appreciate what the ages meant. I could understand how grand and solemn the monument and the message were. In this sacred place my fellow Americans and I would immerse ourselves in historical greatness and be filled with inspiration—perhaps to go into public service, to try following in Lincoln's footsteps.

It never occurred to me that some of my fellow Oak Ridge pilgrims might actually be tourists—people looking less for vision than for vacation photos. They took quite a few; some even laughed and chattered away, in flagrant violation of the tomb signs' requests for respectful silence. Outside, boys and girls my age ran across the cemetery grounds and rubbed the nose of its Lincoln statue for good luck. Then, most shockingly of all, I learned that Abraham Lincoln's sarcophagus was empty. The late president's remains were buried ten to twelve feet below, following an attempt to steal his body.

It wasn't the inspiration I'd come for, but, unexpectedly, it was inspiration just the same. There was, I realized, a story behind every grave and every tomb. Soon I wasn't just fascinated with the presidents' lives but with their *afterlives* as well: how we, the ages, choose to remember and memorialize our dead presidents—an ongoing process that inevitably reveals as much about us as about them. To understand this process, I decided to travel across the country to the graves of the presidents and the sites meant to keep their names alive—the stirring and the stupefying, the powerful and the perplexing, the moving memorials and the cheap cash-ins.

In these travels, I've come to learn that the jobs of dead presidents extend well beyond their graves. They frequently serve as namesakes, for example—our towns are full of Washington Streets, Lincoln Centers, and Jefferson Middle Schools. Each February we celebrate Presidents Day by getting great prices on new or used models at our local auto dealers. And we all know the name of our capital city, Washington.

Those are the obvious ones. We pay tribute to president number 34 every time we roll down a US highway; officially, the system is called the Dwight D. Eisenhower System of Interstate and Defense Highways. Anything we dub as "OK" is a tribute to "Old Kinderhook," Martin Van Buren—and he needs the props. Know the folk song "This Land Is Your Land"? It's by a singer from Oklahoma named Woodrow Wilson Guthrie. The teddy bear (named for the first President Roosevelt), NASA's space center (named for the second President Johnson) . . . ours isn't the first society to name people, places, and things after our leaders, but we sure have put our backs into the work.

Dead presidents are fodder for the highest forms of art—like Daniel Chester French's stirring statue at the Lincoln Memorial, or Horace Greenough's slightly less stirring statue of George Washington in a toga, hidden away in the Smithsonian after public outcry—and the lowest forms of commerce, such as the Brooklyn company that sold James A. Garfield medicinal powders ("Headaches with Garfield, Relieved Instantly") and a presidential-themed laxative drink, with the catchy slogan "Flush the bowels with Garfield Tea."

Visiting presidential graves may sound morbid or even a little weird, but once you start looking for the stories behind the stones, it's hard to stop. The first stop on my honeymoon was a return trip to Springfield to see Lincoln, and later in the week we bypassed Graceland in Memphis so we could see James K. Polk in Nashville. My son, by age two, had spent a fair amount of time in cemeteries and started running up to tombstones and shouting, "Dead!" Most presidential history buffs prefer learning about the lives these memorials are intended to honor, lives that have steered and shaped our nation. But the memorials themselves are worthy of attention as well, not only for what they tell us about the presidents but because they leave a record of what we value and believe as a country. In a country founded on the principle that we're all created equal, we've built Mount Rushmore, where we've carved only four of our equals' heads at twelve times normal size—because the president, the one person whom we can all elect, represents and exemplifies all of us. So fairly or unfairly, we make the presidents bigger than the rest of us. And smaller, too: just as we exalt them with statues and sculptures and iconic paintings, we also cut them down to size through kitsch—wax dummies, cartoons, Halloween costumes, and bobblehead dolls. In death, Americans transform their presidents into mythic figures, pillars of virtue who serve as lead characters in the national narrative . . . and then put their faces on action figures and hot sauce bottles.

The postmortem presidential pantheon doesn't put presidents in the same order as the historical one; some of the liveliest stories of life after death belong to obscure or mediocre presidents, like James Garfield, killed not by his assassin's bullet but by his quack doctor sticking his fingers in the gunshot wound, or Zachary Taylor, disinterred almost 150 years after his death to find out if it was, in fact, cherries and milk that did him in, or poor Franklin Pierce, who, in the final months of his single, unsuccessful term as president decided "there's nothing left to do but get drunk." (This, of course, was after he spoke so long at his inaugural address that outgoing first lady Abigail Fillmore caught pneumonia, which killed her several weeks later.) It took New Hampshire, his home state, almost half a century to stop voting down a statue to remember him by.

Because of what we do, being a dead president is about as close to civic *immortality* as one gets in this part of the world. The presidents keep on living, long after they're gone. It's just a little weird. These stories start where most stories about the presidents leave off. And so the chief job of a dead president is to tell us about ourselves, our history, and how we imagine our past and future.

1

MONUMENT MAN

*On George Washington's Transformation
from Mortal Man to Immortal Icon*

THERE'S A pretty good prime directive when it comes to anything presidential: start with George Washington.

Yes, the job has changed quite a bit since Washington's time, but a huge amount of how presidents act today is based on how Washington acted as president back then, from how frequently to use powers like vetoes and executive orders to how many four-year terms to serve. Then, when the first president became the first *dead* president, the way the country dealt with the loss of Washington set a model for how to honor—or, occasionally, dishonor—his successors.

So here I am, at Mount Vernon—or, technically, "George Washington's Mount Vernon Estate, Museum & Gardens." If the house explains the owner, this one explains a lot about the man and his ambitions. George Washington wanted to have the fanciest house in the neighborhood (he turned a relatively modest farmhouse into a twenty-one-room mansion) and the biggest yard, quadrupling the size of the plantation to a peak of 8,000 acres. Washington's mostly enslaved workforce grew wheat and corn, raised livestock, and operated what was at the time the largest whiskey distillery in America.

Mount Vernon today is a huge historic site: it boasts of having a million visitors a year and nearly eighty million since the Mount Vernon Ladies' Association purchased the place from Washington's descendants in the 1850s.

For seventeen dollars a head, visitors to Mount Vernon can spend the day any number of ways. The big draw is the house tour, where one can see Washington's study, the dining room where Charles Thomson informed the general he had been elected president, and the bed where he died, the victim of a nasty cold and/or incompetent, leech-slinging doctors. Historical reenactors stand in the greenhouse, talking about life on the plantation; there's a wharf, walking trails, and a gristmill. Depending on the day, Nicolas Cage fans can see some of the buildings used in the making of the "National Treasure" movies, and liquor connoisseurs can try whiskey based on a recipe used in Washington's time.

Me, I'm staying close to the tomb, a tall, elegant brick structure with a stone sign embedded near the top. "Within this enclosure," it says, "rest the remains of Genl GEORGE WASHINGTON."

Next to me is a docent who answers visitors' questions. She handles most of them with one phrase: "General Washington is in the sarcophagus on the right; Mrs. Washington is on the left." I actually get an emotional charge standing here, this close to the man by whom every president is measured—not so much that I'd describe myself to be in a state of rapturous, patriotic awe, but enough so that I wish I'd dressed a little better. Who wears a broken baseball cap and a paint-stained T-shirt to see the Father of Our Country?

The docent's shift ends at two, and as she heads out another staffer comes on to start the wreath-laying ceremony. As the new docent unlocks the tomb's large iron gate, she points out that the ceremony in which we're about to take part has been host to presidents and queens and dignitaries. She gives a sort of eulogy, explaining that we lay the wreath because Washington spent much of his adult life leaving home to answer the call to public service, from the Revolutionary War to the Constitutional Convention to the presidency. "In total," she says, "twenty-one years." She says this last phrase very slowly so it sinks in, 'cause that's a long time. "Twenty. One. Years." We all look around at each other with "we haven't been anything for twenty-one years" expressions.

The wreath is modest and unadorned, sitting on a thin green tripod, and volunteers from the audience are needed to place it next to the Washingtons. I'm eager to volunteer until I hear the docent ask the question that disqualifies me: "Do we have any veterans or active members of the military with us today?" Two veterans raise their hands, a fortysomething guy with graying hair and a blue polo shirt, and a thin, smiling woman in her thirties, wearing a long-sleeved khaki top, a red headband atop her short hair, and bright pink polish on her fingernails.

The docent turns back to the crowd to ask for one more volunteer, to read George Washington's prayer. She looks past my outstretched hand and chooses a long-haired girl in her early teens, who reads as the veterans walk the wreath into the tomb:

*I now make it my earnest prayer, that God would have you, and the
State over which you preside, in his holy protection; that he would
incline the hearts of the Citizens to cultivate a spirit of subordination and
obedience to government; to entertain a brotherly affection and love for
one another, for their fellow citizens of the United States at large, and
particularly for their brethren who have served in the field; and finally,
that he would most graciously be pleased to dispose us all, to do Justice,
to love mercy, and to demean ourselves with that charity, humility and
pacific temper of mind, which were the characteristics of the Divine
Author of our blessed religion, and without an humble imitation of whose
example in these things, we can never hope to be a happy nation.*

We wrap up with the Pledge of Allegiance, and the docent invites us to take pictures of the tomb before she closes the gate. I walk back toward the main entrance next to the wreath-laying woman and her three kids. She seems tickled to have been chosen for the ceremony, but the oldest kid, at maybe eight or nine years, is unimpressed that his mom laid a wreath at the tomb of George Washington. "Can we get lunch now?" he asks.

This ceremony plays out at Mount Vernon twice a day, every day of the year. It's short; it's dignified; it doesn't keep kids away from their lunches for too long. Had the country left it at that, Washington probably would have been OK with it. Knowing that his death would set the norm for how the country would treat its late chiefs of state, he stated in his will: "It is my express desire that my Corpse may be Interred in a private manner, without parade, or funeral Oration." In effect: *I gave you twenty-one years of my life—but now that I'm dead, I'm done.*

Private? No parades? No speeches? That's not how we roll. The citizens were so eager to honor Washington's memory, they didn't want to wait for his death to get started. Shortly after the Revolutionary War, the Continental Congress voted to build "an equestrian statue of General Washington . . . at the place where the residence of Congress shall be established . . . the General to be represented in Roman dress, holding a truncheon in his right hand, and his head encircled with a laurel wreath."

This was not the bright start Washington wanted for the United States. He'd spent years tamping down efforts like these to turn him and the presidency into something larger than life; a statue would undo all of that work to emphasize that America was a republic with a chief executive, not an empire ruled by a king. And Washington remembered well what men from his Continental Army did to celebrate the passage of the Declaration of Independence in New York: they found a large equestrian statue of King George III, pulled it down, cut off its head, and held a mock parade across town. He didn't want his own head in such a parade if the new country fell apart.

Washington got his fellow citizens busy building a nation, and talk of equestrian statues and other such honors wound down. The one exception came on September 9, 1791, when the commissioners overseeing construction of the country's new capital renamed the "Federal City" as the city of Washington. The president let this one honor go forward because he had been trying not to micromanage the men he'd personally chosen to lead the construction project. But he pointedly continued to use the city's old name in all his papers.

The city's new name gave it a crucial new purpose. While the design for the Federal City included some space for monuments and memorials, it was, as its name suggested, about functionality—a giant office park for the national government to do its business. Naming the capital for Washington made the entire city a memorial, in effect making DC not only the seat of government but a kind of repository for our national memory.

What—and who—we honored as a country, we would put there, with gusto. All the nation needed now was a corpse.

It got one on December 14, 1799, after General Washington succumbed to a throat infection, though it should also be noted that his doctors, in trying to treat the illness, took something like five of his eight pints of blood while simultaneously trying to get him to throw up. He didn't, but he might have, had he lived to see how the country reacted to his requests for no speeches, no parades, and no public funeral.

For one thing, there was a massive public funeral at Mount Vernon, starting with a large procession. Organized by Washington's Masonic lodge, this parade included musicians, clergy, troops, and a riderless horse, a military tradition reportedly dating back to the age of Genghis Khan. The unwanted funeral included unwanted speeches, too, by no fewer than four ministers. The ceremony concluded with a final viewing of the body and "three general discharges of infantry, the cavalry, and eleven pieces of artillery, which lined the banks of the Potomac." Later, the plantation's farm manager outfitted the slaves and servants with mourning clothes.

The rest of the country followed Mount Vernon's lead upon learning that our first president was gone. It's said the mourning was so deep there were shortages of black cloth in some parts of the country for months. The House and Senate immediately adjourned out of respect; Senate President Pro Tempore Samuel Livermore wrote to President John Adams, "Permit us, sir, to mingle our tears with yours. On this occasion it is manly to weep." The manly tears continued to flow through the official congressional eulogy, as Virginia representative Henry "Light Horse Harry" Lee dubbed Washington "first in war, first in peace, and first in the hearts of his countrymen." Having missed the actual funeral, cities simply held their own. Boston not only held a mock funeral, it struck coins to mark the occasion. "He is in glory," the coins said, "the world in tears."

All of this, remember, was the exact opposite of what George Washington had asked for in his will. And while it's incredibly American for the people to thumb their noses at authority, that's not what was going on here—the country was trying to hold on to a figure they saw as truly indispensable. In his epic biography *Washington: A Life*, the historian Ron Chernow suggests Americans were worried that national unity, and maybe the country itself, might start to crumble without the general there. If Washington was a mere man, he could die, and America would have to carry on without him. But if America simply honored Washington enough, he would become *more* than a man, and then we wouldn't really lose him at all. So, Chernow writes, "Washington was converted into an exemplar of moral values, the person chosen to tutor posterity in patriotism, even a civic deity." You can see evidence of the "civic deity" today if you stand in the Rotunda of the US Capitol and look up: at the center of the Capitol dome, you'll see a painting called *The Apotheosis of Washington*, in which angels welcome the general into heaven and elevate him to godlike status. Apotheosis images, which showed up in engraved prints, textiles, and even pottery for home consumption, were huge hits shortly after Washington's death. So was a book by Parson Weems called *The Life of Washington*, in which the author invented from whole (and probably not black) cloth the story of how honest young George chopped down the cherry tree and quickly confessed the deed to his father. Stories like this helped people feel like Washington was still watching over the country from his new perch in the great beyond.

While Washington the myth was ascending to heaven, Washington the corpse was not faring so well. Again, George Washington had left specific instructions about the handling of his remains in his will:

> *The family Vault at Mount Vernon requiring repairs, and being improperly situated besides, I desire that a new one of Brick, and upon*

1. Angels welcome George Washington into the heavens in Constantino Brumidi's *The Apotheosis of Washington.*

a larger Scale, may be built at the foot of what is commonly called the Vineyard Inclosure, on the ground which is marked out. In which my remains, with those of my deceased relatives (now in the old Vault) and such others of my family as may chuse to be entombed there, may be deposited.

"Requiring repairs" was probably putting the situation mildly; the tomb was in bad shape and getting worse. A visitor to Mount Vernon in 1820 described the vault's entryway as "formed of half inch fir board, now rotting away. Such a door would disgrace an English pig-stye. Were pigs to range here, they would soon enter the tomb." "Improperly situated" was the general's way of saying the Old Tomb was prone to flood damage: for decades the Potomac had invited itself in to the vault, causing thirty or so wooden coffins to rot. There were bones literally spilling onto the ground around Washington's remains. The general was intact—his coffin had been laid on a wooden table, to keep the water away—but tree roots had found their way into the vault as well, and they had started to cause damage. In time, even George Washington's bones might have ended up on the Old Tomb's floor.

Yet even given the urgency about flooding and tree roots and bones, and given Washington's very explicit instructions to move the tomb elsewhere, his body spent the next thirty years right where it was, near the river, in a little vault that was slowly falling apart. Part of the problem was that *everything* was falling apart at the huge and unprofitable Mount Vernon, meaning there wasn't much money to spare on restoration work. The other problem with building a new tomb was that Washington's nephew Bushrod, who had inherited the enormous plantation, was busy enough showing visitors around the existing one. "To that spot," the historian Emma Willard wrote of Washington's resting place, "will every true son of America, in all future ages, be attracted, in mournful, filial pilgrimage." Indeed they were; just as the living Washington had never been short on unexpected guests, a steady stream of visitors invited themselves to Mount Vernon to pay their respects at Washington's tomb and to be shown about the house, whether the Washington family wished to host them or not. Playing host and tour guide became one more giant task on Bushrod's already full plate; while he tried, unsuccessfully, to make the enormous plantation profitable, he was also serving as an associate justice of the Supreme Court. No surprise that when Bushrod died in 1829, he had put in place none of what his uncle had requested.

As a result, George Washington very nearly became the victim of the first presidential grave robbery. Bushrod left the plantation to his nephew John Washington, who soon after fired one of the men who tended the grounds at Mount Vernon. The ex-gardener decided to take his revenge by breaking into the tomb and trying to steal George Washington's head. He got one of Bushrod's in-laws' skulls by mistake, and was apprehended shortly thereafter, but it convinced John

Washington and the surviving executors of the president's will that they had to get a new tomb in place.

All this time, Congress had been asking to bring the former president's body to the Capitol. They even built a crypt under the Rotunda, with a big hole in the center so visitors could peer down and see the coffin. Shortly after the general's death, Congressman (and future Supreme Court legend) John Marshall had managed to get a grieving Martha Washington's approval, though as yeses go, it was a pretty passive-aggressive one:

Taught by that great example which I have so long had before me never to oppose my private wishes to the public will, I must consent to the request made by Congress. . . . In doing this, I need not, I cannot say what a sacrifice of individual feeling I make to a sense of public duty.

Go ahead, take my husband's body away from me, she said, and the Congress, completely oblivious to Mrs. Washington's disappointment, was like, *Sure!* But instead of moving forward, lawmakers wrangled over costs and designs; John Washington, who may have been the only person in America to actually read George's will, finally put a stop to the plan when officials dropped by Mount Vernon to pick up the body. The dejected builders went home to plug the hole between the Rotunda and the Capitol Crypt, which is used today by Capitol tour guides to corral their groups.

It was John Washington who finally got a new tomb together, three decades after Washington's death. The president's coffin was showing signs of wear, possibly from the general turning over in his grave because it took so long to build the new tomb, so the architect William Strickland designed a new sarcophagus, which the artisan John Struthers carved out of white marble. It was strong, sturdy, and beautiful. It was also too big to fit through the doorway to the new crypt. Masons had to add on a whole new front section to house it. Once they did, in 1831, Strickland, Struthers, and some relatives had to get Washington's body in there, which *Harper's New Monthly Magazine* described:

> *When the sarcophagus arrived the coffin of the chief was brought forth.*
> *The vault was first entered by Mr. Strickland, accompanied by Major*
> *Lewis. . . . When [Washington's] decayed wooden case was removed*
> *the leaden lid was perceived to be sunken and fractured. In the bottom of*
> *the wooden case was found the silver coffin-plate, in the form of a shield,*
> *which was placed upon the leaden coffin when Washington was first*
> *entombed. "At the request of Major Lewis," says Mr. S. [Strickland],*
> *"the fractured part of the lid was turned over on the lower part, exposing*
> *to view a head and breast of large dimensions, which appeared, by the*
> *dim light of the candles, to have suffered but little from the effects of*
> *time."*

Ostensibly these fellows were verifying that the would-be grave
robber hadn't disturbed the president's remains. But the next part of
Strickland's account suggests they had probably opened up the coffin
so they could be the first people to see George Washington in over
thirty years:

> *The eye-sockets were large and deep, and the breadth across the temples,*
> *together with the forehead, appeared of unusual size. There was no*
> *appearance of grave-clothes; the chest was broad, the color was dark, and had*
> *the appearance of dried flesh and skin adhering closely to the bones. We saw*
> *no hair, nor was there any offensive odor from the body; but we observed,*
> *when the coffin had been removed to the outside of the vault, the dripping*
> *down of a yellow liquid, which stained the marble of the sarcophagus. A*
> *hand was laid upon the head and instantly removed; the leaden lid was*
> *restored to its place; the body was carried by six men, was carried and laid in*
> *the marble coffin, and the ponderous cover being put on and set in cement, it*
> *was sealed from our sight on Saturday the 7th day of October, 1837.*

I love the phrasing here: "a hand was laid upon the head." Whose
hand? Certainly not any of our hands, just, um, a hand that was hanging around! And while Strickland says he "saw no hair," somebody
seemed to, as hairs purportedly taken in 1837 have gone up for auction, sometimes for tens of thousands of dollars. Nonetheless, the

crew, having sealed the sarcophagus for all time, went back to the Mount Vernon mansion. George Washington had become the first president to be exhumed, patted on the head, then reinterred.*

HAVING BEEN unable to bring George Washington's body to the Capitol, Congress decided to build a Washington of their own instead. In 1832, marking a hundred years since Washington's birth, lawmakers commissioned a statue of Washington from the sculptor Horatio Greenough, offering twenty thousand dollars for the work.

Greenough knew he'd gotten the job of a lifetime and "determined to spare neither time nor expense to make his work worthy of the country and himself." Early America saw itself as the heir to Greek democracy and the Roman republic, and Washington was its version of Cincinnatus, the Roman farmer who handed back the reins of power to civilian authority at the end of a war. Greenough, who had left his native Massachusetts to work and live in Italy, was happy to run with the comparison, and he used a famous statue of Zeus at Olympia as the basis for his Washington at, uh, Washington. Zeus was one of the Seven Wonders of the World, so what better model to choose?

The statue took Greenough nearly ten years to complete. Like Zeus on his throne, Washington is seated; his chair features Native Americans and Columbus—meant to place the general between the New World and the Old. He wears Roman-style clothes, shirtless and in sandals. In his left hand he holds a sheathed sword; the handle points away from him. His raised right hand points toward heaven. He is literally larger than life—and if that wasn't symbolism enough, the work also includes depictions of Apollo, god of the sun, and Her-

---

* There's some debate about whether this actually happened: according to an account from a Washington relative, told secondhand to an author in 1916, "There was a small circular hole immediately over the face, through which several persons attempted to look on Washington's face, and some of them claimed that they saw it, but . . . on attempting to look through the hole could see nothing." If so, Washington was the first president to be exhumed, gawked at through a small hole in the sarcophagus, then reinterred.

2. Horace Greenough depicted George Washington in a toga and looking, according to Charles Bullfinch, as if "entering or leaving a bath."

cules (in infant form, but still). The artist's inscription explains all this in Latin.

If Greenough was excited to bring *Washington* to the Capitol Rotunda in 1842, his excitement was short-lived. The classical imagery did not go over as intended. Instead of seeing a timeless Washington as heir to the ancients, visitors saw the beloved Father of Their Country in a toga, trying to stab himself. "It is a ridiculous affair, and instead of demanding admiration, excites only laughter," said one visitor. Charles Bulfinch, the third Architect of the Capitol, wrote, "I fear that this statue will give the idea of Washington's entering or leaving a bath." The only ones who weren't laughing were the Capitol maintenance workers, who worried the Capitol floorboards would buckle under the sculpture's weight. A friend of Greenough's clicked his tongue at the unappreciative DC rabble: "This magnificent production of genius does not seem to be appreciated at its full value in this metropolis."

Hearing this, Congress decided the Rotunda was too good for a "marble absurdity" like *Washington* and moved the statue outside to the Capitol grounds, where visitors in off-peak months joked the shirtless president was reaching for his clothes. It was moved again to the Patent Office and then was finally donated in 1908 to the Smithsonian, where it was kept relatively out of sight until the bicentennial in 1976. No statue has dared to show presidential nipple since.

Say what you want about a George Washington toga party—at least Horatio Greenough got his work done. The Washington Monument was the other great project aimed at honoring the first president, and even though political heavyweights like Chief Justice John Marshall and former president James Madison were among the most prominent members of the new Washington National Monument Society, formed in 1833, this project moved at the slowest pace imaginable: Toga George had been built, mocked, and moved outside before the Washington Monument even got started. Perhaps that's for the best, though, because the monument's initial design, by the architect Robert Mills, called for an Egyptian-style obelisk surrounded by an oversize statue of Washington on a chariot leading a team of Arabian horses, with a base shaped like a circular Greek temple (not too different from the look of today's Jefferson Memorial). The team of horses would be "driven by Winged Victory." If Toga George went over badly, imagine how the public would have reacted to Ben-Hur George.

Disputes between Congress and the Monument Society went on for several more years, which meant the cornerstone wasn't laid until Independence Day 1848. Even then there was a delay: the cart carrying the six-ton-plus cornerstone got stuck in a mud patch near the National Mall, and it took forty workers from the Navy Yard to pull it out. It set a maddening pattern for the rest of the project: even when it moved forward, it still got stuck.

Mills had designed what was then the tallest structure in the world; he needed more marble than his suppliers could feasibly deliver by rail. And funds were as short as supplies: the project frequently ran

3. By 1854, funding had dried up for the Washington Monument. Construction halted where it was, and the grounds became pasture for pigs and sheep.

out of money. The society staged a fund-raiser on July 4, 1850, with a guest of honor: President Zachary Taylor, who was worn down by the extreme heat and died less than a week later. In honoring one dead president, the monument helped to create another.

By 1854 funding had completely dried up; the builders simply stopped where they were, about 152 feet up, and the long, painful "stump era" of the Washington Monument began. The shrine to the country's greatest hero was now known best as a decent grazing spot for the District's sheep and pigs. Robert Mills died in 1855, around the time the anti-immigrant, anti-Catholic Know-Nothings muscled their way into the leadership of the Monument Society so as to stop the builders from adding a stone sent as a gift by the pope. They probably smashed it to bits and dumped it in the river. They did add about twenty-one feet of stone to the tower, but the work was shoddy and had to be removed. By the time the Know-Nothings relinquished power, the Civil War was about to begin. The country had fallen apart before the Washington Monument could come together.

There was, at last, a turning point around Independence Day 1876—the American centennial. Lawmakers started to realize that almost all of the people who were alive at the start of this project, not to mention sixteen of Washington's successors, were now dead, and they finally put forward long-awaited funds and put the US Army Corps of Engineers in charge of construction. Cost concerns meant all the adornments were scrapped—no Washington on a chariot, no team of horses—and the color difference between old and new marble was (and still is) highly visible. But it was done, albeit after taking some ninety years, absurd sums of money, and the life of Zachary Taylor. The Washington Monument was finished in 1885, dedicated by President Chester Arthur—twentieth successor to Washington—that year, and opened to the public in 1888.

There were concerns the nation might be too exhausted by the building process to care about the monument. "Here is the memorial," wrote the *Atlantic* in the final years of construction, "begun on such a scale that all our other monuments are toys to it, . . . yet nobody outside Washington shows any interest in it." But they needn't have worried: the 555-foot tall obelisk, the tallest human-made structure in the world at the time, was hailed as a marvel of engineering and design, and included innovations like a steam-powered elevator that allowed visitors to take in the view without having to climb all 897 steps. Some critics even considered the monument as a metaphor for a country on the rise, surpassing, as one put it, "the highest cathedral spires designed by the devout and daring architects" of Europe in the Middle Ages.

Even with the many design changes over the decades, Robert

Mills's vision for the monument as the centerpiece of a national pantheon ended up being fulfilled. The architect had hoped to put murals and depictions of historic figures and national heroes in place around a statue of Washington, all of which was scaled back because of cost concerns. But in 1902, a Senate commission studying the park system of the District of Columbia proposed an expansion of the city's monument space, including a memorial to Abraham Lincoln, a bridge to Arlington Cemetery, and several other areas designated for future monuments. The McMillan Plan, as it was known, put the Washington Monument in the center of the civic space, the anchor of what it envisioned as a "Pageant to American History." Hundreds of thousands of people take the elevator to the top each year, while millions more see the monument as they travel about the capital city, a constant reminder of the man for whom the Federal City is named.

Periodically, of course, the ravages of time and nature have to be repaired. After an earthquake in 2011, more than a year's worth of work had to be done. The public used this downtime to take pictures of themselves lying on the ground, with the tall, stiff shaft of the monument positioned behind them in a way that eighth-grade boys find really, really funny.

WASHINGTON SET the precedent for dead presidents—almost everything that happened to him, and for him, happened again to his successors. But even knowing how strange this story got, I'm reassured when I see the tomb, and Mount Vernon, and the monument today. We may go bigger with our presidential funerals than necessary, or than the president wanted; our monuments may be large, controversial, expensive, and hard to build; we may open the presidents' coffins (a lot); there may be thievery and bad behavior . . . but we generally get it right in the end. Even if it takes nearly a century to do it.

2

WELL-TIMED EXITS

On the Postmortem Fortunes (and Misfortunes)
of John Adams, Thomas Jefferson, William Henry Harrison,
Ulysses S. Grant, and Andrew Johnson

GEORGE WASHINGTON'S successor, John Adams, knew well
that the second president would have a hard time measuring up
to the first, both in and out of the job. "Mausoleums, statues, monuments will never be erected to me," he wrote to a friend in 1809. He
added, "I wish them not," which was almost absurdly untrue. Adams
very much wanted to be remembered—maybe painters wouldn't show
him rising to the heavens, as they'd done with Washington, but he
thought he at least deserved recognition for his important work during
the struggle for independence and the early years of the nation.

Adams would get this recognition, and even a few statues and
monuments, too—and his historical reputation would get a huge
boost from an extremely memorable death.

The second president lived at a place he called Peacefield, in
Quincy, Massachusetts, south of Boston. "It is but the farm of a
patriot," Adams said of his country estate, but that's understating the
place. While it's a large house—the Adamses doubled its size after
moving back to Quincy in 1788—they somehow kept its intimate

New England character intact. As a result, Peacefield lives up to its name: it's a serene place, inside and out, which was probably good for its owner. Even his closest allies would admit Adams the politician could follow moments of true genius with incredible pettiness, but at home in Massachusetts, surrounded by family and the country, he was almost a different man.

Adams even had a farmer alter ego—"Humphrey Ploughjogger"—which he'd used for a series of essays in Boston newspapers in the 1760s. The uneducated Ploughjogger persona satirically weighed in on political issues such as the Stamp Act and religious squabbles in Boston, but the character also had a serious agricultural agenda: hemp. "I do say it would be a nice thing if we could raise enuff Hemp to pay our rates, and bye a little rum and shuger, which we cant well do without, and a little Tea, which our Wifes wont let us have any peace without." Adams channeled his inner Ploughjogger barely a week after becoming president, writing to his wife, "It would do me good like a Medicine to See Billings"—the gardener—"one hour at any sort of Work."*

As a historic site, Peacefield is unique in that most of what you see here actually belonged to the occupants. I've gotten used to guides at other sites describing furniture and wallpaper and brickwork and interior trim as "of the time" or "restored to period style." Peacefield stayed in the family until 1946, when the Adamses turned the property and what was inside it over to the government. That means you can see the big, boxy grandfather clock Adams's father gave to John and Abigail as a wedding present, the dishes John Quincy Adams cracked while trying to grow fruit trees in the house, and the family's portraits of George and Martha Washington, hanging in the formal dining room. The guides describe the staircase railing, the one item visitors can touch, as an "opportunity to hold hands with the family."

---

* Aside from hemp, Adams was also fond of manure; he developed his own compost recipe and would write home from Europe about manure piles he'd seen there. "This may be good manure," he told his wife of one European compost heap, "but is not equal to mine."

The pieces I want to see are upstairs in the study, the room where John Adams would start his day, often at five in the morning, to keep up with his letters at a tall, ornate drop-front desk. He would wrap up the day here, too, reading until well past dark in his floral-patterned armchair before retiring for the evening. It's here that, on July 4, 1826, John Adams became part of the most famous death duet in American political history.

That date was the fiftieth anniversary of the signing of the Declaration of Independence—a particularly well timed exit for a man whose fiery pro-independence speech had convinced the Continental Congress to adopt the Declaration. By 1826 the ninety-year-old patriot could barely speak at all. When asked for a toast to mark the anniversary, he could only offer two words: "Independence forever!" Adams slipped in and out of consciousness for days leading up to the Fourth, but when told the anniversary had at last come, he was clearly pleased. "It is a great day," he said, sitting in his reading chair. "It is a *good* day." Adams quietly passed away a few hours later, but not before making reference to the other great voice of 1776: "Thomas Jefferson survives."

While no one around Adams's deathbed in Massachusetts knew it then, Jefferson had already gone, shortly before one o'clock that afternoon. The author of the Declaration of Independence had, like Adams, seen his body fail in the run-up to the anniversary. Jefferson's family knew the former president had hoped, as one relative put it, "to breathe his last on that great day, the birthday of his country." On his deathbed he more than once asked, "Is it the Fourth?" On the morning of the third it looked like Jefferson wasn't going to get his wish, so Nicholas Trist, Jefferson's grandson-in-law, lied and told the old man the Fourth had come. "An expression came over his countenance," Trist recalled, "which said, 'just as I wished.'" But he lingered, and the actual end came on the actual anniversary, several hours before Adams took his final breath.

Many Americans saw the deaths of Adams and Jefferson as evidence that God was smiling down on their country. After all, it couldn't just be coincidence that two Founding Fathers and two presidents should die on the same day—a day that happened to mark fifty years since the

Declaration they brought about. Adams's son President John Quincy Adams noted in his diary, "The time, the manner, the coincidence with the decease of Jefferson are visible and palpable marks of divine favour."

History has largely chalked the two deaths up to just plain coincidence, an only-in-America, one-in-a-million shot to lose Adams and Jefferson on the same day, but a professor at the University of Utah, Dr. Margaret Battin, has suggested that there may be more to July 4, 1826, than either divine intervention or coincidence. Battin, who studies end-of-life issues, looked at the two deaths and noted that Adams and Jefferson may have, amid extremely precarious health, hung on long enough to reach the special day, and then allowed themselves to pass on. Adams's doctors had predicted his demise for weeks leading up to the Fourth, but he defied their expectations until that "good day" arrived. Jefferson had been using the narcotic laudanum every night for almost a year to manage chronic pain, but on the evening of the third, he said, "No, Doctor, nothing more."

There's no way to know for sure, of course, and Battin notes there's no consensus among researchers about whether it's even possible to "hang on." But studies suggests some people seem to hold off death until a birthday, anniversary, or holiday passes. Two other presidents, Ford and Truman, died December 26, and those close to Ford were convinced he'd willed himself not to die on Christmas.

Whatever brought Adams's and Jefferson's deaths about also tied them together in history even tighter than they already had been. When Adams said "Thomas Jefferson survives" on his deathbed, it was a reminder to the nation that the two had once been fierce rivals as well as friends—the heads of the country's first two political parties, who barely spoke for a decade after Jefferson beat Adams for the presidency in 1801. Their political rivalry, egged on by each man's supporters, wore on their friendship: Adams once described Jefferson—who was at the time his vice president—as having a mind "eaten to a honeycomb with ambition, yet weak, confused, uninformed and ignorant." The veep gave as good as he got: "Mr. Adams is vain, irritable, stubborn, endowed with excessive self-love."

The badmouthing largely came to an end after the election, and the friendship picked up not long after Jefferson left the White House, but a "feud" between two presidents and Founding Fathers was too dramatic for the public imagination not to take up. And so the already-high drama of their dual death became the final chapter in a Great American Reconciliation, and we remember the parts of their deaths that fit the story and downplay the ones that don't.

For example: Jefferson's last words are often reported as "Is it the Fourth?" although relatives say the last time he spoke was to call out for some of his enslaved servants. Adams's actual last words had nothing to do with Jefferson: he turned to his granddaughter and said, trying to breathe, "Help me, child! Help me!" While Adams and Jefferson certainly were close, Jefferson was probably even closer to the fourth president, James Madison, and his next-door neighbor for years was president number five, James Monroe. But we think of him in relation to Adams more than to either of those distinguished Virginians. Conversely, we think of Adams first and foremost in association with Jefferson, even more than Adams's own son, President John Quincy Adams.

The Great Reconciliation, in fact, has played out with several other presidential odd couples over the years. Harry Truman and Dwight D. Eisenhower barely spoke to each other at Ike's inauguration in 1953, but they patched up most of their differences at John F. Kennedy's funeral in 1963. Gerald Ford and Jimmy Carter didn't like each other much after the bitter election of 1976, but at his inauguration Carter singled out Ford by name, "for all he has done to heal our land." Almost thirty years later, Carter repeated those words at Ford's funeral; not only had the two become friends after leaving office, they had an agreement that when one died, the other would speak at his funeral.

The Fourth of July, by the way, came very close to becoming the official death day of US presidents. Five years after Adams and Jefferson made their remarkable dual check-out, James Monroe died in New York City on the Fourth—"he seems to have lingered until this time," wrote the city's mayor, Philip Hone, "to add to the number of the Revolutionary patriots whose deaths have occurred on this memorable anniversary." In the summer of 1836, James Madison appeared on course for a fourth consecutive Independence Day death; in fact, he was being treated by Dr. Robley Dunglison, who had seen to Jefferson as his health failed. The doctor offered Madison stimulants and other drugs that would keep him alive until the Fourth, but Madison declined the offer. One morning in late June he went to breakfast, but couldn't swallow any of the food. When Madison's niece asked what was wrong, he answered, "Nothing more than a change of *mind*, my dear," and slumped over, dead.

A WELL-TIMED death can make a president larger than life. A poorly timed one can turn him into a buffoon.

William Henry Harrison is Exhibit A here.

Old Tippecanoe died a month into his term in 1841 and has become the presidency's Darwin Award winner, a fool who gave a long, dull inaugural speech in a snowstorm without a hat or a coat on, and succumbed to pneumonia a month later as a result. History describes his death in the same "there's a lesson to be learned from this" tone teachers and parents use when they tell kids not to stick their arms out of bus windows. *If only the man hadn't been so stupid as to go out in the cold without a coat on, he wouldn't have died.* The story even became part of family lore: President Benjamin Harrison, William Henry's grandson, took his oath of office in 1893 on a cold and rainy day. Mindful of Grandpa's fate, he wore long underwear made of chamois leather to keep dry.

The conclusions are unfair, but the question isn't. Why *didn't* William Henry Harrison just put on a coat?

Probably partly due to habit—Harrison was a military man and a farmer, used to spending time outside in less than ideal conditions— and partly out of a need to prove himself. The sixty-eight-year-old Harrison was the oldest president elected up to that time, and along with the questions about his age, there were concerns about his abilities. Political insiders saw Harrison as an intellectual lightweight, a well-meaning war hero who would sign whatever Whig party leaders put in front of him. Outgoing president Martin Van Buren told associates that Harrison "does not seem to realize the vast importance of his elevation. . . . He is tickled with the presidency as a young woman is with a new bonnet." Others were less considerate: Andrew Jackson, never one to mince words, called Harrison "the present imbecile chief"; Harrison's critics during his presidential campaign had called him "Granny," to imply the old man had gone senile, and said that a frontier dullard like Old Tippecanoe would be happier sitting in a log cabin drinking hard cider.

Harrison's house, by the way, is far from a log cabin, and it proves the theory that a house reveals its owner. The design of Grouseland, in rural Vincennes, Indiana, shows Harrison "thinking like a general," as a guide there put it. Harrison's job as governor of the Indiana Territory was to acquire land that had historically been home to Native Americans, and some of them weren't interested in selling. Grouseland still looks like a fancy-pants country house, but it doubles as a fort. The thick brick walls are curved in some places, so that if Harrison and his men had to take up positions during an attack, they would have multiple angles from which to shoot. The well is in the basement, rather than outside, to keep the water supply safe from poison, and there are panic rooms and hidden back corridors and roof lookouts, all of which would come in handy in a confrontation.

You don't come away from Grouseland thinking of William Henry Harrison as a senile old fool. Then again, the guide there does tell me that Harrison named his house Grouseland because grouse was his favorite food. He named his house after a meal. "Sometimes," she says, "we have school tour groups come in here and we ask them what they'd name their houses if they named them after their favorite foods. And so we get answers like Pizza Hut, or Brownie House."

I will also note that Harrison's will includes a sentence about what is to be done for his grandchildren "if my life should be spared," which is kind of useless in a final testament.

Harrison wanted to prove he was still as vigorous as he was during the days decades before when he fought and won the Battle of Tippecanoe. And he wanted to show he was every bit as smart as the snobs who bashed him as the candidate of illiterate frontier farmers and drunken backwoodsmen. So at his inauguration the hatless, coatless president stood under the East Portico of the US Capitol and talked. For two hours.

He talked about the history of the veto power under the Constitution, about the pros and cons of allowing presidents to seek reelection, about the different currencies states were using . . . on and on and on. When he ran out of things to say about American history, he moved on to Roman history. The speech would have been even longer and duller had it not been for Daniel Webster; the longtime politician, one of America's finest orators, helped Harrison edit down his address, saying wryly of his revisions that he'd "just killed seventeen Roman proconsuls as dead as smelts." It wasn't enough. In all, Harrison's inaugural address comprised 8,445 words; no president before or since has come close.

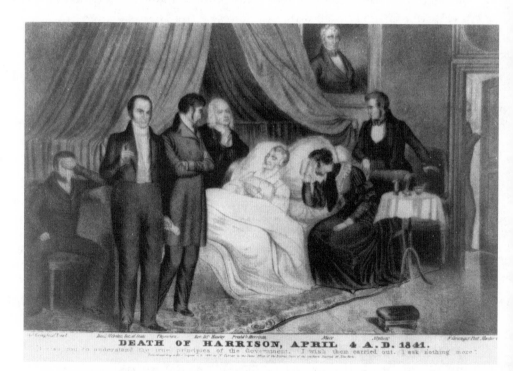

DEATH OF HARRISON, APRIL 4 A.D. 1841.

4. After William Henry Harrison's death in 1841, just a month into his presidency, America forgot his military exploits and political career and remembered only that he'd died of his own inaugural address.

A two-hour speech in the snow makes a president's clothes wet. Harrison's day was just getting started, too: he took part in a parade and three inaugural balls, a record for the time. Then the office-seekers closed in on him, accosting the man until "he staggered upstairs to revive himself with 'stimulants.'" In trying to look vigorous, Harrison had worn himself out. A month later, apparently suffering from pneumonia, Harrison sank into delirium, told his doctor (whom he apparently mistook for Vice President John Tyler) to carry out the principles of government, and then died so abruptly that his body had to be stored in Congressional Cemetery's public vault until a train could ship it back to Ohio. That took three months—three times as long as he'd stayed in the White House.

It is true that loud, coatless street oratory in cold wind and snow is not wise. But if everyone who went outside without a coat and hat on died within a month, how many of us would make it to sixty-eight like Harrison? I bet if he hadn't died thirty days into his term, we wouldn't be calling him stupid.

Timing matters.

This is true not only for presidents but for those visiting them. Harrison is buried in North Bend, Ohio, near Cincinnati, and on the way there I decided to stop in neighboring Cleves to see the Harrison-Symmes Memorial Foundation Museum, the closest thing to a Harrison library. The museum is open Saturday mornings and Sunday afternoons. I showed up Sunday morning, *thinking* it was Saturday, and couldn't figure out why there was a big padlock on the front door.

Fortunately I wasn't the only one who showed up early: a pickup truck and a red Subaru pulled into the driveway just a few minutes after me. "Did you want to see the museum?" said a middle-aged man with a graying beard and glasses. "Joe and I were going in to do some remodeling. You can go in and look around if you like."

Museum director Terry Simpson and his friend and colleague Joe Large had been planning to build a new reception desk, until I showed up. Instead, these two affable gents stop their woodworking and proudly show off the history of Ohio's Three Rivers region, from when a young Harrison met and courted Anna Symmes, daughter of a local land baron ("Her father didn't like that Harrison had no career 'but that of arms,'" Simpson says. "So they snuck off and got married while he was out of town," Large adds with a laugh), to an 1865 train robbery that locals hint might have been done by Frank and Jesse James. "Most of the research I've done says it's the first one [in the country]," Simpson says. "And even if it isn't, I'm claiming it!"

Simpson is technically part of this history—he served as mayor of North Bend, Harrison's town, until a few years ago. "He got married and moved out of town," Large explains. "Residency requirement."

We take a look through the Harrison items in the back room, including something called an ophicleide, which looks like the love-child of a tuba and a bugle, played when Harrison was interred in North Bend in 1841 and brought out again at the renovation of the tomb in 1922. "Have you been to the tomb?" Joe asks. "It's just a few minutes from here."

"It's my next stop."

Large nods, then suggests I make a stop along the way. "There's a church just down the road a little ways where the Harrisons went to church. You'll want to see that."

"I can show him over there," Simpson adds, "and over to the tomb." The interior part of the Harrison tomb isn't always open to visitors— unless you happen to be with the director of the Harrison-Symmes Museum, who has the key. He jumps into his car, and I follow in my rental, touring the Harrison sites and historic markers in the area.

These sites don't get many visitors. Take the Presbyterian church Large mentioned: "It's hard, really hard," Simpson says of its struggles to keep going. "There's a megachurch coming in a few miles from here, and they're going to get people to come in. To be honest, nobody cares that William Henry Harrison went to church here." For a while, few cared that William Henry Harrison was buried here either. The original structure, brick with a sod roof, started falling apart soon after it was built; a restoration in 1879 replaced the roof and covered the brick with cement, but grass started growing between the stones. Locals lobbied the government for funds to restore the tomb, but with little success.

The tomb hit its lowest point in 1912, when newspapers reported a story with the headline "Youth Imprisoned for Four Hours in Burial Place." A sixteen-year-old, George Smedley, was goofing off with two friends at the tomb. "Finding the door open," they went in; Smedley's friends, "as a joke, shut the heavy iron door and braced it with a heavy stick, and they ran away, in the belief that a little effort on George's part would open the door." Instead, Smedley spent the next few hours screaming for help. A Mrs. Gabriel happened by the place and heard a voice from behind the closed door of William Henry Harrison's tomb, shouting "Help! Help!" "She realised now that the voice came from within," the report said, and "was almost on the verge of collapse," before Smedley convinced her to open the door.

Fortunately Harrison's tomb is in fine shape today, which is obvious as Simpson opens the metal gate to the interior. There's a large gold marker placed over the old, worn brick where Harrison and his wife are entombed; it was placed there during another twentieth-century renovation. In place of the sod roof is a tall stone obelisk, with not a speck of grass between its stones, looking south toward Kentucky. "Secretary of the Northwest Territory, Delegate of the Northwest Territory to Congress, Territorial Governor of Indiana, Member of Congress from Ohio, Ohio State Senator, United States Senator from Ohio, Minister to Colombia, Ninth President of the United States." That's a résumé few of President Harrison's better-remembered successors can match. "This is the man who opened up the Midwest to development," Simpson says, staring out at the river. "You can disagree with the methods he used to do that, but that's what he did." It's only here that you'll see anything about it, though. Harrison might have been remembered as a key figure in westward expansion, had he lived. But he didn't, and that badly timed death has left him a badly remembered president.

Simpson still has work to do on that reception desk, so he shakes my hand and drives back to the museum. He put aside his building project for two hours to show me around, because I happened to show up at the museum at the same time he did. I take one last look at the tomb before driving off to my next stop. *Harrison's timing may have been terrible*, I think to myself, *but mine has never been better.*

I WISH I could say my timing was always as good as it was when I visited General Harrison, but more often I'm the guy running up to the door of the museum asking, "You're not about to close, are you?" As a result, I plan out my trips to the letter, so that I'll have extra time in case of a flight delay, or a missed turn, or just a plain old distraction. Usually the planning works out about right and I have just enough time for all my stops; occasionally I even run ahead of schedule, but that was not the case as I drove to a place in upstate New York known as Grant Cottage. This gem of a historic site is open seasonally, and my family and I were bumping up against closing time on the season's final day—a race against time, in a way, which is appropriate because Ulysses S. Grant, the namesake of the cottage, was in a much more dramatic, and tragic, race against time when he came here. The former president was settling into a comfortable retirement in Manhattan, serving as a well-paid figurehead for a finance firm known as Grant and Ward, when he learned that Ward had been running a proto-Ponzi scheme and that he, like the other investors, had been swindled out of his life savings. Worse yet, doctors told the former president they'd found an inoperable cancer in his throat.* He had a year to live and about two hundred dollars to his name.

Fortunately, he had an idea, too: a memoir telling the stories behind the mammoth battles of the Civil War as only the Union's most famous general could tell them. In 1884, after taking offers from several pub-

---

* Grant once noted he'd only become a regular cigar smoker after his well-publicized attack on Fort Donelson. He happened to have a cigar on hand at that moment, which the newspapers reported. "Many persons, thinking, no doubt that tobacco was my chief solace, sent me boxes from everywhere in the North. I gave away all I could get rid of, but having such a quantity on hand, I naturally smoked more than I would have done under ordinary circumstances, and I have continued the habit ever since." Essentially the public thanked Grant by jump-starting the habit that eventually killed him.

5. Ulysses S. Grant, in a photo taken four days before his death in 1885—and one day before he finished his memoirs.

lishers, Grant signed with Mark Twain, who offered enough money to keep the general's family secure for years to come. Grant could barely eat most days or sleep most nights, but he could write thousands of words a day. Friends said the book was keeping him alive.

Aside from debilitating pain, Grant's biggest obstacle was the crowd of people outside his house on East Sixty-sixth Street, which started building after a *New York Times* headline that read "GRANT IS DYING." Seemingly everyone in America felt the need to say good-bye. Choirs stood outside the house to honor the general in song. Others just stood outside and stared at the house. Those who couldn't come got news of the hero's condition thanks to the flock of reporters who hovered outside (or, when they could swing it, inside) Grant's house.

Deliverymen brought huge bouquets of flowers and gifts from all over the country. There were stacks of telegrams—from friends sending their love and concern; from Union soldiers, who remembered Grant for his victories in war, and ex-Confederates, who recalled his dedication to reconciliation in peacetime; from schoolchildren, just writing to say they were praying for his good health.

Grant tried to be gracious about all this, appearing at the window from time to time to greet and thank the crowds, but distractions are distractions, and Grant had a book to finish. The doctors didn't think the city air was doing him much good, either, and the family decided to head north to Mount McGregor, a rural area north of Albany known for its rejuvenating mineral baths.

A family friend, Joseph W. Drexel, had offered Grant use of an eleven-room house in the woods near the luxurious Balmoral Hotel. One of the Balmoral's owners, W. J. Arkell, had lobbied his neighbor Drexel hard to bring the Grants north, but not out of any concern for the general's health. "I thought if we could get him to come to Mount McGregor," he said years later, "and if he should die there, it might make the place a national shrine—and incidentally a success."

The motives weren't pure, but the setting was. The scenery was gorgeous, the crowds were scarce, and Grant could settle in and work on his memoirs for hours while sitting out on the long wraparound porch. The race against time was on.

There are only a handful of rooms on the Grant Cottage tour, but each one is significant in the story of the general's final days. "This was Grant's sickroom," the guide explains, bringing us to a room with two brown leather armchairs facing each other. "That was where he slept—he couldn't lie down because he would choke. So they pushed these two chairs together and slept here." The cancer had also affected Grant's voice; by this point he couldn't speak above a whisper and usually communicated by writing notes. "You can see several of his notes on the wall behind you," the guide says, pointing to the corner.

Also in Grant's room: his top hat, his robe, his toothbrush, and a large glass vial of bluish liquid with some kind of sandy, snow-globey residue. "That was his cocaine water," the guide tells us. "The cocaine is still in it." To ease Grant's pain, doctors would swab his tongue and throat with the solution. "Has anyone here ever had their throat painted?" she asks us. One guy raises his hand. "Doesn't feel very good, does it?" the guide asks. "I had my throat painted as a child. It's very uncomfortable and makes you want to gag." And that was without throat cancer. Toward the very end, the doctors jabbed the cocaine water in with a hypodermic needle.*

It wasn't pretty, but it worked. On July 20, 1885, Ulysses S. Grant declared his manuscript finished. Three days later, so was he: the end came in the front room of the house. Grant's son marked the moment by stopping the hands of the clock at 8:08 a.m. They have stayed in that position ever since—proof that Grant won the race against time.

The book, by the way, provided for Grant's family and then some, earning royalties that would be worth tens of millions of dollars today. And the joke was on W. J. Arkell: the Balmoral Hotel, the one he hoped to boost by having Grant's death site nearby, burned down several years after the president's death. It was just as well, Arkell said later, given that the crowds he'd envisioned never came. "Instead of making the place," Arkell said years later, "Grant's death killed it absolutely." Let that be a lesson to those who try to squeeze a few bucks out of a dead president.

Grant Cottage has run its own race against time—several of them, in fact. Its remote location, coupled with a succession of not-tourist-friendly facilities on the surrounding land (tuberculosis sanitarium, mental hospital, and, most recently, medium security prison), has kept visitors to a minimum; the place gets about five thousand visitors each year. "In the 1980s," the guide explains, "the state of New York wanted to either turn it into office space for the prison or tear it down altogether. A group of us got together against that, and the Friends of the Grant Cottage organization was born."

---

* Are there any worries about a desperate addict buying a ticket for a tour, hoping to score a little of the cocaine water? Yes. Grant Cottage director Tim Welch told CBS News in 2013, "Every year the New York State Department of Parks and Recreation measures this and makes sure that none of it is gone."

There was a new challenge when I visited: "The prison is closing. That's a problem because that's where we get our power and water hookups. Not to mention it's good for security."

"So what happens when they close?"

"That's the question," she says. The state added most of the mountaintop land to Moreau Lake State Park and left forty-three acres and a new private well for Grant Cottage to use. The arrangement has headed off the immediate crisis, but there's no guarantee the cottage's future will be a bright one.

I can't be the only one surprised to discover that a place like this, full of scenery and history, has to worry about its future. Grant memorials, though, don't seem to have an easy time of it; variations of Grant Cottage's story run through quite a few Grant sites. In Washington there's a Ulysses S. Grant Memorial—a huge installation, one of the largest of its kind in the world. It's a highly visible installation, too, sitting just across the street from the US Capitol. But I defy you to find a DC landmark list with the Grant Memorial at the top. This is probably because the Grant Memorial is the most grisly presidential landmark you can imagine: the statue of the general himself looks calm, determined, and majestic atop his horse, Cincinnatus, but below him is battlefield chaos; the *Washington Post* described the installation as "mud, exhaustion, horrible suspense, screaming plunging horses, broken reins, swollen veins, all of this in bronze." Its sculptor, Henry Merwin Shrady, spent two decades and a then-record quarter of a million dollars laboring over the piece, going so far as to dissect horse remains to get the equine anatomy just right. While these studies paid off in unprecedented horse-tongue verisimilitude, Shrady might have been better served by a break now and then; he died just before the memorial was dedicated, on April 27, 1922—General Grant's hundredth birthday.

Dramatic depictions of flailing horses and sculptures of soldiers in their death throes are not always suitable for general audiences, so mostly the Grant Memorial serves as a staging ground for tourists looking to take photos of themselves with the Capitol in the background. I saw one woman work quite a long time directing her adult son, his wife, and their daughter into the perfect wish-you-were-here pose for the folks at home. "Now, *dance!*" she shouted, snapping another set of photos.

Even Grant's Tomb in New York has seen its share of hard times. Shortly before his death in 1885 the general told his son, "It is possible that my funeral may become one of public demonstration." It was a massive understatement: he had a funeral procession five miles long through Manhattan—an island that is just over thirteen miles long. More than a million people were on hand to send him off, including the sitting president, Grover Cleveland, and former presidents Hayes and Arthur. The pallbearers included Union generals as well as Confederate officers. The tomb built in his honor was 150 feet high, and remains the largest mausoleum in North America. Yet it gets so little attention in our time that I almost missed seeing it.

Grant is just up the hill from Columbia University, in a neighborhood known as Morningside Heights, west of Harlem. New York City won the general's approval for a burial site because it agreed to his lone demand for a place for his wife. The mayor offered a spot in one of New York's parks for a tomb, and the family opted for the uptown location in Riverside Park over one in Central Park because they felt the latter spot would have been too busy.

The neighborhood was quiet on the day my family and I dropped by. With hours to go before the tomb closed, and nowhere else we needed to be, my wife and I took our son on the scenic route through Morningside Heights, just because we could. We zigzagged from corner to corner; we paused to read the signs people had posted up on light posts and windows; we pushed the stroller up a steep hill instead of a flat street. Why rush? We had nothing but time in front of us.

We made it to 122nd Street at 2:48 p.m.—plenty of time to explore, so I offered to stay with the stroller and let my wife take the first peek inside.

She came back almost immediately. "You better go in there first," she said. "They're closing in ten minutes."

"What? I checked the website, they close at five!"

"There's a sign on the door. Sequestration."

We were visiting while the federal government made across-the-board cuts aimed at shrinking the budget deficit. Grant's Tomb was doing its part for future generations by closing every other hour. In this case, we could visit from 2 to 3 p.m., but from 3 to 4, it would be locked tight. So much for taking our time.

Other presidential sites changed their schedules during this period, too, but none as noticeably as Grant's Tomb. Frankly, you'd expect closings for a lot of presidents before you'd even think of Grant—and in his own time, closing the place up would have been unthinkable. But as those who lived through the Civil War died off, Grant's reputation faltered. "The post–World War I generation feared, rather than celebrated, the endless sacrifices of the Civil War," wrote UCLA historian Joan Waugh in her biography, *U. S. Grant: American Hero, American Myth.* "In their minds, such sacrifice was associated with the seemingly mindless slaughter that had marked the First World War." A generation that remembered war as mustard gas and trenches and wounds was not going to look back fondly on the high body counts Grant's offensives racked up. Grant's presidency did his memory no favors, either, as it was remembered mostly for the many greedy subordinates who took advantage of the president's honesty and trusting nature to plunder public money. And as Grant's reputation faltered, so did the tomb.

Just decades after that five-mile-long procession came to Morningside Heights to bury Grant, the tomb was covered in graffiti and grime, and there was even talk that it should be torn down. The Grant Memorial Association turned the site over to the National Park Service in the 1950s, hoping for a turnaround, but if anything, its condition grew worse. "Workers arrived one morning last May," wrote an Associated Press reporter in 1993, "to find someone had defecated outside the tomb's entrance and run a garbage can up its flagpole." According to the government, Mrs. Grant had specifically asked for no public bathrooms on-site, understandably hoping to avoid having toilets running in her mausoleum. She might have rethought that request, had she been around to see (and smell) the place a century after it had been built.

For decades the only pleasantness around Grant's Tomb was its role as a punch line on the 1950s quiz show *You Bet Your Life*. Where the joke "Who's buried in Grant's tomb?" started is hard to say; it appeared in newspapers at least as early as 1930, but it was *You Bet Your Life* that made it a catchphrase. Host Groucho Marx didn't want contestants to walk away from the show empty-handed, so if a pair of players failed to answer questions correctly and lost all their money, Groucho would offer them a few bucks if they could answer an easy one: "Who's buried in Grant's Tomb?" Sometimes Groucho would, for variety's sake, ask other softball questions, like "What color is an orange?" And after the contestants would respond, sometimes he would shout, regardless of the question *or* the answer, "General Grant is right!"

Of course, what makes the joke so perfect is that it's a trick question: no one is buried in Grant's Tomb. President Grant and his wife are entombed there . . . but aboveground.

Criticism of the National Park Service's handling of Grant's Tomb grew to the point that the congressional delegation of Illinois, where Grant had once lived, offered to take Grant's body off the city's hands, and Grant's descendants backed them up. The Park Service took the hint and, with $2 million in federal funds, restored Grant's Tomb to its former glory in 1997.

With the clock running, I raced in, took my hat off, put my camera on, and started taking pictures, from the murals of Grant's Civil War deeds atop the high ceilings, to the bronze busts of Union generals on the lower level, to the dark granite sarcophagi where the Grants rest. I was back outside before the rangers closed the doors.

WHEN IT comes to well-timed events, there's one story we like even more than the Race Against Time that Grant was on, or the Great Reconciliation that Adams and Jefferson went through together. It's the Great Comeback.

One of the greatest Great Comebacks starts in the hills of eastern Tennessee, on winding country roads with mountain views and bright fall colors in the trees. "Fall is like a postcard from God," read one of the church signs on the road into the town of Greeneville. Fall colors are a point of pride in New England, where I live, and there are plenty of similarities between there and here, from the redbrick sidewalks to the way people describe residents as "hardy" or "independent." In 1784 eastern Tennessee tried to declare independence from the rest of the state; had the effort succeeded, I would now be driving through the great state of Franklin, with Greeneville as its capital. After four years of quasi-statehood, Congress rejected the petition, but the area has retained its independent streak.

So it's fitting that the president from Greeneville, Andrew Johnson, trusted nobody and butted heads with everyone. He was so feisty and independent, in fact, that he even turned his wrath on the town that now features a statue of him just above Richland Creek in the downtown district: once, in a fit, Johnson wrote to a friend, "If I should happen to die among the dam spirits that infest Greeneville . . . take my dirty, stinky carcass after death, out on some mountain peak and there leave it to be devoured by the vultures and wolves, or that it might pass off in smoke and ride upon the wind in triumph over the god-forsaken and Hell-deserving, money-loving, hypocritical, back-biting, Sunday-praying, scoundrels of the town of Greeneville."

At least Johnson came by his insecurity honestly: he grew up dirt poor and was one of the few major politicians of his day who had neither a military background nor legal training. In fact, Johnson had no formal education at all and was trained as a tailor. Some of the suits he made are still on display in Greeneville. He came into his own in politics, starting as an alderman and mayor in Greeneville and working his way up into national prominence, where he won a reputation as a fiery and effective public speaker on the floor of the US Senate. But he never quite shook the feeling that the better-educated types sneered at him as a "mudsill," a nineteenth-century slur something along the lines of "white trash" today.

So Johnson became a politician who was hard to classify. He was no fan of anti-slavery Northern Republicans, nor of the African Americans whose rights they championed, but he hated the South's white planter class for looking down on working-class whites like himself. When Tennessee tried to leave the Union, Johnson carried on in the Senate as if nothing had changed; then, as military governor of Tennessee, he stood his ground against Confederate assaults—Tennesseans nicknamed their hilltop state capitol "Fortress Johnson"—and warned staffers made of lesser stuff that "anyone who talks of surrender I will shoot!"

This was just what the country needed in the middle of a war. President Lincoln thought enough of Johnson and his fiery resolve to add him to the ticket in his reelection campaign. But what inspires a person in a crisis can get on that person's nerves when the world has settled down. It's hard to win support for your plans and proposals when you're, as one writer called Johnson, "the most obstinate man in America." This was a big reason why Johnson, who ascended to the White House after Lincoln's death, was the first president to be impeached—though *not* removed from office, as the rangers at the Andrew Johnson National Historic Site in Greeneville constantly correct visitors who tour the former president's house on Main Street. Burke Greear, the goateed, bespectacled ranger who shows me around, says of his tours, "We're not even into the first room before they start saying, 'So why did they kick him out of office?' And I have to back up and correct it."

Greear is circumspect about the man whose life he's describing. "Johnson usually gets ranked as one of the worst presidents," he says, "and we don't try to act like he's one of the best. But we do try to show what he was like." Any president, he says, would have had a tough time presiding over post–Civil War reconstruction, but it's no surprise that the one who went out of his way to butt heads with Congress ended up nearly getting thrown out of office.

Johnson's own house was caught up in the massive struggles of the 1860s. While he was away serving in Nashville and Washington, the Johnson homestead was playing host to a lot of uninvited and unimpressed guests. "The Civil War history of Greeneville isn't about big battles," Greear explains. "It was about troop movements." A key railroad in Tennessee ran through the area; as a result, he says,

"Greenville changed hands more than thirty times during the course of the war. Both Union and Confederate troops occupied the house at different times.

"Johnson is caught in the middle," he continues. "He's a southerner who's pro-Union, or maybe more accurately he's anti-secession; he believed the South would better have its grievances addressed within the Union. So he's treated with disgust by the secessionists and distrust by the North."

Both sides left their marks on the house. "All the doors? Gone. There are no doors left. All the windows are gone, or broken. All the furniture is gone. The soldiers who have used this house have come from Michigan to Florida. And they know whose house it was, and they aren't shy about leaving messages on the walls to say what they thought of Andrew Johnson.

"We've left up the only section that you can show in polite company," Greear says, pointing to a section of wallpaper-less wall. "People have invented a few swear words over the years, and these walls had all of 'em!" Some of the messages were in cartoon form. "One person drew a monkey—and of course that has its own connotations as well—and the monkey is facing with its backside out, and on one cheek it says 'Andrew' and on the other it says 'Johnson.'" Johnson's daughter Martha oversaw the house repairs and made a point of using wallpaper to cover up these messages, to ensure her famously suspicious father wouldn't see them when he came back from Washington. "If Johnson only knew that even in the walls of his own bedroom...," Greear says, and he doesn't have to finish the sentence.

Of course, Johnson could give as good as he got. In the midst of his fights with Congress, Johnson decided to go straight to the public to make his case, only to get into shouting matches with hecklers. To be fair, most of the speeches went smoothly, but the press coverage of the ones that didn't made Johnson sound unhinged as he moved about the country. "Can any sane man read his Cleveland and St. Louis speeches," wrote one Illinois paper, "and believe the Chief Magistrate sober when he made them?" The tenth article of impeachment against

Johnson actually refers to these speeches, accusing him of demeaning the presidency by delivering, "with a loud voice, certain intemperate, inflammatory, and scandalous harangues" against Congress.

Johnson was eventually acquitted, by one vote, in his 1868 impeachment trial, but it was hardly vindication. To keep his job, he essentially promised to acquiesce to Congress's wishes on Reconstruction, which were vastly different from his own policies, and stay out of the way. The president spent the end of his term with a new constituency: a group of White House mice. "The little fellows give me their confidence," Johnson told an aide, "and I give them their basket and pour upon the hearth some water that they might quench their thirst."

Johnson found true redemption in 1875, when he became the only former president to win a seat in the US Senate. "I'd rather have this information than to learn that I had been elected President of the United States," he said of the election win. "Thank God for the vindication." He came back to a Senate desk covered in flowers, and some of the same men who voted to remove him from the White House welcomed him back to their ranks.

Shortly after the Senate session, Johnson headed home to Greeneville, where, in July 1875, he succumbed to a series of strokes. Sad, yes, but the timing couldn't have been better. Just as he had been graciously welcomed back to the Senate, news of Johnson's death was met with sadness. Nashville, the city where Johnson had been called a dictator and a tyrant, held a public forum so residents could pay homage to their former governor and president.

Johnson would have reveled in this last round of vindication. But his burial wishes prove he hadn't forgotten his travails, and that he didn't want anyone else to forget what he had been up against and what he saw himself protecting in that fight. "When I die," he wrote, "wrap my body in the flag of my country, pillow my head on its Constitution and carry it to one of those beautiful hills in Greene County and there let me sleep until resurrection morning." That's what he got—and on a high hill looking down toward Greeneville, with a white marble obelisk to mark the spot.

Those who come to the visitors center for the Andrew Johnson National Historic Site not only hear the story of Johnson's trials, they get to take part. After learning about Johnson and his life, the rangers hand out "ballots," which are placed into one of two clear plastic bins, one marked "Guilty" and the other marked "Not Guilty." Everyone in my tour group chose to put the ballots in "Not Guilty," save for a two-year-old who chose to dance in place rather than vote. Ranger Daniel Luther says, of each year's Visitor Impeachment Vote Tally, "Invariably the vote runs ten to one in favor of acquittal." Johnson, I reply, must get a kick out of this annual vindication. "Wherever he is," Luther says with a laugh, "the inscription on his tomb has been proven right: 'His faith in the *people* never wavered.'"

3

———◆•◆———

THE FIRST PATIENT

On James Garfield, Herbert Hoover, Zachary Taylor,
and the Doctors Who Keep Presidents Alive
(and Occasionally Make Them Worse)

FOR ALL its flaws, Andrew Johnson's administration did make one important change: it hired Dr. Basil Norris, a US Army surgeon who became one of the first official presidential doctors. Previously presidents had turned to respected private physicians for treatment, and the idea of the president using government-funded doctors was somewhat controversial at first. But the practice continued, mostly out of convenience. Unlike doctors in private practice, military physicians could be summoned at any time, or could accompany the president when he traveled. And, since they were already on the government payroll, their services didn't cost any extra money. In time the executive branch replaced the on-call military doctor with an in-house presidential doctor, providing round-the-clock care.

Most presidential doctors have followed the first rule of the profession and done no harm to their charges, but a few have done more harm than good. Some have misled the country about the president's health. Franklin Roosevelt's doctors, for example, let the public believe the president was healthy enough to run for a record fourth term in 1944, knowing full well that his blood pressure was dangerously high. Others have just been lousy doctors. When Warren Harding fell ill in 1923, most of his medical team were convinced the president's symptoms proved he was about to have a heart attack, and they called for a cardiologist. Harding's lead physician, Charles Sawyer, insisted the president had merely eaten tainted crabmeat, gave him stimulants and laxatives, and put him to bed—where he promptly died of a heart attack.

There is a presidential medical story even worse than that of Warren Harding, and the end result of that tale rests in the National Museum of Health and Medicine in Silver Spring, Maryland, just north of DC. The museum was founded in 1862 to collect and study "specimens of morbid anatomy" from the ultra-bloody battlefields of the Civil War, so to tour it is to embark on an expansive, highly visual trip through the human body and the horrible things that can be done to it. If you've ever wanted to see, for example, the effects of a "penetrating ice pick wound of skull and brain," you'll feel right at home here. The notorious, eccentric Union general Daniel Sickles sent this museum the leg he lost to a cannonball at Gettysburg—and then proceeded to visit his old friend each year on the anniversary of its amputation.

Along one of the walls is a large glass case, and on one of its shelves, mounted on a small wooden pedestal, is item #13: a section of the backbone of President James A. Garfield. Of the limited number of presidential bones we have aboveground, this is by far the largest. Not far from the backbone are several small pieces of Abraham Lincoln's skull, found on medical tools used during Lincoln's autopsy but apparently not noticed until the rest of Lincoln was already on a train back to Illinois. These fragments are unquestionably historic and valuable, but they're also small enough that visitors can pretend they're something more benign.* Not so with Garfield: these are big human bones,

---

* A nearby container holds a tiny lead ball, with a sign that says "The bullet that took the president's life." The display used to contain the spinal cord of his assassin, John Wilkes Booth, as well, until, as one staffer put it, "the decision was made that it wasn't appropriate, and Booth was put into storage."

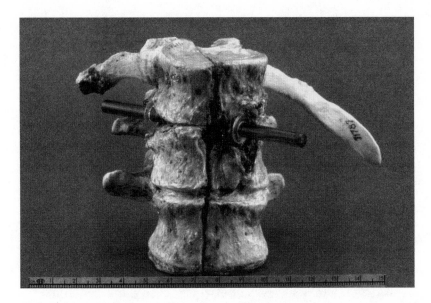

6. After James Garfield's assassination in 1881, medical examiners removed the vertebrae through which the bullet had passed and sent them to prosecutors, who used them as evidence in the assassin's murder trial.

three vertebrae and several rib pieces. Once, during a political tiff, Ulysses S. Grant snorted that Garfield was "not possessed of the backbone of an angleworm." That was just a figure of speech, of course; I'm no expert on bones, but these are more than an angleworm could ever hope for.

These bones are sitting in a museum of "morbid anatomy," with a red tube running through them, pointing out the trajectory of a bullet fired into the president's back. Garfield never shared in the esteem the public held for Lincoln; the best nickname the country could offer Garfield as he joined the Father of Our Country and the Great Emancipator in the pantheon of dead presidents was "the Heroic Sufferer."* Make no mistake, he earned the title: Garfield spent nearly half of his brief, two-hundred-day presidency in agony, thanks to the bullet

---

* It's not much as nicknames go, though it's a step up from the appellation Garfield earned as a young man working on the waterways of northern Ohio: "Canal Boy."

wound and the appalling medical care that followed. His legacy to the nation was a miserable death.

And an entirely avoidable one. Not to discount the pain that comes with gunshot wounds, but Charles Guiteau's shots wouldn't have killed Garfield on their own. The president almost certainly would have lived had his doctors done what their colleagues had done for countless soldiers who had been shot in Civil War battles: keep the patient comfortable, hydrated, and clean while his body healed itself. Dr. Ira Rutkow, a medical historian who wrote a biography of Garfield, told the *New York Times* in 2006 that "in today's world, he would have gone home in a matter of two or three days." But these doctors were treating the president of the United States—and they couldn't just leave the president of the United States alone to heal. These doctors were going to *cure* President Garfield, even if it killed him.

Which is pretty much what happened. The chief architect of this "cure" was a prominent Washington medical man named Doctor Willard Bliss—his legal first name was "Doctor," as Ma and Pa Bliss had named him for the Dr. Willard who had delivered him. Shortly after the shooting, people from the Baltimore and Potomac railroad station raced out into the capital city to find medical men, and Dr. Doctor Bliss was one of the swarm of doctors who rushed over to help the wounded president. This swarm, like most American doctors of the time, was highly suspicious of the theory that microscopic germs caused illnesses and infections and that hand-washing and other precautions could save lives. They celebrated the "surgical stink" that we now recognize as the sign of severe internal infection.

Determined to find the bullet in case it had hit anything vital, Bliss stuck his finger right into Garfield's wound. Eleven other doctors who rushed to the president's aid that day did the same thing; apparently none of them could take the others' word that the bullet was somewhere in there. A few used their fingers; others used special probes that changed colors on contact with bullet lead, sort of like a ghastly murderous pregnancy test. One of Bliss's probes got stuck in the wound; the only way he could get it out was to press down on Garfield's bullet-damaged ribs. From the inside.

A dozen doctors, probing the president's bullet wound, one after the other, with no anesthetic and no relief. It sounds like an absurd comedy sketch, with each new doctor making to check the wound and the patient begging off. Even after they pulled Garfield off the grimy train station floor and brought him back to the White House, the doctors kept probing!

And all of this was done for a bullet the doctors never found, because it had dodged the president's internal organs and landed in some fatty deposits near his pancreas. Garfield's own system had protected him from the bullet.

What the president needed was something to protect him from his doctor. How Bliss ended up in charge of Garfield's care isn't entirely clear; according to another doctor on the scene, Bliss "just took charge of it" and began giving orders to the other practitioners. When Garfield's actual doctor objected, Bliss chased him out of the White House, shouting, "I know your game. . . . You wish to sneak up here and take this case out of my hands." Would that he had, as Bliss's hands had been among those jabbing around inside the president's gunshot wound.

And it was at Bliss's hands that the ailing president took his last meals, shall we say, in through the out door. Apparently oblivious to the president's chronic digestive problems, Bliss swapped out Garfield's bland, low-drama diet for mutton and other heavy foods, then had him wash the stuff down with regular doses of liquor. The food made the patient vomit; the booze made his already severe dehydration worse. Bliss's Plan B was "enemata," a concoction made of beef broth, milk, hydrochloric acid, whiskey, and opium. "For the first five or six days the yolk of an egg was added to the injections," Bliss noted in his 1882 book *Feeding per Rectum*, "but in the judgment of the surgeons was the cause of annoying and offensive flatus."* The doctor replaced the egg yolk with an even more appetizing ingredient: charcoal.

---

* Bliss's book is, for obvious reasons, tough reading—though it does feature a sentence that may qualify as the understatement of the nineteenth century: "We must admit that rectal feeding has been a plant of slow growth."

Tallying up the president's medical treatment thus far: doctors sticking unsterilized fingers into a gunshot wound, giving liquor to a severely dehydrated patient, administering rectal feeding every four hours for weeks on end. The doctors' fingers had managed to open a germy highway in Garfield's lower back that led to raging internal infections and huge, painful abscesses, while the dietary misadventures caused Garfield to lose some eighty pounds in eighty days. On the plus side, Bliss and his medical team managed to put a stop to Garfield's flatulence; then again, they'd caused that problem in the first place. Garfield, who had given Bliss the benefit of the doubt and bravely endured all manner of painful and humiliating procedures, used Latin to describe his condition to a visiting friend: "Strangulatus pro Republica." Tortured for the Republic.

In each torturous moment there was an entire country following along with a ghoulish euphoria usually saved for the teen characters in slasher movies. "The nineteenth century was the morbid century," explains Evan Michelson, who sees ghoulish euphoria daily at her shop, Obscura Antiques & Oddities, and as scholar in residence for the Brooklyn-based Morbid Anatomy Library. "The 1880s was probably the most garish era there was."

"And that's when he died," I tell her, "1881."

"Eighteen eighty-one was dead center for Victorian morbid excess."

Britain's Queen Victoria, in the four decades following the death of her husband in 1861, helped turn the Western world into a death pageant. "She mourned excessively," Michelson says, noting that the queen wore almost nothing but black for the rest of her life and insisted that her husband's living quarters be maintained exactly as they were when he died. "The whole period—forty years—plunged into mourning. They really followed Victoria's lead. The black fabrics they used . . . they weren't reflective. You weren't even supposed to glint with light. Even the pins had to have black heads. It was deeply, deeply dark."

Garfield, Michelson explains, "died at the height of the public aesthetic of death. It was the height of not only public mourning, but the business of mourning. There were mourning emporiums which sold nothing but mourning goods—this was also the beginning of mass production. We could make things and they were widely distributed, very widespread. And then it became expected, with big funerals and black bunting and horses with plumes of black feathers.

"I mean, anyone dying at that time would have had a big event."

Indeed he did. In the wake of the July 2 shooting, for the first and only time, the United States essentially canceled Independence Day. "There were no festive demonstrations at all here to-day," said a dispatch from New Jersey, "the Mayor having prohibited the explosion of fireworks or powder, because of the nation's impending calamity." Instead of celebrating their independence, huge crowds gathered outside newspaper offices—and anywhere else there was a telegraph—for updates on the president's health. The Fifth Avenue Hotel in New York found its lobbies "filled to overflowing with an anxious, surging crowd"; hundreds of men tried to squeeze into telegraph rooms that would normally hold a half dozen. The site of the shooting, the Baltimore and Potomac railroad station in Washington, put a large bronze star on the floor where the president stood at the moment of the tragedy, and a plaque in the shape of an eagle on the wall. Thousands stood not far away at the White House, pressing each official who came out of the mansion for news of the president's condition.

One news report even suggested the shooting had driven a New Jersey woman, already grieving a relative's death, over the edge: "She was much excited and unnerved by the [shooting], and it was the one constant topic that engaged and absorbed her mind. . . . In a fit of despondency she took her life."

And, of course, the eighty days of suffering took Garfield's. On September 19, 1881, the president woke from a nap clutching his chest and begging his friend General David Swaim, "Can't you stop this?" Swaim ran for help, but Garfield was gone. An autopsy revealed the doctors' unsterilized wound–poking spree had filled Garfield's dehydrated, malnourished body with infections it couldn't fight off.

The medical examiners removed the vertebrae closest to the bullet wound and sent them to prosecutors, who introduced them as evidence in the murder trial against gunman Charles Guiteau. This proved useful, as the highly unstable Guiteau managed in a moment of clarity to argue to the court that he couldn't be convicted because the doctors, not his bullets, had finished Garfield off. "I just shot him," he told them. Prosecutors produced the backbone, showed off the bullet hole, and convinced them the assassin was responsible after all.* The backbone ended up at the Army Medical Museum, now known as the National Museum of Health and Medicine—a Victorian-era relic in a Victorian-era medical museum.

"It wasn't uncommon to have some kind of physical remembrance of a person," I ask Michelson, "but it was usually a lock of hair, right?"

"The lock of hair was the most common," she says. This is true for presidents, too: we only have a few presidential bones, but we might have enough hair from our past leaders to put together a presidential toupee.

D. W. Bliss held the president's vertebrae in his hands while on the witness stand at Guiteau's trial, which must have been mighty awkward. Americans blamed the gunman for the president's death, but they didn't exactly absolve his doctor. Bliss had spent a lot of Garfield's eighty-day agony jabbering to reporters about his own medical prowess—"If I can't save him," he told one newspaper, "no one can"—and about Garfield's almost certain recovery. When the public realized Dr. Doctor had cured the president into oblivion, they were furious. Bliss didn't help himself by presenting Congress with a $25,000 bill, worth roughly half a million dollars today, for his services. They didn't pay it.

Money was no object when it came to Garfield's tomb, at Lakeview Cemetery in Cleveland. For starters, it's a castle—180 feet high, made of Ohio sandstone, towering over acres and acres of gravestones and mausoleums that would be huge and impressive in almost any other cemetery. The exterior shows scenes of his careers in teaching, the military, politics, and death. Seriously, there's a relief of his funeral bier. As the Garfield Memorial Association described it:

---

* Guiteau switched his defense to a claim of insanity—a stronger tactic in that the man was almost certainly delusional—but the jury convicted anyway, and Guiteau was hanged shortly thereafter.

The last panel . . . is a composition that will touch the sensibilities of the coldest beholder. Death is the impressive incident. The grief of age, the tender sympathy of the child, the warmth of woman's sorrow, the sturdy pain of the old soldier, the tear of the young boy, the silent grief of the sentinel Knight—all is graphically portrayed.

Mourning, after all, is what the Victorians did best. "This is over-simplifying," Michelson explains, "but American mourning was known for its restrained tombs—and a sort of Puritanical approach to headstones. The 1870s and 1880s is when you started to see draped urns and weeping angels and huge alabasters. And then the angel becomes a skull—you see even this huge marble, out of control, massive mausoleums."

When I suggest that Garfield's tomb is probably the most Victorian presidential burial site, I hear Michelson clicking her Web browser open on the other end of the phone to take a look. "Is it the one with the Moorish arches and the inlaid floors?"

"Yeah, that's the central room with the big statue."

She takes about two seconds to reach a verdict on the Victorian-ness of Garfield's tomb: "Yeah. Absolutely." The Victorians, she explains, "were magpies, culturally—they borrowed Moorish designs and various cultural styles. It's considered rather vulgar. I love it, but especially after the early Victorian period, it explodes and gets quite garish. Architecture became garish. Everything had turrets and towers, and everything was Moorish and Grecian."

The interior continues in this vein. There's a massive white statue of Garfield inside, and above his head are twelve "colossal allegorical statues, representing the twelve signs of the zodiac which mark the sun's path, signifying that the memory of Garfield shall be as enduring as time." There are stained glass windows representing each state in the Union, and massive columns under pointed Moorish arches. The Garfield Association again: "There is a popular idea that color and decoration are entirely out of place in a Memorial, and nothing but cold, white marble, black lines and general gloom should pervade such an interior."

OK, perhaps, but I still question why the tomb of an assassinated president needs a mural of the shooting on its walls. There really is one: it shows the dapper Garfield strolling through the train station with his walking stick, oblivious to the menacing Guiteau firing behind him. It's worth noting that the other two people in the mural—Garfield's companion, Secretary of State James G. Blaine, and a guy working behind a counter—both see Guiteau and his gun but are neither able to stop him nor to alert Garfield to his impending doom.

I suppose this is just one more indignity for Garfield, lying in his flag-draped coffin in the basement of America's only presidential death castle. Just a week before I came to see the tomb, police announced somebody had broken into the monument and made off with several dozen memorial spoons. A few years prior, two guys drove out to a Garfield statue at the college he'd once led, in the town of Hiram, and cut its head off. Even statues to the Heroic Sufferer aren't safe.

The worst indignity for Garfield, though, is that his death became a period piece. The enormous tomb was in place by 1890, when, Evan Michaelson says, the nineteenth-century death aesthetic had "started to die down. Then two world wars sort of put an end to that—there were too many people dying—and the twentieth century put an end to the public display. They used to publish memorials, with all of the speeches from the presidents' funerals. I see them at flea markets all the time. They sell for usually like a dollar. They're not really worth anything, because there are so many of them."

It was around this time that the Baltimore and Potomac railroad station quietly took down the large assassination markers from the waiting room floor and walls; as the culture became less morbid, highlighting the station's role in a national tragedy was increasingly bad for business. The star and plaque disappeared entirely after President Theodore Roosevelt ordered the station demolished in 1908. Garfield's presidential assassination spot is the only one that's unmarked.*

---

* The B&P station was located near where the Newseum and the National Gallery of Art's West Building sit today. The closest we can come to the precise

———

FORTUNATELY NOT all presidential doctors have been terrible. At least one has arguably saved a president's life that might have been lost. Almost exactly a century after Garfield was cut down, a would-be assassin shot Ronald Reagan outside a hotel in Washington. The bullet that went through Reagan did much more damage than the one Garfield took: it went through Reagan's left lung and missed his heart by only an inch or two. The president was close to (if not actually in) shock, was having trouble breathing, and was losing blood quickly; he would lose more than half of his blood volume before surgery.

Reagan's doctor, Daniel Ruge, didn't probe the wound, as Garfield's doctors had done, or assemble a team of prominent experts to assist him. Instead, he let the ER doctors at George Washington University Hospital do their work. "Ruge was a strong advocate for making sure the president got the same care anyone else got," according to GWU's Dr. Dennis O'Leary. "He wasn't loud, but he was very firm."

This no-nonsense approach was, in fact, how he'd ended up as Reagan's physician. Nancy Reagan's stepfather, who was a neurosurgeon, recommended his former partner Ruge and convinced him to take the role on the grounds that "you won't let anybody do foolish things to Ronnie." And he didn't: the GWU docs handled the president's care with the same routines and protocols they used on patients who didn't lead the free world. "When a physician needs help," Ruge said years later of the shooting, "it is best to choose physicians in institutions who are dealing with the particular problem at hand. I did not consider myself the sole provider. I felt it was my duty to see that the president got good care." Reagan, who was in grave condition when he first came to GWU Hospital, was back at work at the White House twelve days after the shooting, largely thanks to the trauma team who worked on him, and Dr. Ruge, who let them do their jobs.

———

spot of the shooting is an estimate from DC engineers in 1936, which placed it in the middle of Constitution Avenue, 30 to 40 feet west from Sixth Street's west curb.

There was, by the way, one morbidly funny moment during Reagan's stay at the hospital. The ER team had put a tube into the president's windpipe to help him breathe; as he stabilized, a member of the team prepared to take the tube out, saying, "This is it." Hearing this, Reagan nervously scrawled out a note, asking, "What does he mean—this is it?"

President Reagan got great medical care, and lived, because his doctors had a plan and followed it. The White House Medical Unit, like the Secret Service, prepares for every kind of contingency, including shootings. There is always a doctor on call at the White House medical office; when the chief is on the road, a doctor is always close by, although not *too* close. The Secret Service prefers medical personnel stay outside of what they unnervingly call the president's "kill zone." (After all, says former White House physician Dr. Connie Mariano, "you can't treat the president if you are dead.") It's a highly streamlined operation—too streamlined, in the end, for Dr. Ruge, who left after four years because he felt the job was too "boring and not medically challenging." He said he would sit outside state dinners doing crossword puzzles on the off chance that the president fell ill.

The White House Medical Unit is a tight ship, probably because it was founded by a navy man, and a decorated one at that. Dr. Joel Boone served in France during World War I, earning a Medal of Honor for treating wounded marines in the middle of a live battlefield, with poison gas in the air. After the war, he served as a White House assistant physician in the 1920s for both Warren Harding and Calvin Coolidge and moved up to the top job for Herbert Hoover. Back then the "president's doctor" set up shop in what had been a White House linen closet; Boone moved headquarters to a space across from the elevator the president uses when coming and going from the residential quarters, which allows the doctors to keep a closer eye on the president's health. Boone helped convince Congress to formally recognize and fund the office as a full-on medical practice, and may have been the first White House doctor to schedule regular physical checkups for the president. He's also the inventor of the first sport named for a president. This is my favorite of Dr. Boone's many accomplishments: he gave us Hoover-Ball.

At first glance you wouldn't expect West Branch, Iowa, to be a sports mecca. Yes, this community of about 2,500 is just down the road from the University of Iowa, home of the Hawkeyes, but the vibe in West Branch is low-key and friendly. This was Quaker country when it was founded in the mid-nineteenth century, and Hoover himself remembered a childhood "filled with accounts of defeat and victory over animate and inanimate things—so far as they were permitted in a Quaker community." Hoover's presidential library is here, as is his burial site: two flat marble slabs for him and his wife, Lou, against a backdrop of rows of shrubs. They face the 14' by 20' cottage where Hoover was born, the president's way of showing that in America, even those born in the most modest of circumstances can make something of themselves. This you'd expect to find in West Branch. Competition? Not so much.

Nevertheless, standing in front of the grave of this accomplished and historic figure, I hear the not-too-distant sound of a PA system and a voice shouting out team names. "Court 2," it says. "Optimistic Noodle Club, you'll play Bull Moose Party."

I'm at the Hoover's Hometown Days festival, which West Branch hosts each August. Young kids are jumping in bouncy houses and eating shaved ice, while older residents take in history and birthday cupcakes at the Herbert Hoover Life Celebration. And there's a field just on the other side of downtown marked off into what looks like four grass volleyball courts, outlined in chalk.

This is home to the National Hoover-Ball Championships, and the voice belongs to Jared Tylee, a former national Hoover-Ball champion and one of the tournament organizers. There are nineteen men's teams and nine women's teams shuffling on and off the four courts, and, as it turns out, the Optimistic Noodle Club is one of the more normal team names; there are also the Marshmallow Pterodactyls, the Original Hoover Huckers, and a few names that might make you blush to say out loud.

I turn to Tylee. "Herbert Hoover probably never expected a team called Slutty Manatees to play his game, do you think?"

He laughs. "Doubtful."

Dr. Boone wanted to keep the president active; as Hoover himself noted in his memoirs, "getting daily exercise to keep physically fit is always a problem for Presidents." (There was another problem, according to Boone's daughter. Hoover, she said, "was always snacking and reaching for nuts.") While traveling through South America years before, Hoover had seen naval officers using a medicine-ball game called "bull-in-the-ring" to keep in shape, so he "suggested to some . . . colleagues that we start a medicine-ball game for seven-thirty in the morning on the White House lawn." Boone mixed the drill with elements of volleyball and doubles tennis to make a new

7. Herbert Hoover's doctor developed Hooverball to give the president regular exercise. It worked: Hoover dropped twenty-five pounds playing with White House associates known as the "Medicine Ball Cabinet," pictured here, on the White House lawn.

sport; the president, who played nearly every morning of his four years in office, found Boone's game "faster and more rigorous [than other sports], and therefore [it] gave more exercise in a short time."

There are a handful of rules, but essentially it comes down to what co-organizer Tony Senio tells two of the men's teams as they start a point. "It's as simple as catching the ball, and throwing the ball. Notice which one of those comes first." Of course, the ball sails beyond the sideline a few throws later. "Catch the ball, then throw the ball *inbounds*," Senio says, laughing, "I should have said."

Dr. Boone was clearly onto something; this game is an intense workout. I'm told local gym teachers and personal fitness coaches often have their charges play Hoover-Ball because it gets them working hard. Heaving a four-pound medicine ball over a volleyball net hundreds of times is bound to build muscle, while having just three players on the court at a time means participants are running to cover a lot of ground. A lot of throwing and a lot of running, in Iowa, in August. At least one player appeared to wipe his sweat onto the medicine ball, hoping that would make it harder for his opponent to catch, and I think it worked.

I ask Tylee which teams to watch as the round robin play gives way to the tournament round, and he doesn't hesitate. "This team right here," he says, pointing to the posterboard where the organizers have been tracking results all day. "They're the three-time defending champions, 21 and 0 today." Hoover-Ball is scored like tennis, and round robin matches are played as a best-of-five series, so 21–0 means the team not only won all of its round robin matches, it won without losing a single game.

The only thing larger than their winning streak is the spectacular irreverence of their team name: Got Hoover's Balls. "We were part of this training program at a gym called Got Strength," explains team member Kelley Trimble, "and when we started this we sort of played off of that."

"But instead of, say, Got Hoover-Balls, you went with this name?"

"The parents didn't like it that much at first," says teammate Kelli Vaughan, laughing. "But they came around."

It's a dynasty that could go on for years, if Hoover-Ball produces the same effects on Got Hoover's Balls and the West Branch players as it did on the sport's namesake. Hoover dropped twenty-five pounds during his presidency, no doubt helped along by the vigorous mornings on the Hoover-Ball court, and lived thirty-one busy years after leaving the White House. He started his postpresidency in 1933 no longer the hero who had saved Europe from starvation after the Great War but the heel who presided over the Great Depression. In the waning days of his doomed reelection campaign Hoover got a twenty-one-gun salute in Charleston, West Virginia; an old man in the crowd groused about the guns. "Hrumph!" he said. "They missed him!" Comedians could always get a laugh when the stock markets rose, by asking, "Did Hoover die?"

But Hoover put his head down and worked, figuring that in American politics, "if you live long enough, the wheel turns, the pendulum swings." And it did: former president Hoover worked twelve-hour days into his seventies and eighties, leading a team of six assistants from his suite at the Waldorf Astoria in New York. He organized another round of famine relief after World War II, led two efforts to streamline the federal government, and wrote numerous books, including a best-selling biography, *The Ordeal of Woodrow Wilson*. By 1951, Herbert Hoover was the fifth-most-admired man in the country. Asked how he'd redeemed himself after being turned into a villain, Hoover gave a simple explanation: "I outlived the bastards."

The final opponent for Got Hoover's Balls is a new team called Haley's Heavers, which got to the finals by upsetting the Heave Hoes (!). Despite the champs' dominance in the early rounds, those in the know are expecting a tough final match—and no one here is more in the know than Mike Johnston. He's played in twenty-two of the twenty-seven national Hoover-Ball tournaments and could tell quite a few of the participants here today that he was playing Hoover-Ball before they were born. Not that he's the type—Johnston occasionally steps out of his own team's tournament games to reline the chalk outlines of the Hoover-Ball courts, or even just to cheer on someone who made a good play on another court. He likes the looks of this championship match. "This is more of a competition than they've had in the past," Mike says of the reigning champions. "And two of them," he says, pointing to the Heavers, "are new—Haley and Megan."

"Is it the competition that brings players out each year to the Hoover-Ball courts? I mean, you've got all these athletes; are they looking for a competitive outlet?"

"It's competition and it's community," Johnston says. "For Hoover it was for fitness, and like you said, we've got that here. For us it's about community. What would West Branch be like without Hoover-Ball? It would be devastating. This is our sport, this is our tradition. Almost every team here is a West Branch team."

Johnston says that when he started playing in the tournament two decades ago, "we'd have like sixty teams or more. There was six-pound and four-pound games, and there was four-pound mixed as well as men's and women's like we have now. What we need now is for teams from other places to come in. Let's have teams from Iowa City come in. Let's have teams from Regina come in. If we 'hate' Regina so much, how about if we have some teams come in from Regina and play. That'll make it even more of a national championship. You take three good athletes from somewhere else and put them against one of the teams here, and we'll beat 'em. It's our job to keep this going, to keep this tradition alive. This is our game."

Keeping the tradition alive can be pretty exhausting. Eight hours of running back and forth to catch and hoist medicine balls has definitely taken its toll on both teams. Players who were lobbing the ball overhand earlier in the day are now using a kind of hammer-throw, starting from the hips and using the whole body to haul the ball back over the net. Others actually turn around, facing the back of the court, and toss it back over their heads. Haley's Heavers keep pace with the champions in the early going, but Got Hoover's Balls picks up the pace. McKenna Sexton starts furiously hurling the ball at every opportunity, shaking up the game, Paige Donohoe drops shots in with precision, and soon Jared Tylee is on the microphone to put this match in the books: "For the fourth year in a row, your women's national Hoover-Ball champions, Got Hoover's Balls!"

There's a brief championship ceremony; in addition to keeping the championship cup for another year, all four team members get individual trophies and split $100 in cash. They pose for photos. The press scrum is me, an intern from the Hoover Foundation, and a couple of friends. The only one of the champs to speak after all is said and done is McKenna Sexton, who says, of the photos, "You guys, it hurts to smile."

OFFICIALLY HERBERT Hoover died in October 1964 from upper gastrointestinal bleeding, but with the usual caveats about how "he had been in ill health for some time." The term is "debility," also known as plain old age, and it's taken quite a few of our leaders over the years. John Adams, Gerald Ford, and Ronald Reagan are among the presidents who have lived past ninety, as Hoover did, and several others, including Harry Truman, Thomas Jefferson, and James Madison, lived well into their eighties. A 2011 study suggested that presidents have a life expectancy several years longer than the rest of us. It's hard to say what accounts for the extra time; it probably doesn't hurt that presidents tend to be wealthier and better educated than the average American. Some analysts suggest the rigors of the job and campaigning for it weed out the less vigorous, leaving us with fitter-than-average leaders. Whatever the reason, presidents know how to stick around.

In the nondebility category, we've lost quite a few presidents to strokes and their complications, including Woodrow Wilson, Richard Nixon, and John Quincy Adams, who collapsed on the floor of the House of Representatives while voting a very vocal "NO!!!!" on a Mexican war bill. Heart disease is another common killer of presidents: Eisenhower had six known heart attacks, and Lyndon Johnson had at least three. The deaths of Andrew Jackson and Theodore Roosevelt are both blamed on coronary events, though each man had been getting progressively sicker over time. Jackson, in particular, was in bad shape—short of breath, in constant pain, and puffed up from fluid retention; "I am a blubber of water," he said, a phrase that luckily did not end up on his tombstone. Cancer is one of the biggest killers in America, but only one president—Ulysses S. Grant—has died of it.

Then there's the case of Zachary Taylor, the grizzled, unkempt Kentuckian who parlayed battlefield success in the Mexican War into a stint in the White House despite never having voted until his election in 1848. Taylor died of a euphemism: "cholera morbus" was a nineteenth-century catchall term for stomach and intestinal problems. Antebellum doctors confronted with abdominal cramps, diarrhea, or other gastrointestinal complaints could throw up their hands and say, "That's probably cholera morbus." That's what Taylor's doctors did in July 1850, when he fell ill and died after a fund-raiser for the still-unfinished Washington Monument. Legend would have you blame the iced cherries and cold milk the president ate and drank after sitting out in the hot DC sun all day—after all, residents of Washington had been warned to avoid eating and drinking precisely those otherwise refreshing items because of concerns about disease—but several other prominent politicos had similar gastrointestinal issues in July 1850. The water and sewer system in the capital city could have been called a sewer and sewer system, and that might have been at the root of Taylor's illness. It might have been something else entirely, too; Taylor had trouble sleeping the night before the fund-raiser, which might have been a sign of illness, and he'd had serious stomach troubles the previous summer as well.

There was no way to know for sure what had done the president in. No autopsy was conducted, and Margaret Taylor refused embalming, instead directing that her husband be placed in a coffin filled with ice before being sent on its way. The remains eventually came home to Taylor's Louisville, Kentucky, plantation, on a plot of land now part of Zachary Taylor National Cemetery.

Military cemeteries are poignant places for obvious reasons—and there are two Medal of Honor recipients among those here—but at this one the contrast between the white marble headstones in exact rows and the gentle slope of the hills on which they were placed amplifies the beauty even that much more. "On Fame's eternal camping-ground / Their silent tents are spread," notes one of the signs, quoting from Theodore O'Hara's poem "The Bivouac of the Dead." There are similar signs at Arlington National Cemetery, but the ones here are a little more poignant because the poem was written to honor Kentuckians. I hesitate to call any place perfect, but I can say that I only found one flaw here: the fifty-foot granite monument to Taylor, with a life-size statue of the president on top, includes a list of his biggest military victories on the sides, and it misspells one, though Taylor, an uneven speller himself, probably doesn't mind being listed as the hero of "Beuna Vista."

So what *was* it that put Zachary Taylor in the cemetery? The "cholera morbus" on Taylor's death certificate was a best guess but hardly an ironclad answer. Maybe it was bad cherries that cut the president down. Maybe it was a chronic intestinal problem. Or maybe it was the heat. For dead presidents, "maybe" isn't good enough. We have to *know*, and that's why Americans in 1991 exhumed a president who died in 1850.

The story of Zachary Taylor's unlikely reentry into the world starts with Clara Rising, who taught humanities at the University of Florida. Rising wrote novels as well; her first, *In The Season of the Wild Rose,* is set in the Civil War. At a book event in Louisville in 1990 she met Bill Gist, who lived in Taylor's boyhood home, Springfield. "It was Bill's wife Betty who first told me that the family had some severe doubts about the diagnosis of gastroenteritis at Taylor's death," Rising said in a 1999 interview. "So I went back to Florida and started to research with that, and that's how I got interested in it."

Sixteen months of research convinced her Taylor was poisoned— no "maybe" about it—by pro-slavery forces convinced the Whig president was in cahoots with anti-slavery northerners to block slavery in the far western territories won in the Mexican War. She was particularly struck by a book recounting how, in Taylor's final hours, "green matter was thrown from his stomach at intervals," which to her sounded like a sign of arsenic poisoning. "I brought the symptoms to Dr. Maples, a pathologist at the University of Florida," Rising said, "and he said the symptoms are classic arsenic."

Dr. William Maples was a forensic anthropologist who, in 1994, wrote a fascinating memoir about his field called *Dead Men Do Tell Tales*. His take on the meeting was slightly different.

> *I told Rising that I wasn't a pathologist but that the symptoms she had described certainly could have resulted from arsenic poisoning.*
>
> *She said: "Well, could this be proven?" And I explained that arsenic and other metallic poisons are quickly deposited in the skeletal system and hair of poisoning victims, if they live for a few days after the initial intake of the poison. Such metals would remain in the hair and bones, even after death.*
>
> *She asked: "How could this be proven?" I told her it would be a fairly simple matter, given access to the remains, to have tests done that would prove the presence or absence of arsenic.*

"Access to the remains" may have sounded like a pretty big caveat to this "fairly simple matter" of pulling an American president out of his coffin 140 years after his death. But Clara Rising was, as Maples puts it, "an extremely persistent and single-minded individual," and you'd have to be to do what she did. Rising looked for Taylor's descendants and "wrote to every address and name [she] could find" until she obtained family permission for an exhumation. She also won over the coroner for Jefferson County, Kentucky, Dr. Richard Greathouse. When faced with Rising's research, Greathouse said later, he decided "that it was my duty as coroner of Jefferson County to disinter President Taylor and conduct a thorough examination to ascertain whether he was truly poisoned with arsenic or not."

Rising was also willing to pay the costs, about $1,200 in all, though when the public found out about the plan to exhume President Taylor in 1991, their first question was not "Who's paying for this?" The *New York Times* was stunned that Taylor's body would be pulled out of its coffin essentially on a hunch, with almost no supporting evidence revealed. "All that's been revealed so far," the paper's editorial page complained of the project, "is a cavalier contempt for the dead." Historians questioned why pro-slavery forces would kill off Taylor, a Kentuckian who himself owned slaves, with Vice President Millard

Fillmore, a New Yorker who opposed slavery, waiting in the wings. "Suppose they find arsenic in his system," said the historian Shelby Foote, known far and wide for his role in the PBS series *The Civil War.* "Where does that leave us? I don't think there's any point in engaging in what-might-have-beens."

The government objected, too—Zachary Taylor National Cemetery is run by the Veterans Administration—but Greathouse noted that the corner of land on which the president's body lay was controlled by the Taylor family, and they had consented to the exhumation. They would open the president's tomb, Greathouse said, if it meant sneaking over the cemetery walls.

Meanwhile, Maples played good cop, reassuring the feds that his forensic photos of the corpse wouldn't end up in the tabloids. They might not have won support for the disinterment, but they had enough permission to go forward.

And so, on June 17, 1991, the bronze doors of Zachary Taylor's tomb swung open, with a small, quiet circus about twenty yards away. "We found the fire department at the front gate, directing traffic," Dr. Maples wrote of exhumation day. "Police were everywhere. The main avenue of the cemetery was lined with hundreds of people. Media camera units were positioned in cherry-picker cranes overhead."

There wasn't supposed to be anything for these onlookers to see. Greathouse and Maples, working under a green tarp set up next to the mausoleum, were going to open the marble sarcophagus and the wooden coffin, collect a few samples, take them to labs, and close the tomb back up. Under the marble sarcophagus, beneath a rotting wooden coffin, was a surprise. "He had been enclosed in a lead cocoon," Greathouse recalled, an inner coffin none of the exhumers expected to find. To get inside the cocoon, they had to take Taylor for a ride to the medical examiner's office.

It was here that Zachary Taylor very nearly became the first president to be accidentally cremated. A county maintenance worker brought a blowtorch to melt away the solder that kept the lead casket sealed. "Suddenly," Maples recalled, "I had a horrifying thought. Peering through the opened portion of the seam, I could see that the box was lined with cloth!" Had the cloth gone up, whatever was left of Taylor would have gone up, too. They changed plans quickly. "We had to take a Stryker saw, which is what we cut bone and so on with, and go around that lead cocoon," Greathouse said. Then all they had to do was "lift the top off, like off a can, and here was Zach."

The last time anyone had peered into that lead cocoon, Zachary Taylor had been freshly dead, and looked more or less as he looked in photos; 140 years later, he'd changed a bit. Who wouldn't? "The former President had been totally skeletonized," Maples said. "He presented an austere picture of simple mortality: a skeleton, clad in his funeral attire, his skull pillowed on a bunch of straw stuffed beneath the casket liner." But there was enough of Taylor left to sample for signs of arsenic. "We obtained fingernails—all ten fingernails," Greathouse noted. "We obtained sideburns, hair, pubic hair, even."

Several Taylor descendants got a peek at the bones before a worker sealed the casket back up. So did Clara Rising, who had done more to make this moment happen than anyone else. "She approached the casket with considerable hesitation and no little awe," Maples wrote. "I fixed my eyes on her and I could sense that, at that moment, she wasn't looking at a mere mass of dead bones. She was gazing on the legendary figure of history." They drove the coffin back to the cemetery, and the president was back in his tomb by 4 p.m. Taylor's corpse kept banker's hours.

The samples, meanwhile, went to Oak Ridge National Laboratory— the Tennessee facility built to make atomic bombs during World War II—where scientists placed Zachary Taylor's fingernails, sideburns, and unmentionables into the High Flux Isotope Reactor. Essentially the reactor's neutron beam, added to arsenic, would give off a particular kind of gamma ray. The scientists would then measure whether Taylor had a "natural" level of arsenic in his system or a "secretly poisoned by the Slave Power" level.

It only took a few days for the very clear and very undramatic test results to come in. "He had no more arsenic in him than you or I walking around in the environment today," Greathouse said. Had someone poisoned Taylor, the tests would have found several hundred

times more arsenic in his remains than was there. After all the speculation and conjecture and media outrage and pilfered fingernails and
neutron beams, the evidence showed that Taylor was probably laid
low by cholera morbus. Which was pretty much where his story stood
before Clara Rising came to Louisville and heard about it.

"We have the truth and that's what we were after," Rising told
reporters after the lab released its results, but she was never quite convinced that the testing ruled out murder. Years later she appeared on
C-SPAN explaining how a White House doctor and two southern
lawmakers might have used secret passages between their houses in
Washington as part of a plot to do Taylor in. One commentator sighed
that, with Rising, "you get a strong sense that she's a nice, intelligent
woman who watched one too many episodes of *Murder, She Wrote.*"

It's easy to throw stones now that we know the outcome, but in
a way, we're all part of the conspiracy that gives rise to conspiracy
theories—even those of us who don't believe in the plots. "The United
States puts a lot of emotional and mental energy in the person of the
presidency," says C. Wyatt Evans, a historian at Drew University who
studies conspiracy culture. "When it comes to people dying—very
notable, very famous people—they can't reconcile that event, they
can't make sense of it. The problem with professional historians is that
we don't provide that kind of emotional and psychological closure that
people need. We provide information to the best of our ability, but
we can never provide final answers—and we want total answers. So
where do people go? They go to conspiracy theories."

Americans—some of us, anyway—have turned to conspiracy theories every time a president has died in office. William Henry Harrison
was supposedly poisoned, as Clara Rising had believed about Taylor.
One book suggested Warren Harding was poisoned by his own wife,
in revenge for his philandering. An out-of-control power struggle
in the Republican Party did in James A. Garfield, say the conspiracy
theories, while an anarchist plot took out William McKinley. FDR
supposedly faked his own death; in Abraham Lincoln's murder, where
there actually *was* a conspiracy, a few Americans have maintained John
Wilkes Booth and his associates acted at the behest of some larger,

more hidden force, like the Confederate government, or maybe even the government in Washington.

Often there are multiple theories. John F. Kennedy is the best example of this, having been allegedly the victim of innumerable conspiracies, but there have been other theories about Zachary Taylor, too. Evans notes a book a defrocked Catholic priest wrote about Taylor's death. "His theory was that the Jesuits did him in. Before the Civil War, conspiracy theory was usually couched in some outside, alien force threatening the American way of life. So you have the Illuminati, the Masons, the Catholic Church."

Now, Evans says, "the threat is inside government . . . a group within who brought them down because they were going to do the right thing." The search for this "big *T* truth," as Evans calls it, gives us a way to squirm out of conventional history and explain why things went wrong in our past. We wouldn't have been bogged down in Vietnam, so the thinking goes, if "they" hadn't killed Kennedy. Rebuilding the country after the Civil War wouldn't have turned into such a divisive, violent mess if "they" hadn't killed Lincoln. For Rising, the Civil War might never have happened had "they" not murdered Zachary Taylor. Her novel notes the horrors of the Civil War through the eyes of her protagonist: "Morgan rode wildly, over dead and dying men and horses, headless, armless, legless corpses twisted like dolls pitched down from a great height, splattered, crushed into the blood-soaked mud. With so much death around, it seemed indecent to be alive." Wouldn't *you* rack your brain to find a way to keep that from happening?

Dead presidents become the road not taken, the vessels of what might have been. We can ascribe to them any position, or any potential accomplishment, that we supported or hoped for when they were alive, and no one can prove they wouldn't have taken those positions or achieved those goals. And since presidents couldn't possibly die of normal, natural causes like the rest of us, there has to have been something more sinister at work in their deaths—something that kept them from doing the right thing.

Maybe, then, we're a little more like Clara Rising than we realize.

The proof of this? Not long after the bronze doors had again been closed and locked at Zachary Taylor's tomb, a new theory arose, and its chief proponent was not a writer of historical fiction but one of Taylor's successors. Speaking to a crowd in Marshfield, Missouri, on Independence Day 1991, President George H. W. Bush weighed in on the controversy—and tweaked his least favorite vegetable—by suggesting the following:

"Back in Washington that was the fateful day that Zachary Taylor gobbled down those cherries with buttermilk. It's a little-known fact, not disproven by when they dug the poor guy up the other day and put him back, that his last words were, 'Please pass the broccoli.'"

4

FAREWELL, MR. PRESIDENT

On William Henry Harrison, Woodrow Wilson,
Gerald Ford, and Richard Nixon, and
How the Presidential Funeral Was Born

AMERICANS DECIDED early on that they would send their presidents off in grand fashion, starting with that multitude of ceremonies George Washington didn't want to take place. William Henry Harrison's state funeral in 1841 set many precedents as well, which was especially impressive because the funeral organizers were essentially improvising. Harrison died so early in his term that his family hadn't even made it to Washington yet, and most of the federal government was out of the city as well. It fell to Secretary of State Daniel Webster and the cabinet to cobble a funeral plan together, and to issue a public proclamation sharing the bad news. "We have thought it our duty, in the recess of Congress and in the absence of the Vice-President from the seat of Government, to make this afflicting bereavement known to the country by this declaration under our hands," they wrote. "The people of the United States, overwhelmed, like ourselves, by an event so unexpected and so melancholy, will derive consolation from knowing that his death was calm and resigned, as his life has been patriotic, useful, and distinguished."

Presidents still issue these proclamations today, as the mechanisms that set the quickly moving state funeral process in motion, so it's probably no surprise that most of these proclamations have been lightly edited versions of the proclamations sent out the last time a president died. Since President Taft's death in 1930 the statements have almost always started with the phrase "It is my sad duty to announce officially the death of . . ." The boilerplate language can get a little impersonal; after Benjamin Harrison's death in 1901, William McKinley said, "The country has been deprived of one of its greatest citizens." When Grover Cleveland died seven years later, Teddy Roosevelt issued the exact same statement, with Cleveland's name in place of Harrison's.

Americans had designed the presidency to be different from a monarchy, but when it came to a presidential funeral, Harrison's cabinet chose the spectacle of a royal funeral as their model—out of legitimate grief, of course, but probably in part to show the world that presidents were just as important as kings and queens. They draped the White House in black cloth, and the rest of the city followed suit. (This tradition has been scaled way back: now we only put black cloth on top of the president's official portrait at the White House.)

The cabinet also hired a Washington merchant called Alexander Hunter to head up the official mourning, and Hunter quickly organized an invite-only funeral service in the East Room of the White House. One of those invites went to John Quincy Adams, one of many political figures who had wondered loudly whether Harrison was up to the presidency. But he attended, remembering Harrison as "amiable and benevolent. Sympathy for his suffering and his fate is the prevailing sentiment of his fellow citizens." It may seem obvious now to have a former president laud another on news of his death, but not every former president reacted so graciously: "Let our nation rejoice," the incorrigible Andrew Jackson said of Harrison's demise. Old Hickory then thanked God for pulling the plug on the Whig-backed Harrison administration: "A kind and overruling providence has interfered to prolong our glorious Union and happy republican system, which General Harrison and his Cabinet were preparing to destroy under the dictation of the profligate demagogue, Henry Clay." Politicos ever since have followed Adams's more forgiving lead.

Americans of 1841 were with Adams on this one, too, and so Alexander Hunter and the others made sure the people could mourn Harrison as well. So they organized a massive funeral procession: military companies, diplomats, cabinet members, newly anointed President John Tyler, and Harrison's horse, Old Whitey, were among the mourners (more than a mile of them) who walked with Harrison's body as it left the White House for a public viewing at the Capitol.* There were bells, cannons, and funeral dirges; the late president and his casket rode in a black and white carriage pulled by six white horses, escorted by a pallbearer for each of the country's twenty-six states and held up on a raised dais so the ten thousand people who turned up could see. It was hard to miss; one observer noted that the stark colors of the carriage and those accompanying it "struck the eye even from the greatest distance, and gave a chilling warning, beforehand, that the corpse was drawing nigh."

There was a slight problem with said corpse; namely, what was to be done with it once the funeral pageant was over? Anna Harrison wanted her husband sent back to Ohio for burial, but the ground there was still too cold for interment, and regardless, there was no tomb there yet to house him. Fortunately there was a stopgap solution just a few blocks east of the Capitol, near the Anacostia River: a place known as Congressional Cemetery.

The cemetery's official name was Washington Parish Burial Ground—it was managed by nearby Christ Church—but it picked up the nickname by becoming Congress's go-to burial site at a time when shipping a lawmaker's body home was prohibitively expensive. Railroad networks eventually solved that problem, so the cemetery began erecting cenotaphs—grave markers without bodies—for members of Congress who died in office. It was a nice gesture, but many Capitol Hill eyebrows furrowed at the look of these things: a cone-shaped piece on top of a big cube, which rests on a flat pedestal. In

---

* Harrison's casket included a glass lid so mourners could peer in.

1876 Congress voted to do away with the cenotaph tradition because, as George Frisbie Hoar of Massachusetts told the Congress, erecting monuments as ugly as these was "adding new terrors to death."

"We've had three presidents—dead ones—as guests," explains tour guide Tim Krepp, as he unlocks a metal door to a large structure marked **PUBLIC VAULT**. Harrison was the first; John Quincy Adams and Zachary Taylor also spent time here before returning home. The inside is nondescript but sturdy and dry, the kind of place you'd want to store a president if you needed to. This, Krepp says, was the whole point of the vault: "Congress being older gentlemen—it was hot, they died—they needed somewhere to stash them."

Krepp, by the way, is wearing a green Congressional Cemetery T-shirt that reads "We Will Talk About You After You're Gone" on the back. Irreverence, it turns out, is something this burial ground has in even greater abundance than tombstones: depending on when you visit, you might come across a craft beer tasting, a herd of goats clear-

8. The bodies of three US presidents—William Henry Harrison, John Quincy Adams, and Zachary Taylor—were stored in the public vault at Congressional Cemetery in Washington before being sent home for burial.

ing poison ivy and invasive weeds, or the annual War of 1812–themed "Flee the British" 5K race, complete with costumed "Brits" shouting, "Flee, you cowardly Washingtonians!" "Congressional Cemetery is a very informal place," Krepp says, smiling. "This is a gathering place for the community."

On this humid Washington evening Krepp is leading about a dozen of us on his "spooky tour" of the cemetery. We stop at some of the burial sites of the cemetery's most prominent "guests," and Krepp has a story for every one. My favorite is the tale of William Thornton, the first Architect of the Capitol, who was also something of a doctor. Thornton, Krepp says, was summoned to Mount Vernon when George Washington was dying. By the time he got there Washington was already gone, but according to Krepp, Thornton would not be deterred, telling the Washington family something along the lines of "All I need are eight pints of warm lamb's blood and we can rejuvenate the General." Needless to say, Thornton's "restoration" pitch didn't win any support, and Washington stayed dead.

There was concern Congressional Cemetery might die a slow death of its own. "This place fell into disrepair in the '70s, '80s, '90s," Krepp says. The site, like the surrounding neighborhood, fell on hard times. "It really started to turn around in the last five, ten years." This, he says, is largely due to neighborhood dog owners, who found the cemetery perfect for their pooches provided someone cut the grass and picked up the used syringes. Cemetery staff realized these owners could serve as watchdogs for crime and litter, and so they set up a program by which residents could pay an annual fee to let their dogs run, leash-free, within the cemetery's brick walls and take part in "Yappy Hours." "We have probably six hundred people and seven hundred dogs," Krepp says, remembering to warn us to watch where we walk. "The owners are good about cleaning up after the dogs," Krepp says, "but there's always a chance someone might miss one."

William Henry Harrison stayed in this liveliest of cemeteries for three months—two months longer than his entire presidency, in fact—before his son John escorted the body back to North Bend, Ohio. Tim Krepp says another presidential "guest," John Quincy Adams, may have found a way to stick around the neighborhood even after his body left town. Adams was serving in Congress in his eighties and suffered a massive stroke as he rose to make a speech. "He died in the Speaker's room, just off the old congressional chamber that is now Statuary Hall," Krepp says. "Steve Livengood of the Capitol Historical Society swears up and down that he sees the ghost of John Quincy Adams rising to give that final speech." The space where Adams died is now the Lindy Claiborne Boggs Congressional Women's Reading Room, and Boggs made reference to the legends when she dedicated the space, the first in the Capitol named for a woman, in 1991. "When they finally gave us a room," she said with a laugh, "wouldn't you know that they'd give us one that was haunted?"

FUNERAL SERVICES for modern presidents use some of the same customs and traditions Daniel Webster and his cabinet colleagues worked up on the fly back in 1841, but in the era of mass media and mass transportation they've become even bigger. These multiday extravaganzas are dignified, usually, but never on the quiet side. If a president dies, we're all going to hear about it.

That's just as well, because we're all paying for it. By law, presidential funerals are state funerals; in fact, presidents, former presidents, and presidents-elect are the only Americans automatically afforded such honors. The government is tight-lipped about the full costs, but suffice to say sending presidential aircraft from place to place isn't cheap. Nor is the time of the United States Armed Forces—regulations say up to four thousand military and civilian support personnel can take part in state funeral services, not to mention people who work in other areas of government. And typically the sitting president announces government offices will close for the day of the funeral, and a paid holiday for the federal workforce costs, by most estimates, hundreds of millions of dollars.

At least we get a striking spectacle out of all the expense. The White House proclamation of a president's death directs the Department of Defense to coordinate the many elements of the president's

funeral, which are directed at the ground level by army personnel with the Military District of Washington. Their playbook is a
remarkable hundred-plus-page document called *Army Pamphlet 1-1:*
State, Official, and Special Military Funerals. No detail is too small to
include here, from the speed of the funeral procession toward the
US Capitol ("police escort will move at 3 miles per hour") to the
appropriate attire for the military aide to the president's family (official uniform "w/four-in-hand tie, service gloves" except for summer,
when it's white gloves). Personnel should hold their salutes until the
flag-draped casket has moved "six paces beyond its nearest approach to
the individual," or until the conclusion of musical honors.

The phenomenally detailed mourning process begins when the
military sends a joint guard of honor, including "carefully selected"
personnel from each branch of the armed forces, to attend the remains
until they can be brought to Washington.* After a day of private
repose, a massive, precise procession, complete with a riderless horse
and a flyover in the "missing man" formation, accompanies the horse-
drawn caisson that carries the president's remains to lie in state for
public viewing in the Capitol Rotunda for twenty-four hours.

While in the Rotunda, the casket typically sits on top of a curious
stand called the Lincoln Catafalque. This is quite possibly the most
unlikely item to end up as a holy relic of American mourning. The
catafalque (pronounced *CAT-a-falk*) was hastily put together in 1865
with pine boards and black velvet, just a small part of a grandiose
installation in the White House that those who attended Lincoln's East
Room funeral service nicknamed the "Temple of Death." That might
have been it for the stand, but it occurred to Benjamin Brown French,
who had organized the funeral services, that it might be worth keeping Abraham Lincoln's catafalque, and it ended up in storage in the
US Capitol Crypt. Souvenir hunters picked over its decorative tassels,
and the whole thing nearly blew up in a gas explosion in 1868. But

---

* This is almost always done by plane today; in fact, the tables and chairs in
parts of *Air Force One* are removable to make room for a casket, in case the plane
needs to carry a president's remains for funeral and burial.

9. Built in 1865, the Lincoln Catafalque has been used in every American state funeral since, including James Garfield's in 1881.

after a few repairs the catafalque was put to use in the very next US state funeral, for Pennsylvania representative Thaddeus Stevens, and it has been used whenever an individual has lain in state in the Capitol, including ten of Lincoln's successors.

The catafalque, then, isn't merely holding up each casket; it's symbolically linking each new dead president to the others, lifting them out of the mundane world of politics and into the loftier realm of history. But remember that the Rotunda ceiling features that painting of George Washington being assumed into heaven, so we don't just commit a late president to history in the public funeral process. Before heading to the burial site, the president's remains move in a motorized cortege from the Capitol to Washington National Cathedral, the unofficial headquarters of America's civil religious life. While this cross-shaped Gothic colossus, high on Mount Saint Alban in northwest Washington, is home to an Episcopal congregation (its official name is the Cathedral Church of Saint Peter and Saint Paul), it's also intended as a place where Americans can look for, or pray to, the God in "In God We Trust."

When Pierre L'Enfant designed the Federal City in the eighteenth century, he included plans for "a great church for national purposes," though this one didn't come along until 1893, when the Protestant Episcopal Cathedral Foundation won a congressional charter to establish a cathedral. It took another eighty-three years before workers put the last bit of Indiana limestone in place on what is now the second-largest cathedral in America, the sixth-largest in the world. The sheer amount of *everything* here makes it endlessly fascinating: music lovers will enjoy the Great Organ and its 10,650 pipes, or the ten massive peal bells, the smallest of which weighs six hundred pounds.* Among the more than two hundred installations of stained glass, a cosmic mosaic known as the Space Window has a moon rock at its center. There are nine chapels inside the church, each representing a different facet of American history or spiritual life.

And there is President Woodrow Wilson. The man who led the United States through the First World War, and the only president whose remains are in Washington, rests in a stone sarcophagus on the right-hand side of the nave. A presidential seal is embedded in the floor, and nearby stands a flag of Princeton University, from which Wilson was plucked to start life in politics.

Wilson, by the way, was a devout Presbyterian whose father and grandfather were both ministers. He's entombed in an Episcopal cathedral partly because of his wife, Edith, who was Episcopal, but also because of an effort to make the cathedral the American equivalent to Westminster Abbey. The first Episcopal bishop of the Diocese of Washington, Henry Yates Satterlee, wanted the cathedral to serve

---

* The cathedral's tradition is to ring the bells a certain number of times to represent the president being honored. For example, at the service for Gerald Ford, the thirty-eighth president, the cathedral bells rang thirty-eight times.

not only as a center for national religious life but as a burial site for the country's best and brightest. One of Satterlee's successors, Bishop James E. Freeman, contacted prominent Americans and asked them to be buried within the cathedral. There are more than two hundred people interred here, including Helen Keller and her teacher, Anne Sullivan, military heroes like Admiral George Dewey, and secretaries of state Cordell Hull and Frank Kellogg.

Freeman offered Edith Wilson a spot for her husband in the Bethlehem Chapel, which she accepted. He stayed there until 1956, when the Wilson family asked the cathedral to make room for a more prominent resting place as it expanded. Eighty-five-year-old Edith Wilson was on hand for the reconsecration ceremony. Fittingly, the man who presided was the dean of the cathedral, Francis Bowes Sayre Jr. Even more fittingly, he was Woodrow Wilson's grandson.

I tour the cathedral with about a dozen people on a hot, sunny Washington morning. The guide mentions Woodrow Wilson, but none of the visitors ask about him. No one asks about Helen Keller, or the American Westminster, or the stained glass, or the organ, or much of anything, with this one exception:

"I heard there was a carving of Darth Vader. Why is he there? Did they sneak him in?"

The visitor heard right: as befitting a Gothic cathedral, there are 112 gargoyles and grotesques keeping evil at bay from this sacred space, and one of them, high above the tomb of a president, is a Dark Lord of the Sith. The cathedral held a sculpture competition for kids in the 1980s, and a young man called Christopher Rader pointed out in his entry that if grotesques were originally supposed to be evil and scary, who was more evil and more scary than the lead villain of *Star Wars*?

The Vader carving is so high up on the north side of the west tower (and yes, it was deliberately placed on the "dark" side) that it's difficult to see without help from the Force, and/or a good pair of binoculars. But I like knowing that when we consider the spiritual side of shared national mourning, we're joined by a character from *Star Wars*, as well as the president who fought the war to end all wars.

THERE'S ANOTHER round of private and public ceremonies at the burial site before the casket is put in place and the president officially belongs to the ages. But nearly all of the above is subject to change, because *Army Pamphlet 1-1* also directs that staff "obtain the Presidents' desires as to type of funeral to be offered." Planning often starts before a president has even left office; the military keeps copies of the arrangements on file, and they're updated periodically.* A presidential funeral is the last real chance a legacy-conscious former leader has to grab the nation's full attention, so presidents craft their funeral plans to ensure their send-offs are memorable and meaningful.

Ronald Reagan, as befitting a onetime movie actor, thought of his funeral services in cinematic terms. "He said dusk is the time to do this," said Kenneth Duberstein, Reagan's last White House chief of staff. "He understood that this would be his closing scene." The "scene" brought out the Reagan "cast" one last time. Among those on hand were Reagan's vice president and successor, George H. W. Bush, British prime minister Margaret Thatcher, and Soviet leader Mikhail Gorbachev. Reagan's daughter Patti Davis, who had made public her political disagreements with her dad in the 1980s, was now helping First Lady Nancy Reagan through the ceremonies. Reagan's tomb faces out over a spectacular California vista, with an optimistic quote from the Gipper himself inscribed on the front: "I know in my heart that man is good, that what is right will always eventually triumph, and that there is purpose and worth to each and every life." It was, as he had envisioned, a widescreen send-off.

Gerald Ford, on the other hand, had downplayed grandeur as president—"I am a Ford, not a Lincoln," he famously said of himself—and his 587-page funeral plan played down the pomp and ritual, too. Greg Willard, who oversaw funeral preparations for the Fords, said the president wanted, first and foremost, a family funeral, with lots of personal touches in place of ceremonial ones. "He didn't want a horse-drawn

---

* Bill Clinton was an exception, and opted not to file a plan as he left the White House. Why? "He's an optimist," said a spokesperson.

caisson," Willard said, "so his casket was to be borne by a hearse from Andrews Air Force Base to the Capitol. So we developed a new idea for him to consider: have the hearse come over Memorial Bridge, around the Lincoln Memorial, up Seventeenth Street, and then pause at the World War II Memorial in a moment of mutual tribute to President Ford and his World War II comrades." Ford loved the idea; his hearse also drove through his old Washington-area hometown of Alexandria, Virginia, and he asked the military band to play a somber version of the fight song for his alma mater, the University of Michigan.

Ford's funeral wasn't entirely simple, of course: his funeral hearse was neither Ford nor Lincoln but a Cadillac. And he did, after all, opt for the whole complement of stops, including a viewing at the Capitol and a service at the National Cathedral. Ford's predecessor, Richard Nixon, turned all of it down—the state funeral, the cathedral, the Capitol, the caisson, and Washington, DC. Even his tombstone is understated—a black stone, probably the smallest such marker of any president, saying simply "Richard Nixon, 1913–1994. 'The greatest honor history can bestow is that of peacemaker.'" No obelisk, no list of accomplishments, no presidential seal.

Nixon wasn't opposed to state funerals; he presided over three of them, for Dwight Eisenhower, Harry Truman, and Lyndon Johnson, while in office. And he started putting ideas together—big ideas—for his own funeral during his first four years as president. He wanted two days of viewing in Washington, lots of patriotic music, and forty honorary pallbearers, including top figures from politics ("See who comes out as the head people after the 1972 campaign," he noted to himself) and entertainment (comedian Bob Hope was among those on the list).

But that was before Watergate, the "third-rate burglary" turned national scandal that uncovered a pattern of break-ins, cover-ups, and dirty tricks among the president's men. When the investigation revealed Nixon's own role in the scandals, it brought down both his presidency and his reputation. Barely two years after winning reelection in a huge landslide, Nixon resigned ahead of likely impeachment and removal from office. News-anchor-turned-political-commentator David Brinkley joked that the only role Nixon could ever play in political disgrace would be that of "Official U.S. Government Scapegoat." If there was a scandal, Brinkley said, the current president "could simply say it was Dick Nixon's fault, and Nixon would step forward and say yes, I did it."

"I let the American people down," Nixon said in his famous television interview with David Frost in 1977. "And I have to carry that burden with me for the rest of my life." But that life still had a few rounds to go, even with the burden of Watergate. On the day he resigned, Nixon gave a farewell speech to White House staff. If you listen closely you can hear him thinking about the next act in his public life. He recalls the great personal tragedies of Theodore Roosevelt, whose mother and first wife died on the same day, and how in time TR overcame the lowest point in his life to rise to greatness. "He not only became President," Nixon told them, "but, as an ex-President, he served his country, always in the arena, tempestuous, strong, sometimes wrong, sometimes right, but he was a man."

Nixon knew one thing about himself and about the country: "It is necessary to struggle, to be embattled, to be knocked down and to have to get up," he told *Time* magazine. "Americans are crazy about renewal." And he put together a plan to renew his public reputation and return to "the arena," as Roosevelt had done. He even gave his comeback project a name: Wizard. "He was determined to become someone people listened to—a senior statesman, a sage," wrote Elizabeth Drew of Wizard for the *Atlantic*. "And the best way to be considered a sage, Nixon understood, was to establish one's credentials as an expert in foreign policy, a man known to world leaders." Nixon traveled extensively, wrote even more extensively, and found opportunities to "counsel" sitting presidents on international issues. At home, Nixon courted thought leaders, policymakers, and even the press, hosting parties at his Manhattan town house (he even mixed the martinis himself).

Rebuilding Nixon's reputation didn't happen overnight. "Watergate—that's all anyone wants," he grumbled years after the resignation. Nevertheless, he kept working, and writing, and traveling, and eventually Watergate wasn't the only thing anyone wanted from Richard Nixon. I saw the evidence of this at the Nixon Library in California, as it marked twenty years since his death and funeral with a special exhibit called "Farewell, Mr. President." The display included the light blue suit jacket, dark blue striped tie, and white button-down shirt the eighty-one-year-old former president was wearing when he suffered a massive stroke at his home in New Jersey, as well as the red wrist tag he wore when he was admitted to New York Hospital–Cornell Medical Center—under the name Dick Ryan, to keep his condition private.* The display showed the letters that came in amid hopes that Nixon might recover, including those from fellow presidents ("You're the feistiest one of us all," Ronald Reagan wrote, "and you've got a huge cheering section rooting for you") and lesser-known well-wishers ("I was so sorry to hear that you are in the hospital. . . . Maybe this medal I won in the Special Olympics will help").

And there was this, which I can describe but not quite explain: a purple plush toy raccoon, wearing a pink sun visor and holding an American flag and a Kit Kat bar, sitting in a yellow baby seat covered in black marker messages like "Viva Nixon" and "Nixon's the One." The staff at the Nixon library don't have any answers about the raccoon, either. "People left that outside the doors," supervisory museum curator Olivia Anastasiadis told me. "We have three shelves' worth of this stuff."

When Nixon eventually succumbed to the stroke, on April 22, 1994, Bill Clinton issued a formal proclamation about the news, as presidents always do, but it was much more personal than the usual boilerplate language issued on the death of a president: "He suffered defeats that would have ended most political careers, yet he won stunning victories that many of the world's most popular leaders have failed to attain," the statement read. "On this solemn day, we recognize the significant value of his contributions to our Nation, and we pray that he left us with enough of his wisdom to guide us safely into the next century." Clinton meant this last part literally. "After he

---

* Ryan was Mrs. Nixon's maiden name.

died," he said later, "I found myself wishing I could pick up the phone and ask President Nixon what he thought about this issue or that problem, particularly if it involved Russia. I appreciated his insight and advice and I'm glad he chose, at the end of his life, to share it with me."

As Clinton and every living former president prepared to attend the funeral, forty-two thousand people filed into the Nixon Library in Yorba Linda to get a brief glimpse of the flag-draped wooden casket. They weren't all Nixon supporters, either: self-described enemies were on hand, too. "Every generation needs somebody to hate, and he was ours," said Richard Shilling, a computer programmer. "He politicized us, he incited us, he defined our cause. No one can ever take his place."

It was this kind of talk that surprised me the most as I followed the news coverage of Nixon's death and funeral, the first presidential death in my lifetime. Nixon had always been characterized as the disgraced villain of Watergate, the scandal that shook the country's faith in its own institutions. Now, instead of bringing up his "enemies list," commentators were ticking off a list of the Nixon administration's domestic and international accomplishments. Nixon's opponent in the 1972 presidential election, George McGovern, had called the Watergate break-in "the kind of thing you expect under a person like Hitler." Two decades later, McGovern was praising his old rival. "I think he became a more authentic, open, liberated person after he left politics," he told *People*. "As a person, he was more humane, a better man the day he died than when he was in the White House."

None of the speakers at Nixon's funeral said the word "Watergate," but each of them touched on the peaks-to-valleys-to-peaks arc of Nixon's presidency and postpresidency. "Richard Nixon would be so proud," said former secretary of state Henry Kissinger, "that President Clinton and all living former presidents of the United States are here, symbolizing that his long and sometimes bitter journey had concluded in reconciliation." Clinton went even further, saying words that can now be read as you walk in and out of the Nixon Library: "May the day of judging President Nixon on anything less than his entire life and career come to a close."

The line I remember from watching the funeral came from Stephen Ambrose, the popular historian who wrote a three-volume biography of Nixon. He was serving as an analyst on ABC News alongside Ted Koppel. As military personnel prepared the coffin for burial, Ambrose said, "I think every American over thirty years old is astonished at this outpouring of affection and emotion for Richard Nixon. And thinking back to the summer of 1974—I just don't understand how this happened. No one could have predicted it, except for one person. And I think he saw it. I think that he landed in California after the resignation and he devoted himself to this moment, making this moment happen. And he's done it. He became not just an elder statesmen—to everyone's amazement except his, he's our beloved elder statesman."

Koppel replied, "And maybe it's best that it is that way. Twenty years have passed, and I think everyone will have their memories of Richard Nixon. And those who choose to harbor ill memories will continue to do so, but in a sense that's what a ceremony like this is about, after all, isn't it? It's a chance for the country to come together, and for us to consider all the things, the entire picture, as President Clinton put it, of what Richard Nixon has meant to the United States."

Ambrose agreed. "The whole American democracy is wrapped up in this scene," he said. "Democratic presidents, Republican presidents, men who have gone after each other all their lives, gather together to honor the most controversial of all of our presidents, in a ceremony that has brought the whole country together." This became the main thrust of the coverage of Nixon's death and funeral—that, love him or hate him, it was time to come together and lay Richard Nixon to rest.

Which is, of course, what Nixon had hoped for. It was as if the press, finally without Dick Nixon to kick around anymore, decided to stop kicking. And those who kept at it found themselves outnumbered. Hunter S. Thompson, who had devoted so much of his gonzo energy to Nixon and Watergate, minced not a single word in his eulogy for *Rolling Stone*. "If the right people had been in charge of Nixon's funeral," Thompson wrote, "his casket would have been launched into one of those open-sewage canals that empty into the ocean just south of Los Angeles." He went on to call Nixon "a swine of a man," "a jabbering dupe of a president," and "evil in a way that only those who believe in the physical reality of the Devil can understand it."

Thompson's essay concludes like this: "By disgracing and degrading the Presidency of the United States, by fleeing the White House like a diseased cur, Richard Nixon broke the heart of the American Dream." Not a small charge—but Thompson also knew that this funeral would change the way America saw the former president and judged his reputation. No matter what people remembered of Watergate, no matter what new dirt we might learn about the man in the future, he had that funeral, with every one of his successors on hand, embracing "his entire life and career," and essentially judging him redeemed. The funeral, Thompson wrote, "was Nixon's last war, and he won."

A communications professor at Tennessee Tech University, Russ Witcher, tracked the media coverage of Richard Nixon from when he resigned to when he died, and he found that as Nixon worked to rebuild his public image, coverage about him in news magazines like *Time* and *Newsweek* changed. He was no longer the man who left the White House in disgrace; instead, he was the president who successfully fought to return to "the arena." In the wake of his death, they wrote of reconciliation, respect, and even a measure of vindication. Project Wizard had worked. "Harry Truman once said that a statesman is a politician who's been dead 10 or 15 years," Witcher wrote.[*] "Nixon was ahead of schedule."

---

[*] Truman was paraphrasing former House Speaker Thomas Brackett Reed, who said, "A statesman is a successful politician who is dead."

5

DEATH TRIPS

On the Posthumous Travels of James Polk,
James Monroe, John Tyler, and Abraham Lincoln

R ICHARD NIXON got the funeral he wanted—and the burial, too, which required a little extra work. California limited interments to public cemeteries, licensed private cemeteries, and burial grounds run by churches and religious communities. The Nixons wished to be buried on the grounds of the presidential library; rather than seeking a state exemption, they solved the problem in a deal by which the library deeded the burial sites to the Yorba Linda Friends Church, which a young Richard had attended. In every respect, says Olivia Anastasiadis, supervisory museum curator at the Nixon Library, "the president's wishes were fulfilled."

I figured this would be obvious—that presidents, who had led and shaped and controlled so much in life, would be able to have their wishes carried out for death and burial. But some presidents have had very different afterlives than the ones they'd envisioned.

Take, for example, the story of James K. Polk, our eleventh president, who, at age forty-nine, had been the youngest president elected to that point but ended up having the shortest retirement of any president who made it through his term alive. Polk once wrote in his diary, "No President who performs his duties faithfully and conscientiously can have any leisure." He meant it, too. Polk put in ten to twelve hours a day, six days a week—sometimes more, because he insisted on clearing every item off his desk before retiring for the night. When his own desk was clear, he checked up on his cabinet members' work—or did it himself. "I have conducted the Government without their aid," he wrote in his diary in 1848. "Indeed, I have become so familiar with the duties and working of the Government, not only in general principles but in minute details, that I find but little difficulty in doing this." Not even the urgency of war slowed down the first presidential micromanager, who found time during the conflict with Mexico to ask an army general why he had used wagons to transport supplies when mules would have been better.

Day after day, hour after hour, Polk pushed himself to do more, more, more—and grumbled about how the formalities of the office slowed him down. In one diary entry he complained about having to sit for a portrait artist. "It was very inconvenient of me to lose the time," he wrote of the two-hour session. Never much of a people person, he left most of the meeting-and-greeting part of the job to his wife. Sarah Polk had tried to get her husband to slow down, but failing that, she aimed to clear his plate a little. Mrs. Polk served as an unofficial secretary and assistant, working long hours as the president did, reading newspapers and gathering documents on his behalf, along with handling her social duties as first lady. The Polks basically turned the government of the United States into a mom-and-pop shop for four years.

This was a period in which a president might have used a little help, too. During Polk's term, the country went to war with Mexico, winning vast amounts of Mexican territory that now comprises California and most of the American Southwest, won the Pacific Northwest after threatening war with Britain, built a federal treasury system that stayed in place for decades, and lowered the national tariff. In four years the hardworking Polk accomplished everything on his presidential to-do list. He might have conquered the world, had he learned to delegate.

Polk took just over two dozen days off in his four-year term, and it showed: at the James K. Polk Ancestral Home in Columbia, Tennessee, about an hour south of Nashville, there is a set of portraits on the walls—one made in the first year of Polk's presidency, the other toward the end of his four-year term. First-year Polk has dark hair and a sly smile; while he's definitely a man of smaller build, his features are filled out. End-of-term Polk is a ghost: his hair is now bright white and much thinner, and so is his face, which stares blankly ahead. He looks considerably older than a man of fifty-three.

James Polk was ready for retirement when his term ended in 1849—and he and Sarah had planned for it well. They bought a large home in Nashville, which they called Polk Place, and filled it with red velvet furniture, portraits of Polk's political heroes—Washington, Jefferson, and Jackson—and gifts from admirers, including a heavy round table from Tunis with the American coat of arms inlaid in the center. Perhaps the most interesting item at Polk Place, though, was the fireplace mantel and its telling inscription: "For what I guard is sacred rest." There would be no twelve-hour workdays at Polk Place. This house was where James and Sarah planned to leave Washington behind and enjoy a quiet life together.

They just had to get home first. And that trip proved that Polk was right when he said a president who performed his duties faithfully would see no leisure.

Rather than take a straight path west to Nashville, the Polks did a loop through the South, a sort of "victory lap" where supporters could fete him for his accomplishments in office. After a short boat trip down the Potomac River, the former first couple took trains south to Wilmington, North Carolina, stopping for a day's worth of public events. There were more festivities the next day in South Carolina, and then in Georgia, Alabama, and Louisiana.

These events were good for Polk's ego, but the long rail trips—which he described as "dusty and fatiguing"—weren't so good for his health, and left him more exhausted than ever. Even Mrs. Polk, who tended to hold up better than her sickly husband, had started begging off of some of the public functions out of sheer exhaustion.

But the public pressure to see the Polks was enormous; seeing a president in person was much more rare in the 1840s than it is today. Polk had a bad cold by the time his party had reached New Orleans; he hoped to zip through town without much fanfare, but the local reception committee begged him to reconsider. After all, they told Polk, New Orleans had done so much to prepare for his visit that he simply *couldn't* decline their hospitality. Not wanting to be rude, Polk took part in a procession through the city; after he tried to duck out early, the city fathers again nagged him until he stuck around for the massive dinner in his honor.

Unfortunately, Polk wasn't the only one passing through the Big Easy at the time: the dread disease cholera was also in town, and Polk caught it. Now he was worn out *and* suffering from diarrhea most of the day—"My bowels were affected and the shaking of the Boat had become inconvenient for me," he told a doctor—and *still* local dignitaries browbeat him into attending their Polk parties. The ex-president's nephews even made the man get up and party in Memphis, at a time when he should have been in bed.

By the time the boat reached Paducah, Kentucky, Polk finally saw a doctor—who inexplicably told him he didn't have cholera. There had been numerous reports of cholera coming upriver on ships from New Orleans, and three people on Polk's boat had already died of cholera, but the doctor said, "Nah." The Polks wisely holed up in a hotel for four days to recuperate, and a few days after that they were back in Nashville.

But by that point cholera had made its way to Nashville, too, and this time, no amount of rest could save Polk. As he grew weaker, his seventy-two-year-old mother raced up from Columbia to say her good-byes. Polk, who had always attended Sunday services with Sarah but had never formally been initiated into a faith, was baptized in the Methodist Church. On June 15, 1849, Polk reportedly told his wife, "I love you, Sarah, for all eternity, I love you," and that was it. Just one hundred and three days after leaving office, James K. Polk was dead.

"He sleeps with the great and good who have gone before him," wrote the *Nashville Union* of the shocking news. "May the earth lie lightly over his remains."

It didn't, of course. The first earth to lie over Polk's remains was that of a Nashville city cemetery—Polk wasn't the only cholera victim in town, and to slow the spread of the disease, the city quickly buried all thirty-three of the victims, Polk included, together. He stayed there for nearly a year, until a permanent tomb was built in the front yard at Polk Place. The designer was William Strickland, who had designed both George Washington's tomb at Mount Vernon and the Tennessee State Capitol, which was being built just a few blocks away from Polk Place.

Made of limestone, the square tomb's white canopy was held up by four round Doric pillars. Underneath was a white pedestal, relatively unadorned save for the long inscriptions on each side, prepared by Polk's longtime political ally A. O. P. Nicholson. "He planted the laws of the American Union on the shores of the Pacific," the marker reads on one side. "The excellence of Christianity was exemplified in his death," says another.

A military band led the procession on May 20, 1850, bringing Polk and his walnut coffin from Nashville City Cemetery back to Polk Place which, according to Polk's complicated will, was to pass on to the State of Tennessee after Sarah's death in 1891. Essentially he named the state a guardian of the property to ensure that only true Polk descendants ever lived there and that his tomb would remain in the garden. Tennessee went 0 for 2 on those requests: after briefly considering using the property as the official governor's residence, the state tore down Polk Place; on the grounds of the site today are a Tennessee state historical marker and a Best Western hotel that offers free continental breakfast and in-room wireless Internet.

Polk's remains moved again, coming in 1893 to the grounds of the Tennessee State Capitol, high on a hill above downtown. The tomb, on the northeast side of the capitol building, appears well maintained but a little lonely; it doesn't command attention, for example, like the giant statue of Andrew Jackson, Tennessee's most famous president. Even the statue of Tennessee's least well regarded president,

Andrew Johnson, has a more prominent perch. Nashville's birds have long considered the feisty Democrat's head a tempting target for their droppings.

This obscurity, tucked away in a corner of the capitol grounds, has people back in Columbia saying that maybe the restless Mr. Polk ought to move one more time. Tom Price, curator of the Polk Ancestral Home, says there's been talk in town—talk, he says, "which I've tried to encourage"—that maybe, rather than lying "where he'd never intended to be," Mr. Polk and his tomb might be happier in a town that already burnishes his legacy. In other words, don't be surprised if you see a military band leading a procession into Columbia, followed by a worn and well-traveled walnut coffin, four limestone pillars, and a pedestal with a really long epitaph. For James K. Polk, it'll be just another workday.

SARAH POLK would live on for four decades after her husband's death, and American political figures passing through Nashville made sure to call on her and to pay their respects to the president's tomb. Even during the Civil War, Union and Confederate generals alike came to the "neutral territory" of Polk Place.

Polk's remains stayed put during this period, but the sectional differences that led to the War Between the States did prompt moves for several of his colleagues. It turns out a president's body can be very useful in trying to make a point.

Such is the story at Hollywood Cemetery in Richmond, Virginia, where both James Monroe and John Tyler rest on a hilltop known as Presidents Circle, overlooking the James River. It takes a little wandering to find the circle, and this is on purpose, according to John O. Peters, who wrote a book on the history of Hollywood Cemetery. "Hollywood is, along with a number of other great cemeteries in the country, part of the rural cemetery movement," he says. "Cities were becoming more crowded and more depersonalized and more industrialized. People were losing touch with nature, essentially. Along with a loss of contact of nature, they were losing touch with basic human yearnings and experiences like birth, death, regeneration, that sort of thing. So rural cemeteries were influenced by a great desire by the inclination to reconnect with nature and with human roots.

"Rural cemeteries were not laid out on a grid plan. They were outside of cities. They had curved roadways, they had irregularly shaped lots, they were put largely in pastoral settings, where they put a premium on leafy glades, and frontage on rivers, and peaceful qualities and lakes and that sort of thing. They were the forerunners of America's public parks—there were no public parks before there were rural cemeteries. And someone said, 'Hey, instead of having to go to the cemetery for relaxation, it'd be nice if we could go someplace where we didn't have the funeral processions and gravestones.' And that's what led to the founding of America's public parks. So the rural cemetery movement is an extremely critical sociological movement in the United States."

Hollywood has taken good care of its presidents. The nonprofit foundation that manages the cemetery put Presidents Circle first when it launched a multimillion-dollar fund-raising campaign to repair monuments and paths. And yet neither Monroe nor Tyler planned on ending up here. It was a governor of Virginia, Henry Wise, who dreamed up Presidents Circle—and had it been up to him, there might have been even more presidents on the hill.

Wise is a little-known figure today, but in the 1850s he was well known, albeit not necessarily well liked. Wise saw himself in the mold of his onetime mentor, Andrew Jackson: tall, thin, bold, and decisive. But many in the country thought he was boisterous, unpredictable, and a little dangerous. Before Wise's first two-year term in Congress was up he'd dueled with—and wounded—the man he defeated for the seat in 1833. Later, Wise served as second for a colleague in a duel; after both men fired and missed, satisfying their honor without injury, Wise somehow convinced them to keep shooting. They did, one of them died, and a reputation was born.

Actually Wise helped prevent more duels than he ever fought, but his sharp-tongued speeches in Congress helped further the image of a political pugilist who loved nothing better than to sock it to his opponents. And Wise rarely pulled punches. When New York congressman and future president Millard Fillmore brought up concerns about slavery in the nation's capital, Wise practically spat out his sarcastic rebuttal: "He says that the people of the North are continually shocked by advertisements of slave dealers in the papers of the District. I am sorry, sir, that their nerves are so delicate, when their fathers did more than any other people of the Colonies to establish slavery amongst us."

Wise's chief cause in public office wasn't fighting, and it wasn't even slavery; privately, he wondered whether the institution was doing more harm than good to his state. Wise wanted Virginia to reclaim its place as America's preeminent state. Virginia was, after all, the home state of great leaders like Washington, Jefferson, Madison, and Monroe, a place to which Almighty God Himself gave special attention. "He guards Virginia," Wise said in one speech, "and Virginia guards the Union." After taking office as governor in 1856, Wise pushed for policies that would better Virginia's roads, economy, and school system. But policy changes wouldn't inspire Virginians to rededicate themselves to greatness. Nor would they remind northern abolitionists that the Old Dominion was the Union's most indispensable state. Wise needed a symbol—and soon he had one: a very popular dead president.

James Monroe was popular enough that in 1820 he ran unopposed for reelection, the only president other than George Washington to do so. History now calls his time in office the Era of Good Feelings, but the good times drew to a close in 1825 as the Monroes returned to their Oak Hill estate in Loudoun County, Virginia. The fifth president's years out of office were, as one biographer put it, "one of the most unhappy, and undeservedly so, retirements of any American president." Elizabeth Monroe died in 1830, after which James's health began to decline. Monroe had money problems, too: with presidential pensions more than a century away, the former chief executive had to spend most of his time badgering Congress to repay expenses he was owed for diplomatic work in Europe decades before. Lawmakers eventually paid them, but not before the hard-up Monroe had to sell

Oak Hill and move in with his daughter's family in New York. He died there on July 4, 1831, and a procession of thousands accompanied his body to Marble Cemetery in Lower Manhattan, where it was placed in the vault of his son-in-law's family.

This burial was a sore point for southerners. "Virginians sort of felt left out," explains John O. Peters. "They didn't like the idea of Monroe being buried in a cemetery in New York without any participation by a Virginian, thought he should be buried in Virginia, thought the burial in New York was probably beneath his status. So there were some feelings in Virginia that Monroe had been given short shrift."

And the bad feeling over Monroe's northern burial grew along with the growing tension between North and South. By 1858, with sectional feeling running extremely high, New York officials started talking about building a monument to mark the centennial of Monroe's birth. I can't say for sure that Virginians were rankled about this, but Peters says that when New York officials asked Henry Wise what Virginia was doing for Monroe's hundredth birthday, the plans abruptly changed—suddenly the discussions weren't about monuments but about moving and reburying Monroe's body. "The Virginia General Assembly ultimately appropriated two thousand dollars to have Monroe reburied in Richmond. And the New York officials eventually acquiesced."

Monroe's family had asked for a simple, private transfer from New York to Virginia. But the New Yorkers wanted to ensure no Virginian thought their state was giving Monroe short shrift in his Empire State send-off; they organized a grand military funeral procession, a public viewing of the casket for ten thousand people, and an entire volunteer regiment in dress uniforms to accompany the remains on the steamship to Richmond. "This handsome offer," wrote one northern newspaper, "cannot but give the Southerners a higher opinion than they are accustomed to expect of the liberality and fraternal feeling of the people of the North."

Wise and the Virginians were impressed by the New York festivities, but they weren't about to be upstaged by them, either. The Virginia end of the reburial included a journey south on the steamship

Jamestown, with several massive public receptions for Monroe and his live accompaniment along the way. One of them was in Washington, so President James Buchanan could pay respects to his predecessor. When the group arrived in Richmond, they were met by Governor Wise and a procession that stretched two miles long on the way to Hollywood Cemetery. The Virginians toasted Monroe and the New York contingent with mint juleps; in his speech next to the hilltop burial site he'd chosen for Monroe, Wise gave a nod to national unity at a time when the country was on the verge of breaking apart. "Who knows this day, this hour, here around this grave," he told the crowd, "that New York is of the North and that Virginia is of the South? They are one." But he also reminded the crowd of virtually every-thing Virginia had ever done for the Union—not to mention the tell-ing inscription on Monroe's new sarcophagus:

> *By order of the General Assembly*
> *His remains were removed to this Cemetery, 5th July 1858,*
> *As an evidence of the affection of Virginia*
> *For her Good and Honored son.*

Wise was so proud of pulling off the Monroe move that he started thinking even bigger. Most accounts say he dreamed of adding Mon-roe's friends and fellow Virginia presidents Thomas Jefferson and James Madison to the hilltop. One account even has Wise standing next to Monroe's new grave and exclaiming, "Now we must have all the native Presidents of Virginia buried in this inclosure." To which an alderman from New York replied, deadpan, "Go ahead, Governor, you fetch 'em." It doesn't appear that Wise sent feelers to Madison's people to "fetch" him, but he did write to Monticello, only to be told thanks but no thanks.

That was the end of Wise's dreaming over Hollywood Cemetery, save for hiring a local architect, Albert Lybrock, to design a twelve-foot-tall iron structure atop Monroe's tomb. The intricate design was meant to evoke the detailed ironwork seen around European cathe-drals, but Peters says most visitors have had something else in mind

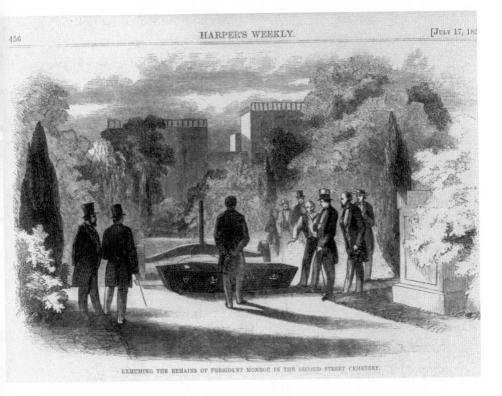

EXHUMING THE REMAINS OF PRESIDENT MONROE IN THE SECOND STREET CEMETERY.

10. James Monroe, a Virginian, was buried in New York, which rankled southerners. So in 1858 the governor of Virginia naturally arranged for Monroe's remains to be exhumed and reburied in Richmond.

when they visit: "People still occasionally call it the birdcage," he says, laughing. "Not much we can do about that."

But even just one president on the hill did wonders for Hollywood Cemetery, which made the most of its new notoriety. "Relatively few burials took place before the reburial of James Monroe," Peters says of the cemetery in its early days. "Financially it was not successful, and it became the battleground, a battleground for debate in the Richmond newspapers and in the Virginia general assembly, when it sought a corporate charter."

After the 1858 reburial, though, "the cemetery began to gain in popularity and became much more appealing and successful finan-cially," Peters says. The reburial "represented a sea change, I think, in the attitude not only of the people who founded and who ran the cemetery, but Virginians in general.

"But," he says, "1858 was three years before 1861. And we all know what happened in 1861."

JAMES MONROE was reburied the year before John Brown and his antislavery "army" raided the federal armory at Harpers Ferry, Virginia. It was Henry Wise who met with Brown for three hours after his capture and then decided the firebrand would hang for the attack. Brown's execution, and his prediction that "the crimes of this guilty land can never be purged away but with blood," sped up the slow march toward secession and war. As governor, Wise had been somewhat reluctant to take the final step of leaving the Union, but after leaving the office he decided secession was impossible to avoid. The man who had declared Virginia and New York "one" just a few years before was now urging local militias to raid the same federal armory John Brown had been hanged for seizing.

Of course, Wise was hardly the only Virginian who had made this kind of switch, and one of them happened to be a living former president. John Tyler, like Wise, had looked at first to avoid a conflict. In 1860, as southern states started moving toward secession after Abraham Lincoln's election, John Tyler headed to Washington to lead a "peace conference" to negotiate a compromise between North and South.

It was a big moment for a man who had only achieved the White House thanks to William Henry Harrison's death in 1841, and one with whom contemporaries had been less than thrilled. Tyler had switched to the Whig Party to oppose some of Andrew Jackson's policies, but in many ways he remained a states'-rights Democrat. While he led Whig leaders to believe he was open to compromise on their differences, Tyler decided in the end to be resolute and started vetoing his own party's bills, infuriating his supporters. Within months of his assuming the office, nearly every member of Tyler's cabinet resigned in protest, and the Whig Party publicly drummed the president out of its ranks. Whig power broker Henry Clay likened Tyler to Benedict Arnold after betraying the Continental Army. "He will stand here," Clay said of the president, "like Arnold in England, a monument of his own perfidy and disgrace." The Democrats didn't want Tyler back either, so in addition to becoming the first president to assume the office after a death, John Tyler became the first presidential pariah. He was the first president to have one of his vetoes overturned and the first president the House considered impeaching.

The country hadn't much cared for the man derisively called "His Accidency" either. At a political dinner in New York honoring the British diplomat Lord Ashburton, the American hosts offered a toast to Queen Victoria, which drew cheers and applause from the guests. The toast to Tyler, on the other hand, prompted nothing but "dead silence." The city of Chicago, which had been naming streets after each of the early presidents, pointedly renamed Tyler Street as Congress Parkway. A newspaper in Ohio said Tyler was "more cordially despised by honest men than any man who ever occupied the presidential chair." A drunken painter tried to prove the point when he showed up at the White House to throw rocks at the commander in chief; Congress had to hire the first presidential bodyguards.* Appropriately enough, one of Tyler's few political allies was another Virginian just as cantankerous and difficult as Tyler was thought to be: Henry Wise.

Despite his reputation, Tyler hoped very much to be remembered as a great man of American history: in his will he appointed a "literary executor" to review his papers so they could be published and future generations could see what an able statesman he was. And Tyler aimed high when he spoke to the delegates of the peace convention, mostly retired political types like himself. Anyone, he said, who managed to stitch the Union back together would be hailed forever as a hero. "Your children's children will rise up and call you blessed,"

---

* Officially they were known as "doormen" so Americans didn't think their unpopular president was building up a personal army. The US Secret Service would not formally take charge of presidential security until 1902.

he told them. "I confess myself ambitious of sharing in the glory of accomplishing this grand and magnificent result. To have our names enrolled in the Capitol, to be repeated by future generations with grateful applause, this is an honor higher than the mountains."

That speech was the high point of the conference. From there, the members seemed to care more about how to run the conference than how to reach a compromise. Tyler, for his part, wasn't nearly as interested in negotiations as his rhetoric had suggested; he was not only opposed to limits on slavery, as Lincoln's party wanted, but he thought slavery needed to be expanded beyond the South. He declared the conference a mistake, threw his lot in with the secessionists, and returned home to Virginia.

Tyler had named his plantation Sherwood Forest, in reference to his life as a political outlaw, and it was here he planned to live out his remaining years with his wife, Julia, and a growing gaggle of kids; he would have fifteen in all, with the last coming when he was seventy. Walk the grounds of Sherwood Forest today and you'll see a large, square patch of lawn marked off with a short white fence and a sign noting that Tyler had asked to be buried here "until the day of my resurrection," under "an uncostly stone of marble or granite."

He never made it. As the southern states left the Union and formed their own provisional government, Virginia elected Tyler to a seat in the new Confederate House of Representatives, making him the only American president elected to serve in a foreign government. Tyler came to Richmond in January 1862 to start his new job, but he soon fell ill in the dining room; it's thought today this was the first of a series of strokes, the last of which proved fatal. The man who had infuriated the country in office had stepped up his game in death by leaving this world at a time when he'd technically renounced his allegiance to the United States. And so the United States ignored Tyler's death entirely. President Lincoln made no proclamation announcing the news. There was no black ribbon over his portrait, because it had been taken down and put into storage.

The *New York Times* was among the few newspapers to devote more than a few sentences to Tyler's death; it wrote that Tyler had died "amid the ruins of his native State. He himself was one of the architects of its ruin; and beneath that melancholy wreck his name will be buried, instead of being inscribed on the Capitol's monumental marble, as a year ago he so much desired."

The North had said, in effect, *John Tyler, you are dead to us*—which, of course, he was.

But the *Times* noted another problem for the late renegade president: "Mr. Tyler's mansion at Hampton, over which he hoisted the rebel flag last Spring, has been for some time occupied as quarters by our troops." Those troops meant Tyler's body would not find his way back to Sherwood Forest. Instead it ended up in the closest possible place of honor: the hilltop at Hollywood Cemetery. The Confederate Congress gave Tyler a state funeral, with over 150 carriages accompanying his Confederate-flag-draped casket to the burial site, just steps away from James Monroe's "birdcage." Oddly, there was no gravestone, uncostly or not, until 1899, and no monument until 1912, when Congress—the United States one—funded the eagle-topped obelisk and bronze bust that mark the burial site today. One last left turn for the saga of John Tyler's burial site, and for the hilltop locals had begun to call Presidents Circle.

Just a short walk from the hilltop tomb, under a flat stone slab, is the man without whom there would be no circle. Henry Wise spent the Civil War as a Confederate military officer, every bit as argumentative as he had been in politics. Just months into the war Wise managed to get himself relieved from duty for refusing to obey orders from his superior officer, an old political enemy. But Wise would rejoin the fight and stay in it until the Army of Northern Virginia surrendered to Ulysses S. Grant in April 1865. After the war Wise wrote books, served on state commissions, and spoke at Confederate commemorations before his death in 1876.

It may seem fitting that Wise is buried so close to the presidential graves he'd envisioned, but there's a certain irony to his burial site, too. One biographer says the former governor hoped to live out his remaining years on his plantation outside Norfolk, but he was unable to regain the property, and his health had deteriorated to the point that he could no longer leave his home in Richmond. The man who moved two presidents wasn't able to move himself.

THE NEXT president to visit Richmond was a living one: Abraham Lincoln, on April 4, 1865, when Robert E. Lee's troops could no longer defend the Confederate capital. As they moved out, Grant's forces moved in to hoist the Stars and Stripes over Virginia's statehouse. Lincoln wanted a Union ship to take him up the James River so he could see the city firsthand. Advisers tried to talk Lincoln out of it, and for good reason: Confederates had placed mines and other obstructions in the river, while the city was partly being looted and partly being torched, as fleeing Confederates had set warehouses and supplies on fire to keep them out of Union hands. Lincoln, who had been stuck in Washington for most of the war, didn't care. "It seems to me that I have been dreaming a horrid dream for four years," he said, "and now the nightmare is gone. I want to see Richmond." So he did, walking the streets of downtown Richmond until he reached the Confederate White House, and then sitting down in Jefferson Davis's chair.

In his time, Abraham Lincoln led a long military campaign to retake Richmond. In our time, he is the face of a campaign to bring more tourists to the city. Yes, Virginia, there is Lincoln tourism in Richmond. The first and only Lincoln statue in a former Confederate state sits at Richmond's historic Tredegar Iron Works, and it shows Lincoln and his son Tad on April 4, 1865. Richmonders were the ones who pushed for the statue: the Richmond-based United States Historical Society commissioned the piece in 2002, and the Richmond city council kicked in $45,000 of the quarter-million-dollar cost. "I'm delighted that it's finally happening, that Lincoln is in Richmond again," said USHS chair Robert H. Kline. "He came on a mission of peace and reconciliation and I think the statue will serve that purpose for a very long time."

The statue was just the beginning. Steven Spielberg filmed nearly all of his 2012 movie *Lincoln* here, and Richmond tourism officials launched "Lincoln: The Movie Trail," including special travel packages, video testimonials from Spielberg and his team about how much they enjoyed the city, and even special mixed drinks. The Lemaire Bar at Richmond's Jefferson Hotel recommends their special Milk Punch, "with vanilla bean, sugar and apple brandy," because "one of President Lincoln's favorite beverages was milk."

He freed the slaves, he put the Union back together, and then he became an icon of tourism, even in parts of the South. Part of this is because Lincoln is Lincoln; Steven Spielberg isn't going to make a biopic about John Tyler, after all. But Lincoln also gave tourists plenty to see and do after his assassination. The Great Emancipator is our most well-traveled dead president.

This wasn't by design. Not only did Lincoln leave no funeral plan, he left no will; the state of Illinois divvied out the Lincoln estate to his widow and surviving sons. But just as the presidents at Hollywood Cemetery had Henry Wise to guide them to Presidents Circle, Lincoln had his own mastermind of mourning, Secretary of War Edwin M. Stanton. And he sent Abraham Lincoln's body on a thirteen-day, cross-country funeral tour that made every other posthumous presidential voyage look pretty quiet by comparison.

In the Lincoln White House, Edwin McMasters Stanton was the coworker who was great at his job but not always great to work with. He was ferociously patriotic, enormously self-confident, and determined to spend every minute of his extremely long workdays putting the rebellion down. While Stanton's subordinates at the War Department certainly believed in the cause, too, it should be noted that they warned each other when his carriage got close to the office, so they'd have time to look busy before he walked in. Stanton's meetings with military brass usually ended with him shouting things like "I'll dismiss you from the service!" Even Lincoln got the Stanton treatment on occasion; once the secretary raged that "we've got to get rid of that baboon at the White House!"

Lincoln waved the story away when he heard it. "That is no insult," he said, "it is an expression of opinion. And what troubles me most about it is that Stanton said it, and Stanton is usually right." Stanton cleared the War Department's decks of incompetent officers and greedy office-seekers; their replacements helped turn the Union war effort from unwieldy to unstoppable. That, Lincoln figured, was worth a few insults.

By the end of the war, Stanton had put the insults away entirely; he had grown to respect Lincoln the president and to love Lincoln the man. He rushed to the president's deathbed at the Petersen House after the shooting at Ford's Theatre and stayed up all night directing the manhunt for John Wilkes Booth and his accomplices. When Lincoln died, it was Stanton who famously said, "Now he belongs to the ages."

And it was Stanton who assigned himself the job of giving Lincoln a massive send-off. The president would, of course, get a state funeral, like the presidents who had died in office before him. But unlike those presidents, Lincoln would not go straight home; instead, Stanton mapped out a sort of Great American Death Tour across the North. Four years earlier, Lincoln had made a long train trip from his home in Springfield, Illinois, to Washington, making stops in cities and towns and meeting the people who he was about to lead. It was fitting, Stanton thought, to send Lincoln's remains back to Illinois on that same train route, so the same people Lincoln met in 1861 could say good-bye. But the secretary of war had more in mind than bringing Lincoln's presidency full circle: he wanted to punish the secessionists, and what better way to stir up public fury against the rebels than to show off the body of the martyred president and point out to the country that a southern sympathizer had pulled the trigger?

The train that undertook this journey, known as the Lincoln Special, was hard to miss. A large black locomotive pulled nine cars; each was "richly draped in mourning within and without," according to one account. One of the last cars was a funeral coach, 42.5 feet long, with an all-hardwood interior and seemingly half the heavy black cloth in the country. Lincoln's casket sat at one end of the coach; at the other end was the coffin of the president's son Willie, who had died at the White House in 1862 and had been disinterred to travel back to Springfield with his dad. The "president's car" had been built to transport the living Lincoln, but he considered it too luxurious in wartime. For this trip, though, it was perfect.

I know this because I rode on the Lincoln Special—sort of. The actual train car fell victim to a fire in March 1911, but Gettysburg, Pennsylvania, has a place called the Lincoln Train Museum, not far from the hallowed Civil War battlefields, and it has a full-size simulator in which people can "ride" on a replica of the funeral train to Springfield. I sat down in a cushy red seat near a black casket as the car swayed back and forth and video screens on the side walls showed fields rushing by on the way to Illinois. Then a screen in front showed "the spirit of Abraham Lincoln," complete with a blue Jedi-like glow, telling us about what he saw while he "watched over our country since my passing." It was, as you'd expect, a pretty general analysis of the country's ups and downs—"though if you're keeping score," he noted, "we'd still come out in the winner's circle." To close, he recited the entire Gettysburg Address, and then gave way to a video montage of patriotic sights set to Lee Greenwood's "God Bless the USA."

11. Over twelve million Americans watched this large black locomotive pull the "Lincoln Special" train that brought Abraham Lincoln's body back to Illinois.

Inspiring stuff, if not quite historically accurate. The actual Lincoln Special had fewer glowing corpses than the simulator, and the mood on the real train was "distinguished, sad and solemn," according to one staff member. "All the conversation was on Lincoln's greatness and untimely demise." There was work to do, too: Edwin Stanton wanted an open casket at every public viewing, so the country could literally see what John Wilkes Booth had done. Before each public viewing the president's embalmer, Dr. Charles Brown, and an undertaker, Frank Sands, had to reapply white chalk and makeup to Lincoln's face to hide the signs of decomposition, and the casket had to be surrounded by fragrant flowers, to mask the growing smell.

They did fine work, but decay and odor probably wouldn't have stopped the people from coming to see, and mourn, Abraham Lincoln. Mourners had placed so many flowers on the train tracks between Harrisburg and Philadelphia that the Lincoln Special slipped and nearly stalled. Virtually all of Philly was on hand to meet the train: "Half a million sorrow-stricken people were upon the streets," wrote one observer, "to do honor to all that was left of the man whom they respected, revered and loved with an affection never before bestowed upon any other." Officials had their hands full at the public viewing at New York City Hall, where "frequent attempts were made by ladies to kiss the placid lips of the corpse."

Those New Yorkers who weren't trying to plant a kiss on Lincoln were calling for swift retribution against the Confederacy. Attorney George Templeton Strong noted in his diary that many New Yorkers thought of the living Lincoln as a well-meaning bumbler, and that the Union would have been better off making a deal with the South. That changed after the murder. "There was no talk of concession and conciliation," Strong wrote. "It would have endured no such talk. Its sentiments seemed like this: 'Now it is plain at last to everybody that there can be no terms. . . . Let us henceforth deal with rebels as they deserve.'" Speakers praised Lincoln for his merciful nature while hailing his successor, Andrew Johnson, as "the Avenger" and encouraging him to bring the South to its knees. Over the next few decades, Republican lawmakers would push for harsh policies toward southern states, and the party's candidates would "wave the bloody shirt," telling voters that Democratic "Copperheads" had enabled the rebellion and led to the deaths of hundreds of thousands, including Lincoln.

Edwin M. Stanton expected these angry calls for justice, and he expected the massive outpourings of grief along the route of the funeral train. What he hadn't expected, though, was for the tour to turn into a sort of grieving contest between cities and towns. If one put up a new building for a public viewing, the next would put up an equally big building, plus gaudier decorations. Smaller towns that weren't hosting viewings set up mourning arches above the tracks or painted huge flags on the nearby buildings. Crowds of thousands showed up in the middle of the night, or in the pouring rain, to mourn and, perhaps, to be seen mourning. It's likely no one topped the woman in Cleveland who did a sort of interpretive dance as "the Goddess of Liberty in mourning" while the train rolled by.

The grand finale was in Springfield. Illinois's capital city not only had to outdo each previous city in its Lincoln mourning, but it had to undo its own mistakes. Mary Lincoln had chosen rural Oak Ridge Cemetery as her husband's burial site, but a group of prominent city and state officials had taken it upon themselves to start developing a different spot, which they thought would better handle visitors. Mrs. Lincoln was so furious that she threatened to turn the train around. "Unless I receive within this next ten days an official assurance that the Monument will be erected over the Tomb in Oak Ridge Cemetery," she told Illinois governor Richard J. Oglesby, "[I will] have the sacred remains deposited in the vault, prepared for Washington, under the Dome of the National Capitol." Oglesby gave in, and Springfield redeemed itself with arguably the grandest funeral display of them all. Residents decorated virtually everything in town—Lincoln's house, his law office, and the state capitol building, in which the president's body was shown one last time before burial. Springfield's public viewing ran a full twenty-four hours, with fresh trains bringing people in from other towns even in the middle of the night. There was not a hotel room to be had in the whole city; some visitors were taken in by residents, but many simply wandered the streets for hours. After an equally large and impressive funeral ceremony, pallbearers placed the remains in the temporary vault, and the crowds went on their way.

It was the longest, strangest death trip America had ever seen—thirteen days, 1,645 miles, seven states, twelve million witnesses to the Lincoln Special, 1.5 million people who viewed the body. But the great genius of the trip was its sheer size and length. In hundreds of towns and cities, people who weren't dignitaries or VIPs could, in a small way, take part in Lincoln's funeral, and they connected with him in a way that they've connected with few presidents before or after. If Abraham Lincoln hadn't belonged to the ages when the funeral tour began, he certainly did when it was over.

The evidence of this is everywhere, as a virtually endless list of towns and cities have been staking their claim to Lincoln since the funeral train rolled west. In Ohio's capitol building, Lincoln appears no less than three times—a lot for a guy who only visited the place, and more than any of the actual Ohioans honored there. The small western New York town of Westfield has a set of statues depicting the meeting between a newly bearded Lincoln and Grace Bedell, the local girl who had suggested he grow whiskers.

Another young New Yorker would remember his view of the funeral parade for the rest of his life: "Lincoln," wrote President Theodore Roosevelt, "has always meant more to me than any other of our public men, even Washington." His secretary of state was John Hay, who had served as one of Lincoln's personal secretaries; for TR's inauguration in 1905, Hay sent the president a ring containing strands of Lincoln's hair, a gift for which Roosevelt could barely find the words to say thanks. "Surely," he wrote Hay, "no other President, on the eve of his inauguration, has ever received such a gift from such a friend. . . . I shall think of it and you as I take the oath tomorrow."

Visitors to Bennington, Vermont, may have a hard time finding the words for the local Lincoln statue. The Great Emancipator, decked out in a top hat and cape, greets two children meant to represent Faith and Hope in "young America." The fact that they're, well, unclothed might make a visitor wonder if the statue should be reported to child protective services. As I took photos, a staffer at the nearby Bennington

Museum raced out to hand me an information sheet about the statue. "It's very easy," she told me, "for people to misunderstand this piece."

In most cases these statues and memorials were set up purely to mark history or pay respects to Lincoln. But they all draw visitors, and so, like the statue marking the president's walking tour of Richmond, the remnants of Abraham Lincoln's great American death train have become fodder for tourism campaigns. It isn't just out of respect, after all, that three states feature Lincoln on their welcome signs. Kentucky welcomes you to the "Birthplace of Abraham Lincoln," while Indiana bills itself as "Lincoln's Boyhood Home." But Illinois, guardian of the president's earthly remains, more than lives up to its "Land of Lincoln" moniker. "Only in Illinois can you fully experience the remarkable life of Abraham Lincoln," explains the state's tourism site. "In this land he called home, Lincoln's legacy isn't contained behind glass. It's alive, up close and personal."

Sometimes it even runs amok. The mascot for the "Enjoy Illinois" campaign is Mini Abe, a tiny animated Lincoln who screams his way across the state's most famous sites. Seeing the sixteenth president shouting down to Chicago from the Willis Tower observation deck may boggle the mind, but apparently it works as intended: the state tourism office said visitor inquiries jumped by more than half after the campaign launched.

The rise of Mini Abe, as well as the more president-specific "Looking for Lincoln" initiative, is good news for downstate Illinois. Rather than let middle-class jobs dry up and drugs move in, small towns and cities across Illinois are highlighting their Lincoln connections to bring in visitors and dollars. After all, among cemeteries, Springfield's Oak Ridge Cemetery is second only to Arlington National Cemetery in the number of visitors; it attracts some 350,000 people each year. The rest of the state wants in on the action. "There are places to come in northwest Illinois," according to Ann Lewis, who helped with the town of Dixon's tourism plans. "To [attract those visitors], we're going to have to bring a good product forward."

The product *is* good, as far as I'm concerned: the towns on the "Looking for Lincoln" map aren't offering mere "Lincoln Slept Here" stories. They each serve as a window into a different facet of Lincoln's life and career. Dixon's statue depicts the Great Emancipator's short and undistinguished military career, as it was one of the places he was stationed during the Black Hawk War of 1832. Visit the Beardstown courthouse for insight into Shrewd Prairie Lawyer Lincoln, who in that very courthouse in 1858 successfully defended a man accused of murder in a pretty clever way: "The key witness," according to the "Looking for Lincoln" information site, "claimed that he saw the whole thing clearly by the bright light of the moon. Using an almanac, Lincoln proved that the moon would have set by the time of this murder, thereby clearing [the defendant] of the charges."

Near the Illinois and Michigan canal site in Lockport visitors can catch a glimpse of State Lawmaker Concerned About Infrastructure Lincoln, which may not sound that intriguing until it's pointed out that the Lincoln statue there appears to have three heads. Its sculptor, David Ostro, says the piece is actually a set of three interlocking Lincoln portraits showing the movement and growth the canal made possible, but I don't think anyone in Lockport is going to stop you from visiting if you want to pretend Three-Headed Lincoln is running around town.

I'm after Dead Lincoln, of course, and his trail begins about thirty miles north of his Springfield tomb. Lincoln, Illinois, named itself for Abraham Lincoln in 1853, when he was but a former member of Congress and a semiprominent prairie lawyer. The town's namesake not only spoke at the launch of the town, he catered it: "Gentlemen," he told the assemblage, "I am requested by the proprietors of the town site to christen it. I have selected the juice of a melon for that purpose, pouring it on the ground. Therefore, in your presence and hearing, I now christen this town site. Its name is Lincoln and soon to be named the permanent capital of Logan County. I have also prepared a feast for the occasion." About a century later, Lincoln the town wanted to recognize its special connection to Lincoln the man. So in 1964, the local Kiwanis, Lions, and Rotary clubs commissioned a steel sculpture of Lincoln's christening watermelon. They painted on black "seeds" and green "rind" and placed the piece on a bright green base just a few feet away from the Amtrak station, a charming, slightly bewildering piece of folk art that stands out even among the crowded field of unusual Lincoln statues.

But Downtown Lincoln is home to something even more unusual than the watermelon—a historic plaque marked SCENE OF CON-SPIRACY. "In the spring of 1876," the sign explains, "a gang of counterfeiters plotted to steal the body of Abraham Lincoln from the tomb in Springfield, Illinois. Hoping to be paid a ransom of $200,000.00 and the release of one of their gang, Ben Boyd, their engraver, who was in the penitentiary. This was the location of their headquarters in central Illinois."

Thievery is nothing new around presidential sites, of course. The big crowds at presidential funerals have long attracted pickpockets, and "relic hunters" have helped themselves to souvenirs large and small. Thomas Jefferson designed his tombstone to deter thieves; he asked that the grave marker be built with coarse stone, which would be less valuable to troublemakers. It didn't work: people chipped off so many pieces of the obelisk that it had to be replaced. Monticello visitors helped themselves to the contents of the famous gardens, too; Jefferson's grandson took out an ad in the *Charlottesville Gazette* asking people to stop stealing plants, but the ad backfired and even more garden weasels came to Monticello. After Ulysses S. Grant died in upstate New York, someone stole the lightning rod from the top of the cottage where he'd been staying—and, of course, lightning struck shortly thereafter, nearly setting the place on fire.

But those thieves were at least only trying to take *things*. Stealing the corpse of a president? Especially the corpse of Abraham Lincoln? That borders on supervillain territory. Fortunately the masterminds of the scheme were anything but super; one of them apparently expected stealing the remains of Abraham Lincoln, lugging them to the Indiana Dunes, and holding them for ransom would earn the group "two hundred thousand dollars, besides the liberation of Ben. Boyd from Joliet penitentiary, and the respect of the American people into the bargain." "They really were knuckleheads," says Thomas Craughwell, who wrote a book on the plot, *Stealing Lincoln's Body*.

The first version of the plot, the one hatched in downtown Lincoln, fell apart almost immediately, thanks to a conspirator who decided to celebrate the heist before actually pulling it off: he bought some booze, went to a brothel, and then started bragging about how he and some friends were about to "steal old Lincoln's bones." The grave-robbery-based pickup line proved massively ineffective; the woman he'd hired told the cops, and the conspirators had to skip town.

Authorities traced the plot back to a counterfeiter known as Big Jim Kennally. Not that they wouldn't have found out anyway: Kennally was openly recruiting another team of Lincoln-stealers out of his Chicago tavern, the Hub, even though Chicago police had been sending paid informants into his place to keep an eye on him. One of them, Lewis C. Swegles, dropped by the bar one day and casually noted that he happened to be "the boss body-snatcher of Chicago." Kennally found this stranger's appearance extremely convenient and not at all suspicious, and hired him on the spot. Swegles was able to send regular updates on the plot to the head of the Secret Service's Chicago office, Patrick Tyrrell, and Lincoln's eldest son, Robert.

That's why when the grave robbers came to retrieve the body on election night 1876, several detectives were already inside Lincoln's tomb at Oak Ridge, waiting to catch the conspirators in the act. The robbers managed to cut through Lincoln's marble sarcophagus and tried lifting the casket out, though it proved heavier than expected and they couldn't get it all the way out. The informant, Swegles, alerted the detectives that the robbery was under way, but unfortunately one of them accidentally discharged his pistol before the tomb could be surrounded, and the authorities started shooting at each other in the dark without realizing that the conspirators had already fled. Fortunately for the cops, the conspirators immediately returned to Big Jim Kennally's club in Chicago, where they were promptly taken into custody. They ended up in Joliet with Ben Boyd, the man they were hoping to spring from prison in the first place. Kennally managed to keep secret his involvement in the caper, but eventually he served time as well.

The plot had been foiled, but that didn't mean Lincoln's body was safe. The custodian of the tomb, John Carroll Power, worried that the next group of criminals might not be incompetent blabbermouths. He and the chair of the Lincoln Monument Association, John Todd Stuart, concluded that the only way to keep Lincoln's body safe was to move it out of public view but pretend that it was still there. After the grave robbers' trials, tomb visitors often asked Power if the president's remains had been returned to the marble sarcophagus; the move meant he had to tell them a creative version of the truth: "'We put it back there the second day after the attempt to steal it,' which is strictly true. If they questioned further [I] would say, 'I suppose you wish to know if there is not further danger, if so, I can assure you that it is absolutely safe.'"

It was safe because Power and Stuart had stashed it in the one part of the monument nobody was interested in visiting. But basements flood, and Power had to unearth the casket to keep it from ending up underwater. For a couple of years Lincoln's remains sat under some spare lumber, just to keep them semidisguised, before Power could find a drier corner to rebury them. Later, work crews would come through the basement to address some serious structural repair, and Power had to stand there silently while they walked on the grave of the Great Emancipator.

Lincoln stayed in the basement for almost a decade—he was joined by the body of his wife, after her death in 1882—until Power and a group known as the Lincoln Guard of Honor had workers build a brick tomb to give the bodies a more distinguished resting place. They held a reburial ceremony on April 15, 1887, the anniversary of Lincoln's death; Power was there, and after the speeches and formality the dignitaries on hand decided that, "after so many changes, it was indisputably necessary to identify the body of the President." To me this reads as "We figured, as long as the casket was out, why not take a look?" Nonetheless, when they opened the casket, they found Lincoln's body had held up pretty well thanks to the thorough embalming in 1865. "Those who stood around and had known Lincoln when alive easily discerned the features," said one account of the event.

This would have been the end of the story, except that water started seeping into the tomb again. Even though the crews had poured cement into the new burial chamber to protect the caskets, the water was on course to eventually eat through the protections and damage the Lincolns' caskets. Around the turn of the century the state decided to spend a hundred thousand dollars to chip the caskets out from the cement, put them back in a temporary vault, and try again—but instead of a below ground burial chamber, Lincoln's casket was going to return to the main floor, in the same marble sarcophagus that held it in 1876, on the night of the attempted robbery.

The last living member of Lincoln's immediate family thought this was a terrible idea. Robert Lincoln had been in close contact with the detectives who had stopped the 1876 grave robbery; he was one of the first people they told about how the Kennally gang had managed to get the casket at least partly out of its resting place. And Robert Lincoln was in no mood for more tragedy and horror: while he'd been unusually successful as a businessman, lawyer, and government official, his only son, Abraham Lincoln II (the family called him Jack), had died at age sixteen. Moreover, Robert Lincoln had been close by for the first three presidential assassinations. In 1865, he stood by his father's deathbed and was the only living Lincoln to ride on the funeral train west. In 1881, while serving as secretary of war, Robert Lincoln was with James Garfield at the Baltimore and Potomac station in Washington when Charles Guiteau shot the president. (It was Robert who sent his driver to fetch D. Willard Bliss, the doctor who oversaw the medical care that killed Garfield. Oops.) Twenty years later, Robert took a train to Buffalo, at President McKinley's request, to see the Pan-American Exposition, but just as he pulled into town, Leon Czolgosz fired. The already highly private Robert Lincoln started staying away from official functions altogether, and understandably so. "There is," he noted, "a certain fatality about presidential functions when I am present."

Robert decided not to attend the 1901 ceremony marking the final reburial of his parents—among other reasons, it took place just weeks after the McKinley assassination—but he played a big role in keeping their caskets out of the reach of any future bands of delusional counterfeiters. Robert had worked for the railroad magnate George Pullman, who had himself buried in a chamber filled with concrete because he feared that his tomb might be desecrated. Robert Lincoln asked for—and received—the same treatment for his parents.

This was going to be it: once the workers lowered Lincoln's casket into the steel chamber, once they poured concrete all around the chamber, Abraham Lincoln's earthly remains would never be seen again. So those on hand for the reburial decided, against Robert Lincoln's wishes, to open the casket one more time. Joseph P. Lindley, who had helped guard Lincoln's body over the years, sent for his thirteen-year-old son, Fleetwood, who raced over from school on his bike. He would be the last living person to look on the face of Abraham Lincoln. "I was allowed to hold one of the leather straps as we lowered the casket for the concrete to be poured," Lindley told a reporter just days before his own death in 1963. "I was not scared at the time, but I slept with Lincoln for the next six months."

Abraham Lincoln's body has remained undisturbed since that day. Being buried under some ten feet of concrete will do that, after all. And while Robert Lincoln's plan means that the hundreds of thousands who visit the tomb each year stare at the red marble sarcophagus with no one inside it, he was right to worry that the original sarcophagus was headed for trouble: in 1930, work crews left it outdoors while they conducted another round of tomb repairs. Souvenir hunters came into the cemetery at night and smashed it to bits.

6

⊷

HIS GOOD NAME

On William McKinley, Ronald Reagan,
and Calvin Coolidge, and the
Large (and Small) Ways Presidents Are Remembered

IN 1868, barely three years after Abraham Lincoln's death and
funeral, the Senate Committee on Territories suggested that the
country establish the Wyoming Territory under a new name: Lincoln.
"The high esteem in which he was held by the country, not only by
his own party, but by the opposite party, suggested his name as a very
appropriate one," said Senator Richard Yates of Illinois. "I think the
committee were unanimous in reporting the name of Lincoln instead
of Wyoming."

Yates was ready to let the change go forward; other senators weren't
so sure, noting that lawmakers had only once before named a territory
after a president, and that was George Washington. "The example
would be unfortunate to name States after our public men," said Indiana's Oliver P. Morton. "We have adopted the system . . . of naming
the western and northwestern States after Indian tribes, or giving to
them the same names that the Indians gave them, and in that way we
have obtained beautiful names for nearly all the western States. I do
not think a prettier name could be found than that of Wyoming, and

for one I would prefer giving this Territory that name." Lawmakers decided not to go with Lincoln after all.

Two decades later, though, Lincoln's name was back before Congress, as a proposed alternate name for North Dakota. Several times legislators considered breaking Idaho up and mashing part of it together with pieces of other nearby states to make a State of Lincoln, with no success.

And that's no knock on Lincoln—this country has loved naming things after him. There's an Abraham Lincoln tomato variety, an asteroid called (3153) Lincoln, and the capital city of Nebraska. The first coast-to-coast highway system in America was the Lincoln Highway—"America's Main Street," as it was known in the early twentieth century. In 2012, firefighters outside the Clermont Presidents Hall of Fame, west of Orlando, rescued a three-week-old kitten stuck inside a statue of Abraham Lincoln; they named the little guy Abe.

The other presidents have done pretty well with names, too. Washington and Grant have their own asteroids, and Herbert Hoover has *two*. In 1920, (932) Hooveria was named by an Austrian astronomer "as a permanent memorial of the great help rendered to the people of Austria" by Hoover after World War I. An asteroid called (1363) Herberta came in 1938, in honor of the former president's visit to Belgium.

There are four state capitals named for presidents—Jackson, Mississippi; Madison, Wisconsin; Lincoln, Nebraska; and Jefferson City, Missouri. George Washington is the namesake for the national capital, and he's the only president with his own state, though there have been plenty of attempts to add other presidents to the ranks. Presidents' names have been given to plenty of children as well: pitcher Grover Cleveland Alexander and blues great Howlin' Wolf (Chester Arthur Burnett) are among the best-known Americans named after our leaders, and there are plenty of lesser-known kids who have carried presidential names as well. As he returned home to Tennessee, Andrew Jackson carried 150 silver half dollars, to give to each child named for him or his late wife, Rachel. He was nearly out of half dollars by the end of the trip.

Some presidents end up as the namesakes for foods. In East Aurora, New York, outside of Buffalo, I stopped for coffee at a place called Taste. The menu there includes a sandwich called the Millard Fill-Me-More, which consists of "chicken salad with walnuts, cranberries, greens and red onions on a bistro blanket." Recipes abound for president-themed dishes, like "puree of wild ducks Van Buren," a rich French-style soup with a lot of duck, a little veal, and plenty of butter. And lots of desserts: Washington Pie (which is actually a pudding-filled cake), a pudding known as "Apricots with rice a la Jefferson," and "Peach pudding à la Cleveland." You could try some of the whiskey George Washington distilled at Mount Vernon, but if you indulge too heavily you might need to join the Washingtonians, an antidrinking movement in the mid-nineteenth century, which, much like Alcoholics Anonymous does today, encouraged the newly sober to attend regular meetings in which they shared personal addiction stories.

We can, on occasion, go a little overboard in naming things after a president, and we have to pull back. In 1901, shortly after the assassination of William McKinley, the *Chautauquan* reported that the United States had considered a proposal "to call the Philippine archipelago by the name of 'The McKinley Islands.'" McKinley had pushed to annex the islands after the Spanish-American War, partly to keep them out of European hands and open to American trade routes, but also, as he told a group of ministers, to "educate the Filipinos, and uplift and civilize and Christianize them, and by God's grace do the very best we could by them, as our fellow-men for whom Christ also died." The idea was eventually dismissed as too ostentatious, and probably not very considerate to the Filipinos, either. "Surely McKinley himself would have been the first to raise his hand," the *Chautauquan* added, "against a proffered honor which would change the map of the world and outrage the sensibilities of a long-suffering people."

McKinley sites, as a general rule, go for size. The town of Niles, Ohio, where the president was born, built a huge Greek Revival memorial building that houses a museum on one side and the town library on the other. The center area is open-air and features a marble McKinley statue, surrounded by a "Court of Honor"—bronze busts of other prominent men of the day. McKinley has the largest monument on the grounds of the Ohio state capitol; while Grant, Hayes, and Garfield have to share a statue, McKinley gets to be out front by himself. Buffalo, New York, put up a giant white obelisk across from the towering Art Deco city hall to remember the president assassinated there. The base features ornately carved sleeping lions, said to represent strength, and one of the facets of the obelisk bitterly explains that the beloved McKinley was the "victim of a treacherous assassin who shot the president as he was extending to him the hand of courtesy."

And then there's his enormous tomb, in Canton, Ohio. "Other memorials have been of a local character," wrote the *Chautauquan*, "but this is national in the interest it has excited. Indeed, it is more than this, for the American consular service throughout all the world reports practical financial sympathy from Americans abroad and from appreciative foreigners, who, even at long range, realized the worth of William McKinley as a man and magistrate." Grant's Tomb in New York is a larger building, but it's on flat land. McKinley's round, double-domed mausoleum is ninety-seven feet tall and built into the side of a massive hill, seventy-five feet higher than the surrounding area. Even William and Ida McKinley's matching dark green sarcophagi are bigger than other presidents' tombs, or at least taller: they sit high above visitors, on a ten-foot stand of black Wisconsin granite.

There are 108 steps from the parking area to the tomb, with a McKinley statue at the halfway point. When I visited, the vast majority of people on these stairs weren't visiting the McKinleys; they were Cantonites looking to get in some exercise. If McKinley is up there watching, he must wonder why so many people come right up to the tomb without going in. I watched one woman trudge up and down, up and down, on an 85-degree day. "How many times do you do this?" I asked. "Ten times, every day," she said. "I've been doing it eight years—it doesn't get any easier."

It takes considerably more than 108 steps to get to the top of what has long been the biggest McKinley memorial—a more-than-20,000-foot mountain, which happens to be the highest point in North America. Calling the giant Alaskan peak Mount McKinley, though, has irritated Alaskans for decades; they prefer the mountain's Athabaskan name—Denali, or "the high one."

McKinley's name didn't come up in reference to the high one until 1896, when a prospector named William Dickey came through the area. His name choice was little more than election-year politics. Dickey, like McKinley, wanted to keep gold as the basis of US currency—not a popular position in the American West, which was open to silver as well as gold. Dickey named the peak after the pro-gold candidate to boost McKinley's campaign and slight the pro-silver prospectors.

By all rights the "Mount McKinley" name should have fallen away from the mountain after the election, given that Dickey "discovered" a peak that had already been found and named by Natives, Russians, the British, and even other American prospectors. None of them, though, wrote about what they saw in the *New York Sun* under the title "Discoveries in Alaska," and so Dickey's name stuck—especially after McKinley's assassination five years later.

But 1901 was a long time ago. In the ensuing decades, William McKinley's star faded, while Native voices grew more influential in Alaska. Yet the official name of the mountain remained Mount McKinley until President Obama moved to change it to Denali in 2015. This was mostly thanks to the process we use for naming natural features. Anyone who wants to name—or rename—a mountain, river, or other natural feature in this country has to go through the US Board on Geographic Names, on which representatives of numerous federal agencies work toward "uniform geographic name usage throughout the Federal Government." "The board doesn't try to dictate the name," explains its executive secretary, Lou Yost; "it's trying to standardize usage," meaning that the board's goal is to make sure the government's maps all use the same names.

Yost says requests for commemorative names, such as for historic

12. In 1896, a prospector named William Dickey named this mountain "Mount McKinley," which annoyed Alaskans for decades.

figures, tend to be recognized if there's local buy-in around the name and the person being recognized has "a long-term or direct association with the feature being named." Someone with "regional or national significance" can trump even that, though the board seems to emphasize local names when possible.

Under this system, the name Denali wins, hands down. Alaskans had already voted to rename the peak, while McKinley's direct connection to the mountain ended with the outspoken and somewhat presumptuous prospector who was passing through the area. But there was a catch here: "If a name for a geographic feature is pending before Congress," explains Yost, "the BGN will not take action on it." And for decades, the members of Congress who have represented Canton introduced legislation to keep McKinley's name in place on the mountain. "We must retain this national landmark's name," Ohio representative Tim Ryan said in a statement accompanying his legislation, "in order to honor the legacy of this great American president and patriot."

The bills don't need to become law, or even come up for votes; they just needed to be in the hopper for the board to keep the Denali name issue in its "later" pile. "Some names will cause some emotions and some consternation," Yost said of the McKinley/Denali standoff, "but I don't think we've had any that have gone on this long." It was a pretty ingenious strategy—if you're from Ohio, that is. Alaskans, of course, found it pretty annoying and responded enthusiastically when the Obama Administration bypassed the stalemate and established Denali as the mountain's only name.

But memorials tend to persist, if only because keeping the status quo is almost always easier than making a change. The northern California town of Arcata has a McKinley statue in the middle of a plaza, even though antiwar locals have compared him to Hitler. "The truth of McKinley is he's just like any of the other people who throughout history caused mass destruction and death," said Michael Schleyer, a resident who launched a petition drive in 2005 to dump the McKinley statue. Schleyer and other residents saw McKinley's pro-imperialist, annexation-heavy foreign policy as exactly the wrong thing to honor. But the town government decided to, as one councilor put it, "grant McKinley amnesty," in part because he would have cost too much to remove.

And so the statue is still there on H Street, still the target of Arcatans' scorn—or, sometimes, worse: "On various occasions," noted a news report around the time of the debate, "the distinguished sculpture has had a gas mask fitted over its head, cheese stuffed in its ears and condoms wrapped around its thumb." The thumb itself went missing for a time—cut off from the rest of the statue. As Arcata officials considered replacement digits, the thumb reappeared; a local man said it had been handed to him by a stranger in nearby Clam Beach. The man alerted the authorities and collected a $500 reward. The thumb was reattached, and no charges were filed in its disappearance, but the *Arcata Union* reported that the man who turned in the thumb thief was arrested after what police called "a drunken brawl."

According to the paper, the man "claimed he'd been surrounded by pro-thumb theft vigilantes who called him a 'snitch.'"

The way I see it, if a monument is surrounded by cheese, gas masks, and "pro-thumb theft vigilantes," it's probably going to stick around.

INERTIA MAY be enough to keep a statue in the ground, but it's not going to make anybody care about the president on that statue. Doing that takes effort—like a movement across the country. Or, alternatively, a lot of little movements in different parts of the country.

This has been the idea behind the Ronald Reagan Legacy Project: rather than let the historic chips fall where they may and leave their man to inertia and thumb vandals, the project wants to keep Ronald Reagan and his ideals in front of the public by naming things for him. Lots of things. How many things? "We want one thing in each county," says the project's architect, Grover Norquist.

America has more than three thousand counties, so he's talking about a *lot* of Reagan.

Norquist is as well suited as anybody for a grand-scale Reagan project: he's the man behind the Taxpayer Protection Pledge, in which lawmakers, almost always Republican ones, promise to block any increase to any tax at any time. That pledge has certainly gone big; signing has been a virtual requirement for Republican candidates, who support the principle behind signing but also know that Norquist's group, Americans for Tax Reform, can pit its considerable influence and resources against them if they don't. Democrats by and large abhor the pledge and complain that Norquist has an "iron grip" on modern conservatives. One critic even called him the "dark wizard" of the right.*

Call him what you want—Norquist has even called himself a "Darth Vader" for the cause at times—but it would be well off the

* Grover Norquist gets his first name from a Democratic president, as the grandfather for whom he was named got his own name from Grover Cleveland. When the media brings this up, Norquist notes that Cleveland was the last fiscally conservative Democrat to win the White House—or as he puts it, "He was a *good* Democrat."

mark to assume he's just a heavy for tax cuts. The Legacy Project is pretty shrewd stuff, using a mostly nonpolitical appeal to advance political principles. "If you want to contend for the future," Norquist said as the project got off the ground, "you have to contend for the public understanding of the past." A big part of that understanding comes from naming things for public figures, and Reagan's naming legacy was, at that point, pretty small. Meanwhile, he said, "everything that wasn't nailed down was named for John F. Kennedy, Martin Luther King or Franklin D. Roosevelt. Conservatives have not done as well in honoring their heroes."

When Norquist started the Legacy Project in 1997, Ronald Reagan was still alive, albeit out of public view because of Alzheimer's disease. And he'd been out of office for less than a decade. Memorials tend to take time, and, by definition, they come after a person's death. Kennedy, King, and FDR had all been dead for decades, and each had died a very public, tragic death; a lot of the memorials that came after those deaths weren't necessarily because of the subject's political persuasions.

Then again, Roosevelt and Kennedy each ended up on a coin within the year after they died, so it is possible to put a memorial together quickly. And if memorials really do shape public perception, then Reagan, with maybe two dozen to his name, wasn't set to shape much. Sure, the Ronald Reagan Building and International Trade Center in Washington was the second-largest government building in the country when it was built, second only to the Pentagon, and the DC emergency room where the Secret Service took the president after the attempt on his life in 1981 had been renamed the Ronald Reagan Institute of Emergency Medicine. But such sites weren't going to capture the public imagination like, say, the Franklin Roosevelt Memorial on the National Mall. And while the Ronald Reagan Boyhood Home in Dixon, Illinois, is a fine place, the statue of Reagan in the side yard is as much about promoting the state's industry as it is about the president's legacy: "Illinois is famous for its production of agricultural products," the statue's information plaque says, "so it seems appropriate for him to be admiring the kernels of corn in his hand."

Hence the effort to put a memorial in every county in the country. If Reagan's legacy lagged in the public imagination, the thinking went, the conservative movement could lag, too. But if the public thought of Reagan, as Norquist did, as a top-tier historic figure, there would be a Reagan mantle for modern conservatives to claim as their own. As the former Legacy Project director Michael Kamburowski put it, "Someone 30 to 40 years from now who may never have heard of Reagan will be forced to ask himself, 'Who was this man to have so many things named after him?'" The project website offers a "strategy guide" for choosing things to name, and it says participants should always keep an eye out for low-hanging fruit: "Many major landmarks and projects are named for physical geography, such as 'Muddy Creek Elementary,'" it advises. "These are easy dedications."

Norquist has often kept a big, high-profile naming opportunity on the table as well, because presidents don't stay top tier solely as a namesake for previously unnamed muddy creeks. "Norquist had learned the lessons of [Reagan's famous speeches at] Normandy and of the Brandenburg Gate," says Will Bunch, a senior writer at the *Philadelphia Daily News*; he wrote about the project in his book about Reagan, *Tear Down This Myth*. "Powerful symbols can mean a lot more than words." The first symbol he chose in launching the initiative in 1997 was National Airport in Washington; he lined up support from then–House Speaker Newt Gingrich and Reagan's son Michael, who called on Congress to "win just one more for the Gipper."

Win they did, though not without opposition. Rep. James Oberstar, a Minnesota Democrat, complained Norquist and company wanted "to turn the airport into a political billboard to greet visitors to Washington." The DC transit authority refused at first to spend money on maps with the new name. And then there was longtime New York senator Daniel Patrick Moynihan, who grumbled, "Washington National Airport is already named after a president—the first one." Even some staunch Reaganites joined in the criticism; commentator George Will wrote there was "something un-Reaganesque about trying to plaster his name all over the country the way Lenin was plastered over Eastern Europe, Mao over China and Saddam Hussein all over Iraq." Nevertheless, the bill passed the House and Senate handily in early 1998, and National Airport became known as Reagan National Airport.

However, opposition has stopped some of the Legacy Project's bigger ideas. Grover Norquist called for Reagan to replace Alexander Hamilton on the $10 bill. "I think it will pass very easily when Reagan passes away," he said in 2001. "I've told the Bush [administration] to expect it." But the effort stalled, even after Reagan's death in 2004. Plan B, to put Reagan on the dime, had less support; even Nancy Reagan declared herself opposed to the idea. And Norquist's wish for a Reagan Monument on the National Mall ground to a halt, ironically because of a bill President Reagan signed in 1986 barring any Mall memorials for people who hadn't been dead for at least twenty-five years.

Sometimes the project has had to play defense. In 2013 the University of Chicago tore down an apartment complex in which Reagan had lived as a preschooler, despite calls from a group of community activists to turn it into "a museum and center." The preservationists proposed a pretty colorful alternative: "Break the walls, floors, ceiling and fixtures of the Reagan family apartment into small fragments and sell them on the Internet for between $100 and $1,000 a chip, depending on the size," suggested a board member of the Hyde Park Historical Society in a letter to the university's newspaper. "This should raise many thousands of dollars for the university, rather like selling fragments of the True Cross." It didn't happen, but not for lack of enthusiasm among the pro-Reagan contingent.

And in the southern California town of Temecula, about an hour north of San Diego, a Reagan statue almost went up in flames. As president, the Gipper liked to tell the story of the town's park—built entirely without public funding or assistance—as an example of what citizens could do without relying on government. Temecula, in response, named the place the Ronald Reagan Sports Park, complete with a Reagan statue. In 2013 someone set the thing on fire, charring the statue and destroying tiles displaying a quote in which Reagan exhorted Temecula to "never lose that spirit" of private-sector freedom and initiative.

More recently the Legacy Project has been on the hunt for a mountain peak on which to hang the Reagan name. In 2003 New Hampshire approved a bill to change the name of Mount Clay, in the White Mountains, to Mount Reagan, but the federal government said no, because of a policy about not naming things after people who hadn't been dead five years; when they tried again years later, the feds said no again because of local resistance to the change. A Legacy Project supporter in Nevada, Chuck Muth, had better luck in his state: he found an unnamed mountain in a mountain range east of Las Vegas, cultivated local support, and even found local connections. ("Reagan was a marquee performer on the Las Vegas Strip for two weeks in 1954," Muth told the *Atlantic* in 2013. "He owed back taxes to the IRS and needed the money. He also filmed a World War II propaganda film with Burgess Meredith at Nellis Air Force Base in Nevada.") But just as the Board on Geographic Names looked set to act on the proposal, a Democratic member of Congress filed a bill to name that mountain after a Nevada lawmaker, blocking the board from taking action just as Ohioans had done so many times to those who wanted to pull William McKinley's name from Denali in Alaska.

Muth has decided to start again with a different mountain in the same range. "It's not the highest peak," he said, "but it's certainly close enough." Maybe someday he'll get Ronald Reagan's name on a mountain. His effort, like many of the Legacy Project's initiatives, has ebbed and flowed. There are hundreds of Reagan memorials on the map now, from Ronald W. Reagan Middle School in Grand Prairie, Texas, to Ronald Reagan Boulevard in Warwick, New York, to the Ronald Reagan Minuteman Missile Site in Cooperstown, North Dakota. But there are still more than two thousand Reagan-less counties, too. Sometimes the Legacy Project aims for a high-profile naming opportunity like the $10 bill; other times it lies low and just reminds supporters to celebrate Reagan's birthday each February.

Even in quiet periods, though, Grover Norquist keeps an eye out for a good opportunity. Shortly after the US Patent and Trademark

Office canceled the Washington Redskins' federal registrations for being "disparaging to Native Americans," sports fans started thinking up new names for the team—including the Washington Reagans. "Great idea," Norquist told *Buzzfeed*. "The former Redskins can be the Ronald Reagans on winning years and the Nancy Reagans on losing years. Unless that gets us in more trouble elsewhere."

Whether or not Reagan gets a football team named for him, or a mountain, or a $10 bill, the ongoing effort to name things after him will at least ensure he lingers in the public imagination, even as other modern presidents fade. In 2000, when the Legacy Project was just a few years old, Gallup Poll respondents ranked Reagan as a better-than-average US president; today, he usually ranks near the top, with John F. Kennedy and Abraham Lincoln. There's a partisan divide in these polls—more than half of Republican respondents choose Reagan, while Democrats give Kennedy a boost—but the poll numbers echo Norquist's hope that Reagan could be a conservative hero in the public's eyes as Kennedy had been for progressives. Ronald Reagan remains, as the Legacy Project had hoped, a big deal.

Almost too big a deal, in fact. In 2012, rumors were flying at the Republican National Convention that a "special guest" on the schedule would be a 3-D hologram version of the Gipper, much like the hologram Tupac Shakur that had "performed" onstage at Coachella earlier in the year. Yahoo! News found a man called Tom Reynolds, who said he'd been developing a hologram version of the Great Communicator, but ran into opposition from Republicans "who asked him to delay the project out of concern it would overshadow Mitt Romney's acceptance speech." "Even in a hologram form," Reynolds said, "I think Reagan's going to beat a lot of people in terms of communicating."

THERE'S NO question there's an overtly political element to the Reagan Legacy Project, but it's hardly the first time someone's tried to name something after a president for political reasons; in fact, the project's playbook isn't that different from the one liberals used in the 1930s to memorialize Thomas Jefferson. The Sage of Monticello's brand of rural individualism fell out of favor after the Civil War, in which Lincoln mobilized a strong central government to keep the country together. But in the 1930s, Franklin Roosevelt and his allies played up Jefferson as a champion of the little guy, a president who stood up for the people against the powerful. Jefferson's face first showed up on the nickel in 1938, and FDR dedicated the Jefferson Memorial the following year, saying, "He lived, as we live, in the midst of a struggle between rule by the self-chosen individual or the self-appointed few." Like the Legacy Project's image of Reagan, this version of Jefferson wasn't always a perfect historic fit, but the politics worked extremely well.

Jefferson has also been used as a symbol by people with very different politics than New Deal Democrats. Several times people in rural northern California have proposed pulling the region out of the Golden State and creating a new, libertarian-themed State of Jefferson with equally rural southern Oregon. "The Jefferson statehood tale appeals to a fantasy Westerners embrace," says journalist Peter Laufer, who's written about the movement. "We're rugged individualists who like to go it alone." And who better to stand as a symbol of that spirit than the most prominent voice for agrarian-style small government?

Ronald Reagan himself made a point of honoring a president for political purposes. Shortly after becoming president, he moved a portrait of New Deal icon Harry Truman out of the Cabinet Room and replaced it with one more in line with the more conservative goals he had in mind: Calvin Coolidge. Silent Cal was, as his biographer Amity Shlaes described him, the Great Refrainer of the American presidency, the guy who would rather get rid of a single bad law than pass twenty good ones. He was known for being frugal with words—the famous Coolidge quote is the one in which a woman tells Cal she made a bet she could get more than two words out of him, and he answers, "You lose." But he was even more frugal with the federal budget, cutting back everything he could, and then trying to cut more. The portrait change was Reagan's way of saying which president he hoped to emulate.

As a dead president, though, the Great Communicator and the Non-Communicator couldn't be more different. The Legacy Project wants to turn Reagan into the country's most memorialized president, while Calvin Coolidge fought the hardest against monuments in his own name. "It is a great advantage to a President," he wrote in his autobiography, "and a major source of safety to the country, for him to know he is not a great man." This wasn't just talk, either: a wealthy supporter offered to build him a large, imposing marble tomb; Coolidge said no.

Even death itself was quiet when it came for Calvin Coolidge. In early 1933, just four years after he left the White House, Coolidge had a heart attack at home, alone, with no reported last words. Upon hearing that Coolidge was dead, the writer Dorothy Parker cracked, "How can you tell?" The answer could be found in his characteristically thrifty arrangements: Coolidge's will was just twenty-three words long, and his funeral ceremony lasted a mere five minutes.* Instead of a showy gravesite that drew attention toward him, Coolidge chose burial at the hilltop cemetery where his family had been buried for four generations. His tombstone is no bigger than anyone else's; its only nod to notability is a presidential seal carved into the top. It's simple, elegant, and perfect for its occupant: "There was a case for monuments to other presidents," Shlaes wrote. "But the best monument to his presidency was no monument at all."

Or maybe there's a monument for Coolidge, too—just not the usual kind. One that's got a lot more cheese in it than the others. Just down the road from Coolidge's grave in Vermont is the village of Plymouth Notch. Getting here means driving on some winding roads next to the towering, tree-covered Green Mountains; it looks like what people outside New England think all of New England looks like. Not that the people who lived there in Coolidge's day had time to look up and enjoy it: snowstorms could cut the village off from the rest of civilization for days back then. People had to be able

---

* The will of Calvin Coolidge, in full: "Not unmindful of my son John, I give all my estate both real and personal to my wife Grace Coolidge, in fee simple."

to rely on themselves. "The neighborhood around The Notch was made up of people of exemplary habits," the president wrote in his autobiography. "The break of day saw them stirring. Their industry continued until twilight." Or, sometimes, later: in 1923, then–Vice President Coolidge learned during a visit to his father's house that President Warren Harding had died. Coolidge took the oath of office by lamplight at 2:47 a.m., with his notary public father, "Colonel" John Coolidge, presiding. Having done what they needed to do, both men returned to bed.

Most of the President Calvin Coolidge State Historic Site is dedicated to preserving Plymouth Notch as Coolidge remembered it: the combination general store and post office, the post-and-beam barn with farm implements of all kinds (including my son's favorite, "Tread Mill for a Horse"), the intimate wooden Congregational church. There's actual industry going on today as well; back behind the Coolidge house, there's a large white building marked THE PLYMOUTH CHEESE CORP. "Colonel" John Coolidge was one of several local farmers who started the cheese operation in 1890, mostly so their surplus milk didn't go to waste. The company went under during the Great Depression, but President Coolidge's son, also named John, revived it in the 1960s and eventually sold it to the state.

The door to this building will take you straight to a cheese case if you just want to buy, but to the left are big picture windows through which visitors can see the Plymouth Cheese Company in action. If you spot a bearded guy dipping blocks of cheese into melted wax, or stirring rennet into big silver vats full of raw milk, you might be looking at Jesse Werner, the artisan behind Plymouth Notch's artisan cheese. This native Vermonter grew up on land that focused on the state's other food group—maple syrup—but says it was cheese that always captured his imagination: "I thought, How can I be here and make this work for me?" The answer didn't come for some time; Werner first headed to Europe to earn an MBA and sample the continent's many cheese varieties. But it became clear once he returned to his native state to take courses at the Vermont Institute for Artisan Cheese. Vermont was looking for a cheesemaker to take over the

13. In 1890, Calvin Coolidge's father helped to found the Plymouth Cheese Company (pictured here seventy-five years later, in 1965), which produces artisan cheese on the grounds of the Coolidge State Historic Site in Vermont.

operation at Plymouth Notch. "I was excited about the possibilities," Werner told the *Boston Globe.* "I really wanted to re-create that early cheese from 1890, to abide by the recipe and try to reposition and rebrand Plymouth cheese."

Re-creating early cheese means Werner and his colleagues use techniques more in line with the antique equipment in the cheese company's second-floor museum than the newer equipment in the production area. Plymouth cheese is made with older, English-style techniques that can't be rushed along, and traditional Plymouth cheese ages for at least ten months before it can be sold. It's not easy starting a business if you can't sell your product for nearly a year, and even now, years later, Werner's workweek can sometimes last six or even seven days. But the hard work is worth it: the Plymouth cheese process gives the end product a smooth, almost buttery texture, not as crumbly as regular cheddar and, for my tastes, even more delicious. Werner has won awards in some high-profile cheese competitions, and his products have ended up in some of Manhattan's finest shops, as well as the excellent grilled cheese sandwiches at the Wilder House restaurant, also on the grounds of the historic site.

When you see Werner and his cheesemakers at work, you see the "exemplary habits" that Calvin Coolidge praised in the nineteenth-century people of Plymouth Notch—patience, dedication, industry, respect for tradition. "Not only do you get to see history, you get to taste and touch and smell it," Werner says of the cheese operation. "It's almost like the cheese is an historical exhibit."

If it's wrong to think this cheese is a perfect monument to a president, then I don't want to be right.

7

ROBOTS AND SPHINXES

On Lyndon Johnson, Rutherford B. Hayes,
Franklin Roosevelt, Harry Truman, Richard Nixon,
and Chester Arthur, and America's Presidential Libraries

IT MAKES sense that someone humble and reserved like Calvin Coolidge would have a relatively small headstone and burial plot. But a gregarious Texan like Lyndon B. Johnson, who has space centers and freeways named in his honor? You'd expect something big and prominent. Yet his grave is unexpectedly small: he's in a walled family cemetery up the road from the LBJ Ranch in Stonewall, a town just west of the Pedernales River in the heart of the Texas Hill Country. The headstone is one in a row of red granite markers, only slightly larger than the others. Mrs. Johnson's marker is the same size and shape; at a distance, the American flag in front of LBJ's stone is the only way to tell them apart.

Johnson wasn't looking for prominence in the afterlife—just quiet. "I come down here almost every evening when I'm at home," he said of the cemetery. "It's always quiet and peaceful here under the shade of these beautiful oak trees."

Now, what Johnson did on the rest of the LBJ Ranch—2,700 acres during his presidency, complete with its own airstrip—was anything but quiet. "This is my ranch and I do as I damn please," he liked to say at home, so often that the family embroidered the line on a pillow for him. In the dining room, the president, over his wife's objections, liked to roll his chair a few feet to the right during dinner to monitor the news on a set of three TVs in the living room (one for each network at the time). If a news story got his dander up, Johnson would roll back to the left and grab the phone, specially installed under the table, to chew the reporter out.

All this noise helped Johnson in other ways, too: often at dinner he would distract guests so that he could switch out the low-fat dessert his doctors wanted him to have with one of their regular desserts.

After taking in Johnson's ranch, I drove back east to Austin to see the LBJ Library, next to the University of Texas. Johnson's library was the first to open with a university affiliation, but it's not all scholarly gravitas when you head inside. In fact, the man at the front desk gave

14. The Lyndon Baines Johnson Presidential Library and Museum has a life-size, joke-telling animatronic version of its namesake.

me four words of advice as I set out on my library tour: "Start with the robot."

The Lyndon Baines Johnson Presidential Library and Museum has a life-size robotic version of its namesake—and it's a joke-telling robot, no less. Mechanical LBJ stands behind a podium, and in front of a wide array of editorial cartoons and caricatures, and cracks jokes, which run on a loop. Johnson's jokes were woven into stories, unlike the one-liners for which John F. Kennedy was known—but they're worth the wait. I heard the robot tell a tale about a man who refused his doctor's orders to quit drinking or he'd lose his hearing. According to the robot, the man told the doc, "I just decided that I liked what I drank so much better than what I heard."

The robot gestured as it spun its tale, and I think that because I grew up in the era of the Rock-afire Explosion, the animatronic animal rock group that performed at Showbiz Pizza, I imagined that the gears made noise as he moved, so he sounded more like this: "I just decided—WRRRRRRRRRRRRRDDDDDDDDD—that I liked what I drank—ZZZZZZZEEEEEZZZZZZZZ—so much better than what I heard.—PSSSSSSOOOOOOOFFFFF."

Nobody here intended a joke-telling animatron to be the big draw at the library of one of the most consequential presidencies of the twentieth century. "It was meant to be an addendum," library director Mark Updegrove told me. In fact, he says, "when we had our renovation we contemplated getting rid of the robot. But the public outcry was such that the robot had almost become like Big Tex out here in Texas, almost as iconic.* And so we kept it." The library not only kept Robot LBJ but gave him an upgrade, including a suit and tie to replace the ranch clothes he'd worn since he started his illustrious career as part of a Neiman Marcus display on Texas history in 1997. Austinites, who take their weirdness seriously, worried whether a suit-and-tie robot would meet their needs, but that robot could keep the city weird all by itself. Even Updegrove has a soft spot for the bot:

---

* Big Tex was the giant talking mascot of the Texas State Fair. He caught fire at the end of the 2012 fair, around the time Robot LBJ's fate was being decided.

"My epitaph may well say 'the man who saved the LBJ animatron,'" he said at the time of the upgrade. "And I am just fine with that."

The LBJ robot isn't one of a kind; Walt Disney World's Hall of Presidents has had talking animatronic presidents since its opening in 1971. It isn't even the only robot on a purely presidential site: I met a William McKinley robot at the McKinley museum in Canton, Ohio. Robot McKinley brushed off his robotic wife's concerns about his plans to greet the public at the Pan-American Exposition in Buffalo. "There is nothing to fear from the American citizens who disagree with me politically," he says. Robots do dramatic irony really well.

But Robot LBJ is the best of the lot, and the hypercompetitive Johnson would undoubtedly approve of that. Presidents tend to be competitive people, and the presidential libraries are where they compete against each other. Speaking at the Johnson Library in 2013, George W. Bush noted that "former presidents compare their libraries the way other men may compare their—well . . ."

Johnson's library takes this metaphor almost literally. The architect, Gordon Bunshaft, described the building this way: "The President was really a virile man, and he ought to have a vigorous, male building. And we have got a vigorous, male building." It's ten stories in all, eighty-five feet high, and about 120,000 square feet. Even the documents here are dramatic: one side of the central room, the enormous Great Hall of Achievement, is a series of glass windows showing off four stories of documents, more than forty thousand bright red storage boxes embossed with gold presidential seals. They're positioned above a massive row of murals showing Johnson with Presidents Roosevelt, Truman, Eisenhower, and Kennedy. Mark Updegrove sums up the building perfectly: "It looks like power."

Johnson didn't just want the biggest building, he wanted the most people, too: he spent inordinate amounts of his time in retirement hounding library staff for the latest admission numbers, or tracking the number of postcards people had bought in the gift shop. Sometimes he ducked out to the parking lot to look at license plates and see who was visiting. And he was forever trying to think of ways to drum up more visitors. Once he suggested the library open at 7 a.m.

15. Lyndon B. Johnson looks closely at an architectural model of his library; he would keep an even closer eye on the library's admissions numbers and postcard sales.

and hand out free doughnuts; another time, he had the University of Texas football announcers remind stadium-goers that there were public bathrooms close by at the library.

LBJ was happy to use his famous powers of personal persuasion to boost foot traffic, too. At a book signing in 1971, Johnson decided the crowd should be bigger—so he went outside to round up passersby. The library staff, dutifully clicking a counter each time a visitor came inside, added these new people to their tally, and counted the large group that followed Johnson outside a second time as they shuffled back in. (Some staffers later admitted that, given the boss's preoccupation with attendance, the final numbers were *maybe*, just maybe, a little tiny bit inflated.)

Johnson's funeral services included a stop at the library. Director Harry Middleton made sure that every last one of the thirty-two thousand people who came to see the president's casket in the Great Hall were counted, because, he said, "I know that somewhere, sometime, President Johnson is going to ask me."

Benjamin Hufbauer, a presidential library scholar who teaches at the University of Louisville, says the development of the presidential library is *the* big turning point in how we memorialize presidents. Previously, he says, "there was a sorting process. History kind of judged—Millard Fillmore doesn't get an obelisk in the middle of Washington." It was up to posterity to decide whether a president was worthy of his own statue on the Mall. Now, Hufbauer says, "they don't wait for posterity to do it. They start memorializing themselves."

Presidential libraries began with one of the most mild-mannered presidents, Rutherford B. Hayes. To be fair, "Rud" was described in his Civil War days as "intense and ferocious"—he was wounded five times on the battlefield, in fact—but as chief executive the reserved, bearded Buckeye president didn't set the world on fire with charisma. It was the same story at home in Fremont, Ohio, where Hayes's favorite pastime was inviting a prominent political figure to stroll the front lawn and place his hands around the trunk of a tree, which Hayes would then name for him.

This wasn't the kind of guy for whom you'd build a joke-telling robot. Nevertheless, without the Rutherford B. Hayes Presidential Center there wouldn't be a robot at the LBJ Library in Texas—or a library at all.

Before Hayes, presidents kept their papers private. George Washington, as usual, established this custom, by lugging his presidential papers back with him to Mount Vernon. Unfortunately, some presidents didn't do as well as others in keeping those papers intact. Rats and moist conditions "extensively mutilated" some of the irreplaceable papers from the first administration. Fire proved to be a hazard for presidential papers as well; many of Andrew Jackson's and William Henry Harrison's papers burned. Union soldiers accidentally destroyed most of Zachary Taylor's papers as they ransacked the Louisiana home of Confederate Major General Richard Taylor, his son. Of the papers that did survive, many stayed off-limits to researchers.

Other presidents sold or donated their papers to the government, or willed them to family members, and these papers were better protected. John Quincy Adams's will charged his son Charles Francis with building a fireproof structure to contain both his and his father's presidential papers. After James A. Garfield's assassination in 1881, his wife, Lucretia, built a sort of memorial addition onto the family home in Mentor, Ohio, with a massive portrait of General Garfield in the stairwell, a spacious wood-paneled reading room to hold Garfield's thousands of books, and a stone vault for his papers, the floral wreath Queen Victoria sent for the funeral, and some of the president's walking sticks.

But these papers stayed out of public view for decades. The Adams descendants eventually donated their papers to the state of Massachusetts, but on the condition that they be kept private for another fifty years, well into the twentieth century. Garfield's family didn't want Americans beating down their door for a look at his papers. Even Lincoln's family required that the Great Emancipator's papers be kept under lock and key until the 1940s.

Established in 1916, the Hayes Presidential Center was the first facility intended to protect a president's papers and artifacts *and* offer them for public viewing. If you find that innovation riveting, you may be Paraguayan, as Rutherford B. Hayes is a bigger name in that country than in his own, and with good reason. Paraguay was in ruins in the 1870s: its leaders had provoked a war with three of its neighbors, who responded by signing a secret treaty to divvy up most of the country for themselves. The Triple Alliance—Argentina, Brazil, and Uruguay—not only had better weapons and modern ships, they had a twenty-five-to-one advantage in troops. The battles were bloody; soon Paraguay was losing soldiers, weapons, and even clothes, and resorted to sending children into battle wearing carpets and carrying sticks painted to look like rifles. Two out of every three Paraguayans died by the end of the war; pretty much everyone else was starving.

Hayes came into the story several years after the war, when what was left of Paraguay was at odds with Argentina over a southwestern area known as the Chaco. The two countries turned to the United States for arbitration, and on November 12, 1878, President Hayes decided in favor of Paraguay's land claims, which amounted to about 60 percent of the country's territory today. Paraguay, having finally won something, decided to name about a fifth of the country after its

American benefactor; the capital of the Presidente Hayes Department (in Paraguay, departments are like states or provinces) is Villa Hayes, there's a soccer team in the area named Club Presidente Hayes, and there's a bust of the former president outside the elementary school, although some of the kids apparently know Hayes simply as "the man without arms."

It was Hayes's second son, Webb Cook Hayes, who made the Hayes Presidential Center happen. Webb served capably as his father's White House secretary, and later made a fortune cofounding Union Carbide, but got restless in his forties and ended up being one of the most daring military men of his age. Webb requested and received the most dangerous assignments he could find: he was wounded twice in the war with Spain, first in an assault on Cuba's San Juan Hill—the same hill Theodore Roosevelt's Rough Riders made famous—and again in an invasion of Puerto Rico shortly thereafter. Later, in China, he helped rescue future president and first lady Herbert and Lou Hoover, who had gotten caught up in the Boxer Rebellion. And Webb once snuck behind the lines of insurgents in the Philippines to aid a US military garrison cut off from the rest of the force; this feat won him the Medal of Honor.

Colonel Hayes, as he was known, offered the family's sprawling thirty-one-room mansion, Spiegel Grove, and the surrounding twenty-five acres to Ohio's State Archaeological and Historical Society, on the condition that they build "a suitable fireproof building . . . for the purpose of preserving and forever keeping in Spiegel Grove all papers, books, and manuscripts left by the said Rutherford B. Hayes." He also required that "said building shall forever remain open to the public." Ohio took the deal and spent $50,000 to fix the roads around the property and construct a 52,000-square-foot sandstone building. Webb Hayes pitched in $100,000 of his own for upgrades and endowments, and offered the library his extensive collection of American weaponry, some dating back to the Revolutionary War. He convinced Congress to give up the old gates to the White House for use at the Hayes Center—it took six years, but he got it done. And he had his parents, buried in nearby Oakwood Cemetery, reinterred in a shady corner of Spiegel Grove, under a tall granite monument Rutherford B. Hayes had dreamed up himself. Walk to the rear of the grave and you'll find markers for Webb Hayes and his wife.

Hayes's 1893 funeral drew figures from all over the country, including Grover Cleveland, the former president who was several months away from returning to the office. Cleveland was riding in a funeral carriage at Spiegel Grove when, as one observer noted, "the crowd of men in uniform caused the horses to plunge forward and for a moment it was feared that President Cleveland would be thrown to the ground." Cleveland "recovered himself promptly by the aid of a mammoth shell-bark hickory against which he leaned and since that time the tree has been known as the Grover Cleveland Hickory." One last tree for the road.

The funny thing is, had one guy voted differently in 1876, Hayes might not have been in the White House to become a Paraguayan hero or have a presidential library. His opponent, New York governor Samuel Tilden, won the most popular votes, but the 1876 election was, as one observer put it, the "Ugliest, Most Contentious Presidential Election Ever." The election included vote fraud of every kind, illicit backroom deal-making, and election boards offering to certify the winner for a price. The dispute got so contentious there were concerns, though probably overblown, that the country would sink back into civil war over the outcome.

Hayes backers fought to claim every last electoral vote; Tilden, inexplicably, spent several weeks writing up a report on the history of electoral college procedures, which he thought would convince a special electoral commission to decide the election in his favor. They didn't, of course, and Hayes ended up in the White House. Tilden, to his credit, kept his head up after the win/loss. "I shall receive from posterity," he said later, "the credit of having been elected to the highest position in the gift of the people, without any of the cares and responsibilities of the office." Then again, Tilden's massive tomb in New Lebanon, New York, very pointedly refers to his status as the man who came as close as a man can to winning the White House without actually getting there: "I still trust the people."

FRANKLIN DELANO Roosevelt was thinking of Hayes and his museum when he started dreaming up his own library, which is the model each president has used since. "FDR was a great fan of saving things," explains library director Lynn Bassanese, who retired in 2015. "He had so much stuff—he had so many ship models, he had so many maps, he had so many books." Roosevelt's stamp collection was one of the most celebrated in the world, and he proudly hung on to what he called "oddities"; his taxidermy collection, for example, included some three hundred species of birds.

The president's biggest and most important collection, of course, was the millions of papers, letters, and documents from his long career in public service. "He wanted a place," Bassanese says, "where historians could look through his documents and write the story of his presidency." He didn't want the collection to be housed in the Library of Congress, though, or even the National Archives, which he'd signed into law in 1934. Roosevelt said he was worried about what might happen if the country housed all of its crucial documents together and an enemy attacked; Spain's civil war had, in fact, led to the destruction of some of the documents in that country's central archives. But Benjamin Hufbauer, the presidential library scholar, says what Roosevelt really wanted was a place to tell *his* story. "Roosevelt," he says, "comes up with this library and says, it's my home, it's my land, I'll be buried there, it will bring everybody full circle. This will be a shrine to my life."

So, on April 12, 1937, FDR sketched out the "shrine": a stone Dutch colonial structure on the grounds of his family home in Hyde Park, New York, to house his official papers and display his personal artifacts for the public. Remember, Roosevelt was still president in 1937. "Only an egocentric megalomaniac would have the nerve to ask for such a measure," groused one Missouri representative. Hamilton Fish, who represented Hyde Park in Congress, called the proposal "utterly un-American, utterly undemocratic. It goes back to the days of the Pharoahs, who built their own images and their own obelisks. It goes back to the days of the Caesars, who put up monuments of themselves and crowned them with laurel leaves, and posed as gods."

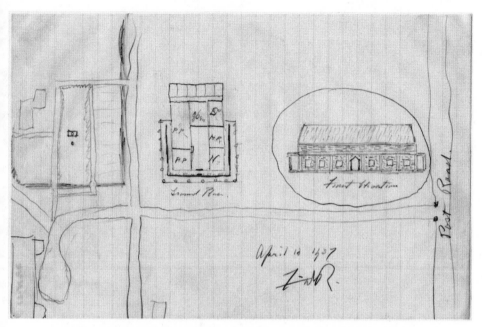

16. On April 12, 1937, Franklin Roosevelt sketched out what would
become the first government-run presidential library: a stone Dutch colonial structure to house his official papers and display his personal artifacts
for the public.

Nevertheless, after some stalling, pro-Roosevelt majorities in Congress approved the library bill in 1939, construction began shortly
thereafter, and the structure was open in 1941.

Roosevelt had intended to help historians sort through his papers
after he retired to Hyde Park. His death in office in 1945 put an end
to that, but his library was the final stop on one of the most unusual
funeral journeys in American history: the mourners on Roosevelt's
eighteen-car funeral train from Washington to Hyde Park included
the new president, Harry Truman, the cabinet, the entire Supreme
Court, and top leaders from Congress and the military. The most
essential personnel in the US government took the same funeral
train—one, mind you, that had its entire schedule printed in the
newspapers—while World War II was going on. It was astonishingly
risky, but fortunately the train arrived without incident, and Roos-

17. When Franklin Roosevelt played coy about whether he'd seek a third term, reporters characterized him as Sphinx-like—and one made it literal, in this papier–mâché bust.

evelt was laid to rest in the family's rose garden—appropriate, given that "Roosevelt" means "field of roses" in Dutch. Eleanor Roosevelt joined her husband after her death in 1962; their burial plots are next to a white oblong stone inscribed only with their names and life-spans, with bright red, yellow, and purple flowers at the stone's base.

"And of course it's not just the grave for the president and the first lady," Lynn Bassanese says, "but underneath the sundial are two of the dogs. There's Fala, and then there's a German shepherd who had belonged to his daughter, named Chief."

The inside of the library has unusual treasures as well. My son galloped from room to room while I perused a wall-sized chart about New Deal government spending. Soon he galloped back to me. "Papa, come here," he said. "I saw a big head." It was Roosevelt's head—made of papier-mâché and shaped like the Sphinx. Bassanese told me the whole story: "It was at the Gridiron Dinner in '39, and FDR had not been very open about whether or not he would run for a third term. It was like he knew all but wouldn't speak, so there had been a lot of editorial cartoons depicting him as a Sphinx. A reporter created this in his basement, and a lot of people might have taken offense to that, but he had a great sense of humor, and when he saw it he laughed and said, when this is all done I want this for my library."

FDR's library might have been one of a kind, had it not been for his successors' decisions to build libraries of their own. "If one or two between then had said 'no, I don't want this,'" Lynn Bassanese said, "then we might have had a very different library system." Each of the following presidents (plus Herbert Hoover, whose library opened in 1962) built upon the Roosevelt model and added his own touches. Harry Truman worked out of an office in his library; he loved to come out and give visitors personal tours, and asked to be buried in the library courtyard, "so I can get up and walk into my office if I want to." Dwight Eisenhower built his library on a tract of land around his boyhood home in Abilene, Kansas.

Every presidential library has its odd side, like the giant Sphinx head in Hyde Park. Gerald Ford's museum, in Grand Rapids, Michigan, chronicles his years in politics and hosts his elegant tomb, a semicircular stone built into the side of a hill overlooking the Grand River. But the library also tells the story of the 1970s, complete with a pair of disco mannequins in mid-hustle, as Marvin Gaye's "What's Going On" plays from the speakers overhead. The Richard Nixon Library in California has a life-size cutout of the president's famous photo with Elvis Presley, as well as the pistol the King brought to the White House as a gift. Bill Clinton's library in Little Rock, Arkansas, has on file ashes from the president's cat, Socks. And, of course, there's Robot LBJ in Austin.

Roosevelt described his library and its contents as "a mine for which future historians will curse as well as praise me." The main criticism of presidential libraries is that there's usually too much praise and not enough cursing. The presidents raise private funds to construct the facilities, which they turn over to the National Archives and Records Administration. Each is part document storehouse and part public museum, using artifacts and official papers to tell the story of the president and his times.

One of Benjamin Hufbauer's favorite phrases to describe the libraries is "archives of spin"; the other is "propaganda museums." "The exhibits in newer presidential libraries often amount to little more than extended campaign commercials in museum form," he says, "because the former president and his supporters essentially control the content." The FDR Library, for example, didn't put in a display about Japanese American internment until the mid-1990s, decades after it took place and nearly a decade after the US government formally apologized for the internment camps. Originally Ronald Reagan's library showed plenty of movie memorabilia and little about the Iran–Contra scandal, and the LBJ Library avoided discussion of Vietnam at first. Its founding director, Harry Middleton, described the dynamic at work in a first-generation library: "We really wanted to do a good job, but we also surely wanted to make sure it was OK with [President Johnson]."

But the libraries have a life cycle: as the president and his contemporaries leave the scene, scholars move in and fill in some of the gaps in a museum's narrative. Lynn Bassanese says this was one of the big goals of the 2013 renovation at the Roosevelt Library: "We wrote the exhibit script with a committee of historians and asked, what's the story here? What are the essentials here? And we crafted the exhibit script that way. Then we took it a step further and created ten computer stations called 'Confront the Issues,' and they're touchscreen stations. And what they do is include excerpts from historians about some of the more controversial issues, like Japanese-American internment, the Holocaust, his health—whether or not he was healthy enough to run for the fourth term.

"What we can do," she continues, "is show lots of the documents the president saw, what his advisers said he should do, and then in hindsight, show what historians have said about those decisions. And that gets us away from those complaints that the libraries are telling just one side of the story." The new FDR Library doesn't stop at the issues—it has no less than three panels about the president's extramarital relationships, as well as a note about Eleanor Roosevelt's "closeness to pioneering newspaperwoman, Lorena Hickok."

The earliest of the presidential libraries have come the longest way in giving both praise and criticism for their subjects. Harry Truman's hometown of Independence, Missouri, lauds its most famous citizen plenty; the downtown historic district lets visitors tour the Truman family home, get an ice cream soda at the shop where young Harry worked, or stop by the men's shop called Wild About Harry. But the president gets no free ride at the Truman Library: the exhibits sometimes disagree with him. One of the walls includes a list of Truman's legislative failures next to his accomplishments; another says pointedly that the Truman Doctrine may have "helped guide the nation into a conflict in Vietnam that did not involve America's national security." The exhibit on the atomic bomb includes plenty of prominent voices who say Truman's decision to use atomic weapons in World War II was the wrong one.

In his book on presidential libraries, Benjamin Hufbauer pointed toward the Truman Library to show how these museums can balance out over time. He's not so sure now, though. "I think my position has changed," he says. "I think the idea that historians are going to push it and modify it and make it more balanced isn't the case. Truman was, as presidents go, relatively modest. The way that it used to work was that the presidential foundation would be established, [the foundation] would raise money for the library, and when it was finished, it would turn the library over to the government and exhaust itself and stop fund-raising.

"That model no longer exists. With Carter, Clinton, Reagan, the two Bushes, the foundations are still active. The children and grandchildren are still involved, and they're not going to let historians—

they're not going to let go of control, long after the president is dead." Hufbauer says these families-vs.-historians struggles will play out much like the struggle over the Watergate exhibit at the Richard Nixon Library in California. Originally this was a private facility run by the Nixon Foundation, so its exhibit on the scandal, "The Last Campaign," made the president sound more like a victim of the scandal than one of the perpetrators. That changed in 2007, when the library formally affiliated with the National Archives and Records Administration. Its new, NARA-appointed director, Timothy Naftali, almost immediately moved to dismantle "The Last Campaign" and spent years developing a new take on Watergate.

The new exhibit, unveiled in 2011, starts with a Nixon quote—"This is a conspiracy"—and continues in that unflinching tone through the long national nightmare of break-ins and cover-ups and Supreme Court cases and resignation. There are some forty hours of video in which those involved in the scandal and the investigation share their memories, and there's a look at the legislation that came out of Watergate, from changes to campaign finance and open records laws to the Presidential Records Act, which formally put all presidential papers into the library system.

(My favorite part of the Watergate exhibit is called "Listen to the Gap," where you can listen to the portions of a White House recording from June 1972 that someone erased, destroying potentially important evidence in the Watergate investigation. Since it's been erased, all you hear is the erasure clicks and occasional buzzing.)

The revamped display won mostly accolades from the public, but foundation backers fumed. Bob Bostock, a former Nixon staffer who had written most of the original exhibit, complained that the Nixon Library had now launched "an unapologetic attack" on its namesake. "It is as much a polemic as the original exhibit was," he wrote in the foundation's lengthy and very public response to the exhibit. "The difference is that the original exhibit never claimed to be impartial." Archivists and volunteer docents quit in protest; for a while, some foundation staff and library staff didn't speak, even though they worked in different parts of the same building. Naftali joked with one reporter that he worked out to cope with stress, and that working at the Nixon Library had gotten him into peak physical condition. He ended up quitting himself, barely six months after the opening of his Watergate exhibit.

The relationship between private foundation and public entity clearly can get complicated. So why not just leave the libraries entirely private, as the Nixon Library used to be? "So they can have the government pay for it," Hufbauer says. "We're talking maybe three to four million dollars a year for staff, keeping the lights on, and so forth. But also because [NARA affiliation] gives it official sanction. If you were to just run it by yourself and say 'We're going to run this propaganda museum,' you wouldn't have that official sanction." Conversely, no library is moving to cut out the private foundation, either, not when they're the biggest financial backers and cheerleaders the libraries have.

Hufbauer says the "sheer weight of the documents" is the biggest problem facing the system today. "Eighty, ninety million documents, and increasingly in digital forms—it's a labor-intensive process to go through those," he says. "It takes eyes and hands and minds of trained archivists to look at these. And they've simply not kept up with the hiring of archivists with the level of documents." At the current rate, the Bill Clinton and George W. Bush libraries aren't expected to finish sorting through their documents for decades, or maybe even a century—and an executive order Bush signed in 2001 allows presidents to block the release of virtually any documents for virtually any reason, including plain old politics. Meanwhile, the museums, which the presidents and their backers shape, get bigger and fancier and more enticing for visitors. Presidential libraries are growing larger *and* smaller at the same time.

They're also more in demand than ever—at least by the potential host sites. A huge presidential library can serve as an economic anchor for a city or a neighborhood; the construction of Bill Clinton's library in Little Rock spurred a billion dollars of private investment in the surrounding area. And most libraries affiliate with nearby colleges or universities. "It is a prestige builder," says Skip Rutherford, dean of the Clinton School of Public Service at the University of Arkansas. "It is a recruiter. People look to the program, even if it's not directly on the campus." No president has been short on bidders for a library site.

Only one president has been short on enthusiasm for placing his name in history. Chester A. Arthur never wanted the top job; he was content to be a nondescript machine politician in New York. But in 1880 the Republicans nominated Arthur as James A. Garfield's running mate to smooth out a squabble between two party factions. In less than a year, Garfield was a martyr and Arthur was the mutton-chopped, well-dressed "Dude President." His first act in office was to lock himself in the bedroom and cry.

To Arthur's credit he rose to the occasion, winning over a skeptical public, and enraging the political bosses, by refusing to do any more dirty work for the machine. Former friends wondered what happened to their man Chet Arthur. "He isn't 'Chet' Arthur anymore," one concluded. "He's the president."

Perhaps the president's former friends didn't know about the non-flunky side of his personality. Arthur served with distinction in the Civil War, efficiently overseeing housing and provisions for hundreds of thousands of New York soldiers. As a young lawyer in Manhattan, he had successfully defended an African American woman called Elizabeth Jennings, who faced a charge of refusing to get off a streetcar to make room for white riders. This was in 1854, a century before Rosa Parks. Even so, Arthur played his cards pretty close to the vest, telling one White House guest, "I may be President of the United States, but my private life is nobody's damned business."

And he meant it. The president's grandson, Chester A. Arthur III, told the Library of Congress that "the day before he died, my grandfather caused to be burned three large garbage cans, each at least four feet high, full of papers which I am sure would have thrown much light on history." Because of that, Chester Arthur is one of the least well known presidents. There is no Chester Arthur Foundation raising money for exhibits at a Chester Arthur Presidential Center, and there are few historic sites retracing Arthur's life or career. His tomb, just outside of Albany, is the most striking of all the president's graves—

there's a weeping angel standing over his sarcophagus—but it doesn't give up many answers. Arthur's Manhattan home is equally impressive, but there's no museum there, just a small plaque on the outside of the building at 123 Lexington Avenue; the twenty-first president's lone National Historic Landmark is better known as Kalustyan's international grocery, "a landmark for fine specialty foods." There are only two Arthur statues, and the one in New York City shows the president holding up a pair of eyeglasses—which aren't there, because somebody swiped them from his hand.

Chester Arthur got the obscurity he wanted, but without another like him in the White House, the presidential library is going to be with us for a while. Presidents just want them too much to let them go. "In America," Benjamin Hufbauer says, "there is an obsession with the presidency. And presidents are the people most obsessed with it."

8

━━ •••━━

UNINTENDED LEGACIES

*On William Taft, Andrew Jackson, Thomas Jefferson, and
How Presidents' Reputations Change over Time*

A MERICANS' OBSESSION with the presidency has its limits.
"It's important to remember that we remember our presidents
in a very cursory manner," Mark Updegrove of the LBJ Library told
me. "Clare Boothe Luce"—writer, two-term member of Congress,
diplomat, and activist in the mid-twentieth century—"used to tell
presidents that they were going to be remembered in one sentence.
And she used to tell them, what will your sentence be?" He laughed
as he recalled the story. "It got so bad that JFK started avoiding her at
parties."

Presidents can try to write their own sentences to sum up their
careers for posterity, and sometimes they're successful. More often the
shorthand version of a president's life ends up changing over time, and
not always for the better. Lyndon Johnson, for example, wanted to be
remembered for launching the War on Poverty and his other Great
Society programs, but the war in Vietnam changed his sentence.

I got a lesson in how presidents are remembered in an unexpected
place: Nationals Park, the Major League Baseball stadium in Washington. The Nats play up their capital connections in a big way, including

a pregame video montage of presidents throwing out the first pitch at Major League games and presidential trivia questions on the big screen during the game. "Who was the First Lady of Baseball?" read one, with four possible answers listed below. "I'm gonna choose Florence Harding," said the fan chosen to answer on our behalf. Unfortunately for the fan, the right answer was Grace Coolidge.

I was sitting in front of a group of four women in their twenties who had been following the baseball action pretty closely, but the trivia questions got them thinking out loud. "Wait," one said to her companions. "Which one was the president who died like after thirty days? Was that Taft?" I couldn't resist piping up. "You're thinking of William Henry Harrison. He's the one who died a month into his term."

"Yeah, Harrison," she said. "Not Taft. Taft was the really fat president."

Of course she was right. But oh, the indignity! A long and distinguished career in public service, and it boils down to being remembered as the Fat President—the only one who weighed over 350 pounds, the only one with a body mass index in the clinical "obesity class 3." I saw this over and over on my trips. The University of Cincinnati has a statue of Taft behind the law school, where he once served as dean; the sculptor had to add more heft to the likeness so visitors would recognize who it depicted. Taft is the only president to also serve as chief justice, but at one of the wax museums I visited, the scale next to the figure wasn't the kind Lady Justice famously holds. A hotel in southern California has a chair specially built for Taft's visit there in 1909; it looked like it could hold three regular-size people. ("Did you have to make the chair so large?" Taft reportedly asked.)

Taft's big achievements always seemed to come with a mention of his big frame. "When he laughs," wrote one reporter, "the surrounding furniture shakes and rumbles." Even Theodore Roosevelt, one of Taft's closest friends, wasn't above using the man's weight as a punch line. When associates worried about who would keep an eye out for problems while he was out of town, Roosevelt said, "Things will be all right. I have left Taft sitting on the lid."

People were forever comparing Taft to Roosevelt, and the sup-

18. Newspapers ridiculed photographs of William Howard Taft on the golf course, which were perhaps less than flattering; a century later, he's still remembered as the "fat president."

posedly jolly fat man "sitting on the lid" paled in comparison. The charismatic Roosevelt charged up hills in battle, took on the captains of industry in the White House, and personified "the strenuous life" on his hikes and hunting trips. As for Taft? "I don't think he had an ounce of charisma," said Lewis Gould, who's written several books about Taft's life and career. "He really didn't stir the heart the way

Roosevelt did. Taft was seen as this genial, honest, competent guy, but he didn't have the magic that Roosevelt had instinctively." Taft was a golfer, not a Rough Rider, and he liked to think through issues more like a judge than a politician. And the issues he chose to tackle, like tariff policy and the organization of the courts, didn't grab headlines the way Roosevelt did with his efforts to clean up the meatpacking industry and build the Panama Canal.

Then again, Taft didn't want to chase headlines. "I simply can't do that sort of thing," he said. "That isn't my method. I must wait for time and the result of my labors to vindicate me naturally." But the opposition didn't wait: as Taft deliberated, they called him lazy. Roosevelt brought about the teddy bear, thanks to a story about one of his hunting trips; the idea for a highly unsuccessful Taft toy, the Billy Possum, came from a banquet. And they ridiculed photos of the president on the golf course, which weren't flattering to his size. "Taft just had no idea of how to market himself in a way that made him seem interesting and attractive," said Gould. "Golf was an aristocratic game played by wealthy fat cats, and the fattest of the fat cats was the president himself."

Taft was a stress eater in office, and as the critics' voices grew louder, he gained weight, which medical historians now believe led to his developing a case of sleep apnea. Taft started falling asleep in important meetings, which convinced more people that he wasn't up to the job. In 1912, as Taft ran for reelection, Roosevelt decided to launch a comeback and seek a third term against his old friend; TR's third-party campaign split the Republican vote and opened the White House door for the Democratic candidate, Woodrow Wilson. Taft finished a distant third.

Taft's postpresidency was much more successful. After spending several years lecturing and teaching, Taft was nominated by Warren Harding for the job he'd always wanted most, chief justice of the United States. He made the high court more efficient, clearing a backlog of cases, and he successfully lobbied Congress to build a separate building for the judicial branch; previously the justices had to work in the Capitol. He reconciled with his old friend Theodore Roosevelt, and his health improved, too: Taft lost seventy pounds in his first year out of office and kept it off for the rest of his life. "I can truthfully say that I never felt any younger in all my life," he told reporters. "Too much flesh is bad for any man." He died in 1930, after nearly a decade as chief justice. Thousands attended his funeral in Washington, and many more listened in on radio; it was the first presidential funeral to be broadcast. As Taft was laid to rest at Arlington National Cemetery, Will Rogers lionized him as the consummate public servant. "We are parting with three hundred pounds of solid charity to everybody, and love and affection for all his fellow men."

This is the crucial point: Americans remembered Taft's weight first and foremost, even as they recognized his gifts. It's worth noting that Taft, the Fat President, was born a year earlier than Roosevelt, the Strenuous President, but he ended up outliving TR by more than a decade. But Taft gets short shrift in the comparison because the era in which they lived was when society's attitudes toward weight made a big shift. "Size in those days was a sign of gravitas and maturity," Lewis Gould says, "in ways now that we would see him as obese." For centuries, artists and thinkers had characterized "flesh" in positive terms, because it meant a person had avoided malnutrition and hunger. Beginning in the late nineteenth century, however, food became more accessible, and medical research started showing the negative health risks connected with obesity. Big was no longer beautiful, and those who were big were characterized as lazy and greedy, clumsy and dumb.

Take, for example, the most famous story about Taft—the one in which he supposedly got stuck in the White House bathtub. This story didn't circulate until after Taft had died, and its first appearance came in a book by a longtime White House usher, Ike Hoover, whose memoir dished dirt on a number of presidents. Researchers say there's no documentary evidence other than Hoover's book about a bathtub story, and anyway, the White House had installed a tub so large that even someone of Taft's size couldn't have gotten stuck in it. But the story of Taft and the bathtub fit what society already believed about weight.

As Taft's size became a bigger part of his story, the rest of the man was diminished. Taft could, and did, crack jokes at his own expense, even about his weight. He personally released to the press the famous telegrams in which he wired a friend to say he'd gone horseback riding and had "stood [the] trip well," only to have the friend wire back, "How is the horse?" But Taft's son Charlie said that the jolly fat man image was "a complete misrepresentation. . . . He was not that kind of genial [person]. . . . His humor had a point to it all the time." William Howard Taft was witty and perceptive, but the culture says large men can't be perceptive, so it reduces his wittiness into self-deprecating fat jokes. Taft's descendants have served as senators and mayors, but they've been overshadowed by the Roosevelts, Kennedys, Bushes, and Adamses—all of whom, of course, happened to be thinner.

Taft isn't the only president to be obese—*Forbes* magazine once ranked the presidents by body mass index, and while Taft was at the top of the list, Grover Cleveland, Zachary Taylor, and William McKinley all had BMIs in the "obesity class 1" range. Even Teddy Roosevelt put on enough weight by the end of his term to qualify as obese. Society's attitudes on obesity have grown more negative since the rise of mass media; only one president in the television age, Bill Clinton, has had any kind of weight issues, and he ended up making a very public show of dieting and exercising.

All of this may be about to change, albeit slowly. As the obesity rate has risen, public attitudes about size seem to have softened, at least a little. There's also increased recognition in the public health community that hectoring people about being overweight doesn't suddenly make them lose pounds. For me, the best sign is that William Howard Taft has started to reemerge in pop culture, joining Theodore Roosevelt, Washington, Jefferson, and Lincoln as one of the Washington Nationals' famous Racing Presidents mascots. These five start each evening's race on the big screen, running through some historic landmarks, including the William Howard Taft Boyhood Home in Ohio, before emerging from the center field wall and barreling down the warning track.

Taft didn't win the running of the presidents on the night I visited Nationals Park, but he didn't lose because of his size. The Baltimore mascot, the Oriole Bird, had interjected himself into the race and knocked three of the other presidents silly. Fourth-place Taft was so incensed by the injustice that he grabbed the Oriole Bird and wrestled him to the grass. It knocked him out of contention—Thomas Jefferson strolled across the finish line and began a surprisingly funky victory dance—but the Nats fans cheered Taft for taking one for the team.

ONE THING is clear walking up to Andrew Jackson's Nashville home, the Hermitage: our seventh president wanted the world to see him as the genteel Tennessee squire he occasionally was, rather than the shrewd but uncouth frontiersman he more often was. The Hermitage was largely designed to round off Old Hickory's rough edges: an elegant, tree-lined "War Road" leads to the house, with signs noting that "each tree came from a battlefield where Andrew Jackson fought," and the large white columns in front of the house are made of wood but painted to look like expensive marble.

But Jackson would be Jackson no matter what his house looked like; legend has it that Old Hickory's funeral featured an impromptu and highly profane eulogy by his pet parrot, Poll, who "commenced swearing so loud and long as to disturb the people and had to be carried from the house."

Younger visitors to the Hermitage can take a kid-friendly audio tour narrated by Poll, who gives his side of the story: "Parrots do love to talk. But that day I said too much. Have you ever had a temper tantrum and felt bad about it later? Well, that's what happened to me. I loved the general and when he died no one could calm me down. Some things I said were in parrot, some were in English, and some in Spanish. Certain things were not so polite. I'm afraid that many things were better suited to the ears of sailors than the many ladies who had gathered to pay their respects. They finally had to lock me up in a room inside until I could control myself. After that day I promised never to use bad language again."

The Hermitage audio tours also include a great deal of information about the hundreds of enslaved people who lived and worked on the plantation. Dead presidents have unexpectedly become an important resource for studying the lives of those in slavery, because presidential houses have been unusually well maintained. "That's especially true in the case of the Hermitage," says Marsha Mullin, chief curator and vice president of museum services. "It's never had anyone else live here—the land hadn't been developed in any way. It's remarkably well preserved. Another factor is that there's so much more written material," which helps researchers who go back over the land find artifacts connected to enslaved people there.

Even so, the physical evidence of those individuals is slim. The slave quarters themselves are long gone, and there are only slivers of evidence of what life was like; for example, scholars uncovered fish bones and fishing tools, suggesting the enslaved people were allowed to catch their own fish. To find the remnants of African American cemeteries, researchers look not for headstones—there usually weren't any—but for flat impressions in the grass, signs of coffins that collapsed due to time and deterioration.

Judging by the outlines in the grass, these houses were remarkably tiny buildings. It looked like you could fit all three in the main hallway of Jackson's house. It was probably the saddest moment on all my travels, to stand there and think of how one man was remembered with a giant house and tons of artifacts while hundreds of people whom he enslaved were remembered with the faintest of ruins and a few fish bones. I walked back toward the rear of Jackson's house; Andrew and Rachel are buried in the back corner of the garden.

Just off to the south side of the cupola is a small headstone, surrounded by a small black chain: "Uncle Alfred. Sept. 4, 1901. 99 years. Faithful servant of Andrew Jackson."

Alfred was born at the Hermitage and worked in slavery there for decades. The tombstone makes it sound like Alfred was Jackson's personal servant, but Marsha Mullin says "it's a little unclear what his job was," adding that it probably had more to do with horses and carriages. Alfred, she says, "may have enhanced his role in his later storytelling." Alfred stayed on in a cabin behind the main house even after Jackson's death and after the Thirteenth Amendment did away with slavery. He rented twenty-four acres at the Hermitage to grow food and to sell butter and cotton. His wife, Gracie, worked for the Jackson descendants as well.

Alfred was still on hand when a group known as the Ladies' Hermitage Association won state sanction to own and operate the Hermitage as a museum. As this group began restoring the house and the grounds, Alfred found a new calling: as Mullin puts it, "he became basically the first tour guide." Hermitage visitors often wanted their picture taken with him and drank in his stories about life with the famous general.

Much of what we know about Alfred comes from a book called *Preservation of the Hermitage, 1889–1915*, which describes him in tour guide mode. Much of it is in language that's considered racist today; Alfred comes off as a kind of rustic savant—his nickname, "Uncle" Alfred, brings to mind the stereotypes associated with Uncle Remus. The author, Mary Dorris, writes Alfred's dialogue in a sort of pidgin slave dialect: "Dis center table was presented to General Jackson an' Mis' Jackson in 1815 by de citizens of New Orleans," she has him saying to visitors. "It is one o' de things saved when de house got burned down in 1834." The author also notes, in a patronizing way, that Alfred's strong suit was his dates. "He would give dates for everything, remembering marvelously, and was generally correct"— though, of course, she points out how Alfred occasionally mixed up his facts about the house and its history.

Still, Alfred comes off as smart and charismatic, a good storyteller who could read visitors well. A white tutor to the Jackson children once gave Alfred the tired line about how life in slavery wasn't all bad, since he got room and board for free. "How would you like to be a slave?" Alfred replied. The man didn't answer.

The Hermitage fell on hard times as the years went on, and after the death of Andrew Jackson Jr. in 1865, many Hermitage items went up for auction to settle debts. Alfred ended up buying some of them, including a mirror that had belonged to the Jacksons. This purchase, curator Mullin says, led to the most interesting part of Alfred's story: "He basically traded the mirror back to [the Ladies' Hermitage Association]—in exchange for a promise that he would be buried next to the Jacksons."

Mullin says we don't know precisely why this was Alfred's sole condition for the deal. His biological family wasn't buried in the garden—in fact, Hermitage researchers don't know where Gracie is buried. Mary Dorris's book suggests two ideas. One is that Alfred had become such a beloved figure that the ladies of the association were glad to have the chance to honor him. Mullin says this isn't likely—after all, "these were southern ladies in the nineteenth century" and wouldn't likely have put an African American man near a white burial ground. The other idea Dorris's book floats is that Alfred was a snob:

> In his way Uncle Alfred was a haughty aristocrat. He had always been
> a faithful and trusted servant in a wealthy and prominent family, which,
> coupled with the fact that "old marster" was President of the United States,
> warranted him in thinking "a powerful sight o' hisself," as he expressed it.

Dorris suggests Alfred saw some of the other enslaved people as "second class," and wanted to distinguish himself and his deep personal connections to the Jacksons and the Hermitage with a burial away from the other former slaves. "Whatever the reason," Mullin says, "they honored the deal and had his funeral in the mansion and buried him next to the Jacksons in the garden."

Whether he intended it or not, Alfred's deal made a powerful statement for all the enslaved people on this plantation and the others. Sites like the Hermitage do meaningful work to bring to light the contributions of the enslaved people, but it's easy for visitors to choose not to look. You don't have to go down that extra path to the slave quarters, or to see Alfred's cabin behind the giant mansion. You can skip past the section about slavery on the audio player. But if you want to see the president's tomb, you can't overlook Alfred. You can't pretend he's not there. If you want to see the final resting place of Andrew Jackson, to see his house and to pay your respects to his tomb, you'll have to see the grave of a man he enslaved, too.

Andrew Jackson may have been unschooled and unrefined, but he was shrewd and knew how to get what he wanted. The tomb next to his suggests he wasn't the only one.

———

WHAT WE know about the enslaved community at the Hermitage is being compiled into something called the Digital Archaeological Archive of Comparative Slavery. The project, which started up in January 2000, combines the historical paper trail with archaeological findings to create a centralized storehouse of information about enslaved people in the American South and the Caribbean. The work isn't quick and it isn't easy, but over time we'll have a fuller picture of this world than we've ever had.

What a change from the early days of the country, when one solution to the slavery problem was literally to send it away. The colonization movement—as in "start a colony in Africa and send the slaves there"—appealed to white northerners as a way to effectively end the institution of slavery, while southerners thought colonization would head off a future in which people of African descent, enslaved or free, would overwhelm whites with sheer numbers, which they believed would end in a bloody race war. Virginia's presidents were especially enthusiastic about the possibilities. James Madison served as one of the first presidents of the American Colonization Society and left it two thousand dollars in his will. James Monroe championed the movement while president; when the ACS set up the West African colony of Liberia in 1822 for some twelve thousand emancipated people, they named the capital city Monrovia—the same Monrovia that has been the subject of long-running tensions between the America-Liberians and native West Africans, multiple civil wars, foreign exploitation, coup d'etats, and, most recently, the worst Ebola outbreak on record. Not all of this is due to the colonization movement, but it sure didn't help.

But it's easy to see why people were looking for an answer: in addition to being morally indefensible, slavery was proving economically unsound as well. Virginia was early America's economic engine, population center, and intellectual powerhouse, but by the 1820s the Commonwealth was in decline, in large part because of the high costs, many inefficiencies, and growing national unease around bondage. Thomas Jefferson, the most prominent voice for America's country mice and an inveterate Virginia booster, backed colonization, but he also wanted to create a world-class university to level the playing field for his state. The university, he thought, would allow (white) Virginia to once again produce the best minds, which would even out the deficiencies with the North and keep the state self-sufficient. Jefferson spent his final years working to raise funds and public support for the school, often while in a sickbed and pumped full of laudanum. Jefferson even used his grave marker as part of this effort; he left exact details for a nine-foot-tall obelisk, on top of a cube-shaped base, with this inscription and "not a word more":

> Here was buried
> Thomas Jefferson
> Author of the Declaration of American Independence
> of the Statute of Virginia for religious freedom
> & Father of the University of Virginia.

It's often noted that Jefferson didn't include his presidency on the obelisk, but the more interesting question is why he *did* include the university, which was only getting off the ground at the time of his death, as one of the three achievements of which he was proudest. For Jefferson, it was just as important as the other two: the university was the means by which Jefferson's beloved home state could turn itself around. In fact, one of his last public appearances was at an event for the university, in which he toasted his guest, the Marquis de Lafayette, by saying of the school, "Could I live to see it once enjoy the patronage and cherishment of our public authorities with undivided voice, I should die without a doubt of the future fortunes of my native State, and in the consoling contemplation of the happy influence of this institution on its character, its virtue, its prosperity, and safety." In death he put his prestige and historical reputation to work on the school's behalf. "Father of the University of Virginia" was his last sales pitch to new students.

I was describing some of my other presidential grave visits to a Monticello staff member as we walked back from the burial ground toward the main house. "You know our story, right?" she asked. It's a memorable story, and hardly the one the third president had inscribed on his stone obelisk. But no president's legacy goes unquestioned, especially not a president with so many varied interests, so much talent and such significant flaws. In the post–Civil War world, race has remained the central question in our national narrative, and as the acclaimed historian John Hope Franklin noted, Jefferson's feelings and actions regarding race seem to personify the country's own struggles with these difficult questions. "Thomas Jefferson was a person who declared that all men were created equal, and at the same time he owned slaves," Franklin said in an interview with PBS in 1997. "Jefferson set standards for himself that make it impossible to reconcile these two things."

Each generation asks new questions of Jefferson's life and legacy. Over time, the questions have gotten tougher, and interestingly, they lead right back to the burial ground at Monticello. There is a tall black iron gate around the cemetery, complete with an intricate family coat of arms on the entrance, and a small gold sign: "This graveyard plot is the private property of Thomas Jefferson's descendants." The Jefferson family held on to the graveyard when they sold Monticello in 1836; today it's managed by a descendants group called the Monticello Association, which cleans the graves and grounds and sees to it that descendants can be buried with their famous ancestor.

Who qualifies as a descendant—and, by extension, who can be laid in the graveyard with Thomas Jefferson—is up to the members of the Monticello Association. And those decisions resonate far outside the big black cemetery gates.

The best illustration of this is the story of an African American man named Robert H. Cooley III, who was on hand at the University of Virginia on October 17, 1992. It was day four of the "Jeffersonian Legacies" conference, which organizers had promised would undo the many myths and misconceptions surrounding the third president, especially over slavery. Robert Cooley had felt a deep connection to the world of slavery at Monticello since his grandfather had taken him aside as a kid and told him what the Cooleys called "the family secret." "I was ten years old," Cooley said in 1995. "He said, 'You are a part of a special family. And you are a special person. Through your mother and me, and my mother and so on, you are a descendant of Sally Hemings and Thomas Jefferson.'

"I didn't know who Sally Hemings was," Cooley said, "but I knew who Jefferson was. And, for a moment, I was very thrilled by that revelation."

But Cooley's grandfather wasn't finished. "He went on to say, however, this is a family secret. And we don't discuss it outside the family. I said, why not? And he said, because people won't believe you, first of all. And it's really not anybody's business."

Cooley took the story—and his grandfather's advice—to heart. He earned two Bronze Stars in Vietnam and, despite the prejudices of the time, became a prominent lawyer and judge in Virginia. "The army has a law school on the grounds of the University of Virginia," he recalled. "When I went into the library and sat down, the kids got up and left, the students, in protest. . . . And I thought, you know, what irony. My great-great-grandfather founded this university."

Cooley also served as president and general counsel of the Thomas Woodson Family Association, which holds that Woodson was the first child born to Jefferson and Hemings and was either allowed or told to leave Monticello for a life in Ohio. (Other oral traditions suggest the first child died in infancy.)

During one "Jeffersonian Legacies" seminar, scholar after scholar spoke about the long-running story that Jefferson had fathered children by Sally Hemings, an enslaved woman at Monticello. Cooley said later his body started to "tingle" during the discussions, so much so that he couldn't help but speak up. And so he did. "Sally Hemings is the seventh great-grandmother of mine," he told the audience. "It's not a story. It's true. There are hundreds of us."

At that "the whole place went silent," he said.

Cooley's grandfather was right: some people—at least the white ones—*didn't* believe the stories about Thomas Jefferson fathering children by Sally Hemings. The rumors started in the early 1800s, when a political mudslinger called James Callender went public with some of the president's supposed secrets. "It is well known that the man, *whom it delighteth the people to honor*, keeps, and for many years past has kept, as his concubine, one of his own slaves. . . . By this wench Sally, our president has had several children. There is not an individual in the neighbourhood of Charlottesville who does not believe the story; and not a few who know it." Callendar's story came at a time where Jefferson's critics were leveling all kinds of incredible charges at him, so people outside of the "neighbourhood" largely read the story as the usual character assassination. And Callendar's credibility was suspect in part because he went to the press after trying to shake Jefferson down for a postmaster's job.

Decades later, abolitionists would turn to the Jefferson/Hemings story to illustrate the evils of the institution, but their accounts weren't ironclad either, because, in addition to using the story to further their goals, the details were different in each account. One abolitionist newspaper accused Jefferson of not only fathering children with an enslaved woman, but then putting those children up for auction: "The DAUGHTER of THOMAS JEFFERSON SOLD in New Orleans," the *Liberator* wrote, in indignant capitals, "for ONE THOUSAND DOLLARS." It wasn't true. Other accounts were admittedly fictional, like William Wells Brown's 1853 novel *Clotel; or, the President's Daughter*, whose title character leapt to her death in the Potomac River rather than return to slavery. "Thus died Clotel," Brown wrote, "the daughter of Thomas Jefferson." The book, one of the first novels by an African American to be published, did well with the public but didn't convince those studying Jefferson that the claims were true.

Then again, historians didn't believe accounts from real people, either. Madison Hemings told an Ohio newspaper in 1873 that Sally Hemings had come to France while Jefferson served as a diplomat there, and that it was in Paris that "my mother became Mr. Jefferson's concubine, and when he was called back home she was *enciente* [*sic*] by him." His account was dismissed outright because Madison Hemings had been enslaved. Scholars compared what they saw as unreliable sources to Jefferson and his character and concluded that he didn't seem the type to take up with Sally Hemings. And the family had its own explanation for the Hemings kids; in letters they pointed to Peter Carr, one of Jefferson's friends and a frequent Monticello guest, as the father of her children.

Attitudes started to change in the mid-twentieth century. For one thing, historians rediscovered, and reconsidered, two important documents: the personal account of Madison Hemings and Thomas Jefferson's Farm Book. Researchers had rejected Hemings's account because of his background and because it had been presented as oral history, without documentary evidence to support it. But in a time when Americans were confronting issues of race and equality, a number of scholars remembered that enslaved people *had* to pass history on through oral tradition, because they had been denied the chance to read and write. And, they added, the Jefferson family's speculation about Peter Carr had just as little supporting evidence as Madison Hemings's account. Why was one considered valid and the other not?

The Farm Book, meanwhile, was full of details about life at Monticello, but in some cases it was notable for what *wasn't* included. The writer and gardener Jamaica Kincaid has noted that in the Farm Book, Jefferson's crops "come to table," with no mention of who put them there. "There's no involvement of labor, there's no soiling of . . . there's no soil at all. It's as if it's Eden. It doesn't have any evil in it."

Monticello itself is like this. In designing his house, Jefferson had emulated the sixteenth-century Italian architect Andrea Palladio, who advised the following: "Contrive a building in such a manner that the finest and most noble parts of it be the most exposed to public view, and the less agreeable disposed in by places, and removed from sight as much as possible." Jefferson removed from sight the activity of the enslaved workers. Monticello is built into the side of a hill; Jefferson could walk guests out onto the north terrace to peer through a telescope at the University of Virginia, and they might never know that underneath them, enslaved people were carrying out the essential tasks of the house. In the dining room, Jefferson could put an empty wine bottle into a dumbwaiter, and a fresh one would appear. If you wanted to pretend the wine had just "come to table," you could.

So researchers began to look at what *wasn't* in the documentary record, like oral histories, reconsidered what was, and reached some intriguing and important conclusions. Fawn Brodie's 1974 best seller *Thomas Jefferson: An Intimate History* delved into Jefferson's inner life (too much for some historians' tastes) and introduced those who hadn't heard the oral histories to the story of Sally Hemings, who accompanied Jefferson's daughter to Paris and came back to Virginia pregnant barely two years later. She was where Jefferson was each time she conceived, she looked after Jefferson's bedchamber (a private sanctuary even his acknowledged family rarely saw), and she sought—and received—freedom for her children when they turned twenty-one. Two decades later, the prizewinning historian Annette Gordon-Reed delved deeper into Jefferson's history. In her books *Thomas Jefferson and Sally Hemings: An American Controversy* and *The Hemingses of Monticello: An American Family*, she questioned some of the biggest historical assumptions about Jefferson, like a common claim that, his extensive slave-owning notwithstanding, the president's morals were somehow too pure for him to have a sexual or romantic relationship with an enslaved woman. Depictions of Jefferson and Hemings in popular fiction and television miniseries were heavy on speculation but captured the popular imagination. The stories about children at Monticello weren't accepted as truth, but they weren't being so quickly dismissed, either.

All the while, Robert Cooley III continued to speak up about his history and heritage. So did others: a woman called Minnie Shumate Woodson organized the family history into a book, which led to a Woodson descendants reunion, which reinforced Cooley's desire to see his ancestors recognized. "Monticello has been noted as the finest example of American architecture," Cooley said in his interview for Ken Burns's documentary about Jefferson. "Mr. Jefferson received the highest award from the American Institute of Architects. But black people built this building. And so we have a share in that celebrity. We have a share in America. We were the bulldozers. We were the ones who built the building, who made the gardens that Mr. Jefferson loved so much." "Official" Jefferson descendants took issue with Cooley's story, but he kept telling it—even to then-President Bill Clinton, who said he believed it. And in 1998, Cooley said in a television interview that, once the world recognized his family as Jefferson descendants, he hoped to be buried in Monticello's graveyard.

No one in the family thought much of the comment at the time. But just a few weeks later, on July 20, Robert Cooley unexpectedly died. He was fifty-eight. It was left to one of his daughters, Michele Cooley-Quille, to call the Monticello Association and ask if her father's last wish could be fulfilled. The Monticello Association turned her down; Cooley-Quille said an official told her the graveyard was "not prepared to admit Hemings descendants." Robert Cooley was buried in the veterans section of Forest Lawn, a private cemetery in Richmond.

As the family carried out that burial, Eugene Foster, a retired pathologist, was conducting a research project that would upend the debate of which Robert Cooley had been such a prominent part. "A friend wondered if DNA might be used to solve the Jefferson/Hemings controversy," Foster recalled in a 2000 interview. "After reading about it for a year, I concluded that it was probably not possible. . . . A parent passes on only half or less of his or her DNA to the children, so with each generation, it begins to disappear. So even if we knew what was specifically characteristic of Thomas Jefferson's DNA, we would have very little chance of finding it in people who are his descendants or think they're his descendants."

But a former colleague suggested Foster take another look: new Y-chromosome research, he said, suggested he might be able to do some testing after all. "Y-chromosomal DNA is passed unchanged from generation to generation, from father to son only," Foster said. "No one had thought of using it for these purposes, because it had not been thought to have enough variation." With DNA samples from the right people, Foster realized, he could look at the Y chromosomes and see if they matched.

None of Jefferson's recognized sons had lived to adulthood, so Foster obtained DNA samples from descendants of Thomas Jefferson's uncle Field Jefferson. "We found that, of the five people in this line, they all had the same Y-chromosomal type, which meant that we had identified the Jefferson family chromosome," he said. "In conjunction with historical evidence, that piece of evidence could be used to arrive at an opinion as to whether Thomas Jefferson was the father of the various people in dispute." Foster took the Jefferson DNA data and compared it to a series of samples taken from the "people in dispute": a descendant of Sally Hemings's son Eston, five descendants of Thomas Woodson's sons, and three relatives of Peter Carr, the man whom Thomas Jefferson's immediate family had suggested as the father of the Hemings children. Foster also took samples from several longtime Virginia families, as a control group, and sent everything he'd collected to geneticists at the University of Oxford in England for analysis.

Foster had found something stunning: the Y chromosome markers in the samples from Eston Hemings's descendants matched the "Jefferson chromosome" Foster had identified. Just as importantly, the testing found no match between the Hemings and Carr samples; the DNA had ruled out the Jefferson family's story about who had fathered Sally Hemings's children. The possibility of these results being random, the researchers said, was less than 1 percent—and that was without considering the historical evidence along with the genetics. The findings, Foster wrote, meant a Jefferson male had almost certainly fathered Eston Hemings.

The study found no direct link between Jefferson DNA and descendants of Thomas Woodson, including Robert Cooley III and his daughter Michele Cooley-Quille. But in many ways it had confirmed the oral histories that the Woodson descendants had passed down for hundreds of years: that Hemingses and Jeffersons were related. "I know that in the end—and I don't know when that end will be—Daddy's mission and his quest will be successful," Cooley-Quille said. "That's why the DNA stuff doesn't worry me, because we know who we are."

The publication of Foster's research in the journal *Nature* in late 1998 was a watershed moment in the debate over Thomas Jefferson and Sally Hemings. This was partly because the headline that accompanied the study read "Jefferson Fathered Slave's Last Child"; Foster quickly clarified that his study showed a link between the Hemings family and *a* Jefferson male, but not which one: "Thomas Jefferson can neither be definitely excluded nor solely implicated." Nonetheless, he largely concurred with the conclusion. "From the historical knowledge we have," he wrote, "we cannot conclude that . . . any other member of the Jefferson family was as likely as Thomas Jefferson to have fathered Eston Hemings." Many news articles treated the report as proof of a liaison between a president and an enslaved woman. Public attitudes continued to shift in favor of the story, and historians who had been skeptical of the Hemings connection before the DNA study now declared themselves convinced of its truth.

But would the members of the Monticello Association, the keepers of the Jefferson burial ground, be convinced? One of the acknowledged Jefferson family members, Lucian Truscott IV, decided it was time to find out. Shortly after Foster's report was made public, Truscott appeared on Oprah Winfrey's television show with Jefferson-and-Hemings descendants and made an invitation to the men and women he now saw as his cousins: "It's time to stop testing all that stuff and just open up the Monticello Association," he said. "Go with us to the Monticello Association meeting in May."

And they did. About thirty-five Hemings descendants were among the two hundred or so participants in the eighty-sixth annual meeting of the Monticello Association. There were dozens of reporters waiting outside for news; the normally low-key group was suddenly being treated as a symbol of American race relations at the end of the twentieth century. "The things that are being asked of this little family association are bigger than anything it's ever had to do before," said Joy Rotch Boissevain, who looked after the Jefferson family cemetery. "In the past, its most important concerns have been repairing the graveyard fence and where to go to dinner on Saturday night at the annual meeting."

Now it had Eugene Foster explaining his DNA findings, and several Hemings descendants speaking, and Michele Cooley-Quille formally applying for membership in the association. "I think the Hemings had the impression that they were going [to] simply bulldoze their way into the Monticello Association without any resistance whatsoever," said John Works, a former association president. When it came time to consider the membership requests, Works called for a members-only discussion and vote; he says it was only to "try to make a distinction between a social gathering and the start of a business meeting." But it amplified the tension. "It was absolutely awful," said Shay Banks-Young, a descendant of Madison Hemings. "I was really disgusted that someone would invite me to something and then turn around and act like I crashed their party."

The motion failed, and the discussion went on. Michele Cooley-Quille recalled that the mood in the room changed "from tension to excitement to humor to animosity." Lucian Truscott IV proposed admitting the Hemings descendants as honorary members for the time being, but the chair refused to put the idea to a vote. So Truscott went to the press, denouncing his relatives as "chicken" and accusing them of being motivated by racism. Another acknowledged descendant walked through the crowd of reporters to challenge Truscott. "We'd like more thorough research," she said. "We're not racists. We're snobs."

The president of the association, Robert Gillespie, called for the association to take time and study both the Hemings evidence and its own criteria for membership. "More evidence is coming forward, and we invite it," he said. "But let's make sure we make the correct decision, not a quick decision." In the meantime, the public debate continued, and it remained largely contentious. For example, in April 2001 President George W. Bush invited descendants from all lines to the White House for a Jefferson birthday celebration. A few blocks away, a new group known as the Thomas Jefferson Heritage Society—which stated as one of its purposes "to stand always in opposition to those who would seek to undermine the integrity of Thomas Jefferson"—released a report in which some scholars found reason for "serious skepticism" of the Hemings story and others declared it "almost certainly false." Those who discount Thomas Jefferson as the likely father of Sally Hemings's children point to his brother Randolph as the most likely candidate for paternity.

"Each side has assumed the worst about each other," University of Virginia historian Edward Ayers said in 2007 about the struggle, and it's been an ongoing one. Over the years, Michele Cooley-Quille said there were "dedicated deniers" in the Monticello Association. John Works said defending Thomas Jefferson against claims that he fathered children by an enslaved woman "has come to mean defending what

America means, and we feel compelled to rise to that defense." Replying to that line of argument, Lucian Truscott wrote, "It's hard for me to understand how you do further damage to the reputation of a man who owned slaves." When a historian proposed exhuming a descendant of Madison Hemings to conduct another genetic study, the descendants said no. "My family doesn't need to prove themselves," Shay Banks-Young said. "If they want to dig up Thomas Jefferson at the same time, maybe I'll reconsider." Finally, in 2002, the members of the Monticello Association voted 67 to 5 against admitting Hemings descendants as members, saying they had not proven their Jefferson lineage.

That meant the gates of the Jefferson family cemetery would stay closed to those descendants, but they found the doors to Monticello wide open: the Thomas Jefferson Memorial Foundation not only accepted the evidence connecting the president to Sally Hemings and her son Eston, but its researchers concluded that Jefferson was "most likely the father of all six of Sally Hemings' children appearing in Jefferson's records." The Hemings side of the family began holding its own reunions at Monticello, with Lucian Truscott and a few other acknowledged descendants joining them. "I think a lot of my family would have more fun if they came to this one," descendant David Works said.

A separate event for Hemings descendants isn't what Robert Cooley III and so many others had envisioned or hoped for. But maybe the story of the Jeffersons and Hemingses, which has been unfolding since 1802, isn't finished unfolding yet. Shay Banks-Young, who described the 1999 Monticello Association meeting as "awful," also called it an important first effort. "I have experienced so many things based on the racial attitudes of America all my life," she told the *New York Times*. "I sure didn't expect this to be different. But I'm hopeful more might come of this, and it will. A mile begins with a single step."

9

ETERNAL FLAME

*On John F. Kennedy, the City of Dallas, and
What Ties Them Together Every November 22*

H ENRY ROEDIGER is a psychology professor at Washington University in St. Louis, and he's been researching how—and sometimes if—we remember presidents. He says our brains remember the presidents "like we would recall a list that somebody gave us. . . . Usually you can remember the presidents who were during your lifetime, and you get a few before that, and then of course most people can also get the early presidents. They can get Washington, John Adams, Thomas Jefferson. But after that, except for Lincoln, it kind of falls off."

Roediger has been running these memory tests for forty years—so long, he says, that "we can actually plot for people, from Truman on, how quickly they're being forgotten. For most presidents, they'll live in modern memory for about 50 or 100 years, and then they'll drop down to roughly the baseline of about 20 to 25 percent of people can remember them, if you give them five minutes." A half century from now, once-towering figures like Harry Truman or Dwight D. Eisenhower may be remembered as poorly as Rutherford B. Hayes or Zachary Taylor are today.

The only exceptions, he says, come "if there's something really distinctive" in an administration—like presiding over a war, for example, or getting a major piece of legislation passed. Or, possibly, a president's jarring, tragic assassination, followed by the biggest funeral in national history and an ongoing effort to assure that president's place in history.

John F. Kennedy's grave at Arlington National Cemetery, just outside Washington, has an eternal flame; it's probably the most recognized grave marker of any president. Unlike the other presidential graves, which place their subjects in the past, Kennedy's eternal flame aims for the future. It consciously recalls something JFK once said: "A man may die, nations may rise and fall, but an idea lives on."

It's moving. It's beautiful. It's poignant. It is not, however, eternal: the flame at the grave today is not the one Jacqueline Kennedy lit in 1963. The original structure, essentially a custom-built wire basket

19. Despite its name, John F. Kennedy's "eternal flame" at Arlington National Cemetery has been replaced several times, most recently in 2013.

welded to a tiki torch, was put together the day before the president's funeral by Arlington superintendent John C. Metzler and Lieutenant Colonel Bernard G. Carroll, the post engineer at nearby Fort Myer. "I advised them that such a construction and installation was beyond my capabilities," Metzler said later. "Their answer was, 'Yes, we know but somehow get an eternal flame.'" The contraption had to be hidden under pine boughs, which had been doused twice with water so that the first lady wouldn't catch on fire as she lit the gas-powered torch.

Bill Morris, who served as one of the guards at the tomb, told *CBS Sunday Morning* that "if you were assigned at the eternal flame you had to have a lighter in your pocket. Every time the wind blew, it went out." One visitor tried to sprinkle holy water on the tomb but ended up dousing the flame; the guard reassured the visitor as he relit the torch, saying, "I won't tell if you won't tell."

The permanent torch, installed in 1967, included an electric spark mechanism that would automatically relight the flame in case of wind or holy-water-wielding cemetery-goers. But even the permanent flame wasn't permanent: the system reached the end of its expected life-span in 2013, and crews had to rig up another temporary eternal flame while they conducted repairs. Eternity is a hard thing to come by, even for a president.

Not that the Kennedys haven't given eternity a heck of a try. No one tried harder than Jacqueline Kennedy, who worried her husband's relatively short term would be forgotten. "He didn't even have the satisfaction of being killed for civil rights," she said to her mother after learning about the background of Lee Harvey Oswald, his accused assassin. "It had to be some silly little Communist. It robs his death of any meaning."

Jacqueline Kennedy knew well the power of a good symbol. After all, she'd led a huge restoration of the White House, which she called "the setting in which the presidency is presented to the world." Her plan was to connect her husband's presidency not to its earthly accomplishments but to timeless, universal themes and values. She'd seen an eternal flame at the Arc de Triomphe in Paris, and took pride in how visible JFK's was. "Whenever you drive across the bridge from

Washington into Virginia," she said, "you see the Lee mansion on the side of the hill in the distance. . . . Now, at night you can see his flame beneath the mansion for miles away."

She chose the burial site at Arlington, which was a pretty important piece of the effort to make Kennedy eternal. The president had expected to be buried back in Massachusetts—"Guess I'll have to go back to Boston," he'd told an aide of his funeral plans—and there was a family plot waiting for him at Holyhood Cemetery in Brookline.* As lovely a spot as it was, though, Holyhood wasn't going to make Jack Kennedy's name live on for centuries. The cemetery where Americans bury their most honored dead—*that's* the kind of place where a president can be remembered.

The Kennedy grave is also in a direct line with the National Mall. Visitors who face east on the hilltop will see the Lincoln Memorial, at the other end of the Memorial Bridge, with the Washington Monument and the US Capitol in the distance. And in the bottom range of their vision, almost like a caption, are some of Kennedy's most stirring quotes, like the one from his inaugural address: "The energy, the faith, the devotion, which we bring to this endeavor will light our country and all who serve it, and the glow from that fire can truly light the world."

Jacqueline Kennedy wanted to model JFK's funeral on the one put together for Abraham Lincoln in 1865—an incredibly audacious move, really. Imagine, for example, that Richard Nixon had won the 1960 election and had then been assassinated three years later; a Lincoln-scale funeral would have come off as massively showy and over the top. Even Sargent Shriver, who had been doing most of the Kennedy funeral legwork, warned the first lady that "some people might think [the funeral plan was] a little ostentatious." But she pulled it off. The most memorable moments from the funeral service are the ones Jackie chose: the long, grim procession of world leaders, led by a widow in a black veil, with nothing but the sound of drums accom-

---

* The Kennedys' son Patrick, who had died shortly after birth in August 1963, had already been buried at Holyhood.

panying them; fifty fighter planes, one for each state, roaring overhead in the "missing man" formation, and a flyover by Special Air Mission 26000, the plane the president had known as *Air Force One*, which dipped its wings in tribute as it flew over; Mrs. Kennedy whispering to three-year-old John F. Kennedy Jr., "John, you can salute Daddy now and say good-bye to him," and the boy giving a perfect salute.

The pageant was so big, and so well executed, that even the pieces that didn't go as planned seemed to fit. Viewers of the funeral procession took notice of the riderless horse, Black Jack, who'd been spooked by a loud noise just before the cortege began. His agitated dancing seemed to mirror the nation's grief. Army Sergeant Keith Clark cracked the sixth note of "Taps" on his bugle during the services at Arlington; this was because his lips had gone numb from standing in the cold for hours, but to the 175 million Americans watching on television, it sounded like his "voice" was breaking with emotion.

By the time she lit the eternal flame at Arlington, Jacqueline Kennedy and her funeral planners had made this enormous pageant look not only good but obvious, as if anything else would have been too little. "Jacqueline Kennedy," wrote the London *Evening Standard*, "has given the American people from this day on one thing they have always lacked—majesty."

The reporter was speaking figuratively, but Mrs. Kennedy had something like majesty on her mind. One week to the day after her husband died, she called Theodore White, who had covered the Kennedy campaign in his best seller *The Making of the President 1960* and covered the majestic funeral for *Life* magazine. White said Mrs. Kennedy brought him to Hyannis Port because "there was something that she wanted *Life* magazine to say to the country, and I must do it." When he arrived, the thing the former First Lady wanted said was that she was "worried Jack would be forgotten by history." Then she brought up a popular song lyric that has characterized Kennedy ever since.

"At night, before we'd go to sleep," she told White, "Jack liked to play some records; and the song he loved most came at the very end of this record. The lines he loved to hear were: *Don't let it be forgot /*

that once there was a spot / for one brief shining moment that was known as Camelot."

Whether it was real or not is hard to say. A number of top Kennedy administration officials derided the comparison, and Kennedy's private secretary claimed later that the president "never listened to 'Camelot' in his whole life." Even Jacqueline Kennedy told White that "when Jack quoted something, it was usually classical." Real or not, the metaphor doesn't quite gel, either. "Don't let it be forgot," wrote Richard Woodward for the *Daily Beast* in 2013, "that Camelot, despite what Jackie wanted us to think, was a story about infidelity by beautiful people who brought down a government. It does not end happily." The *Life* editors thought the Camelot talk was too sentimental and tried to cut it down in Theodore White's piece, but the first lady stood her ground. White ended up mentioning Camelot in his thousand-word essay three times.

Once again, Jacqueline Kennedy's instincts for symbols were right. It may have been contrived, but Camelot gave the country a hook upon which to hang its image of Kennedy: "a magic moment in American history," White said years later, characterizing Mrs. Kennedy's concept, "in which gallant men danced with beautiful women, when great deeds were done, when artists, writers and poets met at the White House, and the barbarians beyond the walls held back." News stories still talk of the Kennedy years as Camelot, a term no one used to describe them when Kennedy was alive.

Jack Kennedy's father had a saying: "Things don't happen, they are made to happen." That's what Jacqueline Kennedy did with symbols like the eternal flame and Camelot. Her genius wasn't just that she placed these symbols in our cultural memory. She could also make those symbols look like they were there all along.

PRESIDENT KENNEDY had the same talent, especially in dealing with the press. After the funeral, *Newsweek* wrote that "no President had ever been so accessible to the press; no President ever so anxious for history to be recorded in the making; he even let TV cameras peek over his shoulder in moments of national crisis." But that image, too, was constructed: the family had been media-savvy going back to the days when patriarch Joseph Kennedy would arrange for himself and his kids to appear in newsreels, just to put their names and faces before the public. President Kennedy brought reporters home with him and let them linger while he "relaxed"; the informal conversations *sounded* like candor, but Kennedy was consciously choosing what to share with the press and what to withhold. "I don't tell anything to the press, on any basis, that I don't expect to see in print," he said. "When you're president, you are president twenty-four hours a day."

Kennedy practiced one-liners and jokes ahead of each press conference so they'd sound more spontaneous, and his press people would suggest questions for reporters to ask. Again, these techniques aren't unique to Kennedy, but because he *sounded* unrehearsed and off-the-cuff, the media gave more coverage to his news conferences than to any president's to that point—which is just what the president wanted. "We were props in a show," one reporter complained later. "We should have joined Actors Equity."

If Kennedy's was, as TV critic Tom Shales suggested, "an Administration that was also a TV series," then it was at least a good one, and Kennedy was a success as one of TV's leading men. Unfortunately, his assassination became his highest-rated episode. "It's the moment where we became a television nation," says Patty Rhule, senior manager of exhibit development at the Newseum, which looked at media coverage of the assassination in an exhibit called "Three Shots Were Fired." During the four days between Dallas and Arlington, Rhule says, "the press really did what it's supposed to do, informing and calming a nation."

The assassination became an especially important part of the creation story of broadcast news. "Not only did television surpass print for primacy as a news source for the first time," *Entertainment Weekly* said years later of the coverage, "it created a focal point for the public's grief." A 1964 study found that within an hour of the shooting, 68 percent of Americans knew about it, and over 90 percent knew by the end of hour two. Most had heard about it on television or radio, and about 175 million of them followed the four days of special network coverage that ensued.* In the Newseum exhibit, Rhule and her team put together a video wall of reports from the frenetic moments right after the shooting. "No one goes past that," Rhule says, "without watching that whole nine-minute roll," and I did see several middle-aged visitors stop at the screen, clearly reliving the experience of 1963 as they watched. But were they remembering what they'd actually seen at the time of the assassination, or were they remembering how we had come to remember that news coverage as a culture?

Time has shaped the way we remember how TV covered the Kennedy assassination—sometimes accurately, sometimes not. The most famous news clip from the coverage shows Walter Cronkite fighting back tears as he gave the CBS audience official word of Kennedy's death. Yet in 1963, more viewers probably tuned in to NBC's news coverage; their anchors, Chet Huntley and David Brinkley, had been beating Cronkite and CBS for several years and didn't lose the top spot until the end of the decade. We remember the Cronkite moment, though, because he went on to be the "most trusted man in America" as CBS anchor in the 1970s and early '80s.

And while our culture fondly remembers the assassination coverage on TV, that coverage actually got off to a shaky start. No journalist in Dallas said he or she saw President Kennedy's assassination firsthand, and none of them got the event on film. The only person who filmed the assassination as it happened was Abraham Zapruder—a Dallas dressmaker. At CBS in New York, Walter Cronkite had a bulletin in hand, but no easy way to get the momentous news on the air. "Our nearest camera was down in the studio in the Grand Central Building and they had to get the camera up to the newsroom," he said later. "In those days, it took twenty minutes for the camera to warm up to be ready to go on the air. So besides lugging the camera up to the newsroom, then you had to turn it on, and then you had to wait twenty minutes for this thing to be ready to go. . . . So instead, we went into the radio booth, a small booth that had radio capability, to

---

* Only the wall-to-wall coverage of the September 11, 2001, attacks was longer.

get on the radio network. We interrupted the program in progress on the television network, which was *As the World Turns*, for a bulletin, which I ad-libbed." From that point forward, Cronkite said, there was always a camera in the CBS newsroom, and it was always on.

The troubles continued: a TV reporter from Dallas managed to film police apprehending Lee Harvey Oswald in the Texas Theatre, but the camera had been set up incorrectly, causing the footage to come out overexposed and unusable. Days later, a live CBS interview ran so long that the network missed the police transfer during which Jack Ruby shot Oswald. One of the correspondents got the suspect/victim's name wrong, telling viewers, "Lee Harold Oswald has been shot!"

You wouldn't expect shaky coverage like this to get its own museum exhibit, or stick in people's minds for decades. But there are plenty of reasons it has. Barbie Zelizer teaches and studies journalism and culture at the University of Pennsylvania's Annenberg School for Communication. She told PBS that even shaky coverage, from a medium "seen as the fluff journalists," was something a person or a family could turn to during an enormously important news moment. "What you got," Zelizer said, "was an ongoing attentiveness to the event that print could not provide. We got ongoing continuous coverage of the story."

The coverage got better as the four days went on. CBS's problems aside, NBC *did* broadcast Oswald's shooting live, and all the networks covered the president's visually striking funeral and burial. When you focus just on the immediate aftermath of the shooting, the media coverage is uneven, but when it's presented as "four days of special coverage," it seems much stronger.

And, Zelizer says, TV news has had a vested interest in keeping alive the story of great assassination coverage, especially given that many of those who had covered the tragedy became the titans of broadcast media for the coming generation. There was Cronkite, of course, but Zelizer says the Exhibit A in this story is Dan Rather, the man who succeeded Cronkite in the CBS anchor chair. "His career was built on the fact that he was in Dallas on that day," she says. "Every CBS special that would retell the Kennedy assassination story on anniversary dates would show Rather and showcase his understanding of what had happened." He was far from the only one. Peter Jennings, who anchored ABC News in the 1980s and '90s, defied his editors in Canada and took a plane to Dallas to cover the shooting. Robert MacNeil, who would coanchor PBS's nightly news with Jim Lehrer, was the NBC News White House correspondent. Looking for a phone after the shots, he ran into, of all places, the Texas School Book Depository, and may have run into Lee Harvey Oswald as he fled the building. "As I ran up the steps and through the door, a young man in shirtsleeves was coming out," MacNeil said. "In great agitation I asked him where there was a phone. He pointed inside." Lehrer, too, was in Dallas, covering the president's visit for the *Times Herald*, then covering the Dallas police as they brought Lee Harvey Oswald into a news conference. He happened to be standing near Jack Ruby, who would shoot Oswald days later.

CBS stalwart Bob Schieffer faced perhaps the weirdest situation of them all: he answered the phone at the *Fort Worth Star* newspaper to hear a woman ask him for a ride to Dallas. "Madam, this is not a taxi service, and besides, the president has been shot," he said. "Yes, I know," the woman said. "I think my son is the one they've arrested." Schieffer not only drove Marguerite Oswald to Dallas, he stayed with her in the police station, using a wide-brimmed, detective-style hat he'd bought to disguise the fact that he wasn't actually a police officer. He very nearly got to interview Lee Harvey Oswald before police figured out who he was and sent him away.

"This is the most ambitious exhibit we've ever done here," Patty Rhule says of the Newseum installation, and I can see why: they had to document not only what the news media covered in 1963 but also how we've come to remember that coverage. As for the famous CBS clip? "We had to have the big Walter Cronkite moment," Rhule says, because "whether you saw it or not, you *feel* like you saw it."

THAT CRONKITE clip got a lot of play in the fall of 2013, during the enormous—and profitable—buildup to the fiftieth anniversary of the Kennedy assassination. Publishers put out book after book to coincide with the half-century mark; TV news put out the usual documentaries looking back, and the National Geographic Channel got its highest ratings ever with a miniseries adapting Bill O'Reilly's book *Killing Kennedy*, with Rob Lowe as JFK.

Seemingly every writer, reporter, photographer, and curiosity seeker in the universe, me included, headed to Dallas to mark the occasion. Dallas has tried hard to move forward in the last fifty years; the Dallas Convention and Visitors Bureau slogan, "Big Things Happen Here," points out that Dallas–Fort Worth International Airport is the third busiest in the world, and that the area is home to eighteen Fortune 500 companies. Still, one of the city's most popular tourist attractions is the Sixth Floor Museum, formerly the Texas School Book Depository. And every November 22 the media and the world take a moment to remember that the biggest thing that happened here had nothing to do with international flights or big business.

It's mostly on the anniversaries that Dallas seems to get uneasy about its status as an assassination site; the rest of the time, you can find an undercurrent of irreverence even about Dealey Plaza. My friend RaeAnna, for example, is a member of a JFK-themed Roller Derby league; the Assassination City Roller Derby has teams with names like Ruby's Revenge, which has as its team logo a showgirl from one of Jack Ruby's nightclubs, riding atop a freshly fired pistol. The league has grown to over a hundred competitors since launching in 2005, and it counts real estate firms, car care centers, and radio stations among its sponsors. As the anniversary drew closer, though, RaeAnna said Assassination City Roller Derby chose not to hold any special public events. "People," she said, "are still touchy about the assassination. People try not to talk about it."

"Don't talk about it and it will pass" could have been Dallas's unofficial strategy for dealing with the first forty-nine anniversaries. Aside from an event in 1993 to recognize Dealey Plaza's newly acquired status as a National Historic Landmark District, the city left the site of Kennedy's murder each November 22 to the public—meaning mostly assassination buffs, tourists, and reporters, as well as those trying to sell things to them. But 2013 was going to be different. After fifty years of this painful dance, Dallas decided to make a deal: we'll tolerate your obsession with the Kennedy assassination, as long as you check out our arts district while you're in town.

The event known as The 50th would be Dallas's first full city-sanctioned commemoration ceremony of John F. Kennedy and his assassination. Mayor Mike Rawlings had repeatedly stressed this would be a "serious, respectful, understated" affair, and I'd be hard-pressed to prove it *wasn't* serious and respectful—they had bagpipers and the historian David McCullough—but the word "understated" raised some eyebrows in town. "We want it to be very classy," Rawlings went on to say, but people were concerned "understated" actually meant the city would mark the assassination without mentioning it. And, technically, the name of the event—"The 50th"—*didn't* mention the assassination. It sounded like a Mad Lib: The 50th *what?*

There was nothing understated about getting into The 50th: the general public was limited to five thousand tickets, distributed to those who went through a lengthy request process. Getting press credentials was even more complicated: I've covered the actual, live, sitting president, and getting in to see him was a lot less cumbersome than getting into this. Dallas police had cordoned off Dealey Plaza and the surrounding area with blocks and blocks of metal security fencing, patrolled by uniformed officers. Even the official John F. Kennedy Memorial was off-limits to the general public during The 50th; the Dallas City Council had earmarked more than $150,000 for security trailers with surveillance cameras, just for this one day.

It wasn't much different inside the plaza; reporters could only talk with ticketholders over the fence, and those who stopped in the wrong spot might be shooed along by event staff. "We have to keep the chute clear," one said, over and over. A few of us had to clear out of the grassy knoll because, as we were told, "NBC News has *exclusive*"—the guy emphasized the word the way they do on TV—"access to this area."

The press tent was just behind the grassy knoll's picket fence, a spot where those who believe there was a conspiracy to kill Kennedy think a second shooter may have done his grisly work. The fence was covered in messages. THE DRIVER DID IT! said someone who signed her name as "Libertarian Anne." Another pointed the finger at LBJ. Others had left more general messages, like YOLO JFK or RIP, while one person wrote two angry messages in blue marker: FUCK OSWALD and FUCK JACK RUBY.

Inside the press tent I joined several reporters who were loading up on coffee and cinnamon rolls. I overheard one of them mention that "the X is gone"—for years tourists had been ducking into traffic to get their picture taken next to one of two big white X's on the approximate locations where Kennedy had been shot. But two days before The 50th, the city repaved just the sections of Elm Street that had been marked—"to level out the streets," according to the official explanation. Rodger Jones of the *Dallas Morning News* wasn't so sure; he'd bet money that the city would remove the "gruesome little tourist magnets" ahead of November 22. "The city's big ceremony next week is trying to focus on Kennedy's life, not on the patches of ground where bullets slammed into his body," he wrote. "The X's were bad 'optics' for what the city wants to project."

Much like the Kennedys, and much like the news media that covered them, Dallas has tried to project a narrative about itself, one best summed up by University of Texas English professor Don Graham as the City That Worked—a place full of big ideas and bigger plans. "Everybody in Dallas in that area at that time was optimistic about getting jobs and getting education," Graham said. "Dallas was interested in protecting the business climate." The city had started to diversify beyond oil and land sales; Texas Instruments had made the city a player in the early tech sector, and its defense industry was growing as well. You could imagine newsreels with names like "Dallas: A Future as Big as Texas!" and scores of smiling Dallas residents on the go toward progress and initiative and civic pride and prosperity.

A journalist in the 1940s said of the city, "Dallas doesn't owe a damn thing to accident, nature or inevitability. It is what it is . . . because the men of Dallas damn well planned it that way." And the extremely reputation-conscious city leaders didn't like it when a news story didn't reflect well on the Big D—like news footage of furious protesters holding up signs that said things like "LBJ Sold Out to Yankee Socialists." That sign became famous in the 1960 campaign, when Dallas congressman Bruce Alger and his supporters accosted Kennedy's vice presidential nominee, Lyndon Johnson, and his wife at the Adolphus Hotel. For a full half hour they screamed, shouted, and spat not only at the candidate but at his wife (a big no-no in the gallant South).

There were others besides Alger. H. L. Hunt, the original eccentric Texas oil baron, put out pamphlets and radio programs excoriating Kennedy for his "soft" policies toward Communists; the ultraconservative John Birch Society, which designated Dallas its regional headquarters, did the same. There was *Dallas Morning News* publisher Ted Dealey, who famously told the president to his face that in a time where the United States needed "a man on horseback," Kennedy was instead riding his daughter Caroline's tricycle in halfhearted "charges" against the Reds.* Dealey's preferred "man on horseback" was former army general Edwin Walker, who accused the administration of tossing him out of the military because they were in league with Moscow and he was standing in the way of a Communist takeover.

Walker supporters heckled UN Ambassador Adlai Stevenson during a speech at Dallas's Memorial Auditorium Theater; one famously smacked Stevenson over the head with a sign. "Are these human beings or animals?" Stevenson asked, and he told the president to reconsider his trip to Dallas. He wasn't the only one: US senators and prominent Dallas leaders thought the atmosphere in town might be too hot to control, and citizens wrote to the White House to dissuade the president from visiting their city. "No number of policeman, plainclothes men nor militia can control the 'air,'" Dallas resident Nelle M. Doyle wrote to White House press secretary Pierre Salinger on October 28, 1963, less than a month before Kennedy's visit. "It is a dreadful thought, but all remember the fate of President McKinley."

---

* Dealey Plaza, where Kennedy was shot, is named for Ted Dealey's father, George.

The Stevenson incident was the final straw for official Dallas. If strident voices like these convinced others this was a city where they could do business, the image of Dallas as the City That Worked would stop working. Mayor Earle Cabell, who had welcomed General Walker on his arrival, now denounced "so-called patriots" as a "cancer on the body politic"; he would run, and win, against Bruce Alger for Congress in the next election. And a hundred prominent Dallas leaders joined the mayor in sending Adlai Stevenson an official and very public apology, pointing out that "a small group of extremists" were responsible for his troubles. The rest of the city, they wrote, was "outraged and abjectly ashamed of the disgraceful discourtesies you suffered."

It's hard to say how much of this sinister reputation would have stuck to Dallas without the assassination. It's fair to question why city leaders didn't stand up to these voices earlier, but the news coverage had probably made these figures look bigger than they probably were. Take Bruce Alger; his protesters at the Adolphus Hotel won a lot of attention, but their attacks on the Johnsons backfired. Lyndon Johnson chose to walk directly through Alger's foaming mass of protesters, knowing full well the cameras would make him look sympathetic and make Alger and his people look nuts, just weeks before Election Day 1960. The Kennedy-Johnson ticket narrowly won Texas, and the Republican nominee, Richard Nixon, blamed Alger, whom he called "that asshole congressman from Dallas," for costing him the state. General Edwin Walker made a vaunted run for governor, but the campaign was a flop (when you're running in Texas, don't hold your campaign kickoff in Chicago); he finished sixth out of six candidates in the primary.

Not to minimize Dallas's problems: racial integration, for example, started later here than in other cities, and it took longer to achieve. The Big D had a high murder rate and an ongoing problem with organized crime. But none of this was unique to any city in 1963—it was the era of George Wallace telling Alabama that he stood for "segregation now, segregation tomorrow, segregation forever," and the era of sit-ins at Birmingham lunch counters and riots in Cambridge,

Maryland. Civil rights activist Medgar Evers was murdered in the summer of 1963. The March on Washington is known today for Martin Luther King Jr.'s "I Have a Dream" speech, but at the time it was better known as a protest for jobs and civil rights. It was the year of the brazen bombing at the 16th Street Baptist Church in Birmingham that killed four African American girls at Sunday school.

Don Graham of the University of Texas said most Americans in 1963 wouldn't have thought of Dallas as an outlier. "If you want to pick a city where Kennedy might have been assassinated," he says, "it would be Miami—because of all the anti-Castro [sentiment]. Dallas went all out to try to make [Kennedy's] visit successful. The last thing they wanted was something like this to happen."

But it did happen, and that sealed Dallas's fate. Of *course* Kennedy had been murdered in Dallas, people across the country said after the shooting; look at what they'd done to Lyndon Johnson and Adlai Stevenson. The City That Worked had become the City of Hate, a place so lawless and unhinged it wasn't just the site of the assassination but the accomplice. "The world decided that Kennedy had died in enemy territory," reflected the journalist and author Lawrence Wright, who grew up in Dallas. "No matter who had killed him, we had *willed* him dead." The *New York Times* made note in its Kennedy assassination coverage that in 1865 most southern newspapers had expressed sorrow at the assassination of Abraham Lincoln, but the *Dallas Herald* had triumphantly declared the murder holy: "God Almighty ordered this event or it could never have taken place." Even Kennedy got in on the act from the grave; Jacqueline Kennedy recalled her husband's response to a foaming-at-the-mouth political ad in one of the Dallas papers: "We're heading into nut country today."

It took its toll. In the years after the assassination, Dallas saw its already high murder rate go up. The suicide rate spiked, too, and more people died of heart disease—all at a time when those trends were *not* climbing anywhere else. Dallas residents told stories for years about traveling and being told by fellow Americans that "you all killed our president," or being refused cab service simply for mentioning where they lived.

At first the city tried to defend itself. "There are maniacs all over the world," Mayor Cabell said. "It could have happened in Podunk as well as in Dallas." Apologists for Dallas stressed that Lee Harvey Oswald was no John Bircher; he was a Marxist who had lived in the Soviet Union and confessed to his (Russian-born) wife that he once tried to kill General Edwin Walker. They pointed to the enormous crowds, two hundred thousand strong, and noted that the last words Kennedy ever heard were from Texas's first lady, Nellie Connally, who said, "Mr. President, you can't say Dallas doesn't love you." "I think it is significant that the president received a warm and genuine reception by thousands of its residents before he was shot by a single emotionally disturbed man," a minister told the *New York Times*. "Dallas cannot be explained in a few words. It is a lot of things."

People tried a lot of things to get Dallas out of the shadow of Dealey Plaza. In 1970 the magician Gene De Jean drove up from Houston, claiming that a "malignant black coven" had put Dallas under a curse and that it couldn't move forward until the curse was lifted. The city got some positive vibes from the success of the Dallas Cowboys, known as "America's Team," and from the TV show *Dallas*, featuring Larry Hagman as lovably wicked oil tycoon J. R. Ewing, an anti-hero modeled in part on H. R. Hunt. More recently the city tried emphasizing Dealey Plaza as a historical site well beyond its Kennedy ties, with one official describing the plaza as "a major public green space on the west side of downtown." (Reporter Eric Nicholson of the *Dallas Observer* summed up the message behind this effort as "One Unfortunate Afternoon Shouldn't Overshadow Dealey Plaza's Decades of Not Murdering Presidents.") Time, too, softened the public attitude toward Dallas. But a nickname like the City of Hate, even if unfairly earned, is hard to shake.

The 50th was about shaking the last lingering traces of that foul reputation and reintroducing Dallas to people who thought only of the violence of November 22. If nothing else, they got to see how cold it can get in Texas: temperatures hovered around the freezing point, freezing rain turned to light snow and then back to freezing rain, and the organizers called off the symphony orchestra performance and the

200   DEAD PRESIDENTS

"missing man" flyover. Reporters got into a routine of interviewing one or two people in the crowd and then scurrying back to the press tent to stand near space heaters. I shivered on the lawn as the outdoor video screen showed clips of Kennedy's inaugural address—I realized I'd basically turned into William Henry Harrison and noted sadly to myself that if I, too, were to expire thirty days after the event I would miss Christmas.

Fortunately the event got under way before I succumbed to the elements. There was a video welcome from Ruth Altshuler, a long-time Dallas civic leader and philanthropist and chair of the planning committee for The 50th. In 1963 she was at the Trade Mart, waiting to hear President Kennedy speak at a lunch event of the Dallas Citizens Council; several days later she served as the only female member of the grand jury that indicted Jack Ruby for murder. She said in a video message that she got involved in the event because "I was so tired of people running Dallas down . . . and I wanted people to see how exciting Dallas is." The Big D, she said, is the "volunteer center of the world." And "the arts district is fantastic."

Other speakers echoed these ideas. In the invocation, Bishop Kevin Farrell talked about how the city "suffered and was implicated . . . a place that was disgraced, scarred and ruthlessly judged." The closing prayer by the Rev. Zan Holmes Jr. urged the city to focus not on "where we have been and what we have done, but where we're going."

Mayor Rawlings gave the keynote speech, and even though he'd talked about The 50th being an understated event, he admitted that he'd been working on the speech for almost a year. "It's something I've had many sleepless nights about," he told the *Dallas Morning News*. "Public recognition of history is an important way for people . . . to see themselves. They see themselves through that historic moment." How did Dallas see itself? What was it the city of now?

The mayor dropped a few clues when he talked about what he'd been reading to prepare for the speech. One was *Profiles in Courage*, a choice obviously aimed to show that Dallas hadn't hated Kennedy in 1963 and surely didn't now. The other was more intriguing: a 1964 initiative known as "Goals for Dallas." It was proposed (and funded) by Earle Cabell's successor as mayor, J. Erik Jonsson, the cofounder of tech giant Texas Instruments and, in his seven years as mayor, the architect of post-assassination Dallas. It was a cosmic coincidence that Jonsson would be the one in this role, given that he was born on the day President McKinley was shot.

His work began almost immediately; as president of the Dallas Citizens Council, Jonsson had to tell the audience at the Trade Mart about the shooting, glumly saying, "I feel like the fellow on Pearl Harbor Day." Jonsson attended Kennedy's funeral in Washington because, as he said, "the city should be represented"; not long after he returned, the city council chose him to succeed Earle Cabell as mayor. And Jonsson put Dallas back to work, building the mammoth Dallas–Fort Worth Airport, pushing for a new city hall and a mass transit system, improving libraries and schools, and urging Dallas to "dream no small dreams."

After paying tribute to Erik Jonsson as the man who "re-energized" Dallas, Rawlings quoted a Dallas rabbi, Levi Olan, who gave a famous radio address in the midst of the "City of Hate" talk. "The city is not guilty of the crime," Rabbi Olan had said, but he also noted that "as the powerful light shone upon it, the city, it was learned, had been inhospitable to honorable debate." Rabbi Olan, the mayor said, "captured the heartbreak and hurt the city felt; he stated plainly the defects and failings that were laid bare before the world. But most important, he called for Dallas to use this tragedy to seek a true transformation. Look around today, and I believe we have heeded that call. . . . Today, because of the hard work of many people, Dallas is a different city."

That's when I realized what was happening. Mayor Rawlings was proposing that Dallas, which had aspired to be the City That Worked, and had been vilified as the City of Hate, had become the City That Changed—a place that saw something it didn't like in itself and did something to fix it. Rawlings even suggested the transformation showed Dallas had fulfilled Kennedy's legacy: "As the people of Dallas did then," he said, "each of us must meet our oncoming challenges head-on, with courage—honoring but not living in the past . . . and never flinching from the truth. We must meet the future with the same vigor, optimism, and unfailing sense of duty that our young president embodied."

It was a tricky line to walk, because if Dallas changed after Kennedy's death, then it would almost confirm what the critics had said about the city all along. It might have made Dallas look like a suspect who, after hours of interrogation, threw up its hands in exhaustion and said, we could have sworn we didn't do it, but maybe we really *did*. But I think Rawlings was trying to recognize that Dallas was never going to be able to outrun November 22 or pretend it didn't exist. "He and our city will forever be linked," Rawlings said. "In tragedy, yes. But out of that tragedy an opportunity was granted to us: the chance to learn how to face the future when it is darkest and most uncertain." Dallas had to acknowledge the hate before anyone would believe hate wasn't what the city was about.

Of course, this is all built on the presumption that people actually still thought of Dallas as the city that killed John F. Kennedy, and Don Graham at the University of Texas wasn't convinced of that. "They still think that there are people in America that think Dallas hasn't changed," he said. "They're still reacting to it. If you find a place where nothing has changed since 1963, you're in Cuba."

And it also presumes that the Kennedy legacy, of which Dallas is now a part, is forever. It's not going anywhere for the time being: millions of people continue to take in the Eternal Flame at Arlington, and I don't expect visits are going to drop off at the Sixth Floor Museum anytime soon. The documentaries and books and theories are going to keep coming out. And the big white X's, the ones the city removed ahead of the ceremony, were back in place on Elm Street even before I got home to New Hampshire. But there's a little bit of evidence that the Kennedy era might be starting to recede, albeit very slowly. In 2013 Public Policy Polling asked Americans about conspiracies and found that people under thirty were about half as likely as older individuals to believe there was a larger conspiracy behind the assassination. It's one poll, obviously, but if it's a meaningful poll, Dealey Plaza may someday be as quiet on November 22 as Buffalo, New York, is each September on the anniversary of McKinley's assassination.

Dealey Plaza did get back to its current normal as the official ceremony ended: as I left I saw a group of protesters shouting "No more lies!" on the street, and apparently they went on to confront some police, but the city's tight lid on the proceedings held: nobody inside the plaza saw or heard them. As the plaza emptied out I walked over to a restaurant called Lee Harvey's, a mile and a half from Elm Street and the grassy knoll and white X's and debates over what kind of city Dallas was, or is. The TV next to the bar was replaying the CBS assassination coverage from 1963; by the time I got my grilled cheese on jalapeño bread and crispy onion rings, the woman behind the counter had turned the screen off and put the jukebox back on. "We've already listened to this once," she said.

10

———◆◆◆———

THE REST OF THE SET

*On the Many Types of Presidential Obscurity and Mediocrity,
with Millard Fillmore, Franklin Pierce, Martin Van Buren,
James Buchanan, and Warren Harding*

HERE IS one rule when it comes to gift shops at presidential sites: you must carry at least a couple of items that highlight all the presidents. Coffee mugs, playing cards, place mats—as long as they have portraits of every president on them, they will end up on the shelves. Lately there's been a set of presidential PEZ dispensers making the rounds; they're part of something called the PEZ Education Series. I don't know how much education we're spurring with candy dispensers, but had Chester Arthur seen his handsome whiskers emblazoned on a PEZ holder, he might have rethought his quest to be the most obscure president ever.

My parents' generation didn't have presidential PEZ, but they had something similar: little presidential figurines produced by toymaker Louis Marx. My mom gave me the three she had as a kid—adorably cheap and plasticky replicas of Lincoln, Wilson, and Eisenhower. Marx sold these figures in grocery stores in the early 1950s, to honor the election of his friend Dwight D. Eisenhower.

They sold well, but Marx ran into the usual problem with "sets" of presidents—once the current guy leaves office, you're out of date. Marx added figures of John F. Kennedy, Lyndon Johnson, and Richard Nixon and played off each new election cycle with figures of some of the potential candidates—including Bobby Kennedy, Hubert Humphrey, and Ronald Reagan. But by the early 1970s Marx was out of the presidential figurine racket; for the set to stay up to date, Richard Nixon would have to stay president forever. (I suspect at least a few of the votes against Nixon's impeachment in the House were cast by Marx collectors.)

Today you can buy an up-to-date set of the whole cast, thanks to the collector and television writer Patric Verrone, who kept his old presidential figurines in the writing room for the show *Futurama*. Despairing that Marx had never cast a little Gerry Ford or Jimmy Carter, Verrone casts his own, selling copies on his website. The secret? New heads on top of Marx presidential bodies. "I turned Nelson Rockefeller into Clinton," he told *Wired* in 2009. "The first Bush was based on a George Romney, and the second, George W. Bush, was an alternative Eisenhower." President Obama is the John F. Kennedy figure with "a different arm." (The only difference is the *arm*?)

Some presidents get monuments, libraries, and museums; others have to settle for PEZ dispensers and Marx figurines. I have a soft spot for some of these guys. Take Millard Fillmore—now there's a president who could use a little love. The Charlie Brown Christmas tree of presidents, Fillmore ended up leading the nation after Zachary Taylor spent too much time at the unfinished Washington Monument. The thirteenth president served in interesting times—he took office just before Congress passed the Compromise of 1850, fueling the already hot national fire around slavery—but no one accuses him of being interesting. Even his official White House biography calls him an "uninspiring man." His most notable paper in office is his first message to Congress, in which he makes an impassioned plea to bring more bird crap into the country. Seriously:

Peruvian guano has become so desirable an article to the agricultural interest of the United States that it is the duty of the Government to employ all the means properly in its power for the purpose of causing that article to be imported into the country at a reasonable price. Nothing will be omitted on my part toward accomplishing this desirable end.

Now, guano was hot stuff for farmers in the 1850s, and knowing that, you can read the above as a trade policy of some seriousness. Still, as slogans go, "Fillmore: He stood for guano" doesn't exactly rival Woodrow Wilson's "He kept us out of war."

Yet there are plenty of sites named in this uninspiring president's honor. One can visit the Millard Fillmore House in East Aurora, New York—the cottage where Fillmore started his political career, and the only presidential house built by its owner. One can attend Millard Fillmore College in Buffalo. Or, perhaps after being pelted with too much guano, one can obtain medical treatment at Millard Fillmore Suburban Hospital. Fillmore has his own statue in front of Buffalo's city hall, "erected by the State of New York to honor an illustrious citizen of Buffalo." And for decades music fans could see shows at Bill Graham's famous Fillmore clubs in New York and in San Francisco, where the Fillmore West even stood on Fillmore Street.

Not bad for a guy who's best known for being mediocre. But the takeaway here isn't that being mediocre can get your name on a landmark Allman Brothers album; rather, it's the importance of "the presidents" as a group that makes that happen. Fillmore gets his name on schools, streets, and nightclubs because he had the same job that George Washington once had. Like the little Marx figures, he's part of the set.

Fillmore also became something of a hometown hero in later life, following his guano-filled White House years by serving as the first chancellor of the University of Buffalo and helping to found the Buffalo Historical Society. When he died in 1874, Fillmore was lauded more for his community work in New York than for anything he did in Washington. He is known for being an illustrious citizen of

Buffalo. The only area where he had continued to excel at not excelling was politics; he was the very unsuccessful presidential nominee in 1856 for the American Party, nicknamed the "Know Nothings." Even Fillmore's final words—"the nourishment is palatable"—were unremarkable; they were just about the soup.

Even so, I managed to have an inspiring moment at Millard Fillmore's grave, a tall pink obelisk toward the back of Buffalo's Forest Lawn Cemetery. There's a creek that runs through part of Forest Lawn, and on the other side of the creek is the final resting place of funk legend Rick James. As I drove, I had my car radio tuned to a Sunday morning gospel service—church announcements, choirs, and homilies. "We think Sunday school is for children," said one speaker. "But you're nothing but a child, a child of God," he said, to cheers. It was Sunday morning, there was gospel on the radio, I was driving through a cemetery. It was lovely.

Then, precisely at 10 a.m., the station switched formats—in midservice—to the swishes and stings of modern commercial radio. The first song after the switch? Rick James and the Temptations' "Standing on the Top," which includes the line "Where do all the freaks and fancy people go?" Rick James doesn't know, but I do. They go to Forest Lawn Cemetery.

BUFFALO IS full of inspiration, probably because it has, next to Washington, the richest presidential history of any city I've visited. Aside from Fillmore, Buffalo can boast direct connections to Grover Cleveland (a former mayor), William McKinley (who died there), and Teddy Roosevelt (who became president there). Buffalo is also home to my hands-down favorite presidential food connection: a downtown pub called Founding Fathers. You would have to be very drunk to mistake this place for anywhere else. There's presidential memorabilia all over the place—behind the bar, on the walls, on the ceiling. There are classic portraits of George Washington and newspapers declaring "KENNEDY DEAD, SHOT BY SNIPER IN DALLAS." The ceiling is home to large flags from all over the world, gifts from well-traveled regulars. Hockey is on the flat-screen; the stereo is playing Neil Young's album *American Stars 'n Bars* in the corner; people are helping themselves to snacks from a popcorn machine.

For the full effect, you can order the "Hail to the Chef!" sandwich—grilled chicken breast with provolone cheese, mushrooms, spinach, and a sundried tomato pesto—but the real draw here may not be the food or even the drinks. It's owner and proprietor Michael Driscoll. Driscoll once taught history at a Catholic school in Williamsville, some fifteen minutes away; now the pub is his classroom, as he peppers everyone within earshot with trivia questions while tending bar. He carries on three or four conversations at the same time, asking a question before dashing off to refill a glass or mix up a cocktail, then returning a few minutes later to answer the question and ask a new one. Not all of his questions are historical in nature—I hear answers ranging from "*The Golden Girls!*" to "Dr. James Naismith!"—but sooner or later the questions always turn back to the guys all over the walls. Driscoll says he makes trips to the library at least once a week to add new questions to his inexhaustible repertoire.

Driscoll vows to test my knowledge with a few stumpers. "Which president was exhumed in the twentieth century?" This one, of course, I know. "Zachary Taylor is right!" he says, and then tells a tongue-in-cheek version of the story to the rest of the bar. "They thought he might have been poisoned—they didn't find any poison. But had he been poisoned, who was the number one suspect?" he pauses, before roaring, "The man who succeeded him . . . *Fillard Millmore!*"

Driscoll is happy to introduce his patrons to Buffalo's rich presidential history, and they, in turn, are happy to try keeping up with his patter. The pub's monthly trivia nights draw huge crowds, and Founding Fathers has had its share of celebrity sightings: David Sedaris has been here, as has Morrissey. Sedaris I could see enjoying this place, but I can't help but giggle when I think of Morrissey, the Pope of Mope, nursing a drink while Driscoll, the sunny bartender, sprays him with Grover Cleveland trivia.

"Next he's gonna ask you which presidents have one-syllable

names," says Glen, a gray-bearded guy with a beer at my end of the bar. His prediction is right on, so he and I sort out the answer together: Polk, Grant, Hayes, Taft, Ford, Bush, and Bush. Glen's glad to have Founding Fathers in Buffalo. "I grew up learning this stuff," he says, but "kids today don't know any of this. My son"—a relatively recent college grad—"he doesn't know any of this." I add that it's all around us, which in this city is true.

Driscoll's enthusiasm is so contagious that I overhear some of the patrons asking each other history questions. There aren't any trivia cards or books in sight; this is just what you do at Founding Fathers. People are *talking* here—I see at least a hundred people come in and out in the time I'm there, and they're talking, joking, sharing trivia. Only once do I see a cell phone, which is viewed only briefly and then quickly put away.

As I head out, I thank Michael for a fun evening, and he can't resist giving me one more trivia question: "What is the unusual name of the town where Millard Fillmore was born?" The answer is Moravia. I sure hope Buffalo gives this illustrious citizen his own statue somewhere down the road. One that peppers every visitor with a question or two about Millard Fillmore.

BEING PRESIDENT and being a local man made good can get you a few namesakes after you leave the earth—assuming, of course, the community *wants* to honor you. Concord, New Hampshire, was once home to Millard Fillmore's successor, Franklin Pierce. His four years in office were eventful—he was in office when the fight over slavery in US territories turned into actual fights, known today as "Bleeding Kansas"—but unsuccessful. After being snubbed by his own party for a reelection bid, Pierce resumed a quiet life in Concord, where, on November 25, 1914, the state of New Hampshire dedicated a statue in his honor outside the State House.

What's notable about this is that Franklin Pierce died on October 8, 1869—more than forty-five years before the statue's dedication. As a proud Granite Stater, I can say without hesitation that this forty-

20. It took Franklin Pierce's home state of New Hampshire nearly half a century to put up a statue in his honor.

five-year Pierce-less interregnum should not be mistaken as the by-product of some laid-back vibe, 'cause we don't have one (even the surfers here are kind of intense). No, the delay was on purpose. For nearly a half century, New Hampshire thought about putting up some kind of memorial to its only president and said . . . *nah.*

It wasn't always this way. In the 1850s Franklin Pierce was New Hampshire's favorite son; his father, Benjamin Pierce, was a Revolutionary War hero who later twice served as governor. Visit the Franklin Pierce Homestead, in Hillsborough, New Hampshire, and you're actually visiting Franklin Pierce's dad's house. "The father and the son," a campaign poster proudly proclaims on the wall. "The one fought to make, the other labors to preserve the Union."

Franklin did pretty well himself, for that matter—a prestigious, if undistinguished, career that included stints as State House speaker, US senator, Mexican War veteran . . . sure, he was a lawyer, people said, but nobody's perfect. So when Pierce ended up as the Democratic nominee for president in 1852, his New Hampshire supporters didn't spare the hyperbole. "The Statesman. The Soldier. The Estimable Citizen," read one campaign poster. "We Honor New Hampshire in Honoring Franklin Pierce," said another. And then—I am not making this up—there was this one, the dirtiest, and therefore best, campaign slogan of all time: "We Polked you in '44, We shall Pierce you in '52." (This line may be why the 1852 election is called one of the more "ludicrous, ridiculous, and uninteresting" elections in American history.)

The Estimable Citizen also got a huge boost from an old classmate at Bowdoin College: Nathaniel Hawthorne, who had just written *The Scarlet Letter* and *The House of the Seven Gables*, wrote Pierce's campaign biography. He not only explained away some of the rougher patches in the candidate's history, he turned them into virtues. Pierce's war record, for example, was not inspiring in the least: he was promoted to brigadier general largely through personal connections and fainted twice on the field of battle. Doesn't sound too brave, right? But in Hawthorne's book, Pierce only passes out because he's already run his men through a gauntlet that would have killed off inferior soldiers; Pierce, he writes, has a "rare elasticity both of mind and body; he springs up from pressure like a well-tempered sword." Hawthorne quotes from Pierce's own war diary to show how he'd been battling diseases ("June 28. The vomito rages fearfully") and incompetent superior officers; when a general orders the already woozy Pierce off the front, Frank replies, "For God's sake, general, don't say that! This is the last great battle, and I must lead my brigade!" And for Hawthorne, the second fainting spell isn't a sign of weakness but the turning point of the battle: Pierce tells the men trying to move him to safety to get back to fighting. "'Don't carry me off! Let me lie here!' And there he lay, under the tremendous fire of Churubusco, until the enemy, in total rout, was driven from the field."

Pierce's Whig opponent was General Winfield Scott. He had actually won battles in the Mexican War—he commanded Pierce, in fact, and had not fainted in the process—but he didn't have Nathaniel Hawthorne spinning his life story into an epic biography. (The educator Horace Mann, the author's brother-in-law, famously derided Hawthorne's book as "the greatest work of fiction he ever wrote.") Nor did Scott have any saucy wordplay to back his campaign. Pierce won an electoral landslide that November.

If Pierce had known what was coming, he probably would've Pierced his own campaign and voted for Scott. Not even Hawthorne could have made gold out of Pierce's incredibly tragic and depressing transition to high office. Shortly after the New Year, the president-elect and his family—his wife, Jane, and eleven-year-old Benjamin, aka Bennie—were returning to Concord after a funeral when the train's axle broke and it went off the tracks. The parents were unhurt; Bennie was crushed to death. Jane Pierce, who had already become extremely protective of Bennie after losing her first two boys at young ages, was completely (and understandably) inconsolable. Desperately looking for a reason why Bennie had been taken, she concluded God needed to clear Franklin's worry list so he could steer the ship of state without distraction. After all, the country had called him to service; he hadn't sought the job. Except she soon learned that he *had* sought the job, even after having promised her years before to get out of politics. Quickly altering the "God's mercy on America" theory to something akin to "God's wrath on her husband," Jane spent the bulk of Franklin's presidency not speaking to him and trying to speak to Bennie, through letters and, depending on whether you trust the sources or not, séances.

I am unable to confirm or deny the "God's wrath" theory, but I have to say, it's as good an explanation as any. Pierce came to Washington mourning his son. On March 4, 1853, he gave his inaugural address (from memory, no less) but spoke so long that outgoing first lady Abigail Fillmore caught a bad cold and fever, and died before the end of the month. And Pierce's own vice president, William Rufus

King of Alabama, was so sick with tuberculosis that he left the country to recuperate in Cuba; Congress had to pass a special law to allow him to take his oath of office on foreign soil. Not that it made any difference—a few weeks later he was gone, too.

(King's early death brings up an interesting historical what-if: imagine if Franklin Pierce, and not Bennie, had died in the train accident. Upon Vice President King's death, the succession laws of the time would have left the president pro tempore of the Senate in the White House. In 1853 that post was filled by a pro-slavery Missourian called David Rice Atchison, who during the fight over "Bleeding Kansas" would implore his supporters to "kill every God-damned abolitionist" in the area. Would President Atchison have led us to the Civil War eight years earlier? Hard to say, but Pierce's greatest accomplishment may have been simply living through his term.)

Everyone around the new president was dying—and that was just the start of Pierce's presidency, which, sadly, included more deaths thanks to the "Bleeding Kansas" debacle. Pro- and anti-slavery forces poured into the Kansas Territory, each hoping to outnumber and/or outmurder the other. Pierce's poor handling of the crisis convinced Democratic Party leaders he couldn't be reelected, and they decided not to renominate him for a second term.

Pierce took the news of his repudiation well. "There's nothing left to do but to get drunk," he reportedly said. And that he did, for many of his remaining days, dying of stomach inflammation brought on by, as his Whig political opponents liked to say, "many a well-fought bottle." The *New York Times* didn't exactly pour on the love in Pierce's obituary, saying that "his place will not be missed by those actively engaged in political affairs" and "his record as a statesman cannot command the approbation of the nation."

Nor did it command the approbation of New Hampshire residents, who, remember, pointedly voted down any attempt to honor the only president to hail from their state for forty-five years. During this period New Hampshire *did* honor two other native sons with statues at the State House. The best spot, the one right in front of the building, went to Daniel Webster, who, in truth, made his name representing Massachusetts but got his start in the Granite State; his statue went up in 1886. A few years later, in 1892, the state put up a statue of former senator John P. Hale. Two former senators—one who even moved out of the state—got statues, and not Pierce.

Once again, the Civil War provides the explanation. Webster's last and greatest stand on the public stage was during the debate over the Compromise of 1850, in which he implored northern and southern people alike to find a way to stand together. "I speak to-day for the preservation of the Union. 'Hear me for my cause,'" he said. And Hale was one of the first members of Congress, if not *the* first, to explicitly run on a platform of ending slavery. In the days after the bloody War Between the States, New Hampshire was more than a little touchy about the fact that its only president was a "Northern man with Southern sympathies," who very publicly criticized the Lincoln administration during the war and, after the fighting was over, visited Confederate president Jefferson Davis while he was in military prison facing charges of treason. So to rebuild some karma, the state honored one man who fought to preserve the Union and immortalized another who fought against slavery. As for the guy who hung out with the dastardly rebel president? He never existed, and if he did, he didn't live here. Franklin who?

To be fair, Pierce was for preserving the Union, too; he just wasn't very good at it—at least as a president. As a private citizen he was slightly more effective: there's a great Civil War story about an angry mob gathering outside Pierce's home in Concord, demanding to know why he didn't have a flag out. His response was a more eloquent version of "Excuse me? While you clowns were out on a scavenger hunt for flags, I was, oh, I don't know, *fighting in the freaking Mexican War and being president*?!?" The mob collectively went "Oh yeah, never mind" and hit the road.

The anger against Franklin Pierce didn't disperse for quite a while. There was still opposition to a statue in his honor as late as 1913, but that was the year in which America marked fifty years since the Battle of Gettysburg, and at a time when old Union men were embracing old Rebels on the battlefields on which they had once shot at each other. People in New Hampshire apparently figured life was too short to hold a grudge against Frank Pierce any longer, so they voted in May 1913 "with practical unanimity" to put up a statue. Artist Augustus Lukeman of New York City whipped up a fine bronze statue with a granite base. The work was finished the following year, with ceremonies set for November 25, 1914.

The New Hampshire Historical Society chronicled the statue's dedication in a book, so we have a full record of the day's festivities. The speakers tried to thread a very fine needle, explaining why they had gathered to honor a guy who they all agreed led an administration they didn't admire. The speeches were full of qualifying statements, like how Pierce fought for the truth "as he saw it" and how he "should be judged in the light of the conditions as they existed in his time." Frank Carpenter, chair of the Pierce Statue Commission, said, "We honor him to whom was given the task of guiding the destinies of the nation when vast forces were working for the ultimate good, but which, during his leadership, had failed to take form and direction." In short: dude was in the wrong place at the wrong time.

Judge Edgar Aldrich had an even less convincing appraisal: "England puts into her library of the House of Lords a bust of Cromwell, not because he was politically right according to English standards, but because he was a great Englishman and a man of notable achievements." Now that's a hell of a comparison—if *Cromwell* can get a statue, why not Franklin Pierce?

Some speakers brought up Pierce's reputation as a legitimately skilled trial lawyer, and others told of small and large kindnesses he had paid to them and to others. My favorite speech, though, was by then-Governor Samuel Felker, who was clearly stretching in his attempt to laud Pierce. For example: "President Pierce appointed one of the strongest cabinets of any President in the history of the United States." "His messages to Congress, considered from a literary view, were able state papers, clearly and strongly expressed." And best of all: "Everyone admits that aside from the slavery question President Pierce met the expectations of the country." It reminds me of an episode of *The Simpsons* in which Homer thinks he's dying and can't think of anything profound to tell Bart before he dies, so all he says is "I like your sheets." Governor Felker could've written that line.

Thus far, the men honoring President Franklin Pierce had summed up his life and career this way: nice guy; pretty good lawyer; decent technical writer, knew a famous author; had a good cabinet; flubbed the slavery thing.

But several speakers picked up on the premise behind the ceremony, and the statue, and New Hampshire's collective decision to finally recognize Franklin Pierce. Here's Judge Aldrich again: "Franklin Pierce was a New Hampshire man, and he achieved the presidency." He's essentially making the same argument here that underlies the "buy local" movement today. Anybody who's ever been to a farmers market or a craft fair knows some local products are truly great and some are painfully, desperately, obviously not. Franklin Pierce was not a great president, but he *was* a neighborhood guy who served in a great capacity, and there's something to be said for celebrating the achievements of your neighbors. After all, if somebody from your hometown can make it to the White House, maybe you can be somebody, too. Another speaker, William Whitcher, summed up this sentiment perfectly with allusion, perhaps unintentional, to Pierce's campaign posters of 1852: "In honoring him, she [New Hampshire] honors herself."

There was a band on hand for the festivities; after the speeches, they played "America" and several other selections, and the people went on their way, having squared their relationship with their hometown president. In 1946, they even got Pierce a new tombstone, which you can see at the Old North Cemetery in Concord. I see his statue on Main Street almost every Saturday, as it stands next to the downtown farmers market. I always keep an eye out for angry mobs, just in case.

THE EASTERN New York town of Kinderhook is what Martin Van Buren called home. As a lesser-known, one-term president, he has almost the same complement of hometown honors that Franklin Pierce has in Concord, starting with a grave in a small rural cemetery.

The inscription on the stone obelisk has become hard to read in the 150 years since his death, but you can still see that it's the only presidential grave marker to use Roman numerals—Van Buren was the "VIIIth President of the United States." The Little Magician also has a birthplace historic site, a portrait at the state capitol, and a statue in the heart of downtown. Van Buren's statue is sitting on a bench with his walking stick in hand; there's a second seat on which you're clearly supposed to sit down and talk with the president.

Van Buren bought his 200-acre estate, Lindenwald, so he could have a house that looked as big and imposing as those of his predecessors, and one at which he could entertain VIPs from out of town. This was an important enough job for Van Buren to move the main staircase out of the front of the house to make way for a massive dining room, with room for twenty. The French wallpaper depicted hunting scenes; there were portraits of Thomas Jefferson and Andrew Jackson on the walls.

But the most intriguing artistic item I saw was outside. There was a massive downed tree behind a wooden fence on the side of the house; a nearby sign explained, "The National Park Service Olmsted Center for Landscape Preservation and the Rhode Island School of Design Witness Tree Project have joined together to allow students to learn about United States History by creating items out of the hallowed wood of fallen trees."

Witness trees are most often associated with Gettysburg—some of the trees that were alive at the time of the battle in 1863 still have bullets inside—and it was there that the RISD project was born. Professor Dale Broholm was touring the battlefield with a friend from the National Park Service, who mentioned a project to clear trees from a historic site. "What becomes of these trees?" he asked, and that question led to an informal deal: the Park Service tells Broholm when trees might become available. Broholm and his colleague Daniel Cavicchi give their students the wood and a theme upon which to base their research and, ultimately, their artwork. Not all the trees are related to presidents, but when they are the themes usually involve "idealization, canonization, memorialization, respect for the office—

how America looks at presidents after they leave office and after they die, and how they're reflected."

There's a wide range of finished work. In a course with wood from Theodore Roosevelt's house, Sagamore Hill, there are functional pieces, like walking sticks featuring TR quotes about nature, and there are more abstract works, like the necklace called "Beginning and End 2010." "Teddy Roosevelt has always been portrayed as a pillar of strength," wrote artist Athena Lo of her creation. "He was born with serious asthma, which drove him to work harder and become the strong figure that has gone down in history as a 'Rough Rider.' Nevertheless, he was brought down by an affliction of his lungs. The knots in the wood from which this necklace was made represents [*sic*] the blood clot in his lungs that caused his death. The necklace commemorates Roosevelt's life and how one can overcome weakness to find strength."

Once the art is finished the project goes full circle: "The objects are curated," Broholm says, "and go back to the site for exhibition, to engage visitors in a different kind of conversation—something fruitful and different than the normal interpretive staff engagement."

Not every president is the whirlwind of personality that TR was, but Broholm has a plan. "With Van Buren we're going to look at American identity. In his time westward expansion was under way, the dawn of industrialization was right around the corner. We're starting to get into a struggle about *who are we?* You could say, oh, he was a minor president, but his presidency is happening at such an important time that he can't help but leave a fingerprint or a footprint." Preparing the tree takes months; it has to be moved, cut, and dried before the course begins. "That tree had fallen two years earlier, but it kept putting up shoots. And the Park Service propagated it. They wanted to make sure they would continue on with the DNA."

Broholm has a dream witness tree in mind: one from the White House, he says. "And we've heard a rumor that there may be one— obviously there's a lot of layers of bureaucracy, but I believe it's from Jackson's time."

———

THE WHITE House is as good a place as any to find material for presidential art, since it's been amassing one of the great collections of American presidential portraits since acquiring the famous Gilbert Stuart portrait of Washington in 1800, the one that had to be whisked out of the Executive Mansion in 1814 before British troops came and burned the place down. Adding new portraits to the collection has been a matter of course since then—with one notable exception: James Buchanan. The wily Pennsylvanian managed to worsen the already tense relationship between North and South; by the time his term was done, the country was practically sprinting toward armed conflict and disunion. He was so loathed that when the artist George Healy finished Buchanan's official portrait for the White House collection, Congress refused to pay the bill.

So you can imagine my surprise to find that Washington, DC, features not only a Buchanan painting in the National Portrait Gallery but also a full-size James Buchanan Memorial overlooking Meridian Hill Park, also known as Malcolm X Park. A statue of the impeccably dressed Buchanan sits admiring the Constitution, while a side panel hails him as "the incorruptible statesman whose walk was upon the mountain ranges of the law." It's a nice memorial, but a completely inexplicable one. How does a president get a memorial like this if he leaves office without a friend in the world?

The answer, it turns out, is simple: he had a niece. Harriet Lane served as first lady for the bachelor president. A bright and forceful young woman, Harriet lobbied to live with Uncle James after the deaths of her parents, and she got what she wanted. He made sure she was well educated and cultured, exposing her to politics and high society; she, in turn, served as his hostess. Though only in her twenties at the time, she was more than up to the job. Queen Victoria called her "dear Miss Lane" during Buchanan's time as minister to Great Britain, and in the White House, she got northern and southern men who were literally preparing to fight a war against each other to come to dinner together—though she made sure to seat them far apart. The bright, charming "Democratic Queen" was perhaps the brightest spot in an otherwise dismal four years in office.

Her years in the White House were successful, but the years that followed were marked by tragedy. She married a Baltimore banker, Henry Elliott Johnston, in 1866, and they had two sons, named for her uncle and her husband. Then, in one three-year period, both James Buchanan Johnston and Henry Elliott Johnston Jr. died from rheumatic fever, and Henry Sr. succumbed to pneumonia. According to newspaper accounts of the time, Harriet Lane Johnston grieved alone, living "in retirement for some years."

But she was far from finished. Having inherited a sizable estate, Harriet Lane Johnston became a philanthropist, paying tribute to her children by establishing a number of facilities to provide medical care for poor children at no cost. When she died in 1903, she left $100,000 to establish the Harriet Lane Home for Invalid Children, affiliated with Johns Hopkins Medical School. Among its many medical advances, the home, later renamed the Johns Hopkins Children's Center, discovered successful treatments for rheumatic fever. Johns Hopkins still publishes a guide to pediatric diagnosis and treatment called *The Harriet Lane Handbook*.

Uncle James had died at home in Lancaster, Pennsylvania, in 1868, after publishing a rather touchy memoir that blamed everyone else for his administration's difficulties. His grave at Lancaster's Woodward Hill Cemetery was tasteful but not too prominent, so Harriet's will called for two large public monuments in his honor. Knowing these requests would be unpopular, she left $100,000 for the pieces—enough to avoid any need for public funds—and she set a strict deadline of fifteen years for officials to either go forward with the memorials or give the money back.

The first project won approval pretty easily; the James Buchanan Monument Fund built a stone pyramid thirty-eight feet high on the southern Pennsylvania land where Old Buck was born. The monument in Washington was a very different story. Remember, at the time, only George Washington had a monument in DC. There was nothing for

Jefferson, nothing for Lincoln, and Congress was supposed to approve a *Buchanan* memorial? Senator Henry Cabot Lodge of Massachusetts fumed, "This joint resolution proposes at this moment, in the midst of this war, to erect a statue to the only President upon whom rests the shadow of disloyalty in the great office to which he was elected." In the end, though, lawmakers decided free money was free money; they authorized the memorial, and President Wilson signed the legislation six days before Harriet's deadline. The memorial opened to the public in 1930, and President Herbert Hoover noted that even though Buchanan was "engrossed in public and private business, he found time to rear and educate an orphaned niece in a manner that would have done credit to any father. It is due to Miss Lane's devoted appreciation of his kindness that this statue has been erected."

Only one other individual has been willing to give Old Buck's presidency the benefit of the doubt besides Harriet Lane: the acclaimed novelist and native Pennsylvanian John Updike, who wrote a "play intended to be read" called *Buchanan Dying*. It is a tough read, mostly depicting the bedridden former president's life flashing before his eyes. Updike's Buchanan thinks of himself as a man who sought to act slowly and deliberately, so as to head off the hotheads in both North and South and buy the Union more time. No one buys this; Edwin Stanton, who was briefly Buchanan's attorney general before serving in Lincoln's cabinet, shows up to tell Buchanan, "Time does not preserve, it destroys. *Men* preserve!" Former president James K. Polk, in whose cabinet Buchanan served, says Buchanan tried too hard to get everyone to like him. "Any honest man has opponents," he warns. "Opposition demonstrates a steadfast direction." Buchanan's severe father is the harshest, telling his son that the country will throw a huge party when he passes on: "Die, Buchanan, and give us an excuse for a clambake!"

Buchanan Dying is less a commentary on Buchanan than on the year in which it was published: 1974, the final act of Watergate. "In these years of high indignation over unbridled and corrupting Presidential power," Updike wrote, "we can give more sympathy to Buchanan's cautious and literal constitutionalism than has been shown him in history books."

Buchanan doesn't show up in many history books these days, and when he does it isn't because of his politics but because of his sexuality: he is, after all, regularly touted as the first gay president, because he never married and lived in Washington with another bachelor politician, Alabama's William Rufus King. Political watchers called the inseparable duo "the Siamese twins." Buchanan griped to friends when King went overseas to work as minister to France; "I am now 'solitary and alone,'" he wrote in one such letter, "having no companion in the house with me. I have gone a wooing to several gentlemen, but have not succeeded with any one of them."

A few politicians snickered at Buchanan and King—one, Aaron Brown, said that Buchanan acted like King was "his wife." Andrew Jackson called the duo "Aunt Nancy and Miss Fancy"; in fact, mocking Buchanan and King was about the only thing on which Old Hickory and his hated rival Henry Clay agreed. The Great Compromiser mocked Buchanan on the Senate floor, raising the pitch of his voice when addressing the Pennsylvanian to, as Clay put it, "suit the delicate ear of the Senator."

It sounds pretty straightforward, but sometimes clear evidence isn't always so clear. Michael Birkner teaches history at Gettysburg College. He's edited two books on Buchanan and says there's no evidence that Old Buck and King were anything other than emotionally close. Take, for example, the comment about King being Buchanan's "wife." Aaron Brown was a political crony of James K. Polk, who, at the time Brown made the comment, was trying to outmaneuver William Rufus King to end up on the Democratic ticket in the 1844 election. Andrew Jackson had deeply distrusted Buchanan because of some behind-the-scenes scheming during Old Hickory's first presidential campaign. Birkner says of the "Miss Nancy and Aunt Fancy" comment, "That's not evidence—that's a quip. And Buchanan was the kind of guy who it was easy to make quips about. He was foppish, he loved small talk with the ladies."

Even the letter about "wooing" gentlemen is less revealing than it might seem. Here's what comes after the sentence about striking out with "several gentlemen": "I feel that it is not good for man to be alone; and should not be astonished to find myself married to some old maid who can nurse me when I am sick provide good dinners for me when I am well, and not expect from me any very ardent or romantic affection." If anything, Buchanan sounds simply lonely. It wasn't unusual for politicians to room together in those days; heck, it's not unusual today. DC housing doesn't come cheap. It should be noted that Harriet Lane and a relative of King's may have destroyed some of their letters when Buchanan became president, but we can't know whether those letters, if they existed, were about personal secrets or political secrets. Or any secrets at all.

WHATEVER THE nature of his relationship with William King, our culture has come to see in James Buchanan what it's looking to see. It's not the only time society has projected its own questions, concerns, and fears onto presidents and presidential candidates. When Warren Harding ran for president in 1920, he faced accusations that he had African American ancestry from a great-grandparent. The accusations came from a man called William Estabrook Chancellor, a college instructor and supporter of the outgoing Democratic president, Woodrow Wilson. Chancellor, like Wilson, was no fan of the more tolerant racial views of Harding and the Republicans, so he invented a scandal that played on cultural fears of race-mixing. His evidence was nonsense, but the rumor has lingered for decades—and as long as race remains a thorny topic in the United States, it will probably continue to linger.

Not many people have lingered at Warren Harding's beautiful, striking tomb in Marion, Ohio. In office he'd hoped to be the country's best-loved president, and immediately after his death in 1923 it looked like he might be. As many as three million people came out to see his funeral train roll from San Francisco to Washington and then back to Ohio. Virtually every major living political figure joined the Harding Memorial Association, which set funding goals in the millions and drew up plans for a large, open-air tomb with classical columns encircling the Hardings.

But the love didn't last, especially as the public started learning what had been going on in the administration. Some of Harding's highest-ranking officials had been embezzling public money and taking bribes. Harding himself wasn't in on the looting, but a best-selling memoir in 1927 said that was because he was too busy carrying on an affair in the White House coat closet. Fund-raising lagged; since the Memorial Association couldn't point to Harding's accomplishments to raise money, it stuck to extremely vague slogans, like "Human Being Always" and "He Loved to Serve." The prominent politicians who had lined up to help build a Harding tomb started keeping their distance; even Harding's successors, Calvin Coolidge and Herbert Hoover, put off the formal dedication so as not to be too closely associated with their former boss. The country had washed its hands of Warren Harding; *Life* magazine called the tomb a "lonely Ohio shrine" in 1944, barely twenty years after his death, and added, "Not many people go there now."

(I wasn't alone when I visited the Harding tomb. It was late May—prom season—and a young couple had chosen to pose for their prom pictures in front of the grave of the twenty-ninth president of the United States.)

The man who had hoped to be the best-loved president seemed to have lost all his friends. All but one, that is; Harding was a dog lover—when he ran the local newspaper in Marion, he had written a loving obituary to one of his furry friends—and his White House dog, Laddie Boy, had become the White House's first celebrity pet. Harding gave the Airedale terrier his own chair in the Cabinet Room and brought him out to greet official delegations. Newspapers published letters in the dog's voice; in one, Laddie Boy "writes" to a famous stage dog called Tiger and tellingly warns him about how "many a dog is more or less spoiled by his environment and associations."

The news coverage of the dog continued after Harding's death. "There was one member of the White House household today who could not quite comprehend the air of sadness which hung over the executive mansion," wrote the *St. Petersburg Times* on August 4, 1923. "Laddie Boy knows that his master and mistress made frequent jour-

21. Warren Harding's Airedale terrier, Laddie Boy, was the White House's first celebrity pet.

neys away from home and he always watches for their return. Of late he has been casting an expectant eye and cocking a watchful ear at the motor cars which roll up on the White House drive. . . . For, in his dog sense way, he figures 'an automobile took them away, so an automobile must bring them back.'"

This apparently broke the heart of a woman called Edna Bell Seward, who wrote a poem about the national conundrum of explaining to Warren Harding's dog that the president was not going to come back to the White House. Set to music by her husband, the piece was called "Laddie Boy, He's Gone."

Laddie Boy ended up as a work of art, too: newsboys donated more than nineteen thousand pennies, which were melted down and turned into a sculpture of the dog. It ended up in the Smithsonian's collection because the person for whom it was intended, Mrs. Harding, had died by the time it was finished.

Harry Truman famously said, "If you want a friend in Washington, get a dog." In Harding's case he was right.

11

FAMILY REUNION

On the Adamses, the Harrisons, and Presidential Descendants

E ACH YEAR the sitting president marks each of his predecessors by sending wreaths to their tombs on their birthdays. Branches of the US military oversee the formal wreath laying, but many of the presidential gravesites go beyond these already elaborate processions and throw birthday parties for their charges. Wanting to see one, I headed down to Quincy, Massachusetts, for President John Quincy Adams's 246th birthday party. Quincy calls itself the "City of Presidents," and United First Parish Church is at the heart of a "presidential district" where there is an Adams Building and a Presidential Pub and lots of "Discover Adams" banners up on the lampposts. On one side of the street there's a statue of John Adams; on the other, his wife Abigail with a young John Quincy. The city has been working to turn the narrow, congested street into a pedestrian path.

The church throws big birthday parties featuring speeches, music, parish tours, and birthday cake at the big Adams house, Peacefield. And the celebrations are apparently a top national priority: during the government shutdown in 2013, church officials worried that they might have to put off the John Adams party, but they say navy officials told them that the wreath-laying ceremonies were considered an essential government service and would go forward even if the government was partially closed.*

I walked in just behind two young women carrying an enormous floral wreath, made up of red and white carnations, blue irises, and white asters, and addressed only to "The President," and we sat down in a creaky enclosed wooden pew in the front row. The Navy Band Northeast, up from Newport, Rhode Island, played "America the Beautiful," "God Bless America," and a downbeat rendition of "Home on the Range." I studied the wall installations extolling the careers and virtues of the two presidents. My two-year-old son waved his miniature American flag and stacked hymnals on the seat.

The first of several speakers was a man called Peter Boylston Adams, who was listed on the program as "descendant." I didn't need a program to tell me this—the man looked, to a stunning degree, like the man we'd come to honor. This distracted me so much that I could barely focus on his speech, which is a shame because Peter Boylston Adams spoke about the parallels between naval piracy in John Quincy Adams's day and international terrorism of today, and he knows something about war, having won the Distinguished Flying Cross and the Purple Heart flying combat missions in Vietnam. "Terror on the high seas was not what you see in *Pirates of the Caribbean*," said Peter Boylston Adams. These were "angry, cruel young men— absolutely ruthless. . . . Terror was their business."

Still, as he talked, I kept thinking back to the famous daguerreotype of John Quincy Adams, taken when he was a grizzled congressional firebrand, and saying to myself, *Man, this guy looks just like that.*

"By 1735 there were no pirates anywhere. Gone. Except in the Mediterranean . . ."

I wonder if he's ever gone to the National Portrait Gallery in Washington just to stand by the Quincy Adams portrait and freak people out.

"They said, 'If you resist us, we will kill you.'"

---

* Dwight Eisenhower's wreath-laying ceremony was held during the shutdown of 2013 but in a different location, as the federally-run Eisenhower Library was closed.

I might not have been following the speech, but my son had been, and he started repeating some of the lines. "We will kill you!" he shouted, much more gleefully than Peter Boylston Adams had. Fortunately there was no need to shush him, as Adams closed out his speech by asking the audience to honor a man he described as "the gatekeeper for the Adams crypts" with three cheers. Adams, who had spoken rather quietly, suddenly bellowed, "*Hip hip*," and we all shouted, "*HOORAY!*"

After the ceremony we headed downstairs to see the tomb, which, as presidential tombs go, is pretty nondescript. It's basically four big stone sarcophagi marked JOHN ADAMS, ABIGAIL ADAMS, JOHN QUINCY ADAMS, and LOUISA CATHERINE ADAMS. The second president once asked for an epitaph that referred to his proudest accomplishment as president: "Here lies John Adams, who took upon himself the responsibility of peace with France in the year 1800." The tomb has that entire inscription on it, except for the words "here lies" and "who took upon himself the responsibility of peace with France in the year 1800." These tombs are in an underground room that's not that different from, say, my basement. A few of the visitors on this humid summer day made jokes about "the smell," though there really wasn't one—it smelled like a basement in the summer, which is what it was. As far as I'm concerned, when there are two presidents and two first ladies in a room, that room can smell any way it wants.

The Adamses may have been buried together, but as families go they weren't the most cheerful. John Adams was a demanding dad and set impossibly high expectations for his offspring. John Quincy was the only one who met them; the others weren't so fortunate. Daughter Nabby, the first child born to a president, died relatively young after struggling for years with breast cancer; at one point she had to endure surgery without anesthesia. Son Charles had a drinking problem; as his alcoholism grew worse, he abandoned his law practice, left his family, and lost the life savings John Quincy had entrusted to him to invest. In 1798 John Adams disowned Charles; two years later, the president's thirty-year-old son was dead, probably of cirrhosis.

To his credit, John Adams learned from his mistakes and warned John Quincy not to repeat them. But the son was no easier on his children than the father had been on him: John Quincy pestered his kids with long letters about their inadequacies. "I had hoped that at least one of my sons would have been ambitious to excel," he grumbled. "I find them all three coming to manhood with indolent minds." One of the three, Charles Francis Adams, did go on to prominence as a member of Congress, diplomat, and public figure, but the other two buckled: John Adams II died of alcoholism at age thirty-one; George Washington Adams started hearing voices and died after falling—or jumping—off a steamboat headed to New York.

The highs and lows the Adamses saw have come time and time again for presidential families. James Madison spent his retirement years paying off the gambling debts of his stepson, John Payne Todd; as a plantation owner, Madison was already financially stretched, but Payne's debts made things worse. When Madison died, the family had to sell the plantation, Montpelier, and the Father of the Constitution's grave went unmarked for two decades. Like the Adamses, William Henry Harrison and Andrew Johnson each lost sons to alcoholism. And the celebrity press hounded John F. Kennedy Jr. in life and in the wake of the plane crash that killed him.

On the other hand, Webb Hayes (son of Rutherford) and Theodore Roosevelt Jr. each won the Medal of Honor for military heroics. Elizabeth Harrison Walker, Benjamin Harrison's daughter and William Henry's great-granddaughter, was a pioneering lawyer and economic commentator at a time when women weren't expected to practice law or invest. George W. Bush, of course, became the second son of a president to serve in the White House as well. "There's good and there's bad," Doug Wead, author of *All the Presidents' Children*, told CNN. "But there doesn't seem to be much in between."

FAMILIES CAN be complicated, and President Benjamin Harrison's family story was no exception. The twenty-third president was also a presidential descendant, the grandson of William Henry Harrison, and as a politician he seemed to have mixed feelings about the connection. As a presidential candidate in 1888, he vowed, "I will show all that my family's famous name is safe in my keeping," but he also said to aides, "I want it understood I am grandson of nobody."

Harrison saw six states come into the Union during his four years in the White House, more than any other president, but his tenure is barely remembered, partly because he was one of the least personable presidents. Adults called him "the human iceberg," but around kids, he warmed up, and there were three grandchildren living in the Harrison White House. We have a White House Christmas tree because of him; having a natural white beard, he was game to play Santa Claus for his grandchildren. Newspapers wrote glowing stories about how the president sat for dinner at his formal White House table with his two-year-old grandson, Benjamin Harrison McKee, sitting nearby in a high chair.

The second President Harrison lived through his term, but his wife didn't; Caroline Harrison died just before Election Day 1892, after fighting tuberculosis for months. Both the president and his opponent, former president Grover Cleveland, suspended campaigning on account of the first lady's death.

One of those on hand at Caroline's deathbed was her niece and secretary, Mary Scott Dimmick. Several years later, after returning to Indianapolis, Benjamin shocked his grown children by announcing that he and Mary, twenty-five years younger, were getting married. Harrison's adult children were mortified, refused to attend the wedding, and cut off their children's contact with their grandfather. Harrison wrote sad letters about missing baby McKee and the other grandkids: "Grandpa came home from Richmond yesterday afternoon," went one letter, "and there was no little boy to meet him in the hall—but there was your bicycle—the first thing I saw to remind me of you. But the bicycle . . . could not talk and I didn't want to."

Benjamin and Mary had a child of their own, Elizabeth, who sat at a high chair at the big table in the Harrisons' Indianapolis home, much as her nephew had done at the White House. But pneumonia struck the Harrisons again: the twenty-third president, just like his grandfather, succumbed to the disease. There was a sweet-sad little story about four-year-old Elizabeth trying to cheer her fading father by bringing him a pie; the president was so ill he could only smile back at his daughter.

Harrison's eldest children heard that their father was ill and raced to see him before it was too late, but they didn't make it. Perhaps owing to that estrangement, or perhaps owing to the fact that they were both grown, Benjamin Harrison's will made no mention of his adult children. He left everything he owned to Mary and to Elizabeth.

Whatever their differences in life, though, they are together in death: at Crown Hill Cemetery in Indianapolis, Benjamin Harrison is buried at the foot of a large grave marker. Caroline Harrison is on one side of him, Mary Harrison is on the other, and the two eldest children are buried nearby.

I THOUGHT I'd call around to some descendants for their thoughts on life as a presidential relative. Then I got an e-mail from one. "Here's something odd to ponder," it began. "Every year in April, I go to the Marshfield Missouri Cherry Blossom Festival and Presidential Family Reunion and Missouri Walk of Fame Celebration. It's in Missouri at the top of the Ozarks. . . . One of these days you should think about coming." It was signed by George Cleveland, "Grover Cleveland grandson."

George Cleveland lives in Tamworth, New Hampshire, about an hour north of where I live. We'd never met, but he'd been a part of several of my trips: there's a photo of George at the Grover Cleveland Birthplace in Caldwell, New Jersey, and the presidential memorabilia collection at Founding Fathers Pub in Buffalo includes a picture of George as well; it's kept behind the bar. When I mentioned this to him he wrote back, "I think my photo is behind several bars, but not all for the same reason."

George's grandfather died in 1908 in Princeton, New Jersey, where he had been serving on the Ivy League university's board. His stately grave marker stands near the west edge of Princeton Cemetery, and if you look closely you'll find the top of the stone covered in Hawaiian beads.* Cleveland was a big supporter of Hawaiian independence. His successor in the White House, Benjamin Harrison, had pushed for a treaty to annex Hawaii, but when Cleveland won the office back, he withdrew the treaty, on the grounds that America's just character would be impugned "if a feeble but friendly state is in danger of being robbed of its independence and its sovereignty by the misuse of the name and power of the United States."

William McKinley re-reversed course after Cleveland retired, but native Hawaiians never forgot the gesture, and clearly didn't hold a grudge about the "feeble" designation. So each year a group from the Pacific Justice and Reconciliation Center comes to New Jersey to say thanks. George Cleveland is usually there. "Oh, it's nuts, it's great," is how he described the festivities. "They have people doing hula on the front porch of the birthplace. And down [in] Princeton they have a very solemn ceremony where they put leis on the graves of Grover and Frances. They eat a lot. They always eat a lot. And it's just sort of one big party."

The festival in Marshfield is more like a big reunion, with representatives of twenty-six presidential families on hand. "We've got Polks, Washingtons," George tells me. "Monroe is going to be big this year"—a Monroe descendant is giving a presentation on the fifth president. The event schedule is pretty eclectic; there's a 5K road race, a "presidential prayer breakfast" with Billy Graham's daughter Gigi, and a look back at the costumes of *Gone with the Wind*, complete with a recorded greeting from Olivia de Havilland. First Lady Laura Bush is one of the keynote speakers; another is the woman who played Zuzu in *It's a Wonderful Life*. You can meet Princess Diana's butler and descendants of Dred Scott. "It's impossible to explain this event to someone," George Cleveland says, "telling them I'm going to a

---

* Princeton Cemetery is also the final resting place of Vice President Aaron Burr, whose most notable accomplishment in office was killing Alexander Hamilton in a duel.

cherry blossom festival/presidential descendant festival/pop culture adventure—and eating a lot."

Marshfield isn't the town you'd expect to have a presidential-themed anything. The town at the "Top of the Ozarks" boasts six thousand residents, one stretch of historic Route 66, and the longest-running Independence Day parade west of the Mississippi River. But its presidential connections aren't any bigger than anywhere else's: the first President Bush came to Marshfield in 1991, but that's it. The town's most famous native is the astronomer Edwin Hubble; there's a large-scale replica of the Hubble telescope on the lawn of the court-house downtown.

Judging by the local history, you might expect a Tomato Canning Festival; there used to be hundreds of plants in this part of Missouri. Instead, there are presidential grandsons and cousins and great-grandnieces running around Marshfield each spring. This is thanks to Nicholas Inman, a local pastor and presidential history buff who had a dream of putting a museum honoring the presidents in town. "I spent some time in Washington, DC, after I graduated high school," he says. "So I thought, we'll plant cherry blossom trees in Marshfield, and we'll tie them around the museum, and we'll have a history festi-val each year to celebrate American history."

Inman started inviting presidential descendants to Marshfield as a way to publicize the museum idea, but as soon as the descendants got to town the plan started to change. "They'd never had an oppor-tunity like this to all get together," Inman said. "It was so much fun to watch them visit. Suddenly they began to talk, *well, my grandfather ran against your grandfather* and *my grandfather was your grandfather's vice president* . . . they started making all these comments, *can we come back next year?* And I thought, well, wow, I never thought they'd want to come back!" Locals took to it, too, and the one-time festival quickly became an annual event.

George Cleveland has been here nearly every year and has turned into a bit of a rock star. At the prayer breakfast he introduced me to John Ross Truman, great-nephew of Harry and "one of my favorite people in the whole world." John has a quick wit and got us both laughing with stories of President Truman's mother-in-law, who "would come to the White House to visit and tell the staff that the president wasn't good enough for her daughter." He started to tell me about how Great-uncle Harry had shown him the famous Truman Balcony at the White House—"a fun spot and a heck of a view"—and given him personal tours of his presidential library, but then a woman came over with an iPad and asked the two of them for a picture. They get this a lot in Marshfield; to give them and the others time to see each other, there are VIP-only events like the "presidential descendant luncheon." "They lock us in a room," George Cleveland says, laughing, "and we tell each other secrets."

As the descendants bared those "secrets," I headed over to the local diner, Freda's Uptown Cafe, where I ate fried okra, found yet another place with a George Cleveland photo on the wall, and thought about what this wonderful and wild festival would have been like if Nicholas Inman had been born decades earlier. Inman has thought about this, too; when I asked him which historical descendant he most would have wanted to have at the festival, he had an answer right away. "Alice," he says, "would have made a great festival guest."

He was referring to Alice Roosevelt Longworth, first daughter of Theodore Roosevelt and one of America's greatest political wits. TR's first wife, Alice Hathaway Lee, died just days after giving birth to baby Alice, and he was so devastated that he went west to raise cattle and left his new daughter in the care of his sister for the first few years of her life. Alice rejoined the family after her father remarried, but there was always some distance between them; Alice was both fascinated by Teddy and determined to rebel against him.

And rebel she did. The press followed the White House antics of the Roosevelt kids like a reality show, and the teenaged Alice was the breakout star. She placed bets with bookies, snuck movie stars into the Executive Mansion, and occasionally enlivened dull parties by pulling out a cap gun and firing it at the ceiling. Once she waltzed into the president's office with her pet garter snake, Emily Spinach, coiled around her arm. "I can be president of the United States or I can control Alice," TR sighed to his guest. "I can't possibly do both." At Alice's wedding in 1906, at which the bride used a sword to cut the cake, Edith Roosevelt told her stepdaughter: "I am glad to see you leave. You have never been anything but trouble."

Alice made trouble for politicians of every stripe for the rest of her life, including her father; she once visited the Cuban hills TR and the Rough Riders had so famously charged up, and declared them to be "hardly more than mildly sloping." Nonrelatives fared even worse. Warren Harding, she said, "wasn't a bad man, just a slob." As for Herbert Hoover, she said, "The Hoover vacuum cleaner is more exciting than the president. But, of course, it's electric." Politicians courted her anyway; Lyndon Johnson teased Alice about her wide-brimmed hats, saying they made it hard for him to give her a kiss. "That, Mr. Johnson, is why I wear them," she replied.

Alice's wit became so well known that people attributed other people's quotes to her. She wasn't the first to say Calvin Coolidge looked like he'd been weaned on a pickle, and she didn't describe two-time Republican presidential nominee Thomas Dewey as "the little man on the wedding cake," but they sounded like things Alice would have said, so that's how they were remembered. Her most-loved quote, though, was an original: "If you can't say something good about someone, sit right here by me."

By the time Alice Roosevelt Longworth died in 1980, at age ninety-six, she had adored the Kennedys, befriended Richard Nixon, supported gay rights, and chastised Jimmy Carter for giving back the Panama Canal her father had annexed. Unusually perceptive, unafraid to speak her mind, unfailingly entertaining, Alice had earned the nickname the political class gave her: "the Other Washington Monument."

Any of the Roosevelt kids would have made great guests at the festival in Marshfield. Theodore Roosevelt Jr. won virtually every military decoration possible for bravery, including the Medal of Honor, serving in both World Wars. In 1944, the fifty-seven-year old Brigadier General Roosevelt was the only man of his rank to be in the line of fire on D-day, directing the landing on Utah Beach with his cane despite the danger—and despite the fact that he was having a series of minor heart attacks at the time; he would die just weeks later. When asked to describe the most heroic act in the entire war, Omar Bradley answered, "Theodore Roosevelt on Utah Beach." Despite his unparalleled heroism, Roosevelt felt he could never measure up to his presidential dad. "Don't you think that it handicaps a boy," he said, "to be the son of a man like my father, and especially to have the same name? Don't you know there can never be another Theodore Roosevelt?"

For me, the saddest family story is that of Quentin Roosevelt, the youngest brother. As a kid, Quentin was the leader of a group known as the White House Gang, whose hijinks included "redecorating" a portrait of Andrew Jackson with spitballs. Quentin's fuming father made him get up in the middle of the night to undo the damage. All the Roosevelt boys served during the Great War, but Quentin arguably took on the riskiest job: fighter pilot. He won a reputation for his daring and his skill, but on July 14, 1918, his luck ran out; Quentin's plane was shot down by a German squadron behind enemy lines. TR had long championed the virtues of fighting, and even dying, in war; he called the day he charged up San Juan Hill "the great day of my life." But seeing his own son dead in battle was devastating—his health quickly declined, and six months after the tragedy, Theodore Roosevelt died in his sleep.

Vice President Thomas Marshall observed that "Death had to take Roosevelt sleeping, for if he had been awake, there would have been a fight," but maybe not. Quentin's death had hurt him deeply, especially since he felt responsible for sending his sons off to war in the first place. "To feel that one has inspired a boy to conduct that has resulted in his death," he wrote a friend, "has a pretty serious side for a father." The forceful, noteworthy man who, according to Alice Roosevelt Longworth, wanted to be "the corpse at every funeral" is buried on a small, quiet hill overlooking New York's Oyster Bay. There's a rock near the grave with a TR quote: "Keep your eyes on the stars and keep your feet on the ground." When I see that quote, I think of Quentin.

"You know how Billy Graham was the minister for all the living presidents?" Nicholas Inman says. "I feel like I've become minister to all the dead presidents, because I'm often called to do things—funerals and weddings and things—for these administrations now." One of those funerals was at Monticello, in the same burial ground that holds the remains of Thomas Jefferson, and someday might hold the remains of his descendants through Sally Hemings. "It's kind of neat how you develop these relationships, and you have to stop and think about, oh yeah, I know them because of the Cherry Blossom Festival, I didn't just meet them on the street."

The final public event of each year's Cherry Blossom Festival is a panel discussion with some of the descendants. John Truman shared more funny stories about Great-uncle Harry's "holy terror" of a mother-in-law, and George Cleveland said the extended Cleveland family was trying to decide what to do with some newly discovered family letters. Several audience members gasped as Susan Tyler, great-granddaughter of John Tyler, explained that her still-living father, Lyon, is the grandson of a man who led the country in the 1840s.

The most poignant story came from Laurene Anfinson, Richard Nixon's niece. She described taking part in an event in 1988, just ahead of George H. W. Bush's inauguration. New York City was marking two hundred years since the first oath of office at Federal Hall, an anniversary in which there were "forty presidents' families represented. In a carriage came George [Washington], as a reenactor. In a car came George Bush." Each family member wore a badge with the family name on it, and as the families walked by in a procession, people in the crowd called out their names—"Truman!" "Kennedy!" "Roosevelt!"—and the crowd cheered. "Pretty soon," she said, "somebody yelled out 'Nixon!' and everybody booed. So our children walked back to us and said, 'what do we do?'" Anfinson said Luci Baines Johnson, daughter of Lyndon, was incensed that anyone would boo a child for being related to a president that person didn't like, and she mobilized the entire group of descendants to make a statement. "All the kids linked arms," Anfinson said, "four lanes wide—and they didn't let go the whole way."

In a way, the presidential descendants have formed "a family of history," as Nicholas Inman describes them. "This comes from people who may have served beside each other in Congress or may have had strong political differences, but they stand firm together and stand beside each other and they don't criticize each other." The Marshfield festival, he says, has "really become a family reunion. . . . It's really its own community—they're all over the country, and they gather here once a year."

The family reunion always includes a family photo; the descendants and the other festival regulars gather together for a picture before heading off to the "state dinner." Before leaving, George Cleveland comes over to ask for a photo of the two of us. "I hope this has been helpful," he says, with gallons of understatement. "It sure has," I tell him, because now I can add my house to the places with photos of George Cleveland on the walls.

EPILOGUE

G EORGE WASHINGTON'S tomb at Mount Vernon was the obvious starting point for this adventure, so I started there. But where to finish? Where does a person wrap up a tour of the gravesites of the presidents?

I thought about this as I walked the grounds of Dwight D. Eisenhower's presidential library. Ike wasn't going to be my last visit—there were still several names left on my list when I visited him in Abilene, Kansas—but his burial site was the first I sized up as a potential finish. In some ways it would have been a good fit: the Eisenhower site is twenty-two acres, a size befitting his historical stature. Staff members shuttle from building to building in small yellow pickup trucks with "We Still Like Ike" signs on the back. There's a federally managed presidential library for his official papers, and a museum showing Eisenhower's White House desk, the Emmy Award he won for his use of television in office, and some of the paintings he made in retirement.

Outdoors, the centerpiece of the campus is a large statue of the general and a series of plaques marking this as the site in which the president's parents taught their six sons "the ways of righteousness, of charity to all men and reverence to God." Eisenhower's indoor burial site, the Place of Meditation, is styled after military chapels, with stained glass windows, wooden pews, and a bubbling fountain.

In other ways, though, Eisenhower's story isn't the one to bring me full circle. Instead of returning home on *Air Force One*, as presidents do today, Eisenhower came back to Kansas on a train—the last presidential funeral train. More importantly, Eisenhower's posthumous story is still being written. In 1999 Congress authorized a commission to create a memorial in Washington to the thirty-fourth president. In 2005 the commission chose a four-acre site near the National Air and Space Museum; four years later it hired the prominent architect Frank Gehry to design the memorial. Though there was wide agreement on honoring Eisenhower, Gehry's design was less popular: critics compared some of the design's metal columns to missile silos and even Communist-style iconography, while others complained about a statue depicting Eisenhower as a "barefoot boy" in Kansas.* Eisenhower's own children spoke out against the design, and Congress suspended funding for the project until the two sides could reach agreement. "This memorial cannot be built," said House Oversight Committee chair Darrell Issa, "if it is inconsistent with the views of the people who knew our commander in chief as well as his family." Gehry agreed to design changes, and the process picked back up in late 2014, but it will be some time before those in Washington can walk through an Eisenhower Memorial.

This is the issue for me in finding a grand finale: each president's story will grow and change over time, and as long as there's a presidency, there won't be a "last" president whose story can serve as a bookend to Washington's. Part of me wishes that all the presidents who are still with us will live to be five hundred, but I know inevitably we will get word someday that one of them has left us, and the

---

* Gehry explained that the idea for the boyhood statue came from a speech Eisenhower gave in his home state, downplaying his wartime achievements and choosing to "speak first of the dreams of a barefoot boy" from Abilene.

military will carry out a detailed funeral plan and lay that president to rest, and I'll make it a point to stop by.

Many of my last few presidential visits were technicalities, like my visit to see Grover Cleveland, the only president to serve two non-consecutive terms, on a second, nonconsecutive occasion. Or Jefferson Davis: like him or not, the Confederate chief executive is part of the American story now, and besides, he's in the same Virginia cemetery as James Monroe and John Tyler. And there's the story of David Rice Atchison, whose grave marker in Plattsburgh, Missouri, reads "President of the United States for One Day—Sunday, Mar. 4, 1849." Atchison was president pro tempore of the Senate in 1849, when new president Zachary Taylor and new vice president Millard Fillmore declined to hold their inauguration on a Sunday. This led to a theory that, under the laws of succession at the time, Atchison was technically president until Taylor took the oath on Monday. He wasn't: legally, presidents don't have to take the oath to start their terms, and Atchison's own term as president pro tem had expired along with the executive's term. Still, he liked to tell the story—especially in retirement, possibly to rebuild his public reputation (Atchison backed the South during the Civil War). Atchison's administration was, by his own admission, hands off. "I slept most of that Sunday," he said.

But no presidential quest could be complete without a visit to the most iconic site of all: the gigantic presidential heads of Mount Rushmore. The story here, at the so-called shrine of democracy, is enormously ironic: Mount Rushmore was designed not to be a touchstone of American identity but as a tourist trap. In the 1920s, South Dakota state historian Doane Robinson wanted to draw more visitors to the Black Hills, and as he put it, "tourists soon get fed up on scenery unless it has something of special interest connected with it." It worked: the state gets some three million visits a year out of Rushmore, not to mention the economic benefits from the web of tourist-friendly businesses and attractions in the area. Whether Doane Robinson intended mystery spots, wax museums, and mini golf is probably up for debate, but, hey, he wanted tourists and he got them.

His original idea was a monument to heroes of the West, but his

*Gutzon Borglum and Supt.
inspecting work on face of
washington - Mt Rushmore.
#40*

22. "The faces are in the mountain," Gutzon Borglum said of Mount Rushmore. "All I have to do is bring them out." Having brought them out, Borglum and a project superintendent inspect George Washington's nose.

sculptor, Gutzon Borglum, shot the idea down for being too regional. He wanted to carve presidents, which he said would be more time-less, more national, and a lot more inspirational. "People from all over America will be drawn to come and look," he said, "and go home better citizens."

Borglum was a magnificent sculptor and not such a magnificent citizen; from 1927 to 1941, he carved the seemingly impossible into

Rushmore's granite facade but drove nearly everyone around him crazy during the construction process. He fought with everyone, including the "untutored miners" working long, dangerous shifts; Borglum's son, Lincoln, was forever rehiring the men his father had canned, just to keep the work moving along. The lawmakers overseeing construction could barely stand him either. "No one could get along with Mr. Borglum for any length of time without losing his temper, unless one was a saint," said former South Dakota governor and senator William J. Bulow, who dealt with the temperamental artist throughout construction. "I never had so many rows with any other person as I had with him."

Borglum's pre-Rushmore row was so big he had to flee the state of Georgia. In 1925 he was working to carve giant Confederate figures into Georgia's Stone Mountain, but the project's backers fired him for excessive spending and his "ungovernable temper." Some of the people backing Borglum's monument were affiliated with the Ku Klux Klan—and they said *he* was too angry. He proved them right by smashing the models, which technically belonged to the monument association, which called on the sheriff to arrest Borglum. The authorities chased the sculptor right up to the state line into North Carolina.

But despite his temper, Borglum the artist usually won over even those who were exasperated by Borglum the man. "The faces are in the mountain," he said, over and over. "All I have to do is bring them out." And people believed him: the workers kept trudging up 506 steps every day to set dynamite and chisel rock high on the peak, and lawmakers kept raising funds and fending off critics. Engineers told South Dakota's US senator Peter Norbeck it would be too difficult to carve the roads he'd proposed for tourists to access the site, but Norbeck insisted they go forward: "With enough dynamite," he told them, "anything is possible." It's not a slogan you'd want to print on national currency, but Borglum proved it correct, working right up until his unexpected death in 1941. Lincoln Borglum supervised the remaining work and added an extra touch: a bust of his father, which visitors pass by on their way in and out of the site.

On summer days the crowds at Rushmore are enormous, but at night you can breathe a little bit; the Park Service conducts a lighting ceremony at 9 p.m., and you can stroll around without bumping into people or walking in front of their cameras as they take photos. Light piano music plays over PA speakers; the café sells Thomas Jefferson–themed vanilla ice cream. I take a seat in the outdoor auditorium, surrounded by families passing around their smartphones to smile over the day's vacation photos. Several of us try to take a photo of Rushmore in the dark, which proves unsuccessful to a ridiculous degree.

The ceremony starts with a short speech by a park ranger. "Mount Rushmore isn't just a tribute to four presidents," she says. "It's a national symbol that represents the legacy that they leave behind, and how each and every one of us is a part of their legacy."

She ticks down why each of the giant faces is on the mountain. Washington "represents the history of the United States, from the Revolutionary War to our role overseas today." Jefferson, she says, represents not only westward expansion but those who "value education and free thinking." Lincoln "was able to lay the groundwork of the abolition of slavery." Theodore Roosevelt had been one of Borglum's benefactors, and the sculptor probably liked the idea of putting one of his friends on the mountain, but the park ranger says TR championed the national park system.

"Mount Rushmore is for everybody," she says. "It isn't just a tribute to four courageous men in our country's past. It is a reminder that day after day we follow in their footsteps. . . . And though our accomplishments may never be as great as theirs, or as nationally significant, our accomplishments matter. What you do today matters, what you do tomorrow matters." She explains that "the lights will begin to unveil this wondrous sculpture. And as you stare up at Mount Rushmore, think about what this mountain means to you. But know that if it inspires you, makes you hopeful, angry, frustrated, or even sad, that Mount Rushmore is *still* for you, and that you will always be these presidents' legacy."

Mount Rushmore *has* made people angry, frustrated, and sad. The name comes from a New York attorney who was only in the Black

Hills to assess nineteenth-century mining claims; the Lakota people, who lived in the area and believed the hills to be the place where their ancestors were created, called it "Six Grandfathers," for heaven, earth, and the four cardinal directions. They have rarely been thrilled with the four giant white guys on top of their sacred place—which they had to give up to the US government less than a decade after it was promised to the Lakota for all time.*

This tension is what led to the construction of the Crazy Horse monument just minutes from Rushmore. Boston-born sculptor Korczak Ziolkowski had come to South Dakota in 1939 to work on the presidents, but he ended up working on the competing sculpture at the behest of Sioux chief Henry Standing Bear, who told him, "We would like the white man to know the red men have great heroes also." Ziolkowski's work, which began in 1948, has been in progress for decades. When it's finished it will be over five hundred feet high—even higher than Rushmore.

Mount Rushmore has played host to protests, too. In 1970, the American Indian Movement set up camp atop the mountain, demanding the government return land taken for military use during World War II. In 2009, authorities arrested eleven Greenpeace activists who had snuck onto the mountain and unfurled a sixty-five-foot banner next to Lincoln's head, calling for action on climate change. The National Park Service cut off access to the mountain and conducted 3-D scans of the sculptures, just in case the next protesters—or terrorists—brought something more explosive than a banner.

Even these critics of the mountain are part of the legacy of the Rushmore four. I can believe that we're all part of the presidents' legacies. But maybe it works the other way around, too. Without Terry Simpson, the museum director who showed me around William Henry Harrison's tomb in southwestern Ohio, the ninth president might not have much of a legacy to be part of. We wouldn't have Hoover-Ball without Herbert Hoover, but we wouldn't remember it without the teams in West Branch that come out each summer to play

---

* The sudden change came after white settlers discovered gold in the hills.

it. The presidents are fodder for giant, majestic works of art, but we're the ones who build in their images.

We couldn't do a Mount Rushmore today. For one thing, we'd argue too much about which heads to put on top of the mountain. There have been calls at times for carving Ronald Reagan, Franklin Roosevelt, and John F. Kennedy into the mountain; some have even suggested adding nonpresidents, like Frederick Douglass, or Elvis. The mountain can't support a fifth head, but people keep arguing about which head it is that we can't put up there.*

Heck, we even argue about imaginary Rushmores. LeBron James irked basketball pundits by declaring he would be atop basketball's Mount Rushmore by the time he retired. "I'm going to be one of the top four to ever play this game," he said, adding that "architects" would have "to chisel somebody's face out and put mine up there." There is no actual Mount Rushmore of basketball, and the game's Hall of Fame has neither chisels nor a shortage of room for great players, but sports fans went at each other for weeks about whether King James belonged on "basketball's Rushmore." Maybe the park rangers could weave this into their talks before the lighting ceremonies. "If you think LeBron James is better than Oscar Robertson or Magic Johnson, Mount Rushmore is *still* for you."

There's been a big change in the way we honor presidents. Before the twentieth century, before broadcasting brought the voices and faces of national figures into our houses, presidents were pretty remote, so our monuments turned them into icons. Today, presidents are human. We see and hear them all the time. We know historic change doesn't always come from what a president does or doesn't do, and we know their personal and professional failings, sometimes better than they do. We don't even need to build monuments to them anymore; through the presidential library system they can try to build

---

* There was barely room, in fact, for a *fourth* head. Jefferson was originally supposed to go on the other side of Washington, but the rock there proved inadequate for further carving. Workers had to dynamite more than a year of work and start over on George's other side.

their own. Maybe that's why, in 2011, the government announced it would scale back a presidential commemorative coin program due to high cost and low interest. "As will shock you all," said Vice President Joe Biden at the time, "calls for Chester A. Arthur coins are not big."

But maybe America still has room for a presidential monument or two, just on a smaller scale. Down the road from Rushmore is Rapid City, South Dakota, which calls itself "the most patriotic city in America" and shows it with a full set of life-size presidential statues. Some of the figures are exactly what you'd expect, like Harry Truman holding up the "Dewey Defeats Truman" newspaper, or Dwight Eisenhower in his World War II general's outfit. Some are even duplicates of works I've seen elsewhere: the Van Buren sculpture is the same as the one in downtown Kinderhook, New York, and I saw the Jefferson statue at a bus station in Chicago.

Others are pleasant surprises. Rapid City doesn't portray William Howard Taft as large and jolly; instead, he's athletic and shrewd—baseball's first First Fan is hunched over with a baseball in his right hand; he's ready to throw to a batter, and the gleam in his eye suggests he's going to throw a strike. George W. Bush holds his dog, Barney, in one hand and gives a thumbs-up with the other, but with so many cars around, "43" appears to be asking for a ride. Richard Nixon sits under a tree, his hands together, pondering the intricacies of foreign policy—but the pose also makes him look like a supervillain.

The statues face each other on street corners. Jimmy Carter's statue is waving; the wave looks as if it's intended for Ronald Reagan, who's across the street, while Andrew Jackson seems to watch them both from a distance: his statue reminded me of the line in "The Farmer in the Dell" about the cheese standing alone. The glum Millard Fillmore sets down his law book and peers over at Woodrow Wilson, trying to figure out what the fuss is about. The statues also interact with the surrounding buildings: Franklin Pierce, who had troubles with the bottle, stands outside a pub. Teddy Roosevelt, decked out in his Rough Rider gear, stands near a coffee shop named in his honor: Bully Blends. And the sight of John Quincy Adams and Gerald Ford next to banners proclaiming "Welcome Bikers" is as good as it gets.

There is no more space atop Mount Rushmore—the epitome of how we once looked up to our presidents. But in downtown Rapid City, where presidents are honored at our size and at our level, there's room for eighty statues in all—plenty of room to grow.

ACKNOWLEDGMENTS

Thanks first and foremost to my wife, Sonya, who kept our family running while I was traveling, and our kids, the best people in the world to come home to after a trip.

My parents and siblings encouraged my presidential hobby all those years ago and still encourage me today.

Farley Chase at Chase Literary Agency found my project on the Web and reached out on a hunch that a good book might come out of it. I hope this has proven him right. Not only did he patiently walk me through the process of planning and pitching a book, he even made his own trip to Buffalo to visit Millard Fillmore's grave. There's no better sign of dedication than that.

My editor, Matt Weiland, made this book immeasurably better with his ideas and suggestions, and made writing the book immeasurably easier with his kindness and perfectly timed Spiro Agnew references. Thanks also to Sam MacLaughlin, Remy Cawley, and everyone at W. W. Norton & Company.

My friend Mick Walsh let me stay with her during two long trips to DC, helped me find my way around the city, and got my weak stomach through a tour of a museum of morbid anatomy.

Many thanks to those who took the time to talk with me, show me around on my travels, or send me ideas and information. Most of them are mentioned in the book, but a few who aren't deserve to be named here: Karen Bachmann and Joanna Ebenstein of the Morbid Anatomy Museum in New York, Dollie Boyd at Tusculum College, Andrew Clark, Stacy Conradt of *Mental Floss* magazine, Darren Garnick, Rebekah Hinckley, Becky Kraemer, Jann Mirkov, Jacqueline Santos at the Association for Gravestone Studies, Tom Schwartz and Lynn Smith of the Herbert Hoover Presidential Library and Museum, Kristin Sherry of the Hoover Presidential Foundation, Amity Shlaes and Rushad Thomas at the Calvin Coolidge Presidential Foundation, Richard Norton Smith, and Anne Wheeler at the Lyndon Baines Johnson Library and Museum.

Thanks to my friends and colleagues at New Hampshire Public Radio for their encouragement and kindness, especially Rebecca Lavoie Flynn.

Thanks to the earliest backers of my trips: Erin Barnes, Charles and Samantha Behensky, Matthew Cain, Claudia Cowden, Sarah Fraser, Ben Leubsdorf, Mike Ostrego, Michael Saffell, Jonathan and Caroline Carter Smith, and Scott Vesely.

Finally, many thanks to Anna Brandenburg, Deb Baker, and the staff at the Concord, New Hampshire, Public Library, which received an endowment of $1,000 to help fund "the purchase of books" from none other than Franklin Pierce. So, thanks to him as well, I guess.

NOTES

Introduction

3 **"break a horse, dance a minuet."** Sullivan, George. *Mr. President: A Book of U.S. Presidents.* New York: Scholastic, 1984. 28.

3 **charged up San Juan Hill.** Sullivan 101.

3 **"Uncle Jumbo."** Sullivan 93.

5 **an attempt to steal his body.** Craughwell, Thomas J. *Stealing Lincoln's Body.* Cambridge: Harvard University Press, 2009. 195.

5 **Dwight D. Eisenhower System.** Pfeiffer, David A. "Ike's Interstates at 50: Anniversary of the Highway System Recalls Eisenhower's Role as Catalyst." *Prologue* 38.2 (Summer 2006). 26 Mar. 2015. <http://www.archives.gov/publications/prologue/2006/summer/interstates.html>

5 **a tribute to "Old Kinderhook."** Richman, Irwin. *Hudson River: From New York City to Albany.* Charleston, SC: Arcadia Publishing, 2001. 7.

5 **named Woodrow Wilson Guthrie.** Dicaire, David. *The Early Years of Folk Music: Fifty Founders of the Tradition.* Jefferson, NC: McFarland, 2010. 99.

5 **named for the first President Roosevelt.** "The Story of the Teddy Bear." Theodore Roosevelt Birthplace National Historic Site. 26 Mar. 2015. <http://www.nps.gov/thrb/learn/historyculture/storyofteddybear.htm>

5 **named for the second President Johnson.** "JSC History." Johnson Space Center. 26 Mar. 2015. <http://www.jsc.nasa.gov/history/jsc_history.htm>

5 **hidden away in the Smithsonian.** "Landmark Object: George Wash-

253

ington Statue, 1841." National Museum of American History. 1 Oct. 2012. <http://americanhistory.si.edu/press/fact-sheets/landmark-object-george-washington-statue-1841>

6   **James A. Garfield medicinal powders.** Garfield Tea Company. "Label of Garfield Tea." Brooklyn, NY.

6   **at twelve times normal size.** "Carving the Mountain." *American Experience.* 12 Mar. 2015. <http://www.pbs.org/wgbh/americanexperience/features/general-article/rushmore-carving/>

6   **sticking his fingers in the gunshot wound.** Millard, Candice. *Destiny of the Republic: A Tale of Madness, Medicine and the Murder of a President.* New York: Anchor Books, 2011. ePub file. Ch. 22.

6   **disinterred almost 150 years after his death.** "Zachary Taylor's Body Taken from Crypts for Arsenic Tests." *Los Angeles Times.* 18 Jun. 1991. 11 Dec. 2013. <http://articles.latimes.com/1991-06-18/news/mn-1004_1_zachary-taylor-s-body>

6   **"there's nothing left to do but get drunk."** Atkinson, David. "Franklin Pierce (1853–1857)." *US Presidents and Foreign Policy.* Ed. Carl Cavanagh Hodge. Santa Barbara, CA: ABC-CLIO, 2007. 117.

Chapter 1: Monument Man

9   **a relatively modest farmhouse.** Howard, Hugh, and Roger Straus III. *Houses of the Presidents: Childhood Homes, Family Dwellings, Private Escapes, and Grand Estates.* New York: Little, Brown, 2012. 12.

9   **a peak of 8,000 acres.** "Exploring Mount Vernon." *Smithsonian.* 1 Nov. 2006. 12 Mar. 2015. <http://www.smithsonianmag.com/history/exploring-mount-vernon-138174820/?no-ist>

10   **nearly eighty million.** Howard 16.

11   **"I now make it my earnest prayer."** Washington, George. "Circular Letter Addressed to the Governors of All the States on the Disbanding of the Army, June 14, 1783." *Writings of George Washington,* ed. Jared Sparks (Boston, 1835), 8:452.

12   **he stated in his will.** Washington, George. "George Washington's 1799 Will and Testament." George Washington's Mount Vernon. 9 Jul. 1799. 12 Mar. 2015. <http://www.mountvernon.org/educational-resources/primary-sources-2/article/george-washingtons-1799-will-and-testament/>

12   **voted to build "an equestrian statue."** Minta, Anna. "Planning a National Pantheon: Monuments in Washington, D.C. and the Creation of Symbolic Space." *Public Space and the Ideology of Place in American Culture.* Ed. Miles Orvell and Jeffrey L. Meikle. New York: Rodopi, 2009. 25–27.

12   **a large equestrian statue of King George III.** Chernow, Ron. *Washington: A Life.* New York: Penguin, 2010. ePub file. Ch. 20.

12   **renamed the "Federal City."** "Washington, D.C. History F.A.Q." Historical Society of Washington, D.C. 12 Mar. 2015. <http://www.dchistory.org/publications/dc-history-faq/>

12   **continued to use the city's old name.** "To Alexander Hamilton from George

Washington, 1 September 1796," Founders Online, National Archives. 12 Mar. 2015. <http://founders.archives.gov/documents/Hamilton/01-20-02-0199> Source: *The Papers of Alexander Hamilton*, vol. 20, *January 1796–March 1797*. Ed. Harold C. Syrett. New York: Columbia University Press, 1974. 311–314.

13 **succumbed to a throat infection.** "The Death of George Washington." George Washington's Mount Vernon. 12 Mar. 2015. <http://www .mountvernon.org/research-collections/digital-encyclopedia/article/ the-death-of-george-washington/>

13 **a massive public funeral at Mount Vernon.** "Mourning George Washington." George Washington's Mount Vernon. 12 Mar. 2015. <http://www .mountvernon.org/research-collections/digital-encyclopedia/article/mourn ing-george-washington/>

13 **"three general discharges of infantry."** Jeffers, H. Paul. *Freemasons: A History and Exploration of the World's Oldest Secret Society*. New York: Citadel Press, 2005. 60–61.

13 **mourning clothes.** "Mourning George Washington."

13 **shortages of black cloth.** Gragg, Rod. *George Washington: An Interactive Biography*. Gretna, LA: Pelican Publishing, 2012. 8.

13 **"mingle our tears with yours."** "Mourning George Washington."

14 **struck coins to mark the occasion.** Adams, Betty. "Montville Man Has Rare George Washington Funeral Medal." *CentralMaine.com*. 15 Jul. 2012. 12 Mar. 2015. <http://www.centralmaine.com/2012/07/15/rare-washington-me dalmontville-man-has-minted-funeral-coin-for-1st-president_2012-07-14/>

14 **"an exemplar of moral values."** Chernow ch. 19.

14 **angels welcome the general into heaven.** "The Apotheosis of Washington." *LearnNC.org*. 12 Mar. 2015. <http://www.learnnc.org/lp/multimedia/6289>

14 **a book by Parson Weems.** Uva, Katie. "Parson Weems." George Washington's Mount Vernon. 12 Mar. 2015. <http://www.mountvernon.org/ research-collections/digital-encyclopedia/article/parson-weems/>

14 **Washington had left specific instructions.** "George Washington's 1799 Will and Testament."

15 **"half inch fir board, now rotting away."** Faux, W. *Memorable Days in America: Being a Journal of a Tour to the United States, Principally Undertaken to Ascertain, by Positive Evidence, the Condition and Probable Prospects of British Emigrants; Including Accounts of Mr. Birkbeck's Settlement in the Illinois: and Intended to Shew Men and Things as They Are in America*. W. Simkin & R. Marshall, 1823. 471.

15 **the Old Tomb was prone to flood damage.** Craughwell, Thomas J. *Stealing Lincoln's Body*. Cambridge: Harvard University Press, 2009. 77–78.

16 **spent the next thirty years right where it was.** Wineberger, James Albert. *The Tomb of Washington at Mount Vernon*. Washington: T. McGill, 1857. 39–41.

16 **"mournful, filial pilgrimage."** Willard, Emma. *History of the United States, or Republic of America: Exhibited in Connexion with Its Chronology and Progressive Geography by Means of a Series of Maps*. New York: White, Gallaher & White, 1829. 300.

16 **a steady stream of visitors.** Wilstach, Paul. *Mount Vernon: Washington's Home and the Nation's Shrine*. New York: Doubleday, Page, 1916. 234.

16 **the first presidential grave robbery.** Craughwell 77–78.

17 **built a crypt under the Rotunda.** Minta 25–27.

17 **a grieving Martha Washington's approval.** Wineberger 49.

17 **finally put a stop to the plan.** "The Resolution to Bury President George Washington at the U.S. Capitol." History, Art & Archives: United States House of Representatives. 12 Mar. 2015. <http://history.house.gov/Historical Highlight/Detail/36506?ret=True>

17 **designed a new sarcophagus.** Wineberger 44.

17 **which *Harper's New Monthly Magazine* described.** Strickland, William. *Tomb of Washington, at Mount Vernon.* Philadelphia: Carey and Hart, 1840. 33–35.

18 **have gone up for auction.** Associated Press. "George Washington's Hair Sold for $17K." *USA Today.* 26 Feb. 2008. 12 Mar. 2015. <http://usatoday30. usatoday.com/news/offbeat/2008-02-26-washington-hair_N.htm?csp=34>

19 **went back to the Mount Vernon mansion.** Strickland 36.

19 **"a small circular hole."** Wilstach 249.

19 **lawmakers commissioned a statue.** Tuckerman, Henry T. *A Memorial of Horatio Greenough, Consisting of a Memoir, Selections from His Writings, and Tributes to His Genius.* New York: G. P. Putnam, 1853. 55.

19 **used a famous statue of Zeus.** Esteves, Maggie. "Washington on Display." *U.S. Capitol Historical Society—A Blog of History.* 20 Jan. 2012. 1 Oct. 2012. <https://uschs.wordpress.com/2012/01/20/washington-on-display/>

19 **Washington is seated.** Tuckerman 55.

20 **"It is a ridiculous affair."** Esteves.

20 **"entering or leaving a bath."** Callahan, North. *Thanks, Mr. President: The Trail-Blazing Second Term of George Washington.* Cranbury, NJ: Cornwall Books, 1991. 59.

20 **would buckle under the sculpture's weight.** Hughes, Will. "Horatio Greenough's Near Naked Washington." *Boundary Stones: WETA's Local History Blog.* 22 May 2013. 12 Mar. 2015. <http://blogs.weta.org/boundarystones/2013/05/22/ horatio-greenough%E2%80%99s-near-naked-washington>

20 **"This magnificent production of genius."** "Landmark Object: George Washington Statue, 1841." National Museum of American History. 1 Oct. 2012. <http://americanhistory.si.edu/press/fact-sheets/landmark-object-geoge -washington-statue-1841>

21 **shirtless president was reaching for his clothes.** "George Washington, Sculpture by Horatio Greenough, 1840." *Legacies: Collecting America's History at the Smithsonian.* 1 Oct. 2012. <http://www.smithsonianlegacies.si.edu/ objectdescription.cfm?ID=66>

21 **finally donated in 1908 to the Smithsonian.** "Landmark Object: George Washington Statue, 1841."

21 **out of sight until the bicentennial.** Minta 25–27.

21 **the monument's initial design.** Hansen, Brett. "Orchestrating the Obelisk: The Washington Monument." *Civil Engineering* 78.7 (July 2008). 38.

21 **"driven by Winged Victory."** Allen, Thomas B. *The Washington Monument: It Stands for All.* New York: Discovery Books, 2000.

21 **cornerstone wasn't laid until Independence Day 1848.** Hansen 39.

22 **guest of honor: President Zachary Taylor.** Maples, William R., and Michael Browning. *Dead Men Do Tell Tales.* New York: Doubleday, 1994. 223–37.

22 **funding had completely dried up.** Hansen 39.

22 **Mills died in 1855.** Allen.

23 **anti-immigrant, anti-Catholic Know-Nothings.** Hansen 39.

23 **a turning point around Independence Day 1876.** Hansen 40.

23 **finished in 1885.** Allen.

23 **"nobody outside Washington shows any interest in it."** "The Washington Monument, and Mr. Story's Design." *Atlantic Monthly* 43.258 (April 1879). 524.

23 **a marvel of engineering and design.** Minta 26.

24 **a Senate commission studying the park system.** "A Chronology of the Mall." *The National Mall: Rethinking Washington's Monumental Core.* Ed. Nathan Glazer and Cynthia R. Field. Baltimore: Johns Hopkins University Press, 2008. 181–82.

24 **more than a year's worth of work.** Hendrix, Steve. "Washington Monument Reopens After $15 Million Repair Project." *Washington Post.* 12 May 2014. 13 Mar. 2015. <http://www.washingtonpost.com/local/washington-monument-attracts-line-of-eager-visitors-as-it-reopens-after-repairs/2014/05/12/1f71658e-d9d0-11e3-8009-71de85b9c527_story.html>

Chapter 2: Well-Timed Exits

25 **"Mausoleums, statues, monuments."** Adams, John. Letter to Benjamin Rush. 23 Mar. 1809.

25 **doubled its size.** Howard, Hugh, and Roger Straus III. *Houses of the Presidents: Childhood Homes, Family Dwellings, Private Escapes, and Grand Estates.* New York: Little, Brown, 2012. 21–22.

26 **a farmer alter ego.** Saltman, Helen Saltzberg. "John Adams's Earliest Essays: The Humphrey Ploughjogger Letters." *William and Mary Quarterly* 37.1 (Jan. 1980). 125.

26 **a serious agricultural agenda.** Eagle, Corliss Knapp. "John Adams, Farmer and Gardener." *Arnoldia* 61.4 (2002). 10–12.

26 **"raise enuff Hemp."** *Papers of John Adams.* Cambridge: Harvard University Press, 2003. 66.

26 **"do me good like a Medicine."** Eagle 12.

26 **Adams was also fond of manure.** Eagle 10.

26 **Peacefield stayed in the family.** Howard and Straus 27.

27 **asked for a toast.** Grant, James D. *John Adams: Party of One.* New York: Farrar, Straus & Giroux, 2005. 450.

27 **slipped in and out of consciousness.** McCullough, David. *John Adams.* New York: Simon & Schuster, 2001. 645.

27 **"Thomas Jefferson survives."** Grant 450.

27 **had, like Adams, seen his body fail.** Crawford, Alan Pell. *Twilight at Monticello: The Final Years of Thomas Jefferson.* New York: Random House, 2008. 241.

28 **noted in his diary.** Adams, John Quincy. Diary 35, 25 Jan. 1823–31 Oct. 1826, 5 Nov. 1828, and 15 Aug. 1844, 331 [electronic edition]. *The Diaries of John Quincy Adams: A Digital Collection.* Boston: Massachusetts Historical Society, 2005. <http://www.masshist.org/jqadiaries>

28 **allowed themselves to pass on.** Battin, Margaret Pabst. "July 4, 1826: Explaining the Same-Day Deaths of John Adams and Thomas Jefferson." *Historically Speaking: The Bulletin of the Historical Society* 6.6 (Jul./Aug. 2005). 27 Dec. 2013. <http://www.bu.edu/historic/battin.htm>

28 **"No, Doctor, nothing more."** Crawford 241.

28 **seem to hold off death.** Battin.

28 **willed himself not to die on Christmas.** DeFrank, Thomas M. *Write It When I'm Gone: Remarkable Off-the-Record Conversations with Gerald R. Ford.* New York: Penguin, 2007. 241.

28 **Their political rivalry.** McCullough 488.

28 **"eaten to a honeycomb"; "vain, irritable."** McCullough 488–89.

29 **the friendship picked up.** Crawford 85.

29 **"Help me, child."** McCullough 646.

29 **barely spoke to each other.** Gibbs, Nancy, and Michael Duffy. *The Presidents Club: Inside the World's Most Exclusive Fraternity.* New York: Simon & Schuster, 2012. 155-7.

29 **repeated those words at Ford's funeral.** DeFrank 140.

29 **when one died, the other would speak.** Gibbs 351.

29 **"lingered until this time."** Hone, Philip. *The Diary of Philip Hone, 1828–1851.* New York: Dodd, Mead, 1889. 214.

30 **offered Madison stimulants.** Lamb, Brian. *Who's Buried in Grant's Tomb? A Tour of Presidential Gravesites.* New York: PublicAffairs, 2010. 17.

30 **"Nothing more than a change of *mind*."** Jennings, Paul. *A Colored Man's Reminiscences of James Madison.* Brooklyn: G. C. Beadle, 1865. 20–21.

30 **long underwear made of chamois leather.** Manners, William. *TR and Will: A Friendship That Split the Republican Party.* New York: Harcourt, Brace & World, 1969. 33.

30 **an intellectual lightweight.** Kaufman, Bill. "He Died of the Presidency." *American Enterprise* 17.3 (April 2006). 45.

31 **"tickled with the presidency."** Woodworth, Steven E. *Manifest Destinies: America's Westward Expansion and the Road to the Civil War.* New York: Alfred A. Knopf, 2010. 27–28.

31 **"the present imbecile chief."** "What Becomes an Ex-President Most." *Newsweek.* 21 Mar. 1993. 19 Apr. 2014. <http://www.newsweek.com/what-becomes-ex-president-most-190936>

31 **"Granny."** Dacre, Henry. *Granny Harrison Delivering the Country of the Executive Federalist.* 1840. Lithograph on wove paper. Library of Congress Prints and Photographs Division, Washington, DC.

31 **"if my life should be spared."** Collins, Herbert R., and David B. Weaver. *Wills of the US Presidents.* New York: Stravon Educational Press, 1976. 81.

32 **"killed seventeen Roman proconsuls."** Kaufman 45.

33 **"staggered upstairs to revive himself."** May, Gary. *John Tyler: The American Presidents Series: The 10th President, 1841–1845.* New York: Macmillan, 2008. 3.

33 **sank into delirium.** "Death of the President." *American President: A Reference Resource.* 14 Mar. 2015. <http://millercenter.org/president/harrison/essays/bio graphy/6>

33 **to carry out the principles of government.** Greene, Meg. *William H. Harrison.* Minneapolis: Twenty-First Century Books, 2007. 91.

33 **stored in Congressional Cemetery.** Lamb 37.

34 **a restoration in 1879.** "Harrison Tomb." *Ohio History Central.* 20 Nov. 2014. <http://www.ohiohistorycentral.org/w/Harrison_Tomb>

35 **lowest point in 1912.** "Youth Imprisoned for Four Hours in Burial Place." *Mountain Advocate.* 22 Nov. 1912. 20 Nov. 2014. <http://www.newspapers .com/newspage/71204293/>

36 **a year to live and about two hundred dollars.** Rocca, Mo. "Ulysses S. Grant's Last Battle." *CBS Sunday Morning.* 17 Feb. 2013. 15 Jul. 2014. <http:// www.cbsnews.com/news/ulysses-s-grants-last-battle/>

36 **become a regular cigar smoker.** Flood 111.

37 **the book was keeping him alive.** Flood, Charles Bracelen. *Grant's Final Victory: Ulysses S. Grant's Heroic Last Year.* Boston: Da Capo Press, 2012. 164.

37 **"GRANT IS DYING."** Flood 131.

38 **"it might make the place a national shrine."** Howard and Straus 94.

39 **jabbed the cocaine water in.** Olson, James Stuart, ed. *The History of Cancer: An Annotated Bibliography.* Westport, CT: Greenwood Press, 1989. 91.

39 **"Every year the New York State Department of Parks and Recreation measures."** Rocca.

39 **declared his manuscript finished.** King, Gilbert. "War and Peace of Mind for Ulysses S. Grant." *Smithsonian.* 16 Jan. 2013. 15 Jul. 2014. <http:// www.smithsonianmag.com/history/war-and-peace-of-mind-for-ulysses-s -grant-1882227/>

39 **stopping the hands of the clock.** Flood 228–29.

39 **the joke was on W. J. Arkell.** Goldhurst, Richard. *Many Are the Hearts: The Agony and the Triumph of Ulysses S. Grant.* New York: Reader's Digest Press, 1975. 253.

39 **five thousand visitors each year.** Post, Paul. "Saratoga Spa State Park Had Record 2.9 Million Visitors in 2013." *Saratogian,* 26 Feb. 2014. 15 Jul. 2014. <http://www.saratogian.com/general-news/20140226/saratoga-spa-state -park-had-record-29-million-visitors-in-2013>

40 **"The prison is closing."** Yusko, Dennis. "Uncertainty over Grant Cottage." *Albany Times-Union.* 28 Sept. 2013. 16 Jul. 2014. <http://www.timesunion .com/local/article/Uncertainty-over-Grant-Cottage-4853274.php>

40 **Forty-three acres and a new private well.** Yusko, Dennis. "Grant Cottage Reopens Amid a Changed Mountaintop." *Albany Times-Union.* 22 May 2015. 14 Jul. 2015. <http://blog.timesunion.com/saratogaseen/grant-cottage -reopens-amid-a-changed-mountain/24027/>

40 **"mud, exhaustion, horrible suspense."** Richard, Paul. "The Gen. Ulysses S. Grant Memorial." *Washington Post.* 19 Aug. 2001. 5 Mar. 2014.

<http://www.washingtonpost.com/gog/museums/the-gen.-ulysses-s.-grant-memorial,1064187.html>

41   **"public demonstration."** Flood 195.

41   **five miles long through Manhattan.** Flood photo sec.

41   **More than a million people.** Lamb 75–76.

41   **The pallbearers included.** "Grant's Funeral March." *American Experience.* 12 Jul. 2014. <http://www.pbs.org/wgbh/americanexperience/features/gen eral-article/grant-funeral/>

41   **was 150 feet high.** McShane, Larry. "Grant Won the Civil War, but His N.Y. Tomb Is Losing the Urban Wars." *Los Angeles Times,* 19 Dec. 1993. 13 Jul. 2014. <http://articles.latimes.com/1993-12-19/news/mn-3462_1_civil-war>

41   **largest mausoleum in North America.** Lamb 75–76.

41   **opted for the uptown location.** Flood 221.

42   **Grant's reputation faltered.** Waugh, Joan. *U.S. Grant: American Hero, American Myth.* Chapel Hill: University of North Carolina Press, 2009. 303-4.

42   **graffiti and grime.** McShane, Larry. "Grant's Tomb: Graffiti, Budget Cuts Plague Once-Proud Site." *Seattle Times.* 13 Dec. 1991. 13 Jul. 2014. <http://community.seattletimes.nwsource.com/archive/?date=19911213&s lug=1322741>

42   **turned the site over to the National Park Service.** McShane, "Grant Won."

42   **asked for no public bathrooms on-site.** "Frequently Asked Questions." General Grant National Memorial. 14 Mar. 2015. <http://www.nps.gov/gegr/ faqs.htm>

43   **appeared in newspapers at least as early as 1930.** Shapiro, Fred R., ed. *The Yale Book of Quotations.* New Haven: Yale University Press, 2006. 497.

43   **walk away from the show empty-handed.** Gehring, Wes D. *The Marx Brothers: A Bio-bibliography.* Westport, CT: Greenwood Press, 1987. 90–91.

43   **offered to take Grant's body.** Kendall, Peter. "Move on to Put Grant's Tomb in Happier State." *Chicago Tribune.* 1 Apr. 1994. 12 Mar. 2015. <http://articles.chicagotribune.com/1994-04-01/news/9404010278_1_frank -scaturro-ulysses-s-grant-volunteer-work>

43   **restored Grant's Tomb.** "Ulysses S. Grant's Tomb Re-Opens After Restoration." Stan Bernard, correspondent. *NBC Nightly News.* 27 Apr. 1997. On the Web: *NBC Learn.* 5 Sept. 2012. 13 Jul. 2014. <http://archives.nbclearn .com/portal/site/k-12/flatview?cuecard=524#>

44   **the great state of Franklin.** Means, Howard B. *The Avenger Takes His Place: Andrew Johnson and the 45 Days That Changed the Nation.* Orlando: Harcourt, 2006. 42.

44   **"the dam spirits that infest Greeneville."** Means 49–50.

44   **sneered at him as a "mudsill."** Means 39–40.

45   **as military governor of Tennessee.** Means 77.

46   **decided to go straight to the public.** "The Campaign and Election of 1866." *American President: A Reference Resource.* 20 Jul. 2014. <http://millercenter.org/ president/johnson/essays/biography/3>

46   **made Johnson sound unhinged.** Oder, Broeck N. "Andrew Johnson and

the 1866 Illinois Election." *Journal of the Illinois State Historical Society* 73.3 (Autumn 1980). 190.

47 **"intemperate, inflammatory, and scandalous harangues."** "The Impeachment of Andrew Johnson (1868), President of the United States." United States Senate. 14 Mar. 2015. <http://www.senate.gov/artandhistory/ history/common/briefing/Impeachment_Johnson.htm>

47 **acquiesce to Congress's wishes.** "Impeachment of Andrew Johnson." *American President: A Reference Resource.* 20 Jul. 2014. <http://millercenter.org/ president/johnson/essays/biography/4>

47 **a group of White House mice.** Farquhar, Michael. *A Treasury of Great American Scandals.* New York: Penguin, 2003.

47 **"Thank God for the vindication."** "Life After the Presidency." *American President: A Reference Resource.* 20 Jul. 2014. <http://millercenter.org/president/ johnson/essays/biography/6>

47 **a Senate desk covered in flowers.** Hearn, Chester G. *The Impeachment of Andrew Johnson.* Jefferson, NC: McFarland, 2000. 219.

47 **succumbed to a series of strokes.** Lamb 71.

47 **"pillow my head on its Constitution."** Cox, Bob. "Former President John-son Eulogized in Greeneville in 1909." *Johnson City Press.* 14 Oct. 2013. 1 Jan. 2014. <http://www.johnsoncitypress.com/article/111710/former-president-an drew-johnson-eulogized-in-greeneville-in-1909#sthash.1vk1x0Hr.dpuf>

Chapter 3: The First Patient

49 **hired Dr. Basil Norris.** Roos, Charles A. "Physicians to the Presidents, and Their Patients: A Biobibliography." *Bulletin of the Medical Library Association* 49.3 (Jul. 1961). 326–27.

49 **military physicians could be summoned at any time.** Deppisch, Ludwig M. *The White House Physician: A History from Washington to George W. Bush.* Jefferson, NC: McFarland, 2007. 31–33.

49 **Franklin Roosevelt's doctors.** Ferrell, Robert H. *The Dying President: Franklin D. Roosevelt, 1944–1945.* Columbia: University of Missouri Press, 1998. 35–39.

50 **had merely eaten tainted crabmeat.** Deppisch 83.

50 **The museum was founded in 1862.** Ruane, Michael E. "Skulls, Bones and Bullets in Refurbished Military Medical Museum Opening Monday." *Washington Post.* 20 May 2012. 18 Jun. 2014. <http://www.washingtonpost.com/ local/skulls-bones-and-bullets-in-refurbished-military-medical-museum-opening-monday/2012/05/20/gIQAwT1odU_story.html>

50 **sent this museum the leg he lost.** Carlson, Peter. "Rest in Pieces." *Washington Post.* 24 Jan. 2006. 7 Jun. 2014. <http://www.washingtonpost.com/ wp-dyn/content/article/2006/01/23/AR2006012301854_pf.html>

50 **several small pieces of Abraham Lincoln's skull.** "'His Wound Is Mortal; It Is Impossible for Him to Recover'—The Final Hours of President Abraham Lincoln." National Museum of Health and Medicine. 14 Mar. 2015. <http://

www.medicalmuseum.mil/index.cfm?p=exhibits.current.collection_that_
teaches.lincoln.page_03>

50 **Booth was put into storage.** Carlson.

51 **"the backbone of an angleworm."** Flood, Charles Bracelen. *Grant's Final Victory: Ulysses S. Grant's Heroic Last Year.* Boston: Da Capo Press, 2012. 4.

51 **"the Heroic Sufferer."** "He Is Dead." *Chicago Daily Tribune.* 20 Sep. 1881. 3 Jun. 2014. <https://garfieldnps.wordpress.com/2012/08/05/the-tragedy-and-triumph-of-president-james-a-garfield-and-alexander-graham-bell/>

51 **"Canal Boy."** Rutkow, Ira. *James A. Garfield: The American Presidents Series: The 20th President, 1881.* New York: Macmillan, 2006. 10.

52 **keep the patient comfortable.** Millard, Candice. *Destiny of the Republic: A Tale of Madness, Medicine and the Murder of a President.* New York: Anchor Books, 2011. ePub file. Ch. 14.

52 **"he would have gone home in a matter of two or three days."** Schaffer, Amanda. "A President Felled by an Assassin and 1880s Medical Care." *New York Times.* 25 Jul. 2006. 7 Jun. 2014. <http://www.nytimes.com/2006/07/25/health/25garf.html?ex=1311480000&en=82dc6ab325dafec6&ei=5090&partner=rssuserland&emc=rss&_r=0>

52 **his legal first name was "Doctor."** Millard ch. 12.

52 **the swarm of doctors.** Millard ch. 14.

53 **landed in some fatty deposits near his pancreas.** Schaffer.

53 **"just took charge of it."** Millard ch. 14.

53 **the president's chronic digestive problems.** Millard ch. 16.

53 **a concoction made of beef broth.** Roach, Mary. *Gulp: Adventures on the Alimentary Canal.* New York: W. W. Norton, 2013. 270.

53 **"annoying and offensive flatus."** Bliss, Doctor Willard. *Feeding per Rectum: As Illustrated in the Case of the Late President Garfield and Others.* Washington, 1882. 10.

53 **"a plant of slow growth."** Bliss 2.

54 **Tortured for the Republic.** Millard ch. 18.

54 **"the morbid century."** Michelson, Evan. Personal interview. 10 Jun. 2014.

55 **"no festive demonstrations."** Ogilvie, John Stuart. *History of the Attempted Assassination of James A. Garfield.* New York: J. S. Ogilvie, 1881. 170.

55 **"filled to overflowing with an anxious, surging crowd."** "At the Fifth-Avenue Hotel; Eagerly Awaiting the News—Discussions in the Anxious Throng." *New York Times.* 3 Jul. 1881. 14 Mar. 2015. <http://query.nytimes.com/gst/abstract.html?res=9403E6DC103CEE3ABC4B53DFB166838A699FDE>

55 **a large bronze star on the floor.** Foote, Kenneth E. *Shadowed Ground: America's Landscapes of Violence and Tragedy.* Austin: University of Texas Press, 1997. 41.

55 **Thousands stood not far away.** "A Terrible Death-Watch; Scenes in the President's Chamber Saturday Night—His Anxiety About Mrs. Garfield and His Joy on Her Arrival—Touching Incidents." *New York Times.* 4 Jul. 1881. 14 Mar. 2015. <http://query.nytimes.com/gst/abstract.html?res=9903E4DC103CEE3ABC4C53DFB166838A699FDE>

55 **"She was much excited and unnerved."** "General Telegraph News;

Victims of Suicide. Mrs. Pritchard's Death at Asbury Park—Caused by the Attempted Assassination." *New York Times*. 7 Jul. 1881. 14 Mar. 2015. <http://query.nytimes.com/gst/abstract.html?res=940CEFDC103CEE3ABC4F53DFB166838A699FDE>

55 **"Can't you stop this?"** Rutkow 127.

55 **Garfield's dehydrated, malnourished body.** Millard ch. 22.

56 **"I just shot him."** Schaffer.

56 **Prosecutors produced the backbone.** Millard, Epilogue.

56 **"The lock of hair was the most common."** Michelson.

56 **jabbering to reporters about his own medical prowess.** Ackerman, Kenneth D. *Dark Horse: The Surprise Election and Political Murder of President James A. Garfield*. Falls Church, VA: Viral History Press, 2011. eBook file. Ch. 14.

56 **a $25,000 bill.** Millard, Epilogue.

56 **made of Ohio sandstone.** Sancetta, Amy. "Lawnfield Holds Treasures of Garfield's Presidency." *Cincinnati Enquirer*. 21 Mar. 1999. 25 Jul. 2014. <http://www2.cincinnati.com/travel/stories/032199_garfield.html>

57 **"Death is the impressive incident."** *The Man and the Mausoleum: Dedication of the Garfield Memorial Structure in Cleveland, Ohio, May 13, 1890*. Cleveland: Cleveland Printing and Publishing, 1890. 35.

57 **"colossal allegorical statues."** *The Man and the Mausoleum* 35–36.

58 **made off with several dozen memorial spoons.** Philip, Abby. "Someone Broke into President Garfield's Tomb and Stole His Commemorative Spoons." *Washington Post*. 12 May 2014. 25 May 2014. <http://www.washingtonpost.com/blogs/the-fix/wp/2014/05/12/someone-broke-into-president-garfields-tomb-and-stole-his-commemorative-spoons/>

58 **cut its head off.** Sangiacomo, Michael. "Two Arrested for Stealing Head of Garfield Statue at Hiram College." *Cleveland Plain Dealer*. 29 Jan. 2010. 26 May 2014. <http://blog.cleveland.com/metro/2010/01/two_arrested_for_stealing_head.html>

58 **quietly took down the large assassination markers.** Foote 41.

59 **an estimate from DC engineers in 1936.** "Witness Calls Garfield Death Badly Reported." *Washington Post*. 7 Aug. 1936. 15 Mar. 2015. <http://pqasb.pqarchiver.com/washingtonpost_historical/doc/150768039.html?FMT=ABS&FMTS=ABS:AI&type=historic&date=Aug+7%2C+1936&author=&desc=Witness+Calls+Garfield+Death+Badly+Reported>

59 **through Reagan's left lung.** Deppisch 141.

59 **missed his heart by only an inch or two.** Binder, Leah. "One Surprising Legacy of the Reagan Assassination Attempt." *Forbes*. 30 Mar. 2014. 6 Aug. 2014. <http://www.forbes.com/sites/leahbinder/2014/03/30/one-surprising-legacy-of-the-reagan-assassination-attempt/2/>

59 **more than half of his blood volume.** Abrams, Herbert L. *The President Has Been Shot: Confusion, Disability, and the 25th Amendment*. New York: W. W. Norton, 1992. 64.

59 **"got the same care anyone else got."** Binder.

59 **"you won't let anybody do foolish things to Ronnie."** Deppisch 139.

59 **"When a physician needs help."** Ruge, Daniel. "The President's Physician." *Presidential Disability: Papers, Discussions, and Recommendations on the*

Twenty-Fifth Amendment and Issues of Inability and Disability Among Presidents of the United States. Ed. James F. Toole and Robert J. Joynt. Rochester, NY: University of Rochester Press, 2001. 114.

59 **twelve days after the shooting.** Altman, Lawrence K. "Daniel Ruge, 88, Dies; Cared for Reagan After Shooting." *New York Times.* 6 Sept. 2005. 5 Dec. 2013. <http://www.nytimes.com/2005/09/06/politics/06ruge.html>

60 **"This is it."** Abrams 65.

60 **The White House Medical Unit.** Altman, Lawrence K. "The Rigors of Treating the Patient in Chief." *New York Times.* 15 Nov. 2010. 7 Aug. 2014. <http://www.nytimes.com/2010/11/16/health/views/16docs.html>

60 **the president's "kill zone."** Hedger, Brian. "White Coats in the White House: Former Presidential Physicians Reflect on Their Service." *American Medical News.* 23 Mar. 2009. 13 Oct. 2013. <http://www.amednews.com/article/20090323/profession/303239973/4/>

60 **"you can't treat the president."** Altman, "The Rigors."

60 **"boring and not medically challenging."** Deppisch 140.

60 **doing crossword puzzles.** Altman, "Daniel Ruge."

60 **Dr. Joel Boone.** Deppisch 75–81.

61 **Quaker country.** "A Brief History of West Branch, Iowa." *West Branch Chamber of Commerce.* 18 Aug. 2014. <http://showcase.netins.net/web/wbranchcc/history.html>

61 **"accounts of defeat and victory."** Hoover, Herbert. "I Am Proud to be an Iowan." *Annals of Iowa* 38 (1967). 551. <http://ir.uiowa.edu/annals-of-iowa/vol38/iss7/10>

62 **wanted to keep the president active.** Deppisch 81.

62 **"getting daily exercise."** Hoover, Herbert. *The Memoirs of Herbert Hoover: The Cabinet and the Presidency, 1920–1933.* New York: Macmillan, 1952. 327.

62 **"snacking and reaching for nuts."** Thomas, Robert McG., Jr., and Barry Jacobs. "Sports World Specials; Hoover's Legacy." *New York Times.* 8 Aug. 1988. 19 Aug. 2014. <http://www.nytimes.com/1988/08/08/sports/sports-world-specials-hoover-s-legacy.html>

62 **"bull-in-the-ring."** "History of Hoover-Ball." 19 Aug. 2014. <http://www.hoover.archives.gov/education/hooverball.html>

62 **"start a medicine-ball game."** Hoover, "Memoirs" 327.

62 **elements of volleyball.** "Herbert Hoover." *Echoes from the White House.* 19 Aug. 2014. <http://www.pbs.org/wnet/whitehouse/popups/hoover.html>

63 **"faster and more rigorous."** Hoover, "Memoirs" 327.

64 **dropped twenty-five pounds.** Smith, Richard Norton, and Timothy Walch. *Prologue Magazine* 36.2 (Summer 2004). 19 Aug. 2014. <http://www.archives.gov/publications/prologue/2004/summer/hoover-1.html>

64 **"They missed him."** Withers, Bob. *The President Travels by Train: Politics and Pullmans.* Lynchburg, VA: TLC Publishing, 1996. 126.

64 **"Did Hoover die?"** Gibbs, Nancy, and Michael Duffy. *The Presidents Club: Inside the World's Most Exclusive Fraternity.* New York: Simon & Schuster, 2012. 21.

64 **"the wheel turns, the pendulum swings."** Walch, Timothy. "The Ordeal of a Biographer: Herbert Hoover Writes About Woodrow Wilson."

Prologue Magazine 40.3 (Fall 2008). <http://www.archives.gov/publications/prologue/2008/fall/hoover-wilson.html>

64 **leading a team of six assistants.** Phillips, McCandlish. "Herbert Hoover Is Dead; Ex-President, 90, Served Country in Various Fields." *New York Times.* 21 Oct. 1964. 14 Oct. 2013. <http://www.nytimes.com/learning/general/onthisday/bday/0810.html>

64 **wrote numerous books.** Walch.

64 **fifth-most-admired man in the country.** Gibbs 51.

64 **"I outlived the bastards."** Smith.

66 **upper gastrointestinal bleeding.** Phillips.

66 **a life expectancy several years longer.** Jaslow, Ryan. "Do Presidents Age Faster? What New Study Shows." *CBS News.* 7 Dec. 2011. 10 Jun. 2014. <http://www.cbsnews.com/news/do-presidents-age-faster-what-new-study-shows/>

66 **collapsed on the floor of the House of Representatives.** Unger, Harlow Giles. *John Quincy Adams.* Boston: Da Capo Press, 2012. 308.

66 **six known heart attacks.** Hoffman, Brian B. *Adrenaline.* Cambridge: Harvard University Press, 2013. eBook file.

66 **Johnson had at least three.** Nelson, Julie. *American Presidents Year by Year.* New York: Routledge, 2015. eBook file. "1973."

66 **"I am a blubber of water."** Remini, Robert V. *Andrew Jackson and the Course of American Democracy, 1833–1845.* New York: Harper & Row, 1984. 519.

67 **"cholera morbus."** Eisenhower, John. *Zachary Taylor: The American Presidents Series: The 12th President, 1849–1850.* New York: Macmillan, 2008. 132–34.

67 **iced cherries and cold milk.** Montgomery, Henry. *The Life of Major General Zachary Taylor, Twelfth President of the United States.* Auburn, NY: Derby, Miller, 1850. 425–31.

67 **warned to avoid eating and drinking.** Bauer, K. Jack. *Zachary Taylor: Soldier, Planter, Statesman of the Old Southwest.* Baton Rouge: Louisiana State University Press, 1985. 314.

67 **a sewer and sewer system.** Eisenhower 132–34.

68 **she met Bill Gist.** Heard, Alex. "Exhumed Innocent." *New Republic* 205.6 (5 Aug. 1991).

68 **Bill's wife Betty.** "Life Portrait of Zachary Taylor." *American Presidents.* C-SPAN, Washington, DC. 31 May 1999.

68 **"green matter was thrown."** Montgomery 425–31.

68 **"I brought the symptoms to Dr. Maples."** "Life Portrait of Zachary Taylor."

69 **"I told Rising."** Maples, William R., and Michael Browning. *Dead Men Do Tell Tales.* New York: Doubleday, 1994. 223–37.

69 **"wrote to every address and name [she] could find."** "Life Portrait of Zachary Taylor."

69 **"that it was my duty as coroner."** "Exhumation of Zachary Taylor." *American Presidents.* C-SPAN, Washington, DC. 3 Jun. 1999.

69 **willing to pay the costs.** Associated Press. "Zachary Taylor's Body Taken from Crypts for Arsenic Tests." *Los Angeles Times.* 18 Jun. 1991. 11 Dec. 2013. <http://articles.latimes.com/1991-06-18/news/mn-1004_1_zachary-taylor-s-body>

69 **"cavalier contempt for the dead."** "Turned Over in His Grave." *New*

York Times. 20 Jun. 1991. 5 May 2014. <http://www.nytimes.com/1991/06/20/opinion/turned-over-in-his-grave.html>

70 **"Suppose they find arsenic."** "A Tale of Arsenic and Old Zach." *Newsweek* 118.1 (1 Jul. 1991). 64.

70 **The government objected.** Maples 223–37.

70 **a small, quiet circus.** Harrison, Eric. "Zachary Taylor Did Not Die of Arsenic Poisoning," *Los Angeles Times.* 27 Jun. 1991. 11 Dec. 2013. <http://articles.latimes.com/1991-06-27/news/mn-2064_1_zachary-taylor>

70 **"the fire department at the front gate."** Maples 223–37.

70 **working under a green tarp.** Marriott, Michel. "Zachary Taylor's Remains Are Removed for Tests." 18 Jun. 1991. 28 May 2014. <http://www.nytimes.com/1991/06/18/us/zachary-taylor-s-remains-are-removed-for-tests.html>

70 **"enclosed in a lead cocoon."** "Exhumation of Zachary Taylor."

70 **brought a blowtorch.** Maples 223–37.

71 **"take a Stryker saw."** "Exhumation of Zachary Taylor."

71 **"She approached the casket."** Maples 223–37.

71 **went to Oak Ridge National Laboratory.** "Scientists Conduct Tests in Reactor on Remains of Zachary Taylor." *Los Angeles Times.* 23 Jun 1991. 27 May 2014. <http://articles.latimes.com/1991-06-23/news/mn-1984_1_president-zachary-taylor>

71 **High Flux Isotope Reactor.** Munger, Frank. "ORNL Alum Robinson to Join Obama Administration." *Knoxville News Sentinel.* 30 Jan. 2010. 28 May 2014. <http://blogs.knoxnews.com/munger/2010/01/ornl-alum-robinson-to-join-oba.html>

71 **"He had no more arsenic in him."** "Exhumation of Zachary Taylor."

72 **"We have the truth."** Harrison.

72 **she appeared on C-SPAN.** "Life Portrait of Zachary Taylor."

72 **"one too many episodes of *Murder, She Wrote*."** Heard.

72 **"a lot of emotional and mental energy."** Evans, C. Wyatt. Personal interview. 29 May 2014.

72 **William Henry Harrison was supposedly poisoned.** Summers, Mark Wahlgren. *A Dangerous Stir: Fear, Paranoia, and the Making of Reconstruction.* Chapel Hill: University of North Carolina Press, 2009. eBook file. Ch. 6.

72 **suggested Warren Harding was poisoned.** Smith, Richard Norton. "Introduction." In Brian Lamb, *Who's Buried in Grant's Tomb? A Tour of Presidential Gravesites.* New York: PublicAffairs, 2010. xi–xii.

72 **power struggle in the Republican Party.** Millard ch. 15.

72 **an anarchist plot.** "Great Anarchist Plot to Kill President." *New York Evening World,* 11 Sept. 1901, Night Edition. 20 Mar. 2015. <http://www.loc.gov/rr/news/topics/goldman.html>

72 **supposedly faked his own death.** Klara, Robert. *FDR's Funeral Train: A Betrayed Widow, a Soviet Spy, and a Presidency in the Balance.* New York: Macmillan, 2010. 102.

72 **actually *was* a conspiracy.** Swanson, James. *Bloody Crimes: The Funeral of Abraham Lincoln and the Chase for Jefferson Davis.* New York: HarperCollins, 2010. 147.

73 **like the Confederate government.** Hatch, Frederick. *Protecting President Lincoln: The Security Effort, the Thwarted Plots and the Disaster at Ford's Theatre.* Jefferson, NC: McFarland, 2011. 66.

73 **"the Jesuits did him in."** Evans.

73 **Her novel notes the horrors.** Rising, Clara. *In the Season of the Wild Rose.* New York: Villard Books, 1986. 444.

74 **"Please pass the broccoli."** Associated Press. "The Broccoli Did It, Bush Says of Taylor." *Los Angeles Times.* 5 Jul. 1991. 11 Dec. 2013. <http://articles .latimes.com/1991-07-05/news/mn-1779_1_zachary-taylor>

Chapter 4: Farewell, Mr. President

75 **cobble a funeral plan together.** "Public Announcement—Death of President Harrison." 4 Apr. 1841. Online by Gerhard Peters and John T. Woolley, *The American Presidency Project.* 3 Sept. 2014. <http://www.presidency.ucsb .edu/ws/?pid=67332>

76 **Since President Taft's death.** Hoover, Herbert. "Proclamation 1901— Announcing the Death of William Howard Taft." 8 Mar. 1930. 20 Mar. 2015. Online by Gerhard Peters and John T. Woolley, *The American Presidency Project.* <http://www.presidency.ucsb.edu/ws/?pid=22542>

76 **after Benjamin Harrison's death in 1901.** McKinley, William. "Proclamation 454—Announcing the Death of Benjamin Harrison." 14 Mar. 1901. 1 Sept. 2014. Online by Gerhard Peters and John T. Woolley, *The American Presidency Project.* <http://www.presidency.ucsb.edu/ws/?pid=69278>

76 **Grover Cleveland died seven years later.** Roosevelt, Theodore. "Proclamation 813—Announcing the Death of Ex-President Grover Cleveland." 24 Jun. 1908. 1 Sept. 2014. Online by Gerhard Peters and John T. Woolley, *The American Presidency Project.* <http://www.presidency.ucsb.edu/ws/? pid=69625>

76 **the spectacle of a royal funeral.** "Presidential Funerals." White House Historical Association. 4 Sept. 2014. <http://www.whitehousehistory.org/ presentations/presidential-funerals/>

76 **black cloth on top of the president's official portrait.** "Modern Mourning Observations at the White House." White House Historical Association. 20 Mar. 2015. <http://www.whha.org/presentations/presidential-funerals/pre sidential-funerals-modern-observations.html>

76 **a Washington merchant called Alexander Hunter.** Carroll, Rebecca. "Protocol Fills State Funerals." *Cincinnati Enquirer.* 7 Jun. 2004. 29 Aug. 2014. <http://www.enquirer.com/editions/2004/06/07/loc_loc1arwrd.html>

76 **"amiable and benevolent."** Collins, Gail. *William Henry Harrison: The American Presidents Series: The 9th President, 1841.* New York: Macmillan, 2012. 124.

76 **"A kind and overruling providence."** Smith, Richard Norton. "William Henry Harrison." In Brian Lamb, *Who's Buried in Grant's Tomb? A Tour of Presidential Gravesites.* New York: PublicAffairs, 2010. 39.

77 **a massive funeral procession.** Collins 124.

77 **a pallbearer for each of the country's twenty-six states.** Lamb 37.

77 **"struck the eye even from the greatest distance."** "President William Henry Harrison: The Funeral Ceremonies." *National Intelligencer.* 28 Jun. 1841. 4 Sept. 2014. <http://www.congressionalcemetery.org/president -william-henry-harrison>

77 **too cold for interment.** "Presidential Funerals."

77 **The cemetery's official name.** Dick, Jason. "Dog Days at Congressional Cemetery." *Roll Call.* 29 Feb. 2012. 1 Sept. 2014. <http://www.rollcall.com/ issues/57_101/-212696-1.html?zkPrintable=true>

77 **Congress's go-to burial site.** Swiller, Josh. "A Walk Through Congressional Cemetery." *Washingtonian.* 19 May 2011. 2 Sept. 2014. <http://www .washingtonian.com/articles/people/a-walk-through-congressional -cemetery/>

77 **"adding new terrors to death."** Association for the Preservation of Historic Congressional Cemetery. Foreword to United States Senate, "History of the Congressional Cemetery." 59th Cong., 2nd sess. Washington: 6 Dec. 1906. 21 Mar. 2015. <http://www.congressionalcemetery.org/sites/default/ files/CemeteryHistory_Senate-1906.pdf>

78 **craft beer tasting.** Dick, Jason. "Congressional Cemetery's Day of the Dog: It CouldGetRuff." *RollCall.* 29Aug.2014. 1Sept.2014. <http://blogs.rollcall.com/ after-dark/congressional-cemeterys-day-of-the-dog-it-could-get-ruff/>

79 **"we can rejuvenate the General."** Smith, Richard Norton. "George Washington." In Brian Lamb, *Who's Buried in Grant's Tomb? A Tour of Presidential Gravesites.* New York: PublicAffairs, 2010. 7.

79 **Washington stayed dead.** Krepp, Tim. *Capitol Hill Haunts.* Charleston, SC: Haunted America, 2012. 13–15.

79 **due to neighborhood dog owners.** Dick, "Dog Days."

79 **stayed in this liveliest of cemeteries.** Lamb 37.

80 **may have found a way to stick around.** Krepp 20.

80 **the only Americans automatically afforded such honors.** *Army Pamphlet 1-1: State, Official, and Special Military Funerals.* 30 Dec. 1965. 21 Mar. 2015. <http://armypubs.army.mil/epubs/pdf/p1_1.pdf>

80 **sending presidential aircraft.** Goto, Shihoko. "The Cost of Pomp for Reagan's Funeral." *UPI.* 16 Jun 2004. 15 Dec. 2013. <http://www.upi.com/ Business_News/2004/06/16/The-cost-of-pomp-for-Reagans-funeral/ UPI-14211087417177/>

80 **up to four thousand.** "Questions About Military and Joint Force Headquarters—National Capital Region Participation." 15 Dec. 2013. <http://www.usstatefuneral.mdw.army.mil/docs/default-document-library/ faq-sf-military-questions.pdf?sfvrsn=0>

80 **close for the day of the funeral.** Goto.

80 **hundreds of millions of dollars.** Dinan, Stephen. "Bush Holiday Extension to cost $450 Million." *Washington Times.* 15 Dec. 2008. 30 Aug. 2014. <http://www.washingtontimes.com/news/2008/dec/15/bushs-holiday-exten sion-leaves-450-million-bill/>

81 **directed at the ground level by army personnel.** *Army Pamphlet 1-1*, 1.

81 **"police escort will move at 3 miles per hour."** *Army Pamphlet 1-1*, 27.

81 **"w/four-in-hand tie, service gloves."** *Army Pamphlet 1-1*, 57.

81 **"six paces beyond its nearest approach."** *Army Pamphlet 1-1*, 58.

81 **"carefully selected."** *Army Pamphlet 1-1*, 53.

81 **parts of *Air Force One* are removable.** "Aboard Air Force One." *Fox News Sunday*. Host Chris Wallace. Washington, DC. 24 Nov. 2008. 21 Mar. 2015. <http://video.foxnews.com/v/3918511/aboard-air-force-one/?pageid=232 36#sp=show-clips>

81 **a day of private repose.** *Army Pamphlet 1-1*, 2.

81 **hastily put together in 1865.** "The Catafalque." Architect of the Capitol. 7 Sept. 2014. <http://www.aoc.gov/nations-stage/catafalque>

81 **"Temple of Death."** Craughwell, Thomas J. *Stealing Lincoln's Body.* Cambridge: Harvard University Press, 2009. 9.

81 **storage in the US Capitol Crypt.** Swanson, James. *Bloody Crimes: The Funeral of Abraham Lincoln and the Chase for Jefferson Davis.* New York: HarperCollins, 2010. 210–11.

81 **nearly blew up in a gas explosion.** "Lincoln's Bier: An Interesting National Relic, to Be Seen at the World's Fair." *San Francisco Call* 71.35 (4 Jan. 1892). 7 Sept. 2014. <http://cdnc.ucr.edu/cgi-bin/cdnc?a=d&d=SFC18920104.2.79>

82 **the catafalque was put to use.** "The Catafalque."

83 **Cathedral Church of Saint Peter and Saint Paul.** "Cathedral Facts." Washington National Cathedral. 12 Sept. 2014. <http://www.cathedral.org/about/allFacts.shtml>

83 **L'Enfant designed the Federal City.** Meisler, Stanley. "People Thought This Great Church Was Never to Be Finished." *Smithsonian* 21.3 (Jun. 1990). 116.

83 **won a congressional charter to establish a cathedral.** Meyer, Graham. "Mysteries of the Washington National Cathedral." *Washingtonian*. 1 Sept. 2007. 8 Sept. 2014. <http://www.washingtonian.com/articles/arts-events/mysteries-of-the-washington-national-cathedral/>

83 **another eighty-three years.** "Cathedral Figures." Washington National Cathedral. 8 Sept. 2014. <http://www.cathedral.org/about/allFigures.shtml>

83 **10,650 pipes.** Meyer.

83 **a devout Presbyterian.** Cooper, John Milton, Jr. "Times Topics: Woodrow Wilson." *New York Times.* 1 Oct. 2010. 11 Sept. 2014. <http://topics.nytimes.com/top/reference/timestopics/people/w/woodrow_wilson/index.html>

84 **asked them to be buried within the cathedral.** Berg, A. Scott. *Wilson.* New York: Simon & Schuster, 2013. ePub file. Ch. 17.

84 **there are 112 gargoyles and grotesques.** "Cathedral Figures."

84 **a sculpture competition for kids.** "Grotesques: Darth Vader." Washington National Cathedral. 21 Mar. 2015. <http://www.cathedral.org/about/darthVader.shtml>

85 **"desires as to type of funeral."** *Army Pamphlet 1-1*, 1.

85 **the military keeps copies of the arrangements.** Orin, Deborah. "Bill Bury Quiet—Only Ex-Prez Who Won't Plan A Funeral." *New York*

Post. 18 Jul. 2005. 31 Aug. 2014. <http://nypost.com/2005/07/18/bill-bury -quiet-only-ex-prez-who-wont-plan-a-funeral/>

85 **"dusk is the time to do this."** Bumiller, Elizabeth, and Elizabeth Becker. "The 40th President: The Plans; Down to the Last Detail, a Reagan-Style Funeral." *New York Times*, 8 Jun. 2004. 2 Sept. 2014. <http://www.nytimes .com/2004/06/08/us/the-40th-president-the-plans-down-to-the-last-detail- a-reagan-style-funeral.html>

85 **brought out the Reagan "cast."** Associated Press. "Sun Sets As Reagan Laid To Rest In California." *NBC News.* 12 Jun. 2004. 25 Aug. 2014. <http://www .nbcnews.com/id/5144264/ns/us_news-the_legacy_of_ronald_reagan/t/ sun-sets-reagan-laid-rest-california/#.U_vSNGOgbfx>

85 **made public her political disagreements.** "Road to a Reconciliation." *CBS Sunday Morning.* 27 Mar. 2009. 15 Sept. 2014. <http://www.cbsnews .com/news/road-to-a-reconciliation/>

85 **his 587-page funeral plan.** Willard, Greg. Interview. Gerald Ford Foundation. 14 Feb. 2011. 21 Mar. 2015. <http://geraldrfordfoundation.org/ centennial/oralhistory/greg-willard/>

86 **hometown of Alexandria, Virginia.** Smith, Richard Norton. "Gerald Ford." In Brian Lamb, *Who's Buried in Grant's Tomb? A Tour of Presidential Gravesites.* New York: PublicAffairs, 2010. 176-8.

86 **a somber version of the fight song.** Kornblut, Anne E. "Ford Arranged His Funeral to Reflect Himself and Drew In a Former Adversary." *New York Times.* 29 Dec. 2006. 10 Jul. 2014. <http://www.nytimes.com/2006/12/29/ washington/29funeral.html?_r=1&>

86 **a Cadillac.** Gilmore, Gerry J. "Ford's Body Arrives in Washington for Official Honors." *Armed Forces News Service.* 30 Dec. 2006. 15 Sept. 2014. <http:// www.defense.gov/news/newsarticle.aspx?id=2561>

86 **turned all of it down.** Bumiller.

86 **two days of viewing in Washington.** Bitman, Terry. "How Nixon Made His Funeral Plans Perfectly Clear." *Philadelphia Inquirer.* 12 Aug. 1993. 13 Jul. 2014. <http://articles.philly.com/1993-08-12/living/25967509_1_con-artist-state -funeral-vanity-fair>

86 **"the head people after the 1972 campaign."** Kalogerakis, George. "California, Here I Succumb!" *Vanity Fair* 56.9 (Sept. 1993). 142, 144.

87 **"Official U.S. Government Scapegoat."** Brinkley, David. *Everyone Is Entitled to My Opinion.* New York: Random House, 1996. 100.

87 **"I let the American people down."** "I Have Impeached Myself." *Guardian.* 7 Sept. 2007. 15 Sept. 2014. <http://www.theguardian.com/theguardian/2007/ sep/07/greatinterviews1>

87 **"always in the arena."** Nixon, Richard. "President Richard Nixon's Final Remarks at the White House." 9 Aug. 1974. 15 Sept. 2014. <http://www.cnn .com/ALLPOLITICS/1997/gen/resources/watergate/nixon.farewell.html>

87 **"It is necessary to struggle."** Gibbs, Nancy, and Michael Duffy. *The Presidents Club: Inside the World's Most Exclusive Fraternity.* New York: Simon & Schuster, 2012. 366.

87 **"the best way to be considered a sage."** Drew, Elizabeth. "Project Wizard: Dick Nixon's Brazen Plan for Post-Watergate Redemption." *Atlan-*

tic. 15 May 2014. 26 May 2014. <http://www.theatlantic.com/politics/archive/2014/05/project-wizard-richard-nixons-post-watergate-plan-for-redemption/370874/>

87 **"Watergate—that's all anyone wants."** Greenberg, David. "Richard Nixed." *New Republic.* 8 Jun. 2012. 31 Aug. 2014. <http://www.newrepublic.com/article/politics/magazine/103940/watergate-richard-nixon>

88 **amid hopes that Nixon might recover.** Roberts, Sam. "Nixon's Condition Worsens After Stroke, His Doctor Says." *New York Times.* 20 Apr. 1994. 14 May 2014. <http://www.nytimes.com/1994/04/20/us/nixon-s-condition-worsens-after-stroke-his-doctor-says.html>

88 **"People left that outside the doors."** Anastasiadis, Olivia. Personal interview. 17 Jul. 2014.

88 **formal proclamation about the news.** Clinton, Bill. "Proclamation 6677—Announcing the Death of Richard Milhous Nixon." 22 Apr. 1994. 15 Sept. 2014. <http://www.gpo.gov/fdsys/pkg/WCPD-1994-05-02/html/WCPD-1994-05-02-Pg897-2.htm>

89 **"pick up the phone and ask President Nixon."** Associated Press. "Richard Nixon's Quiet Foreign Policy Advice to Bill Clinton Revealed in Newly Declassified Documents." *New York Daily News.* 14 Feb. 2013. 31 Aug. 2014. <http://www.nydailynews.com/news/politics/nixon-foreign-policy-advice-bill-clinton-revealed-article-1.1264304>

89 **"Every generation needs somebody to hate."** "Allies, Enemies Mourn Nixon." *Milwaukee Sentinel.* 28 Apr. 1994. 14 May 2014. <http://news.google.com/newspapers?nid=1368&dat=19940428&id=WasxAAAAIBAJ&sjid=CBMEAAAAIBAJ&pg=3590,7676032>

89 **"the kind of thing you expect under a person like Hitler."** Greenberg, David. *Nixon's Shadow: The History of an Image.* New York: W. W. Norton, 2004. 99.

89 **"a more authentic, open, liberated person."** "Ever the Warrior." *People* 41.17 (9 May 1994). 42.

89 **"Richard Nixon would be so proud."** Clark, Robin. "Leaders, Nation Say Their Last Farewells to Ex-president Nixon." *Philadelphia Inquirer.* 28 Apr. 1994. 31 Aug. 2014. <http://articles.philly.com/1994-04-28/news/25862477_1_watergate-saga-37th-president-richard-milhous-nixon>

90 **"anything less than his entire life and career."** Associated Press, "Richard Nixon's Quiet Foreign Policy Advice."

90 **"astonished at this outpouring of affection."** "Richard M. Nixon, 1913–1994." *ABC News.* Host: Ted Koppel; commentator: Stephen Ambrose. 27 Apr. 1994.

91 **"his casket would have been launched."** Thompson, Hunter S. "He Was a Crook." *Fear and Loathing at "Rolling Stone": The Essential Writing of Hunter S. Thompson.* New York: Simon & Schuster, 2012. 506–12.

91 **Thomas Brackett Reed.** Rawson, Hugh, and Margaret Miner. *The Oxford Dictionary of American Quotations.* 2nd ed. New York: Oxford University Press, 2006. 526.

91 **"Nixon was ahead of schedule."** Witcher, Russ. *After Watergate: Nixon and the Newsweeklies.* Lanham, MD: University Press of America, 2000. 53.

Chapter 5: Death Trips

93   **California limited interments.** Platte, Mark. "Pat Nixon Burial at Library Required State Exemption." *Los Angeles Times*. 2 Jul. 1993. 21 Mar. 2015. <http://articles.latimes.com/1993-07-02/news/mn-9168_1_nixon-library>

93   **"the president's wishes were fulfilled."** Anastasiadis, Olivia. Personal interview. 17 Jul. 2014.

94   **"No President who performs his duties."** McCormac, Eugene Irving. *James K. Polk: A Political Biography*. Berkeley and Los Angeles: University of California Press, 1922. 328.

94   **"I have conducted the Government without their aid."** Seigenthaler, John. *James K. Polk: The American Presidents Series: The 11th President, 1845–1849*. New York: Times Books, 2003. 121.

94   **when mules would have been better.** Seigenthaler 137–38.

94   **having to sit for a portrait artist.** Polk, James Knox. *The Diary of James K. Polk During His Presidency, 1845 to 1849: Now First Printed from the Original Manuscript Owned by the Society, Volume 1*. Chicago: A. C. McClurg, 1910. 211.

94   **everything on his presidential to-do list.** Seigenthaler 102–3.

95   **a large home in Nashville.** Nelson, Anson, and Fanny Nelson. *Memorials of Sarah Childress Polk: Wife of the Eleventh President of the United States*. New York: A. D. F. Randolph, 1892. 141–44.

95   **a loop through the South.** Borneman, Walter R. *Polk: The Man Who Transformed the Presidency and America*. New York: Random House, 2008. 338-41.

96   **cholera was also in town.** Seigenthaler 153.

96   **"My bowels were affected."** Smith, Richard Norton. "James Polk." In Brian Lamb, *Who's Buried in Grant's Tomb? A Tour of Presidential Gravesites*. New York: PublicAffairs, 2010. 47.

96   **The ex-president's nephews.** Borneman 342.

96   **told him he didn't have cholera.** Smith 47.

96   **holed up in a hotel for four days.** Borneman 342.

96   **baptized in the Methodist Church.** Smith 47.

96   **"I love you, Sarah, for all eternity, I love you."** Borneman 342.

96   **"sleeps with the great and good."** "Death of James K. Polk." *Daily Union*. 18 Jun. 1849. 22 Mar. 2015. <http://www.thenashvillecitycemetery.org/news papers-polk.htm>

97   **a Nashville city cemetery.** Smith 47.

97   **until a permanent tomb was built.** Seigenthaler 172.

97   **The designer was William Strickland.** Hoobler, James A. "William F. Strickland." *The Tennessee Encyclopedia of History and Culture*. 1 Jan. 2010. 22 Mar. 2015. <http://tennesseeencyclopedia.net/entry.php?rec=1275>

97   **the long inscriptions on each side.** Heiskell, Samuel Gordon. *Andrew Jackson and Early Tennessee History*. Nashville: Ambrose Printing, 1920. 200.

97   **A military band led the procession.** Byrnes, Mark Eaton. *James K. Polk: A Biographical Companion*. Santa Barbara, CA: ABC-CLIO, 2001. 52.

97   **Polk's complicated will.** Collins, Herbert R., and David B. Weaver. *Wills of the US Presidents*. New York: Stravon Educational Press, 1976. 95.

97   **tore down Polk Place.** Collins 92.

97 **Polk's remains moved again.** Borneman 359.

98 **"neutral territory."** Borneman 359.

98 **"part of the rural cemetery movement."** Peters, John O. Personal interview. 12 Sept. 2014.

99 **put Presidents Circle first.** Calos, Katherine, and Jeremy Slayton. "Volunteers Revamp Virginia Cemeteries." *USA Today*. 5 Jan. 2010. 24 Sept. 2014. <http://usatoday30.usatoday.com/travel/destinations/2010-01-05-richmond-cemetery-repairs_N.htm>

99 **boisterous, unpredictable, and a little dangerous.** "Henry A. Wise (1806–1876)." *American Experience: John Brown's Holy War.* 1 Oct. 2014. <http://www.pbs.org/wgbh/amex/brown/peopleevents/pande05.html>

99 **dueled with—and wounded—the man he defeated.** Tarter, Brent. "Henry Alexander Wise (1806–1876)." *Virginia Memory.* 2010. 29 Sept. 2014. <http://www.virginiamemory.com/online_classroom/union_or_secession/people/henry_wise>

99 **served as second for a colleague.** Tarter.

99 **convinced them to keep shooting.** Zaeske, Susan. "'A Nest of Rattlesnakes Let Loose Among Them': Congressional Debates over Women's Antislavery Petitions, 1835–1845." *In the Shadow of Freedom: The Politics of Slavery in the National Capital.* Ed. Paul Finkelman and Donald R. Kennon. Athens: Ohio University Press, 2011. 110.

99 **helped prevent more duels than he ever fought.** Simpson, Craig M. *A Good Southerner: The Life of Henry A. Wise of Virginia.* Chapel Hill: University of North Carolina Press, 1985. 38.

100 **his sarcastic rebuttal.** Wise, Barton Hextall. *The Life Of Henry A. Wise of Virginia, 1806–1876.* New York: Macmillan, 1899. 48.

100 **more harm than good to his state.** Simpson 7–8.

100 **"He guards Virginia."** Simpson 138.

100 **roads, economy, and school system.** Tarter.

100 **"most unhappy, and undeservedly so, retirements."** Hart, Gary. *James Monroe: The American Presidents Series: The 5th President, 1817–1825.* New York: Macmillan, 2005. 144.

100 **Elizabeth Monroe died.** Smith, Richard Norton. "James Monroe." In Brian Lamb, *Who's Buried in Grant's Tomb? A Tour of Presidential Gravesites.* New York: PublicAffairs, 2010. 23.

100 **Monroe had money problems.** Hart 144–46.

101 **move in with his daughter's family.** Smith, "James Monroe" 23.

101 **"Virginians sort of felt left out."** Peters.

101 **to mark the centennial of Monroe's birth.** Kammen, Michael. *Digging Up the Dead: A History of Notable American Reburials.* Chicago: University of Chicago Press, 2010. 87.

101 **"appropriated two thousand dollars."** Peters.

101 **a simple, private transfer.** Kammen 87.

101 **a public viewing of the casket.** Hall, Larry. "New York, Virginia United to Rebury James Monroe." *Richmond Times-Dispatch.* 4 Jul. 2007. 22 Mar. 2015. <http://www.richmond.com/news/article_305a6cc9-fd8b-576b-b148-05172daf54fb.html>

101 **"This handsome offer."** Kimball, Gregg D. *American City, Southern Place: A Cultural History of Antebellum Richmond.* Athens: University of Georgia Press, 2000. 210.

101 **a journey south on the steamship *Jamestown*.** Rouse, Parke. "Richmond Turned Out for Monroe Reburial." *Hampton Roads Daily Press.* 4 Sept. 1994. 9 Feb. 2014. <http://articles.dailypress.com/1994-09-04/news/9409020413_1_james-monroe-monroe-home-anniversary-of-monroe-s-birth>

102 **so President James Buchanan could pay respects.** Kammen 87.

102 **a procession that stretched two miles long.** Rouse.

102 **"Who knows this day."** Kammen 88–90.

102 **dreamed of adding Monroe's friends.** Rouse.

102 **"Go ahead, Governor, you fetch 'em."** Morgan, George. *The Life of James Monroe.* Boston: Small, Maynard, 1921. 458.

102 **he did write to Monticello.** Moore, Craig. "A New Star: Jefferson in Hollywood?" *Out of the Box: Notes from the Archives @ the Library of Virginia.* 7 Jul. 2010. 25 Dec. 2013. <http://www.virginiamemory.com/blogs/out_of_the_box/2010/07/07/a-new-star-jefferson-in-hollywood/>

102 **a local architect, Albert Lybrock.** Rouse.

102 **meant to evoke the detailed ironwork.** Kammen 90.

103 **"People still occasionally call it the birdcage."** Peters.

104 **It was Henry Wise who met with Brown.** Tarter.

104 **raid the same federal armory.** "Henry A. Wise (1806–1876)."

104 **headed to Washington to lead a "peace conference."** Goodheart, Adam. "The Ashen Ruin." *New York Times Opinionator.* 15 Feb. 2011. 12 Mar. 2014. <http://opinionator.blogs.nytimes.com/2011/02/15/the-ashen-ruin/?_php=true&_type=blogs&_r=0>

104 **led Whig leaders to believe he was open to compromise.** Crapol, Edward P. *John Tyler, the Accidental President.* Chapel Hill: University of North Carolina Press, 2006. 19.

104 **started vetoing his own party's bills.** Abbott, Philip. "Accidental Presidents: Death, Assassination, Resignation, and Democratic Succession." *Presidential Studies Quarterly* 35.4 (Dec. 2005). 638.

104 **resigned in protest.** Simpson 51.

104 **drummed the president out of its ranks.** Crapol 20.

105 **The toast to Tyler.** Crapol 116.

105 **renamed Tyler Street.** Martin, William. "Chicago Streets." Chicago Historical Society. 22 Mar. 2015. <http://www.chsmedia.org/househistory/nameChanges/start.pdf>

105 **"more cordially despised."** Goodheart.

105 **throw rocks at the commander in chief.** May, Gary. *John Tyler: The American Presidents Series: The 10th President, 1841–1845.* New York: Macmillan, 2008. 71.

105 **the first presidential bodyguards.** Fawcett, Bill. *Oval Office Oddities: An Irreverent Collection of Presidential Facts, Follies, and Foibles.* New York: HarperCollins, 2008. 34.

105 **one of Tyler's few political allies.** Simpson 52–53.

105 **"literary executor."** Collins 90.

105 **hailed forever as a hero.** Goodheart.

106 **"higher than the mountains."** "Death of Ex-President Tyler." *New York Times.* 22 Jan. 1862. 5 Oct. 2014. <http://www.nytimes.com/1862/01/22/news/death-of-ex-president-tyler.html>

106 **the high point of the conference.** Goodheart.

106 **elected to serve in a foreign government.** Lamb, Brian. *Who's Buried in Grant's Tomb? A Tour of Presidential Gravesites.* New York: PublicAffairs, 2010. 41.

106 **no proclamation announcing the news.** Crapol 268.

106 **taken down and put into storage.** Goodheart.

107 **"one of the architects of its ruin."** "Death of Ex-President Tyler."

107 **gave Tyler a state funeral.** Crapol 268.

107 **there was no gravestone.** Townsend, Malcolm. *Handbook of United States Political History for Readers and Students.* Boston: Lothrop, Lee & Shepard, 1905. 384.

107 **funded the eagle-topped obelisk.** Lamb 41.

107 **a Confederate military officer.** Tarter.

107 **relieved from duty.** Wise 303.

107 **wrote books, served on state commissions.** Tarter.

107 **on his plantation outside Norfolk.** "Henry Wise." National Park Service. 16 Mar. 2015. <http://www.nps.gov/resources/person.htm?id=138>

107 **health had deteriorated.** Wise 420–22.

108 **could no longer defend the Confederate capital.** Swanson, James. *Bloody Crimes: The Funeral of Abraham Lincoln and the Chase for Jefferson Davis.* New York: HarperCollins, 2010. 6–8.

108 **mines and other obstructions.** Harris, William C. *Lincoln's Last Months.* Cambridge: Harvard University Press, 2004. 204.

108 **partly being looted and partly being torched.** Swanson 28–30.

108 **"I want to see Richmond."** Nichols, Clifton Melvin. *Life of Abraham Lincoln: Being a Biography of His Life from His Birth to His Assassination; Also a Record of His Ancestors, and a Collection of Anecdotes Attributed to Lincoln.* New York: Mast, Crowell & Kirkpatrick, 1896. 235.

108 **sitting down in Jefferson Davis's chair.** Swanson 47.

108 **Lincoln tourism in Richmond.** Johnson, Randy. "Following the Film Lincoln Around Richmond: How One Surprising City Dominates the New Spielberg Blockbuster." *National Parks Traveler.* 19 Nov. 2012. 21 Oct. 2014. <http://www.nationalparkstraveler.com/2012/11/following-film-lincoln-around-richmond-how-one-surprising-city-dominates-new-spielberg-blockbuster10864>

108 **"Lincoln is in Richmond again."** "Lincoln Statue Is Unveiled, and Protesters Come Out." *New York Times.* 6 Apr. 2003. 8 Feb. 2014. <http://www.nytimes.com/2003/04/06/us/lincoln-statue-is-unveiled-and-protesters-come-out.html>

108 **filmed nearly all of his 2012 movie.** Johnson.

109 **even special mixed drinks.** "Specialty Lincoln Items." Virginia.org. 21 Oct. 2014. <http://www.virginia.org/lincoln/specialties/>

109 **left no will.** Collins 124.

109 **extremely long workdays.** Goodwin, Doris Kearns. *Team of Rivals: The Political Genius of Abraham Lincoln.* New York: Simon & Schuster, 2006. 414.

109 **"I'll dismiss you from the service!"** Catton, Bruce. *Glory Road.* New York: Doubleday, 1952. 132.

109 **"Stanton is usually right."** Wilson, Rufus Rockwell. *Intimate Memories of Lincoln.* Elmira, NY: Primavera Press, 1945. 435.

109 **cleared the War Department's decks.** Goodwin, 414–15.

110 **love Lincoln the man.** Thomas, Benjamin P., and Harold M. Hyman. *Stanton: Life and Times of Lincoln's Secretary of War.* New York: Alfred A. Knopf, 1962. 2.

110 **stayed up all night directing the manhunt.** Swanson 110–1.

110 **"Now he belongs to the ages."** Wilson 435.

110 **a long train trip.** Swanson 152–55.

110 **punish the secessionists.** Means, Howard B. *The Avenger Takes His Place: Andrew Johnson and the 45 Days That Changed the Nation.* Orlando: Harcourt, 2006. 182.

110 **known as the Lincoln Special.** "Abraham Lincoln's Funeral Train." History.com. 2009. 23 Oct. 2014. <http://www.history.com/topics/president-lincolns-funeral-train>

110 **pulled nine cars.** Pruitt, Sarah. "Chemist Solves Lincoln Funeral Train Mystery." History.com: History in the Headlines. 9 May 2013. 23 Mar. 2015. <http://www.history.com/news/chemist-solves-lincoln-funeral-train-mystery>

110 **"richly draped in mourning."** Coggeshall, William Turner. *Lincoln Memorial: The Journeys of Abraham Lincoln: from Springfield to Washington, 1861, as President Elect; and from Washington to Springfield, 1865, as President Martyred; Comprising an Account of Public Ceremonies on the Entire Route, and Full Details of Both Journeys.* Columbus: Ohio State Journal, 1865. 142.

110 **a funeral coach.** Withers, Bob. *The President Travels by Train: Politics and Pullmans.* Lynchburg, VA: TLC Publishing, 1996. 326.

110 **Lincoln's casket sat at one end.** Coggeshall 142.

110 **too luxurious in wartime.** Withers 327.

112 **"distinguished, sad and solemn."** Withers 328–29.

112 **wanted an open casket.** Swanson 155.

112 **the president's embalmer.** Soniak, Matt. "Preserving the President: Abraham Lincoln, Grave Robbers, and an Excellent Embalmer." *Mental Floss.* 10 Dec. 2012. 29 Aug. 2014. <http://mentalfloss.com/article/31845/preserving-president-abraham-lincoln-grave-robbers-and-excellent-embalmer>

112 **reapply white chalk and makeup.** Craughwell, Thomas J. *Stealing Lincoln's Body.* Cambridge: Harvard University Press, 2009. 19–20.

112 **surrounded by fragrant flowers.** Swanson 222.

112 **flowers on the train tracks.** Withers 329.

112 **"Half a million sorrow-stricken people."** Morris, Benjamin Franklin, ed. *Memorial Record of the Nation's Tribute to Abraham Lincoln.* Washington, DC: W. H. & O. H. Morrison, 1865. 160.

112 **"kiss the placid lips of the corpse."** Swanson 229.

112 **"no talk of concession and conciliation."** Strong, George Templeton.

"From the Diaries." *Writing New York: A Literary Anthology*. Ed. Philip Lopate. New York: Simon & Schuster, 2000. 238.

112 **hailing his successor.** Means 103–4.

113 **"wave the bloody shirt."** Fulton, Joe B. *The Reconstruction of Mark Twain: How a Confederate Bushwhacker Became the Lincoln of Our Literature*. Baton Rouge: Louisiana State University Press, 2010. 98.

113 **a sort of grieving contest.** Swanson 246.

113 **"the Goddess of Liberty in mourning."** Coggeshall 218.

113 **threatened to turn the train around.** Craughwell 27.

113 **decorated virtually everything in town.** Swanson 270–72.

113 **a full twenty-four hours.** Swanson 280–81.

114 **pallbearers placed the remains.** Craughwell 24–27.

114 **longest, strangest death trip.** "Abraham Lincoln's Final Journey Home." *USA Today*. 17 Apr. 2010. 29 Oct. 2014. <http://usatoday30.usatoday.com/news/nation/lincoln-funeral-train.htm>

114 **"more to me than any other of our public men."** Beschloss, Michael. "When T.R. Saw Lincoln." *New York Times*. 21 May 2014. 29 Oct. 2014. <http://www.nytimes.com/2014/05/22/upshot/when-tr-saw-lincoln.html?_r=0&abt=0002&abg=1>

114 **"received such a gift."** Conradt, Stacy. "How Teddy Roosevelt Ended Up with Abe Lincoln's Hair." *Mental Floss*. 19 May 2011. 2 Nov. 2014. <http://mentalfloss.com/article/27777/how-teddy-roosevelt-ended-abe-lincoln%E2%80%99s-hair>

114 **represent Faith and Hope in "young America."** Perkins, Stephen J. "Essay on Hunt's Lincoln Sculpture." Bennington Museum. 23 Mar. 2015. <http://www.benningtonmuseum.org/lincoln.html>

115 **"Only in Illinois."** "Lincoln's Living Legacy." Enjoy Illinois. 23 Mar. 2015. <http://www.enjoyillinois.com/en-us/tripideas/lincoln>

115 **a tiny animated Lincoln who screams.** Nudd, Tim. "Illinois Tourism Loses Its Mind with a Tiny, Screaming, Hilarious Abe Lincoln." *AdWeek*. 3 Oct. 2013. 1 Sept. 2014. <http://www.adweek.com/news/advertising-branding/ad-day-illinois-tourism-loses-its-mind-tiny-screaming-hilarious-abe-lincoln-152871>

115 **visitor inquiries jumped.** Lazare, Lewis. "Illinois and Mini-Abe Prove a Great Match." *Chicago Business Journal*. 27 Sept. 2013. 1 Sept. 2014. <http://www.bizjournals.com/chicago/news/2013/09/27/illinois-and-mini-abe-prove-a-great.html>

115 **second only to Arlington National Cemetery.** Petry, Ashley. "Spend the Weekend in Abraham Lincoln's Hometown." *Indianapolis Star*. 6 Mar. 2015. 23 Mar. 2015. <http://www.indystar.com/story/life/2015/03/06/abraham-lincoln-springfield-illinois-weekend-getaway/24515537/>

115 **some 350,000 people each year.** Reynolds, John. "Lincoln Tomb Repair Work Continuing, Reopening Set for April." *Springfield State Journal-Register*. 27 Feb. 2014. 16 Jan. 2015. <http://www.sj-r.com/article/20140227/NEWS/140229293>

115 **"There are places to come in northwest Illinois."** Barichello, Derek. "Tourism Officials Bank on Lincoln." *Sterling (IL) Daily Gazette*. 25 Jan. 2013.

16 Jan. 2015. <http://www.saukvalley.com/2013/01/24/tourism-officials-bank
-on-lincoln/a90j8hu/>

116 **successfully defended a man accused of murder.** "Cass County
Courthouse—Beardstown." Looking for Lincoln. 23 Mar. 2015. <http://
www.lookingforlincoln.com/8thcircuit/tours/tour-courthouse.html>

116 **a set of three interlocking Lincoln portraits.** Ostro, David Avi. "David
Ostro's Link: A Contemporary Monument of Abraham Lincoln." Brooklyn
Arts Council. 22 Nov. 2009. 14 Oct. 2013. <http://www.brooklynartscouncil
.org/forum/876>

116 **named itself for Abraham Lincoln.** McEvers, Kelly. "Dwindling Middle
Class Has Repercussions for Small Towns." NPR. 12 Nov. 2013. 1 Sept. 2014.
<http://www.npr.org/2013/11/12/242999770/reinventing-the-dwindling
-middle-class-may-take-a-revolution>

116 **"I have selected the juice of a melon."** "Looking for Lincoln: Lincoln's
Lincoln." Historical marker, Lincoln, Illinois.

117 **presidential funerals have long attracted pickpockets.** "Lying in State
of the Late President." *New York Daily Tribune.* 13 Jul. 1850. 25 Mar. 2015.
<http://chroniclingamerica.loc.gov/lccn/sn83030213/1850-07-13/ed-1/seq-1/
print/image_681x718_from_0%2C2173_to_1490%2C3745/>

117 **built with coarse stone.** Barker, Tim. "Thomas Jefferson Tombstone,
Now at Mizzou, will Be Restored." *St. Louis Post-Dispatch.* 1 Jan. 2013. 2
Oct. 2013. <http://www.stltoday.com/news/local/education/thomas-jefferson
-tombstone-now-at-mizzou-will-be-restored/article_c4e79fb0-9566-5312-
8dad-f0bdd2c9bd20.html>

117 **asking people to stop stealing plants.** Crawford, Alan Pell. *Twilight at
Monticello: The Final Years of Thomas Jefferson.* New York: Random House,
2008. 251.

117 **stole the lightning rod.** Flood, Charles Bracelen. *Grant's Final Victory:
Ulysses S. Grant's Heroic Last Year.* Boston: Da Capo Press, 2012. 236.

117 **"liberation of Ben. Boyd from Joliet penitentiary."** Power, John Carroll, ed. *History of an Attempt to Steal the Body of Abraham Lincoln (Late President
of the United States of America) Including a History of the Lincoln Guard of Honor,
with Eight Years Lincoln Memorial Services.* Springfield, IL: H. W. Rokker Printing and Publishing House, 1890. 45.

117 **"They really were knuckleheads."** Babwin, Don. "Book Details
Plot to Steal Abe's Body." *Washington Post.* 7 May 2007. 2 Nov. 2014.
<http://www.washingtonpost.com/wp-dyn/content/article/2007/05/06/
AR2007050601250.html>

118 **"steal old Lincoln's bones."** Craughwell 80–83.

118 **"the boss body-snatcher of Chicago."** Craughwell 91–92.

118 **accidentally discharged his pistol.** Hinton, Dave. "Conspirators Caught."
Kankakee (IL) Daily Journal. 6 Feb. 2004. 12 Apr. 2014. <http://www.daily-
journal.com/news/local/conspirators-caught/article_407f32f7-02ef-5d69-
81a8-8da47e748f4c.html>

118 **ended up in Joliet with Ben Boyd.** Craughwell 153.

118 **served time as well.** Craughwell 170–71.

119 **"We put it back there the second day."** Power 89.

119 **sat under some spare lumber.** Fitz-Gerald, Charles E. "The Man Who Last Saw Abraham Lincoln." *Yankee Magazine.* Apr. 1980. 20 Aug. 2014. <http://www.yankeemagazine.com/article/history/man-who-last-saw-lincoln>

119 **joined by the body of his wife.** Craughwell 165.

119 **"indisputably necessary to identify the body."** Craughwell 178.

119 **"easily discerned the features."** Craughwell 179–80.

120 **return to the main floor.** Craughwell 182–83.

120 **close by for the first three presidential assassinations.** Crotty, Rob. "The Curious Case of Robert Lincoln." *Prologue: Pieces of History.* 27 Oct. 2010. 6 Nov. 2014. <http://blogs.archives.gov/prologue/?p=2239>

120 **sent his driver to fetch D. Willard Bliss.** Millard, Candice. *Destiny of the Republic: A Tale of Madness, Medicine and the Murder of a President.* New York: Anchor Books, 2011. ePub file. Ch. 12.

120 **"a certain fatality about presidential functions."** Crotty.

121 **the same treatment for his parents.** Craughwell 190–94.

121 **sent for his thirteen-year-old son, Fleetwood.** Fitz-Gerald.

121 **"to hold one of the leather straps."** Craughwell 195.

121 **smashed it to bits.** Craughwell 198.

Chapter 6: His Good Name

123 **establish the Wyoming Territory under a new name.** "A Century of Lawmaking for a New Nation: U.S. Congressional Documents and Debates, 1774-1875." *Congressional Globe,* 40th Cong., 2nd sess. <http://memory.loc.gov/cgi-bin/ampage?collId=llcg&fileName=081/llcg081.db&recNum=748>

124 **alternate name for North Dakota.** Coolidge, Louis Arthur. *An Old-Fashioned Senator: Orville H. Platt, of Connecticut: The Story of a Life Unselfishly Devoted to the Public Service.* New York: G. P. Putnam's Sons, 1910. 140.

124 **breaking Idaho up.** Trinklein, Michael J. *Lost States: True Stories of Texlahoma, Transylvania, and Other States That Never Made It.* Philadelphia: Quirk Books, 2010. eBook file. Ch. 27.

124 **Lincoln tomato variety.** Getsinger, Annie. "A Presidential Tomato." *Baraboo News-Republic.* 10 Oct. 2013. 27 Mar. 2015. <http://www.wiscnews.com/baraboonewsrepublic/news/local/article_a3be36cf-a611-54d5-a771-1ab8f10421a2.html>

124 **asteroid called (3153) Lincoln.** Schmadel, Lutz D. *Dictionary of Minor Planet Names, Sixth Edition.* New York: Springer, 2012. 245.

124 **capital city of Nebraska.** "History of Nebraska's Capitols." Nebraska State Capitol. 27 Mar. 2015. <http://capitol.nebraska.gov/index.php/building/history/nebraska-capitols>

124 **the Lincoln Highway.** Shelton, Kay. Interview. *All Things Considered.* NPR. Washington, DC. 31 Oct. 2013.

124 **rescued a three-week-old kitten.** "Miracle Three-Week-Old Kitten Rescued After Being Stuck Inside Statue of Abe Lincoln for Three Days." *Daily*

Mail. 19 Nov. 2012. 8 Nov. 2014. <http://www.dailymail.co.uk/news/article
-2235080/Clermont-Kitten-rescued-stuck-inside-statue-President-Abe
-Lincoln-days.html>

124 **have their own asteroids.** Schmadel 79, 82, 108, 245.

124 **Grover Cleveland Alexander.** Skipper, John C. *Wicked Curve: The Life and
Troubled Times of Grover Cleveland Alexander.* Jefferson, NC: McFarland, 2006.
10.

124 **blues great Howlin' Wolf.** Epting, Chris. *Led Zeppelin Crashed Here: The
Rock and Roll Landmarks of North America.* Santa Monica, CA: Santa Monica
Press, 2007. 231.

124 **carried 150 silver half dollars.** Remini, Robert V. *Andrew Jackson and the
Course of American Democracy, 1833–1845.* New York: Harper & Row, 1984. 425.

124 **nearly out of half dollars.** Fawcett, Bill. *Oval Office Oddities: An Irreverent
Collection of Presidential Facts, Follies, and Foibles.* New York: HarperCollins,
2008. 74.

125 **"puree of wild ducks Van Buren."** Robbins, Katie. "Top Ten Dishes Named
for Presidents." *Delish.* 21 Feb. 2011. 27 Mar. 2015. <http://www.delish.com/
food/news/a38484/top-ten-dishes-named-for-presidents/>

125 **an antidrinking movement.** Baumohl, Jim. "Inebriate Institutions in
North America, 1840–1920." *British Journal of Addiction* 85.9 (Sept. 1990). 1188.

125 **"the Philippine archipelago."** Flood, Theodore L. "The McKinley
Islands." *Chautauquan* 34 (1902). 119.

125 **"educate the Filipinos."** Harris, Susan K. *God's Arbiters: Americans and the
Philippines, 1898–1902.* New York: Oxford University Press, 2011. 14.

125 **"first to raise his hand."** Flood 119.

126 **"a local character."** Flood 119.

127 **Denali, or "the high one."** Rosen, Yereth. "Century After Peak First
Scaled, Alaska Mountain's Name Still Disputed." *Reuters.* 27 Apr. 2013. 16
Jan. 2015. <http://www.reuters.com/article/2013/04/27/usa-mountmckinley
-idUSL2N0DC02820130427>

127 **a prospector named William Dickey.** Loewen, James. *Lies Across America:
What Our Historic Sites Get Wrong.* New York: New Press, 1999. 52–53.

127 **already been found and named.** Associated Press. "Senator Introduces Bill
to Rename Mount McKinley to Mount Denali." 29 Jun. 2012. 27 Feb. 2014.
<http://www.foxnews.com/politics/2012/06/29/senator-introduces-bill-to
-rename-mount-mckinley-to-mount-denali/>

127 **wrote about what they saw.** Dickey, William. "Discoveries in Alaska."
New York Sun. 24 Jan. 1897. 6.

127 **Native voices grew more influential.** Associated Press, "Senator
Introduces."

127 **"uniform geographic name usage."** United States Board on Geographic
Names. 13 Mar. 2015. 28 Mar. 2015. <http://geonames.usgs.gov/>

127 **"to standardize usage."** Yost, Louis. Personal interview. 25 Feb. 2014.

128 **voted to rename the peak.** Rosen.

128 **"pending before Congress."** Yost.

128 **"We must retain."** Rosen.

129 **don't need to become law.** Loewen 52–53.

129 **"any that have gone on this long."** Associated Press, "Senator Introduces."

129 **"The truth of McKinley."** Associated Press. "McKinley Legacy Remains Unsettled." *Vindicator*. 28 Nov. 2005. 22 Sept. 2014. <http://www.vindy.com/news/2005/nov/28/mckinley-legacy-remains-unsettled/?print>

129 **launched a petition drive.** Wear, Kimberly. "McKinley on the Mind: Arcata Split over New Push to Remove Statue." *Eureka Times-Standard*. 20 Oct. 2005. 22 Sept. 2014. <http://www.times-standard.com/ci_3134628>

129 **"grant McKinley amnesty."** Wear, Kimberly. "Statue Spared." *Eureka Times-Standard*. 21 Oct. 2005. 22 Sept. 2014. <http://www.times-standard.com/local/ci_3138720>

129 **"cheese stuffed in its ears."** Associated Press, "McKinley Legacy."

129 **The thumb itself went missing.** *Arcata Union* and *Arcata Eye*. *On This Day in Arcata*. Charleston, SC: Arcadia Publishing, 2008. 102.

130 **"one thing in each county."** Slevin, Peter. "On Roads, Schools—and Dimes?—Reagan Lives On." *Washington Post*. 6 Jun. 2004. 23 Sept. 2014. <http://www.washingtonpost.com/wp-dyn/articles/A19169-2004Jun5.html>

130 **more than three thousand counties.** Lochhead, Carolyn. "GOP Mission: Name 3,000 Things After Reagan." *San Francisco Chronicle*. 13 May 2014. 13 Nov. 2014. <http://www.sfgate.com/politics/article/GOP-mission-Name-3-000-things-after-Reagan-5475466.php>

130 **its considerable influence.** Stiles, Andrew. "Remember Grover Norquist?" *National Review*. 30 Oct. 2013. 13 Nov. 2013. <http://www.nationalreview.com/article/362556/remember-grover-norquist-andrew-stiles>

130 **from a Democratic president.** Swidey, Neil. "Grover Norquist: Emperor of No." *Boston Globe Magazine*. 16 Mar. 2012. 13 Nov. 2014. <http://www.bostonglobe.com/magazine/2012/03/16/read-grover-norquist-lips/HYhyPVdyay7oMNf3ETRyYI/story.html>

130 **called himself a "Darth Vader."** Swidey.

131 **"to contend for the future."** Borger, Gloria. "In Search of Mount Reagan." *U.S. News & World Report* 123.23 (15 Dec. 1997). 35.

131 **"everything that wasn't nailed down."** Baer, Susan. "Tributes to Reagan Are in the Running." *Baltimore Sun*. 2 Dec. 1997. 16 Nov. 2014. <http://articles.baltimoresun.com/1997-12-02/news/1997336003_1_washington-national-airport-reagan-washington-norquist>

131 **ended up on a coin.** Slevin.

131 **within the year after they died.** Harper, Jennifer, and William Glanz. "Naming Efforts get Renewed Push." *Washington Times*. 9 Jun. 2004. A10.

131 **Ronald Reagan Building**. Slevin, Peter. "Republicans Pushing Adoration of Ronald Reagan Across Country." *San Francisco Chronicle*. 17 Jun. 2001. 16 Nov. 2014. <http://www.sfgate.com/politics/article/Republicans-pushing-adoration-of-Ronald-Reagan-2909554.php>

131 **renamed the Ronald Reagan Institute of Emergency Medicine.** D'Agostino, Joseph A. "Ronald Reagan Legacy Project." *Human Events* 54.38 (9 Oct. 1998). 19.

132 **"'Who was this man.'"** Mechanic, Michael. "A Fitting Memorial." *Mother Jones* 26.2 (Mar./Apr. 2001). 24.

132 **"These are easy dedications."** "What Can I Do?" Ronald Reagan Legacy

Project. 16 Nov. 2014. <http://www.ronaldreaganlegacyproject.org/userfiles /012611ot-reaganwhatcanidohandout.pdf>

132   **"Norquist had learned the lessons."** Bunch, Will. "How Republicans Created the Myth of Ronald Reagan." *Salon.* 2 Feb. 2009. 12 Nov. 2014. <http://www.salon.com/2009/02/02/ronald_reagan_2/>

132   **National Airport in Washington.** Ota, Alan K. "Partisan Rancor Flares in Debate to Rename National Airport." *Congressional Quarterly.* 7 Feb. 1998. 14 Nov. 2014. <http://www.cnn.com/ALLPOLITICS/1998/02/13/cq/airport.html>

132   **The DC transit authority refused.** Slevin, "Republicans."

132   **"already named after a president."** Borger.

132   **"something un-Reaganesque."** Slevin, "On Roads."

133   **passed the House and Senate.** Ota.

133   **replace Alexander Hamilton on the $10 bill.** Page, Susan. "Monetary Memorial? That's the $10 Question." *USA Today.* 8 Jun. 2004. 14a.

133   **"it will pass very easily."** Slevin, "Republicans."

133   **Nancy Reagan declared herself opposed.** Page.

133   **a bill President Reagan signed in 1986.** Slevin, "Republicans."

133   **in which Reagan had lived as a preschooler.** Cholke, Sam. "Ronald Reagan's Boyhood Home Being Demolished by University of Chicago." *DNAinfo.* 3 Apr. 2013. 17 Nov. 2014. <http://www.dnainfo.com/chicago/20130403/hyde -park/ronald-reagans-boyhood-home-being-demolished-by-university-of- chicago>

133   **set the thing on fire.** Juarez, Leticia. "Reagan Statue in Temecula Charred in Arson Fire." *Eyewitness News*, ABC7 Los Angeles. 23 Sept. 2013. 27 May 2014. <http://abc7.com/archive/9259154/>

134   **on the hunt for a mountain peak.** Ball, Molly. "How to Name a Mountain After Ronald Reagan." *Atlantic.* 8 Feb. 2013. 13 Nov. 2014. <http:// www.theatlantic.com/politics/archive/2013/02/how-to-name-a-mountain -after-ronald-reagan/273000/>

134   **change the name of Mount Clay.** Associated Press. "Insignificant N.H. Peak Getting Significant Name: Mount Reagan." *St. Petersburg Times.* 15 Jun. 2003. 17 Nov. 2014. <http://www.sptimes.com/2003/06/15/Worldandnation/ Insignificant_NH_peak.shtml>

134   **local resistance to the change.** Jensen, Chris. "Mount Reagan Is Still Mount Clay—on US Maps." New Hampshire Public Radio. 13 May 2010. 17 Nov. 2014. <http://info.nhpr.org/node/32445>

134   **a mountain range east of Las Vegas.** Flock, Elizabeth, and Kenneth T. Walsh. "Honoring the Gipper." *U.S. News Digital Weekly* 5.12 (22 Mar. 2013). 2.

134   **"Reagan was a marquee performer."** Ball.

134   **name that mountain after a Nevada lawmaker.** Lochhead.

134   **hundreds of Reagan memorials.** "Map & Directory." Ronald Reagan Legacy Project. 28 Mar. 2015. <http://www.ronaldreaganlegacyproject.org/ map>

135   **new names for the team.** Kaczynski, Andrew. "Anti-Tax Crusader Grover Norquist Endorses Naming Redskins After Ronald Reagan." *Buzzfeed.* 18 Jun. 2014. 25 Jun. 2014. <http://www.buzzfeed.com/andrewkaczynski/ anti-tax-crusader-grover-norquist-endorses-renaming-redskins>

135 **Gallup Poll respondents.** Gillespie, Mark. "JFK Ranked as Greatest U.S. President." Gallup. 21 Feb. 2000. 17 Nov. 2014. <http://www.gallup.com/poll/3214/JFK-Ranked-Greatest-US-President.aspx>

135 **ranks near the top.** Newport, Frank. "Americans Say Reagan Is the Greatest U.S. President." Gallup. 18 Feb. 2011. 17 Nov. 2014. <http://www.gallup.com/poll/146183/Americans-Say-Reagan-Greatest-President.aspx>

135 **a hologram version of the Great Communicator.** Pfeiffer, Eric. "Reagan Hologram Is Real, Was Planned for RNC Debut." *Yahoo! News.* 30 Aug. 2012. 17 Nov. 2014. <http://news.yahoo.com/blogs/the-ticket/reagan-hologram-real-planned-rnc-debut-203919642--election.html>

136 **played up Jefferson.** Hamby, Alonzo L. *For the Survival of Democracy: Franklin Roosevelt and the World Crisis of the 1930s.* New York: Simon & Schuster, 2004. 422.

136 **on the nickel in 1938.** "Jefferson Nickel (Five-Cent Coin)." United States Mint. 23 Nov. 2014. <http://www.usmint.gov/mint_programs/circulatingcoins/?action=circnickel>

136 **"in the midst of a struggle."** Hamby 422.

136 **"The Jefferson statehood tale."** Laufer, Peter. "California's Grumpy Secessionists of the Far North." *Los Angeles Times.* 9 Jan. 2014. 8 Feb. 2014. <http://www.latimes.com/opinion/op-ed/la-oe-laufer-jefferson-california-secession-20140109-story.html>

136 **moved a portrait.** Greenberg, David. "Hot for Coolidge." *Slate.* 10 Nov. 2011. 17 Nov. 2014. <http://www.slate.com/articles/life/history_lesson/2011/11/calvin_coolidge_why_are_republicans_so_obsessed_with_him_.html>

136 **Great Refrainer.** Shlaes, Amity. *Coolidge.* New York: HarperCollins, 2013. eBook file. Introduction.

136 **"You lose."** Greenberg, David. *Calvin Coolidge: The American Presidents Series: The 30th President, 1923–1929.* New York: Macmillan, 2007. 10.

136 **frugal with the federal budget.** Shlaes, Introduction.

137 **"a great advantage to a president."** Smith, Richard Norton. "Introduction." In Brian Lamb, *Who's Buried in Grant's Tomb? A Tour of Presidential Gravesites.* New York: PublicAffairs, 2010. X.

137 **a heart attack at home.** Greenberg, *Coolidge* 154.

137 **"How can you tell?"** Fawcett 25.

137 **twenty-three words long.** Scriba, Jay. "Which President Wrote the Shortest Will?" *Milwaukee Journal.* 13 Apr. 1978. 10.

137 **a mere five minutes.** Lamb 129.

137 **The will of Calvin Coolidge.** Scriba 10.

138 **started the cheese operation in 1890.** Kardashian, Kirk. "Uncommon Curds." *Seven Days.* 25 Nov. 2009. 22 Nov. 2014. <http://www.sevendaysvt.com/vermont/uncommon-curds/Content?oid=2138850>

138 **revived it in the 1960s.** Dornbusch, Jane. "Young Cheesemaker Takes Over 120-Year-Old Business." *Boston Globe.* 21 Aug. 2012. 5 Sept. 2014. <http://www.bostonglobe.com/lifestyle/food-dining/2012/08/21/young-cheesemaker-vermont-takes-over-year-old-business/0OtvpyiADUwfvpomHQQJRI/story.html>

138 **captured his imagination.** Kardashian.

138 **to earn an MBA.** Dornbusch.

138 **Vermont Institute for Artisan Cheese.** Gardner, Laura. "Reinventing the Wheel." *Brandeis Magazine.* Summer 2011. 5 Sept. 2014. <http://www.brandeis .edu/magazine/2011/summer/featured-stories/sidebar-stories/wheel.html>

139 **"to re-create that early cheese."** Dornbusch.

139 **older, English-style techniques.** Gardner.

139 **ages for at least ten months.** Dornbusch.

139 **six or even seven days.** Gardner.

140 **"taste and touch and smell it."** Dornbusch, Jane. "Calvin Coolidge and Plymouth Cheese." *Culture.* 23 Sept. 2010. 18 Nov. 2014. <http:// culturecheesemag.com/cheese-talk/calvin-coolidge-plymouth-cheese>

Chapter 7: Robots and Sphinxes

141 **"I come down here almost every evening."** "Johnson Family Cemetery." Lyndon B. Johnson National Historical Park. 24 Nov. 2014. <http://www .nps.gov/lyjo/planyourvisit/johnsoncemetery.htm>

141 **the LBJ Ranch—2,700 acres during his presidency.** Vertuino, Jim. "Johnson Ranch to Become Public." *Washington Post.* 13 Jul. 2007. 28 Mar. 2015. <http://www.washingtonpost.com/wp-dyn/content/article/2007/07/13/ AR2007071300090.html>

142 **"This is my ranch."** Hannaford, Peter. *Presidential Retreats: Where the Presidents Went and Why They Went There.* New York: Simon & Schuster, 2012. 213.

142 **first to open with a university affiliation.** Hufbauer, Benjamin. *Presidential Temples: How Memorials and Libraries Shape Public Memory.* Lawrence: University Press of Kansas, 2005. 74.

143 **"meant to be an addendum."** Updegrove, Mark. Personal interview. 20 Aug. 2014.

143 **giant talking mascot.** Dunbar, Wells. "Photos: State Fair Mascot 'Big Tex' Catches Fire." KUT News. 19 Oct. 2012. 24 Aug. 2014. <http://kut.org/post/ photos-state-fair-mascot-big-tex-catches-fire-updated>

143 **gave him an upgrade.** Silverman, Rachel Emma. "At Presidential Library, LBJ Gets a Makeover." *Wall Street Journal.* 28 Dec. 2012. 12 Dec. 2013. <http:// online.wsj.com/news/articles/SB1000142412788732446160457819180087411 73 48>

144 **since its opening in 1971.** Smith, Dave. *Disney Trivia from the Vault: Secrets Revealed and Questions Answered.* Disney Electronic Content, 2012. eBook file. Ch. 7.

144 **"former presidents compare their libraries."** "When It Comes to Presidential Libraries, Size Matters." NPR. 11 Apr. 2014. 27 May 2014. <http: //www.npr.org/2014/04/11/301749061/when-it-comes-to-presidential -libraries-size-matters>

144 **"a virile man."** Hufbauer 83.

144 **Great Hall of Achievement.** Hufbauer 86.

144 **"It looks like power."** Updegrove.

144 **the latest admission numbers.** Hufbauer 176–77.

144 **tracking the number of postcards.** Gibbs, Nancy, and Michael Duffy. *The Presidents Club: Inside the World's Most Exclusive Fraternity.* New York: Simon & Schuster, 2012. 266.

145 **hand out free doughnuts.** Hufbauer 176–77.

145 **public bathrooms close by.** Gibbs 266.

145 **to round up passersby.** Hufbauer 176–77.

145 **"President Johnson is going to ask me."** Smith, Richard Norton. "Lyndon Johnson." In Brian Lamb, *Who's Buried in Grant's Tomb? A Tour of Presidential Gravesites.* New York: PublicAffairs, 2010. 165.

146 **"there was a sorting process."** Hufbauer, Benjamin. Personal interview. 22 Jul. 2014.

146 **"intense and ferocious."** "Rutherford B. Hayes: A Life in Brief." *American President: A Reference Resource.* 28 Mar. 2015. <http://millercenter.org/president/hayes/essays/biography/1>

146 **around the trunk of a tree.** "Speaking of Pictures: Here Are All U.S. Presidents' Graves, Both Famous and Forgotten." *Life.* 6 Jul. 1953. 3.

146 **"extensively mutilated."** Hufbauer, *Presidential Temples* 25–26.

146 **many of Andrew Jackson's.** O'Neill, James E. "Will Success Spoil the Presidential Libraries?" *American Archivist* 36.3 (July 1973). 343.

146 **William Henry Harrison's papers burned.** Fawcett, Bill. *Oval Office Oddities: An Irreverent Collection of Presidential Facts, Follies, and Foibles.* New York: HarperCollins, 2008. 177.

146 **ransacked the Louisiana home.** Eisenhower, John. *Zachary Taylor: The American Presidents Series: The 12th President, 1849–1850.* New York: Macmillan, 2008. 138.

146 **stayed off-limits to researchers.** O'Neill 344–45.

147 **building a fireproof structure.** Collins, Herbert R., and David B. Weaver. *Wills of the US Presidents.* New York: Stravon Educational Press, 1976. 55.

147 **stone vault for his papers.** Millard, Candice. *Destiny of the Republic: A Tale of Madness, Medicine and the Murder of a President.* New York: Anchor Books, 2011. ePub file. Epilogue.

147 **kept private for another fifty years.** Collins 65.

147 **under lock and key until the 1940s.** Hufbauer, *Presidential Temples* 25–26.

147 **offer them for public viewing.** "About the Museum." Rutherford B. Hayes Presidential Center. 25 Jul. 2014. <http://www.rbhayes.org/hayes/museum/>

147 **Paraguay was in ruins.** D'Angelo, Guillermo Adrian. "The War That Changed South America forever." *Argentina Independent.* 10 May 2012. 2 Mar. 2014. <http://www.argentinaindependent.com/top-story/the-war-that-changed-south-america-forever/>

147 **sticks painted to look like rifles.** "The Never-Ending War." *Economist.* 22 Dec. 2012. 2 Mar. 2014. <http://www.economist.com/news/christmas/21568594-how-terrible-little-known-conflict-continues-shape-and-blight-nation>

147 **Two out of every three Paraguayans died.** Drapkin, Jenny. "Rutherford B. Hayes: The National Hero of . . . Paraguay?" *Mental Floss.* 21 Sept. 2009. 28 Mar. 2015. <http://mentalfloss.com/article/22814/rutherford-b-hayes-national-hero-paraguay>

147   **everyone else was starving.** "The Never-Ending War."

147   **a southwestern area known as the Chaco.** D'Angelo.

147   **turned to the United States for arbitration.** Associated Press. "Paraguay
        Celebrates Rutherford B. Hayes." NBC News. 13 Feb. 2009. 2 Mar. 2014. <http
        ://www.nbcnews.com/id/29186525/ns/world_news-americas/t/paraguay-
        celebrates-rutherford-b-hayes/#.VRdTl-Et5KU>

148   **his father's White House secretary.** Quinn, Sandra L. *America's Royalty:
        All the Presidents' Children.* Westport, CT: Greenwood Press, 1995. 112.

148   **cofounding Union Carbide.** Bowie, Edward L. "Hayes, Webb C." *Amer-
        ica's Heroes: Medal of Honor Recipients from the Civil War to Afghanistan.* Santa
        Barbara, CA: ABC-CLIO, 2011. 134–35.

148   **got restless in his forties.** Wead, Doug. *All the Presidents' Children: Triumph
        and Tragedy in the Lives of America's First Families.* New York: Atria Books, 2003.
        185.

148   **he was wounded twice.** Bowie 134–35.

148   **caught up in the Boxer Rebellion.** Wead 190.

148   **snuck behind the lines of insurgents.** Bowie 134–35.

148   **"a suitable fireproof building."** Keeler, Lucy Elliot, ed. *Dedication of the
        Hayes Memorial Library and Museum in Honor of Rutherford Birchard Hayes at Spie-
        gel Grove State Park, Fremont, Ohio, May 30, 1916.* Columbus, OH: Press of the
        F. J. Heer Printing Company, 1916. 36.

148   **the old gates to the White House.** Zurcher, Neil. *Ohio Oddities: A Guide
        to the Curious Attractions of the Buckeye State.* Cleveland: Gray, 2008. 46.

149   **a shady corner of Spiegel Grove.** Keeler 36–37.

149   **a tall granite monument.** Lamb 81–82.

149   **"caused the horses to plunge forward."** Keeler, Lucy Elliot. "Unveiling
        of the Soldiers' Memorial Tablet on the Hayes Memorial Building at Spiegel
        Grove." *Ohio Archaeological and Historical Quarterly* 29 (1920). Columbus, OH:
        Press of the F. J. Heer Printing Company, 1916. 327.

149   **vote fraud of every kind.** King, Gilbert. "The Ugliest, Most Contentious
        Presidential Election Ever." *Smithsonian.* 7 Sept. 2012. 28 Mar. 2015. <http://
        www.smithsonianmag.com/history/the-ugliest-most-contentious-presi
        dential-election-ever-28429530/>

150   **thinking of Hayes and his museum.** Hufbauer, *Presidential Temples* 25–26.

150   **"a great fan of saving things."** Bassanese, Lynn. Personal interview. 13
        Aug. 2014.

150   **Roosevelt's stamp collection.** Collins 199.

150   **three hundred species of birds.** Margaret, Amy. *Franklin D. Roosevelt
        Library and Museum.* New York: Rosen Publishing Group, 2004. 8.

150   **"write the story of his presidency."** Bassanese.

150   **Spain's civil war.** Hufbauer, *Presidential Temples* 30–31.

150   **"a shrine to my life."** Hufbauer, personal interview.

150   **sketched out the "shrine."** Hufbauer, *Presidential Temples* 23.

150   **"Only an egocentric megalomaniac."** Span, Paula. "Monumental Ambi-
        tion." *Washington Post Magazine.* 17 Feb. 2002. 4 Jul. 2014. W24. <http://ore
        gonstate.edu/instruct/hsts507/doel/preslib.htm>

150   **"utterly un-American."** O'Neill 346.

151 **Congress approved the library bill.** Hufbauer, *Presidential Temples* 32.

151 **open in 1941.** Hufbauer, Benjamin. "Archives of Spin." *New York Times.* 20 Jan. 2007. 31 May 2014. <http://www.nytimes.com/2007/01/20/opinion /20hufbauer.html?_r=0>

151 **intended to help historians.** Hufbauer, *Presidential Temples* 33.

151 **Roosevelt's eighteen-car funeral train.** Klara, Robert. *FDR's Funeral Train: A Betrayed Widow, a Soviet Spy, and a Presidency in the Balance.* New York: Macmillan, 2010. 47-51.

152 **"underneath the sundial."** Bassanese.

153 **built upon the Roosevelt model.** O'Neill 340–41.

153 **"get up and walk into my office."** Lamb 145.

153 **around his boyhood home.** Smith, Richard Norton. "Dwight Eisenhower." In Brian Lamb, *Who's Buried in Grant's Tomb? A Tour of Presidential Gravesites.* New York: PublicAffairs, 2010. 153.

153 **ashes from the president's cat.** Blue, Victoria. "American Archives Month: Kim Coryat, Clinton Presidential Library." *Prologue: Pieces of History.* 28 Oct. 2013. 29 Jul. 2014. <http://blogs.archives.gov/prologue/?p=12937>

154 **"curse as well as praise me."** Roosevelt, Franklin D. "Remarks at a Dinner of the Trustees of the Franklin D. Roosevelt Library, Inc., Washington, D.C." 4 Feb. 1939. Online by Gerhard Peters and John T. Woolley, *The American Presidency Project.* 29 Jul. 2014. <http://www.presidency.ucsb.edu/ws /?pid=15708>

154 **favorite phrases to describe the libraries.** Hufbauer, "Archives."

154 **"extended campaign commercials in museum form."** Hufbauer, personal interview.

154 **a display about Japanese American internment.** Hufbauer, *Presidential Temples* 138.

154 **little about the Iran-Contra scandal.** Nagourney, Adam. "What's a Presidential Library to Do?" *New York Times.* 12 Sept. 2011. 25 Aug. 2014. <http:// www.nytimes.com/2011/09/13/us/13libraries.html?pagewanted=all&_r=0>

154 **"wanted to make sure it was OK."** McKenna, Brendan. "Objectivity Key in Shaping Bush Library, Experts Say." *Dallas Morning News.* 21 Apr. 2008.

154 **libraries have a life cycle.** Hufbauer, *Presidential Temples* 146.

154 **"the more controversial issues."** Bassanese.

155 **sometimes disagree with him.** Hufbauer, *Presidential Temples* 159–60.

155 **"my position has changed."** Hufbauer, personal interview.

156 **more like a victim.** Nagourney, Adam. "Nixon Library Opens a Door Some Would Prefer Left Closed." *New York Times.* 31 Mar. 2011. 29 Jul. 2014. <http://www.nytimes.com/2011/04/01/us/01nixon.html?_r=0>

156 **formally affiliated with the National Archives and Records Administration.** Frank, Jeffrey. "Who Owns Richard Nixon?" *New Yorker.* 20 May 2014. 29 Jul. 2014. <http://www.newyorker.com/news/daily-comment/who -owns-richard-nixon>

156 **a new take on Watergate.** Gumbel, Andrew. "Nixon's Presidential Library: The Last Battle of Watergate." *Pacific Standard.* 8 Dec. 2011. 29 Jul. 2014. <http://www.psmag.com/navigation/politics-and-law/nixons-presiden tial-library-the-last-battle-of-watergate-38176/>

156 **"This is a conspiracy."** Nagourney, "Nixon Library."

156 **legislation that came out of Watergate.** Wiener, Jon. "At the New Watergate Gallery, the Truth Finally Wins Out." *Los Angeles Times.* 5 Apr. 2011. 29 Jul. 2014. <http://articles.latimes.com/2011/apr/05/opinion/la-oe -wiener-nixon-library-watergate-20110405>

156 **"an unapologetic attack."** Gumbel.

156 **"never claimed to be impartial."** Bostock, Bob. "The Facts About the Creation of the Watergate Exhibit at the Nixon Library." Richard Nixon Foundation. 29 Jul. 2014. <http://nixonfoundation.org/news-details.php?id=41>

156 **quit in protest.** Gumbel.

157 **worked out to cope with stress.** Whiting, David. "Nixon Library Director Leaves Mixed Legacy." *Orange County Register.* 17 Nov. 2011. 29 Jul. 2014. <http://www.ocregister.com/articles/naftali-327486-nixon-watergate.html>

157 **"gives it official sanction."** Hufbauer, personal interview.

157 **sorting through their documents.** Hufbauer, Benjamin. "Imperial shrines." *Christian Century* 125.11 (3 Jun. 2008). 12–13.

157 **an executive order.** Hufbauer, "Archives."

157 **a billion dollars of private investment.** Hufbauer, *Presidential Temples* 193.

157 **"a prestige builder."** Epstein, Jennifer. "The Fight for Obama's Presidential Library." *Politico.* 11 Feb. 2014. 1 Sept. 2014. <http://www.politico.com/ story/2014/02/president-obama-library-location-103341.html>

158 **lock himself in the bedroom and cry.** Carroll, Maurice. "Chester Arthur Tour of Old New York." *New York Times.* 18 Sept. 1981. 21 Dec. 2013. <http:// www.nytimes.com/1981/09/18/arts/chester-arthur-tour-of-old-new-york .html>

158 **"He's the president."** Ackerman, Kenneth D. *Dark Horse: The Surprise Election and Political Murder of President James A. Garfield.* Falls Church, VA: Viral History Press, 2011. eBook file. Ch. 15.

158 **served with distinction in the Civil War.** "Chester Alan Arthur." *American President: A Reference Resource.* 28 Mar. 2015. <http://millercenter.org/ president/arthur/essays/biography/print>

158 **As a young lawyer in Manhattan.** Greider, Katharine. "The Schoolteacher on the Streetcar." *New York Times.* 13 Nov. 2005. 21 Dec. 2013. <http://www .nytimes.com/2005/11/13/nyregion/thecity/13jenn.html?pagewanted=all>

158 **"nobody's damned business."** Harris, Bill, and Laura Ross. *The First Ladies Fact Book—Revised and Updated: The Childhoods, Courtships, Marriages, Campaigns, Accomplishments, and Legacies of Every First Lady from Martha Washington to Michelle Obama.* New York: Black Dog & Leventhal, 2013. 316.

158 **"burned three large garbage cans."** *Index to the Chester A. Arthur Papers.* Washington, DC: Library of Congress, 1959. v.

159 **somebody swiped them.** O'Donnell, Michelle. "Neighborhood Report: Flatiron; Some Bronze Stars Shine Brighter than Others." *New York Times.* 27 Oct. 2002. 21 Dec. 2013. <http://www.nytimes.com/2002/10/27/nyregion/ neighborhood-report-flatiron-some-bronze-stars-shine-brighter-than- others.html>

159 **"the people most obsessed with it."** Hufbauer, personal interview.

Chapter 8: Unintended Legacies

161 **"in a very cursory manner."** Updegrove, Mark. Personal interview. 20 Aug. 2014.

161 **remembered for launching the War on Poverty.** Robert Caro, Lyndon Johnson's acclaimed biographer, spoke at the University of New Hampshire on 27 Sept. 2013. After his presentation, he took questions, and I asked him what Johnson wanted his legacy to be. His answer was four words long: "The War on Poverty."

162 **body mass index.** Noah, Timothy. "Fat Presidents: A Survey." *New Republic.* 27 Sept. 2011. 29 Mar. 2015. <http://www.newrepublic.com/blog/timothy -noah/95432/overweight-presidents-survey>

162 **add more heft to the likeness.** Suess, Jeff. "President Statues Tell Our Story." *Cincinnati Enquirer.* 25 Mar. 2013. 17 Feb. 2014. <http://cincinnati.com /blogs/ourhistory/2013/03/25/president-statues-tell-our-story/>

162 **"make the chair so large."** Harvey, Steve. "Riverside's Mission Inn Big on Tradition and History." *Los Angeles Times.* 29 Nov. 2009. 27 May 2014. <http://articles.latimes.com/2009/nov/29/local/la-me-then29-2009nov29>

162 **"the surrounding furniture shakes and rumbles."** Gould, Lewis L. *The William Howard Taft Presidency.* Lawrence: University Press of Kansas, 2009. 42.

163 **"sitting on the lid."** Goodwin, Doris Kearns. *The Bully Pulpit: Theodore Roosevelt, William Howard Taft, and the Golden Age of Journalism.* New York: Simon & Schuster, 2013. xiii.

163 **"an ounce of charisma."** Gould, Lewis. Personal interview. 4 Sept. 2014.

164 **a golfer, not a Rough Rider.** Spragens, William C., ed. *Popular Images of American Presidents.* Westport, CT: Greenwood Press, 1988. 234.

164 **tariff policy.** Gould, Personal interview.

164 **"That isn't my method."** Spragens 232–23.

164 **highly unsuccessful Taft toy.** Reilly, Lucas. "Billy Possum: President Taft's Answer to the Teddy Bear." *Mental Floss.* 10 Jun. 2013. 7 Dec. 2014. <http://mentalfloss.com/article/51030/billy-possum-president-tafts-ans wer-teddy-bear>

164 **"the fattest of the fat cats."** Gould, personal interview.

164 **a case of sleep apnea.** Eknoyan, Garabed. "A History of Obesity, or How What Was Good Became Ugly and Then Bad." *Advances in Chronic Kidney Disease* 13.4 (Oct. 2006). 421–27.

164 **clearing a backlog.** Spragens 217.

164 **build a separate building.** Hall, Timothy L. *Supreme Court Justices: A Biographical Dictionary.* New York: Facts on File, 2001. 277.

165 **lost seventy pounds.** "Mr. Taft on Diet Loses 70 Pounds; Ex-President Weighs 270, as Against 340 on March 4 Last." *New York Times.* 12 Dec. 1913. 7 Dec. 2014. <http://query.nytimes.com/gst/abstract.html?res=9A07E2D9103F E633A25751C1A9649D946296D6CF>

165 **listened in on radio.** Lamb, Brian. *Who's Buried in Grant's Tomb? A Tour of Presidential Gravesites.* New York: PublicAffairs, 2010. 115–16.

165 **"three hundred pounds of solid charity."** Barber, James David. *The Pulse*

of Politics: Electing Presidents in the Media Age. 2nd ed. New Brunswick, NJ: Transaction Publishers, 1992. 223.

165 **outliving TR by more than a decade.** Gould, *William Howard Taft Presidency* 36.

165 **society's attitudes toward weight.** Eknoyan.

165 **"gravitas and maturity."** Gould, personal interview.

165 **Big was no longer beautiful.** Eknoyan.

165 **dished dirt on a number of presidents.** "Fact or Fiction: Taft Got Stuck in a Tub?" *Political Ticker.* CNN. 6 Feb. 2013. 1 Sept. 2014. <http://politicalticker.blogs.cnn.com/2013/02/06/fact-or-fiction-taft-got-stuck-in-a-tub/>

166 **"How is the horse?"** Goodwin, *Bully Pulpit* 390.

166 **"a complete misrepresentation."** Spragens 217.

166 **Taft's descendants.** Wead, Doug. *All the Presidents' Children: Triumph and Tragedy in the Lives of America's First Families.* New York: Atria Books, 2003. 204–13.

166 **ranked the presidents by body mass index.** Kain, Erik. "A History of Fat Presidents." *Forbes.* 28 Sept. 2011. 7 Dec. 2014. <http://www.forbes.com/sites/erikkain/2011/09/28/a-history-of-fat-presidents/>

166 **grown more negative.** Conlon, Kevin. "Bill Clinton and McDonald's: Let's Forgo the Fries and Fight the Fat." CNN. 27 Sept. 2013. 7 Dec. 2014. <http://www.cnn.com/2013/09/26/us/mcdonalds-value-meal/>

166 **only one president in the television age.** White, Chris. "Question 22: Can the President Be Fat?" *McSweeney's.* 5 Oct. 2009. 7 Dec. 2014. <http://www.mcsweeneys.net/articles/question-22-can-the-president-be-fat>

166 **public attitudes about size.** Choi, Candice. "Attitudes on Obesity Are Lightening Up, Poll Finds." *SeattlePI.* 11 Jan. 2006. 7 Dec. 2014. <http://www.seattlepi.com/lifestyle/health/article/Attitudes-on-obesity-are-lightening-up-poll-finds-1192431.php>

166 **hectoring people about being overweight.** Puhl, Rebecca, and Charles A. Heuer. "Obesity Stigma: Important Considerations for Public Health." *American Journal of Public Health* 100.6 (Jun. 2010). 1019–28.

167 **painted to look like expensive marble.** "The Hermitage Mansion Story." Andrew Jackson's Hermitage. 29 Mar. 2015. <http://thehermitage.com/learn/mansion-grounds/mansion/mansion-story/>

167 **highly profane eulogy.** "Stranger than Fiction: Andrew Jackson's Foul Mouthed Fowl." *Jefferson County Post.* 8 Apr. 2013. 29 Mar. 2015. <http://jeffersoncountypost.com/?p=8084>

168 **"remarkably well preserved."** Mullin, Marsha. Personal interview. 20 Feb. 2014.

168 **born at the Hermitage.** Dorris, Mary C. Currey. *Preservation of the Hermitage, 1889–1915: Annals, History, and Stories.* Nashville, TN: Smith and Lamar, 1915. 116–28.

168 **"unclear what his job was."** Mullin.

168 **rented twenty-four acres.** "Alfred's Cabin." Information sign at Andrew Jackson's Hermitage. 25 Nov. 2013.

169 **His wife, Gracie.** Dorris 116–28.

169 **"the first tour guide."** Mullin.

169 **strong suit was his dates.** Dorris 116–28.

169 **"traded the mirror back."** Mullin.

170 **the chance to honor him.** Dorris 116–28.

170 **"southern ladies in the nineteenth century."** Mullin.

170 **"a haughty aristocrat."** Dorris 116–28.

170 **"they honored the deal."** Mullin.

171 **a centralized storehouse of information.** "DAACS Project History." 15 Dec. 2014. <http://www.daacs.org/aboutdaacs/project-history/>

171 **The colonization movement.** "American Colonization Society." *Africans in America*. 30 Nov. 2014. <http://www.pbs.org/wgbh/aia/part3/3p1521.html>

171 **left it two thousand dollars.** Collins, Herbert R., and David B. Weaver. *Wills of the US Presidents.* New York: Stravon Educational Press, 1976. 45.

171 **twelve thousand emancipated people.** "American Colonization Society."

171 **named the capital city Monrovia.** Hart, Gary. *James Monroe: The American Presidents Series: The 5th President, 1817–1825.* New York: Macmillan, 2005. 104.

171 **long-running tensions.** Steinberg, Jonny. *Little Liberia: An African Odyssey in New York City.* New York: Vintage Books, 2012. 36–42.

171 **civil wars.** Barry, Ellen. "From Staten Island Haven, Liberians Reveal War's Scars." *New York Times.* 18 Sept. 2007. 28 May 2014. <http://www.nytimes.com/2007/09/18/nyregion/18liberians.html?_r=0>

171 **worst Ebola outbreak on record.** Tharoor, Ishaan. "This Is the Worst Ebola Outbreak in History. Here's Why You Should Be Worried." *Washington Post.* 28 Jul. 2014. 29 Mar. 2015. <http://www.washingtonpost.com/blogs/worldviews/wp/2014/07/28/this-is-the-worst-ebola-outbreak-in-history-heres-why-you-should-be-worried/>

172 **a world-class university.** Crawford, Alan Pell. *Twilight at Monticello: The Final Years of Thomas Jefferson.* New York: Random House, 2008. 206.

172 **"not a word more."** Barker, Tim. "Thomas Jefferson Tombstone, now at Mizzou, Will Be Restored." *St. Louis Post-Dispatch.* 1 Jan. 2013. 2 Oct. 2013. <http://www.stltoday.com/news/local/education/thomas-jefferson-tombstone-now-at-mizzou-will-be-restored/article_c4e79fb0-9566-5312-8dad-f0bdd2c9bd20.html>

172 **one of his last public appearances.** Crawford 206.

173 **"impossible to reconcile."** Franklin, John Hope. "John Hope Franklin, Historian." Interview. PBS. 9 Mar. 2015. <http://www.pbs.org/jefferson/archives/interviews/Franklin.htm>

173 **held on to the graveyard.** "1826 to Civil War." Monticello Association. 31 Dec. 2014. <http://www.monticello-assoc.org/1826-to-civil-war.html>

173 **on hand at the University of Virginia.** Gallagher, Edward J. "Cooley Stops the Show: An Overview." *The Jefferson-Hemings Controversy.* 22 Jan. 2015. <http://digital.lib.lehigh.edu/trial/jefferson//episodes/list/9_1>

173 **"Jeffersonian Legacies" conference.** "The History of a Secret." *Frontline.* 18 Dec. 2014. <http://www.pbs.org/wgbh/pages/frontline/shows/jefferson/cron/>

173 **"part of a special family."** Cooley, Robert H., III. Interview. *Getting Word:*

African-American Families of Monticello. 6 Oct. 1995. 18 Dec. 2014. <http://slavery.monticello.org/getting-word/people/robert-h-cooley-iii>

174 **"I knew who Jefferson was."** Cooley, Robert H., III. "Robert Cooley, Hemings Descendant." Interview. PBS. 22 Dec. 2014. <http://www.pbs.org/jefferson/archives/interviews/Cooley.htm>

174 **"a family secret."** Cooley, *Getting Word.*

174 **two Bronze Stars.** Hendricks, Melissa. "A Daughter's Declaration." *Johns Hopkins Magazine.* Sept. 1999. 16 Dec. 2014. <http://pages.jh.edu/~jhumag/0999web/roots.html>

174 **"a law school on the grounds."** Cooley, "Robert Cooley."

174 **Thomas Woodson Family Association.** Thomas, Robert McG., Jr. "Robert Cooley 3d, 58, Lawyer Who Sought Link to Jefferson." *New York Times.* 3 Aug. 1998. 17 Dec. 2014. <http://www.nytimes.com/1998/08/03/us/robert-cooley-3d-58-lawyer-who-sought-link-to-jefferson.html>

174 **Other oral traditions.** Lanier, Shannon, and Jane Feldman. *Jefferson's Children: The Story of One American Family.* New York: Random House, 2002. 30.

174 **his body started to "tingle."** Randolph, Laura B. "Thomas Jefferson's Black and White Descendants Debate His Lineage and Legacy." *Ebony.* Jul. 1993. 25–29.

174 **"There are hundreds of us."** Gallagher.

174 **James Callender went public.** "James Callender." *American Experience: John and Abigail Adams.* 26 Aug. 2005. 30 Nov. 2014. <http://www.pbs.org/wgbh/amex/adams/peopleevents/p_callender.html>

175 **"kept, as his concubine."** Callendar, James Thomson. "The President, Again." *Encyclopedia Virginia.* 1 Sept. 1802. 16 Dec. 2014. <http://encyclopediavirginia.org/_The_President_Again_by_James_Thomson_Callender_September_1_1802>

175 **the usual character assassination.** Singleton, Maura. "Anatomy of a Mystery." *UVA Magazine.* Fall 2007. 21 Jan. 2015. <http://uvamagazine.org/articles/anatomy_of_a_mystery/>

175 **putting those children up for auction.** Lepore, Jill. "President Tom's Cabin." *New Yorker.* 22 Sept. 2008. 86–91.

175 **Madison Hemings told an Ohio newspaper.** Hemings, Madison. "Life Among the Lowly, No. 1." *Encyclopedia Virginia.* 13 Mar. 1873. 28 May 2014. <http://www.encyclopediavirginia.org/_Life_Among_the_Lowly_No_1_by_Madison_Hemings_March_13_1873>

175 **account was dismissed.** Patton, Venetria K., and Ronald Jemal Stevens. "Narrating Competing Truths in the Thomas Jefferson–Sally Hemings Paternity Debate." *Black Scholar* 29.4 (Winter 1999). 8–15.

175 **pointed to Peter Carr.** Lepore.

176 **presented as oral history.** Gordon-Reed, Annette. Interview. *Frontline: Jefferson's Blood.* 23 Feb. 2014. <http://www.pbs.org/wgbh/pages/frontline/shows/jefferson/interviews/reed.html>

176 **"no involvement of labor."** "American Icons: Monticello." *Studio 360.* 17 Feb. 2012. 24 Dec. 2014. <http://www.studio360.org/story/96253-american-icons-monticello/transcript/>

176 **Italian architect Andrea Palladio.** Howard, Hugh, and Roger Straus III.

Houses of the Presidents: Childhood Homes, Family Dwellings, Private Escapes, and Grand Estates. New York: Little, Brown, 2012. 31–34.

176 **"Contrive a building."** Wiencek, Henry. "The Dark Side of Thomas Jefferson." *Smithsonian.* Oct. 2012. 30 Nov. 2014. <http://www.smithsonianmag.com/history/the-dark-side-of-thomas-jefferson-35976004/?all>

176 **delved into Jefferson's inner life.** Bringhurst, Newell G. *Fawn McKay Brodie: A Biographer's Life.* Norman: University of Oklahoma Press, 1999. 215–20.

177 **each time she conceived.** Brodie, Fawn M. *Thomas Jefferson: An Intimate History.* New York: W. W. Norton, 1974. 291–94.

177 **the biggest historical assumptions.** Patton 8–15.

177 **popular fiction.** "The History of a Secret."

177 **television miniseries.** Bringhurst 215–20.

177 **Woodson descendants reunion.** Athans, Marego. "A Legacy of Reason." *Baltimore Sun.* 29 May 1999. 23 Jun. 2014. <http://articles.baltimoresun.com/1999-05-29/features/9905290353_1_thomas-jefferson-hemings-cooley>

177 **"finest example of American architecture."** Cooley, "Robert Cooley."

177 **he kept telling it.** Athans.

177 **buried in Monticello's graveyard.** Lanier 44.

178 **unexpectedly died.** Thomas.

178 **"not prepared to admit Hemings descendants."** Lanier 44.

178 **a private cemetery in Richmond.** Thomas.

178 **"wondered if DNA might be used."** Foster, Eugene. Interview. *Frontline: Jefferson's Blood.* 21 Jan. 2015. <http://www.pbs.org/wgbh/pages/frontline/shows/jefferson/interviews/foster.html>

178 **suggested Foster take another look.** Smith, Dinitia, and Nicholas Wade. "DNA Test Finds Evidence of Jefferson Child by Slave." *New York Times.* 1 Nov. 1998. 20 Jan. 2015. <http://www.nytimes.com/1998/11/01/us/dna-test-finds-evidence-of-jefferson-child-by-slave.html>

178 **obtained DNA samples.** Lepore.

178 **"the Jefferson family chromosome."** Foster.

179 **compared it to a series of samples.** Smith.

179 **several longtime Virginia families.** Thomas.

179 **sent everything he'd collected to geneticists.** Smith.

179 **matched the "Jefferson chromosome."** Lepore.

179 **ruled out the Jefferson family's story.** Smith.

179 **"Daddy's mission and his quest."** Lanier 47.

179 **"neither be definitely excluded nor solely implicated."** Lamb, Yvonne Shinhoster. "Eugene Foster; Led Jefferson Paternity Study." *Washington Post.* 25 Jul. 2008. 15 Dec. 2014. <http://www.washingtonpost.com/wp-dyn/content/article/2008/07/24/AR2008072403726.html>

179 **"From the historical knowledge."** Patton 8–15.

180 **historians who had been skeptical.** Smith.

180 **"open up the Monticello Association."** "American Icons: Monticello."

180 **About thirty-five Hemings descendants.** Smith, Leef. "Jeffersons Split over Hemings Descendants." *Washington Post.* 17 May 1999. 8 Feb. 2014. B1. <http://www.washingtonpost.com/wp-srv/local/daily/may99/reunion17.htm>

180 **dozens of reporters.** Hendricks.

180 **"this little family association."** Lanier 122.

180 **explaining his DNA findings.** Hendricks.

180 **formally applying for membership.** Athans.

180 **"bulldoze their way."** "American Icons: Monticello."

180 **members-only discussion and vote.** Athans.

180 **"the start of a business meeting."** "American Icons: Monticello."

181 **The motion failed.** Athans.

181 **honorary members for the time being.** Smith, L.

181 **"More evidence is coming forward."** Jankofsky, Michael. "Jefferson's Kin Not Ready To Accept Tie to Slave." *New York Times.* 16 May 1999. 8 Feb. 2014. <http://www.nytimes.com/1999/05/16/us/jefferson-s-kin-not-ready-to-accept-tie-to-slave.html>

181 **Jefferson birthday celebration.** Singleton.

181 **"to stand always in opposition."** Weil, Francois. *Family Trees.* Cambridge: Harvard University Press, 2013. eBook file. Ch. 1.

181 **"almost certainly false."** Singleton.

181 **point to his brother Randolph.** Hendricks.

181 **"assumed the worst."** Singleton.

181 **"dedicated deniers."** Associated Press. "Not All Are Welcome at Jefferson Family Reunion." *Los Angeles Times.* 7 May 2000. 8 Feb. 2014. <http://articles.latimes.com/2000/may/07/news/mn-27481>

181 **"defending what America means."** Cogliano, Francis D. *Thomas Jefferson: Reputation and Legacy.* Charlottesville: University of Virginia Press, 2006. 183.

182 **"the reputation of a man who owned slaves."** Lanier 81–82.

182 **"maybe I'll reconsider."** Associated Press. "Historian Wants Access to Kansas Grave in Probing Link Between Jefferson, Slave." *Topeka Capital-Journal.* 4 Jan. 2000. 16 Dec. 2014. <http://cjonline.com/stories/010400/new_ksgrave.shtml#.VRinR-Et5KU>

182 **voted 67 to 5.** "American Icons: Monticello."

182 **"most likely the father of all six."** Thomas Jefferson Memorial Foundation. "Report of the Research Committee on Thomas Jefferson and Sally Hemings." Thomas Jefferson's Monticello. Jan. 2182. 22 Jan. 2015. <http://www.monticello.org/site/plantation-and-slavery/report-research-committee-thomas-jefferson-and-sally-hemings>

182 **holding its own reunions.** Associated Press. "Hemings Family Holds Own Reunion at Monticello." *USA Today.* 13 Jul. 2003. 8 Feb. 2014. <http://usatoday30.usatoday.com/news/nation/2003-07-13-hemings-family-reunion_x.htm>

182 **"with a single step."** Jankofsky.

Chapter 9: Eternal Flame

183 **"recall a list."** Roediger, Henry. Interview. *Science Friday.* 1 Dec. 2014. 1 Dec. 2014. <http://www.sciencefriday.com/segment/12/05/2014/how-long-does-a-president-s-legacy-last.html>

183 **for forty years.** Ferdman, Roberto A. "The Presidents We Remember—and the Ones We've Almost Entirely Forgotten." *Washington Post.* 1 Dec. 2014. 8 Dec. 2014. <http://www.washingtonpost.com/blogs/wonkblog/wp/2014/12/01/the-presidents-we-remember-and-the-ones-weve-almost-entirely-forgotten/>

183 **"plot for people."** Roediger.

184 **"an idea lives on."** Kennedy, John F. "Remarks Recorded for the Opening of a USIA Transmitter at Greenville, North Carolina." 8 Feb. 1963. 29 Mar. 2015. Online by Gerhard Peters and John T. Woolley, *The American Presidency Project.* <http://www.presidency.ucsb.edu/ws/?pid=9551>

184 **custom-built wire basket.** Poole, Robert M. *On Hallowed Ground: The Story of Arlington National Cemetery.* New York: Bloomsbury, 2009. 219.

185 **"a lighter in your pocket."** Reece, Kevin. "JFK's 'Eternal Flame' Sits in a Houston Museum." *KHOU News.* 22 Nov. 2013. 7 Jan. 2014. <http://www.khou.com/story/local/2015/05/11/12252942/>

185 **"I won't tell if you won't tell."** Poole 226.

185 **an electric spark mechanism.** Reece.

185 **the end of its expected life-span.** "Corps Begins Repairs JFK Eternal Flame." U.S. Army. 30 Apr. 2013. 29 Mar. 2015. <http://www.army.mil/article/102215/Corps_begins_repairs_JFK_Eternal_Flame/>

185 **"some silly little Communist."** Manchester, William. *The Death of a President.* New York: Harper & Row, 1967. 407.

185 **"presented to the world."** *Jacqueline Kennedy: Historic Conversations on Life with John F. Kennedy.* New York: Hachette Books, 2011. xxvii.

185 **Arc de Triomphe.** Poole 219.

186 **"see his flame beneath the mansion."** White, Theodore H. "For President Kennedy: An Epilogue." *Life.* 6 Dec. 1963. 158–59.

186 **"go back to Boston."** Poole 210–13.

186 **a family plot.** Zimmerman, Rachel. "Tale of the Pediatrician Snatched to Treat the Kennedy Baby." WBUR. 6 Aug. 2013. 29 Mar. 2015. <http://commonhealth.wbur.org/2013/08/tale-of-the-pediatrician-snatched-to-treat-kennedy-baby>

186 **model JFK's funeral.** Carroll, Rebecca. "Protocol Fills State Funerals." *Cincinnati Enquirer.* 7 Jun. 2004. 29 Aug. 2014. <http://www.enquirer.com/editions/2004/06/07/loc_loc1arwrd.html>

186 **"a little ostentatious."** Rubin, Gretchen. *Forty Ways to Look at JFK.* New York: Ballantine Books, 2005. 161–62.

187 **"missing man" formation.** Poole 223–25.

187 **Mrs. Kennedy whispering.** Rubin 160.

187 **the riderless horse.** Gray, Jeremy. "Arthur, Black Jack and Kennedy: At Age 19, Mobile man Led Riderless Horse for Fallen President." Alabama Media Group. 14 Nov. 2013. 29 Aug. 2014. <http://blog.al.com/live/2013/11/arthur_black_jack_and_kennedy.html>

187 **cracked the sixth note.** Poole 223–25.

187 **the 175 million Americans watching.** Rubin 293.

187 **"one thing they have always lacked—majesty."** Semple, Robert B., Jr., ed. *Four Days in November: The Original Coverage of the John F. Kennedy Assassination.* New York: Macmillan, 2003. 485-6.

187   **called Theodore White.** Swanson, James. *End of Days: The Assassination of John F. Kennedy.* New York: HarperCollins, 2013. ePub file. Ch. 1.

187   **"before we'd go to sleep."** White.

188   **"never listened to 'Camelot.'"** Davies, Frank. "The House of Kennedy Revisited." *Chicago Tribune.* 10 Aug. 1995. 10 Dec. 2014. <http://articles.chicagotribune.com/1995-08-10/features/9508118896_1_joe-kennedy-kennedy-brothers-kennedy-lore>

188   **"it was usually classical."** White.

188   **"a story about infidelity."** Woodward, Richard. "Death of JFK Spawned an Industry That Thrived for Decades." *Daily Beast.* 24 Nov. 2013. 10 Dec. 2014. <http://www.thedailybeast.com/articles/2013/11/24/death-of-jfk-spawned-an-industry-that-thrived-for-decades.html>

188   **the first lady stood her ground.** Piereson, James. "How Jackie Kennedy Invented The Camelot Legend After JFK's Death." *Daily Beast.* 12 Nov. 2013. 8 Jan. 2014. <http://www.thedailybeast.com/articles/2013/11/12/how-jackie-kennedy-invented-the-camelot-legend-after-jfk-s-death.html>

188   **a hook upon which to hang its image.** Hitchens, Christopher. "Widow of Opportunity." *Vanity Fair.* Dec. 2011. 1 Feb. 2014. <http://www.vanityfair.com/culture/features/2011/12/hitchens-201112>

188   **"A magic moment in American history."** O'Brien, Michael. *John F. Kennedy: A Biography.* New York: Macmillan, 2006. xii.

188   **"they are made to happen."** Rubin 271.

188   **"accessible to the press."** Zelizer, Barbie. *Covering the Body: The Kennedy Assassination, the Media, and the Shaping of Collective Memory.* Chicago: University of Chicago Press, 1992. 26.

189   **to appear in newsreels.** Rubin 76.

189   **"twenty-four hours a day."** Rubin 133.

189   **practiced one-liners.** Fairlie, Henry. "JFK's Television Presidency." *New Republic.* 26 Dec. 1983. 21 Jan. 2014. <http://www.newrepublic.com/article/115247/john-f-kennedy-television-presidency>

189   **"props in a show."** O'Brien 815.

189   **"a television nation."** Rhule, Patty. Personal interview. 9 Oct. 2013.

189   **"surpass print for primacy."** Newseum, with Cathy Trost and Susan Bennett. *President Kennedy Has Been Shot: Experience the Moment-to-moment Account of the Four Days That Changed America.* Naperville, IL: Sourcebooks, 2003. xiv.

189   **within an hour of the shooting.** Sneed, Tierney. "How John F. Kennedy's Assassination Changed Television Forever." *U.S. News & World Report.* 14 Nov. 2013. 10 Dec. 2014. <http://www.usnews.com/news/articles/2013/11/14/how-john-f-kennedy-assassination-changed-television-forever?page=2>

190   **wall-to-wall coverage.** Newseum xiii.

190   **"No one goes past that."** Rhule.

190   **had been beating Cronkite.** Mickelson, Sig. *The Decade That Shaped Television News: CBS in the 1950s.* Westport, CT: Praeger Publishers. 212.

190   **No journalist in Dallas.** Zelizer 37–38.

190   **"Our nearest camera."** Newseum 42.

191   **always a camera in the CBS newsroom.** Sneed.

191 **overexposed and unusable.** Zelizer 73.

191 **"Lee Harold Oswald."** Newseum 210.

191 **"an ongoing attentiveness."** Zelizer, Barbie. Interview. *American Experience: Oswald's Ghost.* 11 Dec. 2014. <http://www.pbs.org/wgbh/amex/oswald/press/>

191 **presented as "four days of special coverage."** Zelizer, *Covering the Body* 38.

191 **"he was in Dallas on that day."** Zelizer, interview.

192 **defied his editors in Canada.** "Covering Chaos: The Reporters." Sixth Floor Museum at Dealey Plaza. <http://www.jfk.org/go/exhibits/chaos/reporters>

192 **may have run into Lee Harvey Oswald.** Newseum 35.

192 **standing near Jack Ruby.** "Covering Chaos: The Reporters."

192 **CBS stalwart Bob Schieffer.** Newseum 146–47.

192 **"not a taxi service."** "Covering Chaos: The Reporters."

192 **nearly got to interview Lee Harvey Oswald.** Newseum 146–47.

192 **"most ambitious exhibit."** Rhule.

193 **put out book after book.** Woodward.

193 **highest ratings ever.** Kissell, Rick. "'Killing Kennedy' Draws Record 3.4 Million for National Geographic Channel." *Variety.* 11 Nov. 2013. 30 Mar. 2015. <http://variety.com/2013/tv/news/killing-kennedy-draws-record-3-4-million-for-nat-geo-channel-1200819532/>

193 **"Big Things Happen Here."** Dallas Convention and Visitors Bureau. "Dallas: Just the Facts." 12 Dec. 2014. <http://www.visitdallas.com/includes/content/docs/media/Dallas-Facts.pdf>

193 **JFK-themed Roller Derby league.** "About Us." Assassination City Roller Derby. 13 Dec. 2014. <http://www.acderby.com/?page_id=20>

193 **an event in 1993.** Ray, Richard. "JFK Ceremony Will Go On Despite Bad Weather Threat." 21 Nov. 2013. 12 Jan. 2014. <http://www.myfoxdfw.com/story/24032074/workers-prep-for-jfk-50th-anniversary-event>

194 **"serious, respectful, understated."** Parks, Scott K. "Rawlings Names Committee to Plan Commemoration of JFK Tragedy in Dallas." *Dallas Morning News.* 31 May 2012. 5 Dec. 2013. <http://www.dallasnews.com/news/community-news/dallas/headlines/20120530-rawlings-names-committee-to-plan-commemoration-of-jfk-tragedy-in-dallas.ece>

194 **five thousand tickets.** Mezzofiore, Gianluca. "JFK Conspiracy Theorists Threaten Dealey Plaza Lockdown in 50th Anniversary Protest." *International Business Times.* 15 Nov. 2013. 8 Feb. 2014. <http://www.ibtimes.co.uk/jfk-assassination-anniversary-conspiracy-dallas-dealey-plaza-522590>

194 **security trailers with surveillance cameras.** Goldstein, Scott. "Dallas Police to Use Federally Funded Mobile Surveillance Cameras for JFK Assassination Anniversary Events." *Dallas Morning News.* 11 Sept. 2013. 13 Dec. 2013. <http://cityhallblog.dallasnews.com/2013/09/dallas-police-to-use-federally-funded-mobile-surveillance-cameras-for-jfk-assassination-anniversary-events.html/>

195 **"to level out the streets."** Nicholson, Eric. "The City of Dallas Removed

the White 'X' from Dealey Plaza on Monday." *Dallas Observer.* 19 Nov. 2013. 5 Dec. 2013. <http://blogs.dallasobserver.com/unfairpark/2013/11/dealey_plaza_x_removed.php>

195 **"gruesome little tourist magnets."** Jones, Rodger. "'Allegedly' Defaced on JFK Plaque Again." *Dallas Morning News.* 14 Nov. 2013. 5 Dec. 2013. <http://dallasmorningviewsblog.dallasnews.com/2013/11/allegedly-defaced-on-jfk-plaque-again.html/>

195 **the City That Worked.** Graham, Don. Personal interview. 7 February 2014.

195 **diversify beyond oil and land sales.** Ennis, Michael. "Spun City." *Texas Monthly.* Nov. 2013. 7 Feb. 2014. <http://www.texasmonthly.com/story/dallas-in-1963-was-more-than-the-city-of-hate>

195 **"Dallas doesn't owe a damn thing."** McAuley, James. "The City with the Death Wish in Its Eye." *New York Times.* 16 Nov. 2013. 2 Feb. 2014. <http://www.nytimes.com/2013/11/17/opinion/sunday/dallass-role-in-kennedys-murder.html>

196 **"LBJ Sold Out to Yankee Socialists."** Parks, Scott K. "Extremists in Dallas Created Volatile Atmosphere Before JFK's 1963 Visit." 12 Oct. 2013. 22 Nov. 2013. <http://www.dallasnews.com/news/jfk50/reflect/20131012-extremists-in-dallas-created-volatile-atmosphere-before-jfks-1963-visit.ece>

196 **screamed, shouted, and spat.** Wright, Lawrence. "Why Do They Hate Us So Much?" *Texas Monthly.* Nov. 1983. 5 Dec. 2013. <http://www.texasmonthly.com/story/why-do-they-hate-us-so-much?fullpage=1>

196 **in the gallant South.** Minutaglio, Bill, and Steven L. Davis. *Dallas 1963.* New York: Grand Central Publishing, 2013. 64.

196 **eccentric Texas oil baron.** Fernandez, Manny. "50 Years Later, a Changed Dallas Grapples with Its Darkest Day." *New York Times.* 19 Nov. 2013. 22 Nov. 2013. <http://www.nytimes.com/2013/11/20/us/a-changed-dallas-grapples-with-its-darkest-day.html>

196 **its regional headquarters.** Parks.

196 **his daughter Caroline's tricycle.** Wright.

196 **former army general Edwin Walker.** Parks.

196 **"human beings or animals?"** Minutaglio 248.

196 **told the president to reconsider.** Wright.

196 **US senators.** Swanson ch. 3.

196 **"control the 'air.'"** Onion, Rebecca. "In a Prophetic Letter, a Dallas Citizen Begged JFK Not to Visit." *Slate.* 15 Nov. 2013. 5 Dec. 2013. <http://www.slate.com/blogs/the_vault/2013/11/15/jfk_assassination_prophetic_letter_from_dallas_citizen_begged_the_president.html>

197 **"cancer on the body politic."** Minutaglio 255.

197 **run, and win, against Bruce Alger.** Minutaglio 325.

197 **"a small group of extremists."** Minutaglio 251.

197 **the cameras would make him look sympathetic.** Wright.

197 **blamed Alger.** Minutaglio 66.

197 **campaign kickoff in Chicago.** Minutaglio 140.

197 **sixth out of six.** Parks.

197 **racial integration.** Minutaglio 191.

197 **problem with organized crime.** Minutaglio 149.

197 **any city in 1963.** "50 Years Ago: The World in 1963." *Atlantic.* 15 Feb. 2013. 29 Jan. 2014. <http://www.theatlantic.com/infocus/2013/02/50-years-ago -the-world-in-1963/100460/>

198 **Medgar Evers was murdered.** Walsh, Kenneth T. "Turns Out 1963 Was Not So Dreamy a Year." *U.S. News & World Report.* 29 Aug. 2013. 29 Jan. 2014. <www.usnews.com/news/blogs/Ken-Walshs-Washington/2013/08/29/ turns-out-1963-was-not-so-dreamy-a-year>

198 **brazen bombing.** "50 Years Ago."

198 **"it would be Miami."** Graham.

198 **"died in enemy territory."** Wright.

198 **"God Almighty ordered this event."** Semple 307.

198 **"into nut country."** McAuley.

198 **already high murder rate go up.** Applebome, Peter. "25 Years After the Death of Kennedy, Dallas Looks at Its Changed Image." *New York Times.* 21 Nov. 1988. 5 Dec. 2013. <http://www.nytimes.com/1988/11/21/us/25-years- after-the-death-of-kennedy-dallas-looks-at-its-changed-image.html>

198 *not* **climbing anywhere else.** Pennebaker, James W. "Interview with Pro- fessor Pennebaker About the Effects of the JFK Assassination on Dallas." *Enter- tainment Tonight.* 1991. 12 Jan. 2014. <http://texasarchive.org/library/index .php?title=2013_04528>

198 **"killed our president."** Wright.

199 **"maniacs all over the world."** Semple 283.

199 **he was a Marxist.** Fernandez.

199 **his (Russian-born) wife.** Ennis.

199 **tried to kill General Edwin Walker.** Parks.

199 **two hundred thousand strong.** Jervis, Rick. "Dallas Landmarks Still Echo JFK Killing." *USA Today.* 7 Aug. 2013. 12 Jan. 2014. <http:// www.usatoday.com/story/news/nation/2013/08/07/kennedy-assassina tion-oswald-dallas-50th-anniversary/2609763/>

199 **"cannot be explained in a few words."** Semple 348.

199 **magician Gene De Jean.** Byrnes, Mark. "Dallas, 1963: 'City of Hate'?" *City- lab.* 22 Nov. 2013. 30 Mar. 2015. <http://www.citylab.com/politics/2013/11/ dallas-1963-city-hate/7244/>

199 **Dallas Cowboys.** Goodwyn, Wade. "Marking Kennedy Assassination, Dal- las Still on 'Eggshells.'" *All Things Considered.* NPR. 21 Nov. 2013. 5 Dec. 2013. <http://www.npr.org/2013/11/21/246580954/marking-kennedy-assassi nation-dallas-still-on-egg-shells>

199 **modeled in part on H. R. Hunt.** Hannaford, Alex. "Dallas: The Feud- ing Family That Inspired the TV Series." *Telegraph.* 5 Sept. 2012. 29 Jan. 2014. <http://www.telegraph.co.uk/culture/tvandradio/9446483/Dallas-the- feuding-family-that-inspired-the-TV-series.html>

199 **well beyond its Kennedy ties.** Nicholson, Eric. "City Hall: One Unfortunate Afternoon Shouldn't Overshadow Dealey Plaza's Decades of Not Murdering Presidents." *Dallas Observer.* 15 Jul. 2013. 5 Dec. 2013. <http://blogs.dallasobserv er.com/unfairpark/2013/07/city_officials_one_infamous_mo.php>

200 **she was at the Trade Mart.** Farwell, Scott. "With Ruth Altshuler at the Helm, Dallas' Painful JFK Memorial Is in Experienced Hands." *Dallas Morning News.* 2 Feb. 2013. 5 Dec. 2013. <http://www.dallasnews.com/news/community-news/dallas/headlines/20130202-dallas-painful-jfk-memorial-in-experienced-hands.ece>

200 **"many sleepless nights."** Goldstein, Scott. "Dallas Mayor Says He's Worked on JFK Speech Since January." *Dallas Morning News.* 11 Nov. 2013. 5 Dec. 2013. <http://www.dallasnews.com/news/jfk50/discuss/20131111-dallas-mayor-says-hes-worked-on-jfk-speech-since-january.ece>

201 **architect of post-assassination Dallas.** Jervis.

201 **born on the day President McKinley was shot.** Westerlin, Ann F. "Jonsson, John Erik." *Handbook of Texas Online.* Texas State Historical Association. 15 Jun. 2010. 13 Dec. 2014. <http://www.tshaonline.org/handbook/online/articles/fjowh>

201 **"the fellow on Pearl Harbor Day."** Fagin, Stephen. *Assassination and Commemoration: JFK, Dallas, and the Sixth Floor Museum at Dealey Plaza.* Norman: University of Oklahoma Press, 2013. eBook file. Introduction.

201 **"the city should be represented."** Museum placard. "Dream No Small Dreams: How Erik Jonsson Led Dallas from Tragedy to Triumph in the 1960s." Old Red Museum of Dallas County History and Culture, Dallas.

201 **put Dallas back to work.** Jervis.

202 **"They're still reacting to it."** Graham.

202 **back in place on Elm Street.** Wilonsky, Robert. "In Dealey Plaza, the X That Marked the Spot on Elm Street Where Kennedy Was Killed Has Returned." *Dallas Morning News.* 26 Nov. 2013. 5 Dec. 2013. <http://cityhallblog.dallasnews.com/2013/11/in-dealey-plaza-the-x-that-marked-the-spot-on-elm-street-where-kennedy-was-killed-has-returned.html/>

202 **asked Americans about conspiracies.** Weigel, David. "Five Conspiracy Theories and the Americans Who Believe Them." *Slate.* 2 Apr. 2013. 14 Dec. 2014. <http://www.slate.com/blogs/weigel/2013/04/02/five_conspiracy_theories_and_the_americans_who_believe_them.html>

203 **went on to confront some police.** MacCormack, John. "Dallas Puts Past to Rest in Moving Tribute to JFK." *Houston Chronicle.* 22 Nov. 2013. 13 Dec. 2014. <http://www.houstonchronicle.com/news/nation-world/nation/article/Dallas-puts-past-to-rest-in-moving-tribute-to-JFK-5004198.php>

Chapter 10: The Rest of the Set

205 **presidential PEZ dispensers.** Garnick, Darren. "Is Pez Trying to Sugarcoat American History?" *Atlantic.* 3 Jul. 2012. <http://www.theatlantic.com/politics/archive/2012/07/is-pez-trying-to-sugarcoat-american-history/259222/>

205 **little presidential figurines.** Knox, Olivier. "Sculptor in Chief: *Futurama* Writer Saves Line of Tiny Presidents." *Wired.* 19 Oct. 2009. 30 Mar. 2015. <http://www.wired.com/2009/10/st_verrone_futurama/>

205 **his friend Dwight D. Eisenhower.** Saxon, Wolfgang. "Louis Marx Sr. Is

Dead at 85; Toy Maker and Philanthropist." *New York Times*. 6 Feb. 1982. 30 Mar. 2015. <http://www.nytimes.com/1982/02/06/obituaries/louis-marx-sr-is-dead-at-85-toy-maker-and-philanthropist.html>

206 **figures of some of the potential candidates.** Knox.

206 **"uninspiring man."** Freidel, Frank, and Hugh Sidey. "Millard Fillmore." The White House. 2006. 30 Mar. 2015. <https://www.whitehouse.gov/1600/presidents/millardfillmore>

207 **"Peruvian guano."** Fillmore, Millard. "First Annual Message, December 2, 1850." *The Statesman's Manual: The Addresses and Messages of the Presidents of the United States, Inaugural, Annual, and Special, from 1789 to 1854; with a Memoir of Each of the Presidents and a History of Their Administrations: Also, the Constitution of the United States, and a Selection of Important Documents and Statistical Information*, vol. 4. Edwin Williams, ed. New York: Edward Walker, 1849. 1939.

207 **first chancellor of the University of Buffalo.** Prior, Anna. "No Joke: Buffalo and Moravia Duke It Out over Millard Fillmore." *Wall Street Journal*. 18 Feb. 2010. 11 Dec. 2013. <http://online.wsj.com/news/articles/SB10001424052748703444804575071322401554694>

208 **"the nourishment is palatable."** Lamb, Brian. *Who's Buried in Grant's Tomb? A Tour of Presidential Gravesites*. New York: PublicAffairs, 2010. 53.

209 **Morrissey.** "Founding Fathers Pub in the Press." 30 Mar. 2015. <http://www.foundingfatherspub.com/our-press>

210 **snubbed by his own party.** Rudin, Ken. "When Has a President Been Denied His Party's Nomination?" NPR. 22 Jul. 2009. 30 Mar. 2015. <http://www.npr.org/blogs/politicaljunkie/2009/07/a_president_denied_renominatio.html>

210 **dedicated a statue in his honor.** Metcalf, Henry Harrison, ed. *Dedication of a Statue of General Franklin Pierce, Fourteenth President of the United States, at the State House, Concord, November 25, 1914*. Concord: State of New Hampshire, 1914. 8.

212 **"We Polked you in '44."** Roberts, Robert North, Scott John Hammond, and Valerie A. Sulfaro. *Presidential Campaigns, Slogans, Issues, and Platforms: The Complete Encyclopedia*, vol. 1. Santa Barbara, CA: ABC-CLIO, 2012. 529.

212 **"ludicrous, ridiculous, and uninteresting."** "The Campaign and Election of 1852." *American President: A Reference Resource*. 31 Mar. 2015. <http://millercenter.org/president/pierce/essays/biography/3>

212 **"rare elasticity."** Hawthorne, Nathaniel. *The Life of Franklin Pierce*. Boston: Ticknor, Reed and Fields, 1852. 94.

212 **the turning point of the battle.** Lundberg, James M. "Nathaniel Hawthorne, Party Hack." *Slate*. 14 Sept. 2012. 31 Mar. 2015. <http://www.slate.com/articles/news_and_politics/history/2012/09/nathaniel_hawthorne_s_biography_of_franklin_pierce_why_d_he_write_it_.html>

212 **"driven from the field."** Hawthorne 102.

213 **Pierce's Whig opponent.** Eisenhower, John. *Zachary Taylor: The American Presidents Series: The 12th President, 1849–1850*. New York: Macmillan, 2008. 135.

213 **"greatest work of fiction."** Lundberg.

213 **the train's axle broke.** Quinn, Sandra L. *America's Royalty: All the Presidents' Children.* Westport, CT: Greenwood Press, 1995. 88.

213 **Bennie was crushed.** Withers, Bob. *The President Travels by Train: Politics and Pullmans.* Lynchburg, VA: TLC Publishing, 1996. 6.

213 **clear Franklin's worry list.** Martin, Albro. *Railroads Triumphant: The Growth, Rejection, and Rebirth of a Vital American Force.* New York: Oxford University Press, 1992. eBook file. Ch. 2.

213 **"God's wrath."** Quinn 87.

213 **through letters.** Hillinger, Charles. "The Charge of the Pierce Brigade: Group Strives to Rescue the Reputation of 14th President." *Los Angeles Times.* 18 Nov. 1998. 1 Sept. 2014. <http://articles.latimes.com/1988-11-18/news/vw-643_1_president-pierce>

213 **séances.** "Jane Pierce." *American President: A Reference Resource.* 31 Mar. 2015. <http://millercenter.org/president/pierce/essays/firstlady>

213 **from memory.** Hamilton, Neil. *Presidents: A Biographical Dictionary.* New York: Facts on File, 2010. 432.

213 **caught a bad cold and fever.** Deppisch, Ludwig M. *The Health of the First Ladies: Medical Histories from Martha Washington to Michelle Obama.* Jefferson, NC: McFarland, 2015. 50.

214 **sick with tuberculosis.** Purcell, L. Edward, ed. *Vice Presidents: A Biographical Dictionary.* New York: Facts on File, 2010. 135.

214 **a pro-slavery Missourian.** Egerton, Douglas R. *Year of Meteors: Stephen Douglas, Abraham Lincoln, and the Election That Brought on the Civil War.* New York: Bloomsbury, 2010. 25.

214 **"nothing left to do but to get drunk."** Holzel, David. "Five Amazing Facts About Franklin Pierce (in Honor of His 203rd Birthday)." *Mental Floss.* 19 Nov. 2007. 31 Mar. 2015. <http://mentalfloss.com/article/17407/five-amazing-facts-about-franklin-pierce-honor-his-203rd-birthday>

214 **stomach inflammation.** Lamb 56.

214 **"a well-fought bottle."** Cummins, Joseph. *Anything for a Vote: Dirty Tricks, Cheap Shots, and October Surprises in U.S. Presidential Campaigns.* Philadelphia: Quirk Books, 2007. 86.

214 **"his place will not be missed."** "Hon. Franklin Pierce; Death of the Ex-President at Concord, N. H." *New York Times.* 9 Oct. 1869. 31 Mar. 2015. <http://query.nytimes.com/gst/abstract.html?res=9F01E4D8173BE63BBC4153DFB6678382679FDE>

215 **"preservation of the Union."** Wheeler, Everett Pepperell. *Daniel Webster, the Expounder of the Constitution.* New York: G. P. Putnam's Sons, 1905. 164.

215 **a platform of ending slavery.** Robinson, J. Dennis. "Whittier's Anti-Slavery Ode to New Hampshire." *SeacoastNH.com.* 1998. 31 Mar. 2015. <http://www.seacoastnh.com/blackhistory/whittier.html>

215 **"Northern man with Southern sympathies."** Faber, Richard B., and Elizabeth A. Bedford. *Domestic Programs of the American Presidents: A Critical Evaluation.* Jefferson, NC: McFarland, 2008. 59.

215 **very publicly criticized.** Holt, Michael F. *Franklin Pierce: The American Presidents Series: The 14th President, 1853–1857.* New York: Macmillan, 2010. 124–25.

215 **visited Confederate president Jefferson Davis.** "To the Associated Press." *New York Times.* 12 May 1867. 31 Mar. 2015. <http://query.nytimes.com/gst/abstract.html?res=9E05E5D8123AEF34BC4A52DFB366838C679FDE>

215 **an angry mob.** Wallner, Peter. *Franklin Pierce: Martyr for the Union.* Concord, NH: Plaidswede, 2007. 361.

215 **as late as 1913.** "Exterior Statues and Memorials at the New Hampshire State House Complex." New Hampshire Division of Historical Resources. 31 Mar. 2015. <http://www.nh.gov/nhdhr/publications/esm/pierce.html>

215 **embracing old Rebels.** Allen, Scott. "Gettysburg: The Great Reunion of 2013." 3 Jul. 2013. 3 Mar. 2015. <http://mentalfloss.com/article/28128/gettysburg-great-reunion-1913>

216 **"with practical unanimity."** Metcalf 4.

216 **Artist Augustus Lukeman.** Metcalf 20.

216 **"as he saw it."** Metcalf 19.

216 **"in the light of the conditions."** Metcalf 59.

216 **"guiding the destinies of the nation."** Metcalf 19.

216 **"a bust of Cromwell."** Metcalf 28.

216 **"able state papers."** Metcalf 27.

217 **"I like your sheets."** "One Fish, Two Fish, Blowfish, Blue Fish." *The Simpsons.* Writ. Nell Scovell. Dir. Wes Archer. Fox, WFLD, Chicago. 24 Jan. 1991.

217 **"achieved the presidency."** Metcalf 28.

217 **"honors herself."** Metcalf 62.

217 **a new tombstone.** Lamb 57.

217 **complement of hometown honors.** Matthews, Kathryn. "Martin Van Buren Slept Here." *New York Times.* 24 Aug. 2007. 5 Dec. 2014. <http://www.nytimes.com/2007/08/24/travel/escapes/24trip.html>

218 **big and imposing.** Howard, Hugh, and Roger Straus III. *Houses of the Presidents: Childhood Homes, Family Dwellings, Private Escapes, and Grand Estates.* New York: Little, Brown, 2012. 63–64.

218 **French wallpaper.** Hamm, Patricia, and James Hamm. "The Removal and Conservation Treatment of a Scenic Wallpaper, *Paysage à Chasses,* from the Martin Van Buren National Historic Site." *Journal of the American Institute for Conservation* 20.2 (1981). 116–25.

218 **portraits of Thomas Jefferson.** "The Formal Parlor." Martin Van Buren National Historic Site. 6 Dec. 2014. <http://www.nps.gov/features/mava/feat01/>

218 **still have bullets inside.** Barnes, Tom. "Workers Find Civil War–Era bullets in Gettysburg Tree." *Pittsburgh Post-Gazette.* 9 Aug. 2011. 6 Dec. 2014. <http://www.post-gazette.com/home/2011/08/09/Workers-find-Civil-War-era-bullets-in-Gettysburg-tree/stories/201108090199>

218 **"What becomes of these trees?"** Eil, Philip. *Phoenix.* 5 Sept. 2012. 30 May 2014. <http://thephoenix.com/boston/news/143725-risd-carves-up-historys-silent-witnesses/>

218 **"idealization, canonization, memorialization."** Broholm, Dale. Personal interview. 31 May 2014.

219 **"a pillar of strength."** Karppi, Dagmar Fors. "Witness Trees Exhibit Ends

August 19." *Oyster Bay Enterprise Pilot.* 10 Aug. 2012. 30 May 2014. <http://www.antonnews.com/oysterbayenterprisepilot/76-oysterbaynews/24376-witness-trees-exhibit-ends-august-19-.html>

219   **"back to the site for exhibition."** Broholm.

220   **acquiring the famous Gilbert Stuart portrait.** Tederick, Lydia. "How Portraits of US Presidents and First Ladies Are Chosen." The White House. 31 Mar. 2015. <https://www.whitehouse.gov/about/inside-white-house/art>

220   **refused to pay the bill.** "James Buchanan (1791–1868)." National Portrait Gallery. 27 May 2014. <http://www.npg.si.edu/exh/travpres/buchs.htm>

220   **lobbied to live with Uncle James.** Rasmussen, Frederick N. "Remembering the Benefactress of Johns Hopkins Children's Center." *Baltimore Sun.* 29 Nov. 2012. 16 Feb. 2014. <http://articles.baltimoresun.com/2012-11-29/health/bs-md-harriet-lane-johnston-backstory30-20121129_1_sons-franklin-county-newspaper>

220   **well educated and cultured.** "Harriet Lane." *American President: A Reference Resource.* 1 Sept. 2014. <http://millercenter.org/president/buchanan/essays/firstlady>

220   **"dear Miss Lane."** Black, Allida. "Harriet Lane." The White House. 2009. 1 Dec. 2014. <https://www.whitehouse.gov/1600/first-ladies/harrietlane>

220   **seat them far apart.** Roth, Mark. "The First First Lady: Buchanan's Niece Enlivened Social Scene." *Pittsburgh Post-Gazette.* 5 Dec. 2006. 16 Feb. 2014. <http://www.post-gazette.com/life/lifestyle/2006/12/05/The-first-first-lady-Buchanan-s-niece-enlivened-social-scene/stories/200612050130>

221   **"Democratic Queen."** "Harriet Lane."

221   **married a Baltimore banker.** Rasmussen.

221   **died from rheumatic fever.** Roth.

221   **"in retirement for some years."** Rasmussen.

221   **inherited a sizable estate.** Roth.

221   **medical care for poor children.** Rasmussen.

221   **successful treatments for rheumatic fever.** "Our History." Johns Hopkins Children's Center. 2 Dec. 2014. <http://www.hopkinschildrens.org/tpl_rlinks.aspx?id=98>

221   **a guide to pediatric diagnosis and treatment.** Engorn, Branden, and Jamie Flerlage, eds. *The Harriet Lane Handbook.* 20th ed. Philadelphia: Saunders, 2015.

221   **rather touchy memoir.** Abbott, Philip. *Bad Presidents: Failure in the White House.* New York: Macmillan, 2013. 81.

221   **left $100,000 for the pieces.** Ferris, Gary W. *Presidential Places: A Guide to the Historic Sites of U.S. Presidents.* Winston-Salem, NC: John F. Blair, 1999. 87.

221   **deadline of fifteen years.** Roth.

221   **James Buchanan Monument Fund.** "A Pennsylvania Recreational Guide for Buchanan's Birthplace State Park." 31 Mar. 2015. <www.dcnr.state.pa.us/cs/groups/public/documents/document/dcnr_20029707.rtf>

221   **stone pyramid thirty-eight feet high.** Fossett, Katelyn. "The Monuments Men." *Politico.* Jul. 2014. 2 Dec. 2014. <http://www.politico.com/magazine/gallery/2014/07/the-monuments-men/001932-027515.html>

222 **"the shadow of disloyalty."** Roth.

222 **"Time does not preserve."** Updike, John. *Buchanan Dying: A Play.* New York: Alfred A. Knopf, 1974. 134.

222 **"Any honest man has opponents."** Updike 96.

222 **"an excuse for a clambake."** Updike 167.

222 **"cautious and literal constitutionalism."** Kauffman, Bill. "For President Buchanan." *American Conservative.* 31 May 2013. 17 Feb. 2014. <http://www.theamericanconservative.com/articles/for-president-buchanan/>

223 **"the Siamese twins."** Loewen, James. "We Have Had a Gay President, Just Not Nixon." *History News Network.* 22 Feb. 2012. 16 Feb. 2014. <http://hnn.us/blog/144754>

223 **"his wife."** Seigenthaler, John. *James K. Polk: The American Presidents Series: The 11th President, 1845–1849.* New York: Times Books, 2003. 109.

223 **"Aunt Nancy and Miss Fancy."** Loewen.

223 **"suit the delicate ear."** Seigenthaler 109–10.

223 **"easy to make quips about."** Birkner, Michael. Personal interview. 24 Feb. 2014.

224 **"married to some old maid."** Cwiek, Timothy. "James Buchanan: America's First Gay President?" *Washington Blade.* 4 Oct. 2011. 16 Feb. 2014. <http://www.washingtonblade.com/2011/10/04/james-buchanan-america%E2%80%99s-first-gay-president/>

224 **destroyed some of their letters.** Baker, Jean H. *James Buchanan: The American Presidents Series: The 15th President, 1857–1861.* New York: Macmillan, 2004. 25–26.

224 **African American ancestry.** Payne, Philip. "Was Warren G. Harding America's First Black President?" Jim Crow Museum of Racist Memorabilia. Nov. 2008. 3 Dec. 2014. <http://www.ferris.edu/HTMLS/NEWS/jimcrow/question/nov08/index.htm>

224 **best-loved president.** Payne, Phillip G. *Dead Last: The Public Memory of Warren G. Harding's Scandalous Legacy.* Athens: Ohio University Press, 2009. 53.

224 **As many as three million people.** Withers 343.

224 **Harding Memorial Association.** Payne 59.

225 **a best-selling memoir in 1927.** Payne 65.

225 **"He Loved to Serve."** Payne 57–58.

225 **put off the formal dedication.** Payne 65.

225 **"Not many people go there now."** "Harding Tomb Is a Lonely Ohio Shrine." *Life.* 12 Jun. 1944. 88.

225 **a loving obituary.** Sparkes, Boyden. "Warren: Is the Friendly Man from Marion Becoming Just Mr. President?" *Collier's* 70.16 (14 Oct. 1922). 5–7.

225 **chair in the Cabinet Room.** Rowan, Roy, and Brooke Janis. *First Dogs: American Presidents and Their Best Friends.* New York: Algonquin Books, 2009. 84.

225 **"spoiled by his environment."** "Laddie Boy 'Writes' of White House Life; 'Tells' Boston Stage Dog He Has No Political Aspirations After Experiences." *New York Times.* 7 Feb. 1922. 3 Dec. 2014. <http://query.nytimes.com/gst/abstract.html?res=9D07E2DE1E30EE3ABC4053DFB4668389639EDE>

226 **"in his dog sense way."** "Laddie Boy Cannot Understand Air of Sadness in White House." *St. Petersburg Times.* 4 Aug. 1923. 6.

226 **a woman called Edna Bell Seward.** Tedeschi, Diane. "The White House's First Celebrity Dog." *Smithsonian.* 22 Jan. 2009. 3 Dec. 2014. <http://www .smithsonianmag.com/history/the-white-houses-first-celebrity-dog-48373 830/>

226 **more than nineteen thousand pennies.** "National Affairs: Again, Laddie Boy." *Time.* 16 Aug. 1926. 3 Dec. 2014. <http://content.time.com/time/ magazine/article/0,9171,722297,00.html>

226 **in the Smithsonian's collection.** Lopata, Peg. "A Real Political Animal." *Faces* 25.1 (Sept. 2008). 6–7.

226 **"get a dog."** Moser, Don. "All the Presidents' Pooches." *Smithsonian.* Jun. 1997. 31 Mar. 2015. <http://www.smithsonianmag.com/history/all-the-presi dents-pooches-136909816/>

Chapter 11: Family Reunion

228 **Dwight Eisenhower's wreath-laying ceremony.** Associated Press. "Eisenhower Event Moved Because of Shutdown." KSAL.com. 10 Oct. 2013. 18 Jul. 2015. <http://www.ksal.com/eisenhower-event-moved-because-of-shutdown/>

229 **asked for an epitaph.** Grant, James D. *John Adams: Party of One.* New York: Farrar, Straus & Giroux, 2005. 383.

229 **Daughter Nabby.** "The Adams Children." *American Experience: John and Abigail Adams.* 28 Nov. 2014. <http://www.pbs.org/wgbh/amex/adams/peo pleevents/p_adamskids.html>

229 **surgery without anesthesia.** Mathiasen, Helle. "Mastectomy Without Anesthesia: The Cases of Abigail Adams Smith and Fanny Burney." *American Journal of Medicine* blog. 2011 May 16. 31 Mar. 2015. <http://amjmed.org/ mastectomy-without-anesthesia-the-cases-of-abigail-adams-smith-and- fanny-burney/>

229 **Son Charles.** Wead, Doug. *All the Presidents' Children: Triumph and Tragedy in the Lives of America's First Families.* New York: Atria Books, 2003. 34.

229 **disowned Charles.** "The Adams Children."

230 **warned John Quincy.** Wead 14–15.

230 **"with indolent minds."** Wead 298.

230 **did go on to prominence.** "Charles Francis Adams." *Encyclopedia Britannica.* 14 Dec. 2014. 31 Mar. 2015. <http://www.britannica.com/EBchecked/ topic/5100/Charles-Francis-Adams>

230 **John Adams II.** Wead 8–9.

230 **falling—or jumping—off a steamboat.** Wead 15–16.

230 **the gambling debts of his stepson.** "John Payne Todd." James Madison's Montpelier. 1 Mar. 2014. <http://www.montpelier.org/research-and-collec tions/people/john-payne-todd>

230 **had to sell the plantation.** Collins, Herbert R., and David B. Weaver. *Wills of the US Presidents.* New York: Stravon Educational Press, 1976. 49.

230 **unmarked for two decades.** Townsend, Malcolm. *Handbook of United States Political History for Readers and Students.* Boston: Lothrop, Lee and Shepard, 1905. 376.

230 **lost sons to alcoholism.** Wead 8–9.

230 **hounded John F. Kennedy Jr.** "10 Years After Plane Crash, a Look Back at JFK Jr." *Boston.com.* 16 Jul. 2009. 29 Nov. 2014. <http://www.boston.com/news/local/massachusetts/gallery/071609_jfkjr?pg=6>

230 **Webb Hayes (son of Rutherford).** Bowie, Edward L. "Hayes, Webb C." *America's Heroes: Medal of Honor Recipients from the Civil War to Afghanistan.* Santa Barbara, CA: ABC-CLIO, 2011. 134–35.

230 **Theodore Roosevelt Jr.** Wead 8–9.

230 **a pioneering lawyer.** Quinn, Sandra L. *America's Royalty: All the Presidents' Children.* Westport, CT: Greenwood Press, 1995. 144.

230 **"There's good and there's bad."** Wead, Doug. Interview. *Connie Chung Tonight.* CNN. 26 Feb. 2003.

231 **"safe in my keeping."** Wead, *All the Presidents' Children,* 56.

231 **"grandson of nobody."** Wead, *All the Presidents' Children,* 300.

231 **saw six states come into the Union.** "Benjamin Harrison." *American President: A Reference Resource.* 31 Mar. 2015. <http://millercenter.org/president/bharrison/essays/biography/print>

231 **"the human iceberg."** Howard, Hugh, and Roger Straus III. *Houses of the Presidents: Childhood Homes, Family Dwellings, Private Escapes, and Grand Estates.* New York: Little, Brown, 2012. 100.

231 **were getting married.** Howard and Straus 102.

231 **"Grandpa came home."** Howard and Straus 100.

231 **pneumonia struck the Harrisons again.** Lamb, Brian. *Who's Buried in Grant's Tomb? A Tour of Presidential Gravesites.* New York: PublicAffairs, 2010. 99.

232 **bringing him a pie.** Wead 150.

232 **raced to see him.** "Benjamin Harrison Dead; Ex-President's Battle for Life Ended Yesterday Afternoon." *New York Times.* 14 Mar. 1901. 31 Mar. 2015. <http://query.nytimes.com/gst/abstract.html?res=9B0CE1D91330E132A25757C1A9659C946097D6CF>

232 **Benjamin Harrison's will.** Fawcett, Bill. *Oval Office Oddities: An Irreverent Collection of Presidential Facts, Follies, and Foibles.* New York: HarperCollins, 2008. 52.

233 **supporter of Hawaiian independence.** Goldman, Mary Kunz. "Grover Cleveland, a Gentle Giant and 'a Buffalo Guy.'" *Buffalo News.* 9 Feb. 2014. <http://www.buffalonews.com/spotlight/grover-cleveland-a-genle-giant-and-a-buffalo-guy-20140209>

233 **"a feeble but friendly state."** Read, Philip. "First 'Presidential Luau' Is Held in Honor of President Grover Cleveland in Caldwell." *Star-Ledger.* 30 Apr. 2010. 24 Aug. 2013. <http://www.nj.com/news/index.ssf/2010/04/first-ever_presidential_luau_h.html>

233 **"hula on the front porch."** Schonfeld, Zach. "'Beyond Americana': An Interview with George Cleveland." *I Visit Presidential Birthplaces.* 10 Jul. 2011. 29

Nov. 2014. <http://ivisitpresidentialbirthplaces.wordpress.com/2011/07/10/beyond-americana-an-interview-with-george-cleveland/>

234 **came to Marshfield in 1991.** Associated Press. "The Broccoli Did It, Bush Says of Taylor." *Los Angeles Times*, 5 Jul. 1991. 11 Dec. 2013. <http://articles.latimes.com/1991-07-05/news/mn-1779_1_zachary-taylor>

234 **Tomato Canning Festival.** "General History." Webster County Historical Society. 31 Mar. 2015. <https://webstercountyhistory.wordpress.com/general-history/>

234 **"we'll have a history festival."** Inman, Nicholas. Personal interview. 28 Nov. 2014.

235 **after giving birth to baby Alice.** Mallon, Thomas. "Washingtonienne." *New York Times*. 18 Nov. 2007. 30 Nov. 2014. <http://www.nytimes.com/2007/11/18/books/review/Mallon-t.html>

235 **placed bets with bookies.** Collier, Peter. *Roosevelts: An American Saga*. New York: Simon & Schuster, 1995. 118.

236 **used a sword to cut the cake.** Wead 236.

236 **"glad to see you leave."** Mallon.

236 **"hardly more than mildly sloping."** Felsenthal, Carol. *Princess Alice: The Life and Times of Alice Roosevelt Longworth*. New York: Macmillan, 2003. 108.

236 **"just a slob."** Mallon.

236 **"But, of course, it's electric."** Wead 46.

236 **"why I wear them."** Dotinga, Randy. "'Alice' Was Anything but Old Hat." *Christian Science Monitor*. 16 Oct. 2007. 30 Nov. 2014. <http://www.csmonitor.com/2007/1016/p17s02-bogn.html>

236 **weaned on a pickle.** Mallon.

236 **in the line of fire on D-day.** Wead 8–9.

237 **"Theodore Roosevelt on Utah Beach."** Watson, Robert. "Hidden History: Roosevelt's Son a Forgotten Hero." *Sun-Sentinel*. 25 Jul. 2010. 30 Nov. 2014. <http://articles.sun-sentinel.com/2010-07-25/news/fl-rwcol-roosevelt-oped0725-20100725_1_teddy-roosevelt-franklin-roosevelt-hills>

237 **"handicaps a boy."** Wead 7.

237 **the White House Gang.** Wead 210.

237 **a portrait of Andrew Jackson with spitballs.** Fawcett 262.

237 **Quentin's plane was shot down.** Wead 98.

237 **"the great day of my life."** "T.R. the Rough Rider: Hero of the Spanish-American War." Theodore Roosevelt Birthplace. 30 Nov. 2014. <http://www.nps.gov/thrb/learn/historyculture/tr-rr-spanamwar.htm>

237 **six months after the tragedy.** Wead 99.

237 **"Death had to take Roosevelt sleeping."** Bishop, Chip. *The Lion and the Journalist: The Unlikely Friendship of Theodore Roosevelt and Joseph Bucklin Bishop*. Guilford, CT: Globe Pequot Press, 2012. x.

237 **"has a pretty serious side for a father."** Wead 99.

237 **"the corpse at every funeral."** Felsenthal 105.

238 **"minister to all the dead presidents."** Inman.

Epilogue

242 **styled after military chapels.** Hufbauer, Benjamin. *Presidential Temples: How Memorials and Libraries Shape Public Memory*. Lawrence: University Press of Kansas, 2005. 197.

242 **the last presidential funeral train.** Withers, Bob. *The President Travels by Train: Politics and Pullmans*. Lynchburg, VA: TLC Publishing, 1996. 364.

242 **authorized a commission.** Newton-Small, Jay. "Nobody Likes Ike's: Why Congress Just Defunded the Eisenhower Memorial Commission." *Time*, 24 Oct. 2013. 19 Mar. 2015. <http://swampland.time.com/2013/10/24/nobody-likes-ikes-why-congress-just-defunded-eisenhower-memorial-commission/>

242 **a four-acre site.** Recio, Maria. "Eisenhower Memorial Design Passes One Hurdle, but Not at Finish Line Yet." McClatchy DC. 24 Sept. 2014. 19 Mar. 2015. <http://www.mcclatchydc.com/2014/09/24/240957/eisenhower-memorial-design-passes.html>

242 **Gehry's design was less popular.** Newton-Small.

242 **process picked back up.** Zongker, Brett. "Eisenhower Memorial Wins Key Design Approval in DC." *Washington Times*. 2 Oct. 2014. 19 Mar. 2015. <http://www.washingtontimes.com/news/2014/oct/2/eisenhower-memorial-returns-to-dc-planning-panel/>

243 **led to a theory.** Newton, Ken. "Man Examines a Sort-of Presidency." *St. Joseph News-Press*. 27 Feb. 2014.

243 **"I slept most of that Sunday."** Kauffman, Bill. "President Atchison?" *American Enterprise* 16.1 (Jan./Feb. 2005). 47.

243 **shrine of democracy.** "The Making of Mount Rushmore." *Smithsonian*. 30 Oct. 2011. 9 Aug. 2014. <http://www.smithsonianmag.com/history/the-making-of-mount-rushmore-121886182/>

245 **"untutored miners."** "Mount Rushmore." *American Experience*. 9 Aug. 2014. <http://www.pbs.org/wgbh/americanexperience/features/transcript/rushmore-transcript/>

245 **"never had so many rows."** Bulow, William J. "My Days with Gutzon Borglum." *Saturday Evening Post*, 11 Jan. 1947. 24–25, 105–8.

245 **carve giant Confederate figures.** "The Making of Mount Rushmore."

245 **"ungovernable temper."** "Mount Rushmore."

245 **affiliated with the Ku Klux Klan.** Heard, Alex. "Mount Rushmore: The Real Story." *New Republic*. 15–22 Jul. 1991. 16–18.

245 **smashing the models.** "Mount Rushmore."

245 **authorities chased the sculptor.** Heard 16–18.

245 **unexpected death in 1941.** "The Making of Mount Rushmore."

247 **"Six Grandfathers."** Gardella, Peter. *American Civil Religion: What Americans Hold Sacred*. New York: Oxford University Press, 2004. 232.

247 **discovered gold.** "The Making of Mount Rushmore."

247 **to work on the presidents.** Doss, Erika. *Memorial Mania: Public Feeling in America*. Chicago: University of Chicago Press, 2010. 344.

247   **"the red men have great heroes also."** Bernstein, Adam. "Toiled to Turn a Mountain into a Monument." *Washington Post.* 23 May 2014.

247   **over five hundred feet high.** Gardella 243.

247   **arrested eleven Greenpeace activists.** "Greenpeace Ruined It for Everyone." *Mitchell Daily Republic.* 5 Jan. 2010.

247   **conducted 3-D scans.** Gardella 244–45.

248   **carving Ronald Reagan.** "Put Ronald Reagan on Mount Rushmore." *Human Events* 55.15 (23 Apr. 1999). 4.

248   **Franklin Roosevelt.** Jackson, Donald Dale. "Gutzon Borglum's Odd and Awesome Portraits in Granite." *Smithsonian* 23.5 (Aug. 1992). 64–75.

248   **John F. Kennedy into the mountain.** Warner, Gary A. "Why These Four American Presidents Are on Mount Rushmore." *Orange County Register.* 19 Jul. 1999.

248   **like Frederick Douglass.** Price, Robert. "No Room Next to Abe, Even for Overlooked Giant." *Bakersfield Californian.* 2 Mar. 2008.

248   **inadequate for further carving.** Gardella 239–40.

248   **"chisel somebody's face out."** Golliver, Ben. "Heat's LeBron James: I Will Be on NBA's Mount Rushmore of Greats 'for Sure.'" *Sports Illustrated.* 11 Feb. 2014. 9 Aug. 2014. <http://www.si.com/nba/point-forward/2014/02/11/lebron-james-mount-rushmore-nba-greats>

249   **"calls for Chester A. Arthur coins."** Bull, Alister. "US Presidential Dollar Coins Victims of Budget Crunch." *Reuters.* 13 Dec. 2011. 10 Aug. 2014. <http://af.reuters.com/article/metalsNews/idAFN1E7BC0GM20111213>

250   **room for eighty statues.** Montgomery, David. "City of Presidents Project Unveils Statues." *Rapid City Journal.* 9 Oct. 2010. 8 Dec. 2014. <http://rapidcityjournal.com/news/city-of-presidents-project-unveils-statues/article_64535ada-d408-11df-9ac0-001cc4c002e0.html>

ILLUSTRATION CREDITS

INDEX

Note: Italic page numbers refer to illustrations.